SPIES WITHOUT CLOAKS

SPIES WITHOUT CLOAKS

THE KGB'S SUCCESSORS

AMY KNIGHT

PRINCETON UNIVERSITY PRESS

PRINCETON, NEW JERSEY

Copyright © 1996 by Amy Knight
Published by Princeton University Press, 41 William Street,
Princeton, New Jersey 08540
In the United Kingdom: Princeton University Press,
Chichester, West Sussex
All Rights Reserved

Library of Congress Cataloging-in-Publication Data

Knight, Amy 1946–
Spies without cloaks : The KGB's successors / Amy Knight.
p.   cm.
Includes index.
ISBN 0-691-02577-0 (cl)
ISBN 0-691-01718-2 (pbk.)
1. Secret service—Russia (Federation)
2. Russia (Federation). Ministerstvo bezopasnosti.
I. Title.
HV8227.2.A3K59   1996
363.2'83'0947—dc20 95-26281

This book has been composed in Sabon

Princeton University Press books are printed on acid-free
paper and meet the guidelines for permanence and
durability of the Committee on Production Guidelines for
Book Longevity of the Council on Library Resources

Third printing, and first paperback printing, 1998

http://pup.princeton.edu

Printed in the United States of America

10 9 8 7 6 5 4 3

*To all those in Russia who have courageously
fought to reform the KGB and its successors*

CONTENTS

LIST OF TABLES AND MAPS

ACKNOWLEDGMENTS

I BEGAN working on this book in September 1992 as a fellow at the Kennan Institute for Advanced Russian Studies of the Woodrow Wilson International Center for Scholars in Washington, D.C. My ten months there were invaluable, and I want to express my gratitude to Blair Ruble, Charles Blitzer, and the entire staff at the Kennan Institute and the Wilson Center for their help.

I am also indebted to the International Research and Exchanges Board, which awarded me a short-term travel grant to conduct interviews in Moscow, and to the Smith-Richardson Foundation, which provided me with a grant to finish up the writing of this book.

This book would not have been possible with the support and advice of numerous colleagues. I owe much to Robert Sharlet for his encouragement of the project from the beginning and for reading the manuscript before publication, and to Eugene Huskey, who also read and commented on the manuscript. I also want to thank Thane Gustafson, Bruce Parrott, Barbara Chotiner, Yevgenia Albats, and Rod Barker for their support, as well as the staff at the Library of Congress, and my agent, Gail Ross.

Special thanks go to Werner Hahn and Jim Nichol, who have been willing to take time out from their busy schedules to give me the benefit of their expert knowledge of Russian politics, and to my friend Peter Reddaway, whose ideas and writings on Russia are always an inspiration.

Thanks are also due to two excellent research assistants, Joe Proctor and Steve Guenther, and to Florence Rotz, of the Department of Russian Area and East European Studies at Johns Hopkins, SAIS.

I am grateful to my former editor at Princeton, Lauren Osborne, for encouraging the book project and for reading and commenting on the manuscript, as well as to my present editor, Brigitta van Rheinberg, and my manuscript editor, Alice Calaprice, for seeing this book through to publication efficiently and thoroughly. Thanks are also due to Alan Greenberg, who prepared the index.

My final debt of gratitude is to my husband, Malcolm, who read the manuscript and provided invaluable insights and commentary, and to my daughters, Molly, Diana, and Alexandra, who put up with my long hours graciously and patiently.

LIST OF ABBREVIATIONS

(see Introduction for further explanations)

CIS	Commonwealth of Independent States
CPSU	Communist Party of the Soviet Union
CSCE	Conference on Security and Cooperation in Europe
EEC	European Economic Community (European Union)
FAPSI	Federal Agency for Government Communications and Information
FCD	First Chief Directorate (KGB)
FIS	Foreign Intelligence Service
FSB	Federal Security Service
FSK	Federal Counterintelligence Service
GRU	Main Intelligence Directorate (under Ministry of Defense)
GUO	Main Guard Directorate
KGB	Committee for State Security
MB	Ministry of Security
MVD	Ministry of Internal Affairs
NKVD	People's Commissariat of Internal Affairs (USSR)
SBP	Presidential Security Service
SBU	Ukrainian Security Service
SCSE	State Committee on the State of Emergency

SPIES WITHOUT CLOAKS

INTRODUCTION

> Spies, you are lights in state, but of base stuffe,
> ho, when you have burnt your selves down to the snuffe,
> Stinke, and are throwne away. End faire enough.
> *(Ben Jonson)*

THIS BOOK tells the story of what happened to the world's most powerful security and intelligence apparatus, known until late 1991 as the KGB, when the totalitarian Soviet empire that supported it collapsed. How does such an organization survive in a world where the rules of the game have changed dramatically? Why, for that matter, does it survive at all, given that the cold war has ended and Russia has embarked on a path of political and economic transformation? Does the KGB's successor organization still represent a threat to Western interests and an enemy to the development of democracy within the former Soviet Union?

This account is part of the larger story of the post-Soviet political system in transition, and, although the book deals with one element of that system, its ultimate aim is to provide a deeper understanding of domestic and foreign politics in the former Soviet Union. The focus of the book is on the Russian Federation, which emerged as an independent state when the Soviet Union was dissolved in December 1991. But the story of what happened to the KGB also involves the other former Soviet republics, whose security services were part of the KGB and are still closely connected with Moscow.

The former Soviet Union has been in the throes of economic and political upheaval since 1987, when Mikhail Gorbachev initiated his program of *perestroika*. Western observers have followed these events closely, because the outcome will affect the entire world for a long time to come. Yet in many respects the Russian political process remains a puzzle. Despite—or perhaps because of—the overwhelming amount of information on day-to-day developments in Russia, Western experts and policymakers have often been caught off guard by important political events there, such as the August 1991 coup attempt, Yeltsin's violent confrontation with the parliamentary opposition in the autumn of 1993, and the December 1994 invasion of Chechnia. The significance of such events for Russia's long-term political development is not always clear.

It will probably take a substantial interlude, providing the benefit of historical perspective, to understand fully this period of breathtaking change in Russia. Nonetheless, we can learn a great deal about the broader political process and the future of reform in Russia by looking specifically at the fate of the KGB, which always played a key role in Soviet politics. The power and influence of its successor organization serves as a gauge against which to measure the progress of political reform in Russia. Also, the influence of the Russian security services in the other former Soviet republics that now form the Commonwealth of Independent States (CIS) tells us much about the political evolution of the former Soviet Union as a whole.

The development of the Russian security services after the fall of the Soviet Union reflects all the contradictions and discontinuities that have characterized Russia's political development under Boris Yeltsin. On the one hand, the reforms that began under Gorbachev and were continued by Yeltsin have had a significant impact on the security services, depriving them of potent weapons. As a result of *glasnost*, for example, the security police can no longer enforce silence through censorship. The abuses and offenses of the security police are openly criticized in the press. Gone are the days when bothersome dissidents could be dealt with easily by whisking them off to labor camps or psychiatric hospitals without answering to a court or a judge. And the security services do not have the unlimited resources that were at their disposal during the Soviet era. They too have to worry about their budgets. With the West no longer an evil enemy, Russia's spies and agents abroad have had to change their ways. Murder, support of terrorism, and kidnapping are no longer in the arsenal of weapons to be used freely against foreign governments.

Nonetheless, it is wrong to depict the KGB's successor organization as an impotent, shattered bureaucracy that poses no threat to Russia's democratic reform or to Western governments. Along with the difficulties created by the political and economic changes in the former Soviet Union, new advantages and opportunities have arisen for security professionals. The political climate itself has worked in favor of a strong security service. Ever since the August 1991 coup attempt, which set the stage for the collapse of the Soviet Union, a crisis atmosphere has prevailed in Russia. The economy has been weak and unstable, crime has reached epidemic proportions, ethnic conflicts and separatist movements have seriously threatened the viability of the Russian state, and the political leadership has been embroiled in internal struggles. Such an environment of instability and lawlessness makes people yearn for the rigid law and order of the past.

The Yeltsin government, for all its avowed democratic ideals, has been reluctant to rein in the police and intelligence apparatus. Indeed, like Gorbachev before him, Yeltsin chose to co-opt the support of the security services rather than to confront them. He could not risk alienating this key source of support against challenges to him and his government. He has depended on the security organs for reliable information—a crucial function for monitoring what is going on in the periphery and among political opponents. And the special security troops, well trained and more reliable than the regular army, have been valuable assets in the face of violence and unrest. Another important consideration for Yeltsin has been that the security services have extensive files on all members of the political leadership. Judging from the compromising materials that were released about Gorbachev, their files could be highly damaging to Yeltsin, a stalwart communist bureaucrat until 1987.

As a result of Yeltsin's policies, Russia's new security services inherited the bulk of the staff and resources of the former KGB, and they continued to enjoy unrivaled political influence. For many Russian democrats, particularly those who have been involved in the human rights movement, Yeltsin's reluctance to reform the security services has been a great disappointment. As a Moscow journalist bemoaned, "Why did the president go only halfway, outlawing the CPSU, but not touching the no less dangerous monster, the KGB?"[1]

THE KGB'S LEGACY

It is no simple matter to reform a security service that for decades had been so powerful and pervasive. The KGB had been a key component of the Soviet state since it was established by Khrushchev in 1954 to replace the Stalinist security services. Having acquired vast monetary and technical resources, an active personnel that numbered at least 420,000 (not to mention the large network of informers and persons with loose connections to the KGB), and huge archival files with the most sensitive political information, the KGB represented a state within a state.[2] As a former KGB general, Valentin Korolev, observed: "During the years of stagnation [the Brezhnev era] the KGB grew to proportions that nobody but a Chekist [the traditional name for a KGB employee] could imagine. Several years ago whole new departments were created by subdividing departments in the central KGB apparatus."[3]

Thanks to the policy of openness initiated by Gorbachev and continued by Yeltsin, former KGB and party officials have provided accounts of their careers during the Soviet period, and some archival sources on the activities of the KGB and the party leadership have become available. As a result, we know a lot more about the KGB than we did when it was still in existence. But the new information does not change the general perception of this institution as a powerful bulwark of the Soviet regime.

The KGB was a rigidly hierarchical structure, led by a chairman (the most infamous of which was Vladimir Kriuchkov, who was implicated in the aborted August 1991 coup attempt) and several deputies. The various KGB directorates had responsibilities ranging from suppressing political dissent to guarding borders to conducting propaganda campaigns abroad. Unlike the United States government, which has two separate agencies, the FBI and the CIA, for domestic counterintelligence and foreign intelligence, the Soviet system combined these functions within the KGB. This practice reflected the ideological underpinnings of the regime, which blurred the distinction between the enemy abroad and political threats at home on the grounds that the latter were always foreign inspired.

The KGB's tentacles extended far and wide. There were large KGB branches in the non-Russian republics, which duplicated its functions at the Moscow center, and KGB offices in every district, region, and city. Its empire also spread over Eastern Europe, where secret police organizations set up by the Soviets after World War II enforced Moscow's domination and carried out operations on the KGB's behalf.

KGB officials, who bore military ranks, were recruited from the "best and the brightest" and had long been accustomed to the privileges granted to the most elite elements of Soviet society. They were also used to operating without regard to the law, answering only to the Communist Party leadership. Recent sources have revealed, for example, that the KGB channeled money abroad—to be stored in secret accounts—for party bosses. And it was common practice for KGB intelligence officers in foreign countries to purchase "gifts" with state money to bring back to their superiors in the KGB and the party.

The KGB's primary internal functions were spying on the Soviet citizenry—by means of a vast surveillance apparatus—to ensure its loyalty to the regime, and suppressing any expressions of political opposition. It served as the eyes and ears of the party leadership, purveying information to the Politburo on all aspects of Soviet society. So effective was the KGB at keeping a lid on dissent that it did not resort to the widespread terror used by the Stalinist political police. It was often enough just to call an outspoken citizen to KGB offices for a warning "chat."

In some cases the KGB used such chats to persuade people to become informers. Like other secret police agencies, the KGB relied heavily on an extensive network of collaborators, who spied on colleagues and neighbors and then reported periodically to KGB case officers. Because KGB files are still closed, it is not known how pervasive the informant network was. But unofficial reports leave little doubt that, as in Eastern Europe, agents and informers were ubiquitous in the Soviet Union. In some sense, the entire society—with the exception of a small minority of dissidents—collaborated with the KGB by adhering to the rules of a police state in order to avoid trouble.

With all its access to information, the KGB stayed on top of events and was therefore able to adopt better than other Soviet institutions to changing circumstances. This flexibility enabled the KGB to weather the dramatic changes that Gorbachev's policy of perestroika wrought and to retain its substantial influence on politics up until the time of the coup attempt. Even before perestroika the KGB leadership had recognized the need to revamp the KGB's image in keeping with the times and had tried to avoid strong-arm tactics that gave it a bad name. During the late 1970s and 1980s the KGB had moved from coercion to manipulation, emphasizing propaganda and political education over arrests and public trials of dissidents. The KGB also tried to soften its image—and that of the Soviet leadership—abroad by means of sophisticated public relations campaigns.

Toward the end of the Soviet period the KGB had evolved into an institution that appeared to be markedly different from the security services of earlier days—not necessarily more benign, but more complex. It was harder to single out KGB officers than it had been earlier, except that they were more sophisticated and worldly-wise than the average Soviet citizen. They professed democratic values, endorsed economic reform, and complained openly about various shortcomings in the Soviet system. They began speaking about the West in friendly terms. KGB officials went into politics, running for elections to the local and central parliaments, and they became involved in joint ventures. They voiced support for perestroika until it went too far for them to tolerate.

The failed August 1991 coup attempt, which the KGB helped to orchestrate in order to put a brake on reforms, demonstrated the superficiality of the KGB's new image and the hypocrisy of its efforts to portray itself as a progressive institution. Those who had been willing to believe that the KGB was proreform felt betrayed and joined the chorus of demands that it be dissolved once and for all. The KGB was disbanded, but, much to the chagrin of the democrats, it was reconstituted under another name.

AFTER THE KGB

The years 1991–1995 have seen the demise of several important Russian politicians, including Gorbachev. Structures like the Communist Party and the Soviet Union have crumbled. Even the Russian Army is in disarray, demoralized by budget cuts, corruption, and the loss of its traditional strategic mission. The security services, on the other hand, have survived because this has been a time of political struggle and civil disorder, when Russian leaders have depended more than ever on their ability to employ secret police methods. In every political crisis that has occurred in Russia since perestroika began, the security services have played decisive roles.

Herein lies the paradox of Russia's transition toward democracy. Significant economic reforms have been introduced, the media have been unshackled, political parties have formed, and people are experiencing a freedom of movement and expression that was unknown in the Soviet days. Yet the security services continue to play a larger than life role in the political system, just as they did in the past. Can the Russian government free itself from its reliance on these institutions without creating a vacuum of power that could lead to political chaos? Can Russian leaders preserve order and stability without reneging completely on their commitment to protect individual rights? These are some of the questions that this book attempts to answer.

The book begins with an account of the August 1991 coup attempt. Although others have described this event in detail, I offer my own interpretation of the developments that led to the coup and the role that the KGB played because it is essential for understanding the subsequent evolution of the security services and of the political system in general. Although the initial, widely accepted version of this event—that a small group of KGB-led culprits attempted to seize power from Gorbachev and failed because of the courageous resistance of democrats—has been discredited by subsequent evidence, a cover-up of sorts has persisted. As I argue here, the failure of Russian society to come to terms with what really happened in August 1991 has impeded the process of political reform.

The collapse of the coup had an immediate impact on the KGB, which was soon dismantled and replaced by several different agencies performing the same functions. In chapter 2 I describe the new security structure as it evolved under Yeltsin and the various laws that Yeltsin introduced to buttress the powers of this apparatus.

Chapters 2 and 3 provide details on the role of the security services in the power struggles and political crises that occurred during the first two and a half years after the coup. I give particular attention to the actions of the counterintelligence apparatus in the fight against official corruption, which ended up involving some of Yeltsin's closest associates. Chapter 4 continues the saga of the struggle against official crime, describing the new powers that were granted to the security police to deal with this problem and the creation, at the end of 1993, of the Federal Counterintelligence Service (FSK). Its establishment coincided with a new emphasis on fighting nuclear smuggling and on suppressing ethnic separatism, particularly as it related to the recalcitrant republic of Chechnia.

In chapter 5 I turn to the Foreign Intelligence Service (FIS), successor to the former First Chief Directorate of the KGB. What are the goals and purposes of Russia's foreign intelligence apparatus now that the cold war is over? Spying against the West is still an important priority, as the case of Aldrich Ames demonstrates. But the FIS directs much of its effort at the newly independent states of the former Soviet Union. The FIS has played a crucial foreign policy role in the Russian Federation, which has not abandoned its goal of preserving its great power status. In contrast to the KGB's First Chief Directorate, the FIS has moved beyond intelligence gathering and other foreign operations to the actual formulation of policy for the Yeltsin administration.

Chapter 6 describes the situation along Russia's borders and the role of the Border Guard Service, formerly part of the KGB, in protecting Russia's security interests. This is followed by a discussion of the security services of the other CIS countries and the efforts of the Russian Federation to integrate the operations of these services with those of Russia. As I argue, the success of Russia's efforts raises the possibility of a partial reconstitution of the KGB's empire.

I then consider, in chapter 7, the important question of human rights in Russia and the other CIS states. Do the security services still violate these rights? What laws have been established to protect individuals from police persecution? In several of the CIS countries the governments have been slow to institute legal restrictions on the security police, largely because their political leaders are members of the old guard, which had close ties with the KGB. Indeed, Gaidar Aliev, the leader of Azerbaidzhan, headed the republican KGB there for years. And Evhen Marchuk, the new prime minister of Ukraine, was a career KGB official.

Closely tied to the human rights issue is the question of coming to terms with the past, which is still buried in the archives, especially those of the KGB. The archives, discussed in chapter 8, are central to the process of reform in Russia. Without dealing directly with its history of police repression, Russian society cannot expect to solve its political problems today. The KGB archives have been the subject of intense debate because they contain files that are highly sensitive politically, particularly those that pertain to the abuse of human rights by former KGB officers and to the use of informers. In addition, the foreign intelligence archives hold the answers to key issues of cold war history. Although the KGB archives were supposed to be handed over to the state archive committee and thus be screened for the possible declassification of some documents, this has not happened. Instead they have remained in the custody of the security services, whose staffers have profited from the sale of secret documents to the West.

In chapter 9 I provide an overview of political events involving Russia's security services since the beginning of 1995, when authoritarian tendencies in the government came to the fore. In 1995, four years after the August coup attempt, we can finally discern long-term political trends that transcend the personalities of leaders like Yeltsin, who may well not survive in office after the 1996 presidential elections.

In the concluding afterword, I attempt to shed light on the future by looking briefly at what happened to the security services in eastern Europe, where people have for the most part faced up to their past legacies of secret police repression and grappled with questions of guilt and responsibility. Is Russia's situation so different that it can never go the way of some states in eastern Europe and peacefully rid itself of this last vestige of totalitarianism, the all-powerful secret police? Or will it eventually follow in the path of these countries that were once part of the Soviet empire? Russia's future as a democracy depends heavily on the answer to this question. And we in the West have a tremendous stake in the success of Russia's transition to a democratic state. But this transition may not occur quickly and easily, no matter what the outcome of the next parliamentary and presidential elections. Russia's security services, revamped yet still powerful, serve as a reminder that Russia's future political course is highly uncertain.

The dizzying succession of name changes and reorganizations of the security services under Yeltsin have posed a challenge in the writing of this book. I did not want to solve the problem, as other writers have done, by simply referring to the new security services as the KGB. That would not only be inaccurate, but it would also give the false impression of continuity of purpose on the part of the Russian government. I have chosen instead to use the correct terminology for the new agencies, but, in order to avoid inundating the reader with unfamiliar names, I often use the generic term "security services." Table two in chapter 1 should help if there is any confusion.

The reader will also note that in some cases I use abbreviations from the English translation of the organization's name rather than the Russian. This is because some of the names in Russian are so unfamiliar that the reader might have trouble remembering what the abbreviation stands for. Thus, I use FIS for the Foreign Intelligence Service rather than the Russian "SVR" (Sluzhba Vneshnei Razvedki). But at the same time I use "MB" (Ministerstvo Bezopasnosti), rather than "MS" for Ministry of Security, just as the term "KGB" (Komitet Gosudarstvennoi Bezopasnosti) was always used, instead of CSS, for Committee of State Security.

For sources of information I have relied extensively on the Russian media. Glasnost has given rise to a flourishing Russian press, which not only reports the day-to-day details of politics, but also offers lively and perceptive analyses and in-depth investigative reporting. I have also made broad use of interviews conducted in Moscow in 1994–1995, memoirs of Russian politicians and former KGB officials, and Western books, periodicals, and newspapers.

Chapter One

THE KGB AND THE MYTH OF
THE AUGUST COUP

> Men make their own history but they do not make it just
> as they please; they do not make it under circumstances
> chosen by themselves, but under circumstances directly
> encountered, given, and transmitted from the past.
> *(Karl Marx)*

RUSSIA HAS always been prone to historical myths. Take, for example, the widely held nineteenth-century belief that the peasants were the true bearers of socialism, or the portrayal of Lenin as a deity and the Communist Party as infallible. Or consider the most outlandish myth of all, that of the "great leader" Joseph Stalin. In some cases it has taken a long time to dispel the myths. Official acknowledgment of the true extent of Stalin's crimes and public criticism of Lenin, for example, did not occur until the late 1980s. By contrast, the myth of the failed August 1991 coup attempt, presented as a victory of the democratic will of the Russian people, took only a few years to fall flat.

The aborted coup was a last-ditch effort by Gorbachev's hard-line subordinates to stem the tide of reform in the country, which they saw as a threat to political stability and to their own interests as party and state leaders. In particular, they wanted to prevent the imminent signing of the so-called Union Treaty, which would have significantly reduced the powers of the central Soviet government vis-à-vis the republics. On the morning of 19 August 1991, KGB Chief Vladimir Kriuchkov and seven other conservative members of the government, including Defense Minister Dmitrii Iazov and Minister of Interior Boris Pugo, announced that Gorbachev, who was vacationing in the Crimea, had fallen ill. Because of his incapacitation, they said, they had formed an eight-man State Committee on the State of Emergency (SCSE), headed by Vice-President Gennadii Ianaev, to rule the country.[1] Their attempt to enforce a state of emergency and impose martial law was a resounding failure, and within seventy-two hours most of them had been arrested.[2] The coup affair, which riveted the world for several days, had an important impact on subsequent developments, giving impetus to the breakup of the Soviet Union and laying much of the groundwork for the evolution of the KGB's successor agencies. But, viewed from the hindsight of several years, the August 1991 events appear much different from what they seemed at the time.

Part of the appeal of the coup story was that it featured what appeared to be clear-cut forces of good and evil, battling it out.[3] It also had a happy ending—or so it seemed—with the hero, Boris Yeltsin, standing victorious on top of a tank, and the villains, the KGB-led conspirators who had tried to seize power, being marched off to jail. But the dividing line between good and evil, reformers and hard-liners, victors and vanquished that seemed so clear in August 1991 has since become blurred.

By August 1994 all but one of the fourteen accused coup plotters had been granted amnesty, and two of those amnestied, Vasilii Starodubtsev and Anatolii Lukianov, had been elected members of the Russian parliament. The remaining defendant, Army General Valentin Varennikov, had rejected the amnesty and insisted on his day in court. After a highly publicized trial, he was acquitted of all charges. Meanwhile Yeltsin's allies in August 1991, Aleksandr Rutskoi and Ruslan Khasbulatov, who helped him defend the Russian White House, had become his bitterest enemies, even ending up in prison for a short time after their confrontation with Yeltsin in October 1993. As for the KGB, which was blamed for masterminding the coup plot, it survived the upheaval and was still in business, albeit under another name.

One hundred and fifty volumes of investigation and inquiry records, days of court testimony, and numerous eyewitness accounts in the press led many to the inevitable conclusion that things were not what they had seemed to be in August 1991. Not only had the accusations of treason against the fourteen men been effectively refuted; Gorbachev's claims that he was an innocent victim of the coup had lost all credibility; and even Yeltsin's role as the courageous defender of the White House during the August crisis appeared dubious.

Not surprisingly, public opinion about the coup had also changed. Polled on the three-year anniversary of the coup attempt, only a small proportion of Muscovites expressed a favorable opinion of its outcome.[4] Less than a quarter of those polled viewed the changes that had taken place since the coup in positive terms, and close to one-third said they would like to return to the pre-1991 state of affairs. Almost 50 percent said that their opinion of the August 1991 events had changed over the past three years.[5]

In fact, many Russians sympathized with the plotters all along, because they approved of their motivation, that of preventing the Soviet Union from unraveling. After the initial euphoria over the defeat of the coup had died down and people began to face the realities of a disbanded Soviet empire, disenchantment set in. Within a couple of years the Yeltsin administration itself was pushing, with considerable success, for a "reintegration" of the former Soviet republics (with the exception of the three Baltic states).

As it turned out, the crisis of August 1991 did not represent the revolutionary turning point that it was portrayed to be. A decisive break with the Soviet system of the past did not occur when the coup attempt collapsed. The system had begun to unravel well before and, as the postcoup events have shown, it has yet to be completely destroyed. What, then, was the significance of the August coup attempt? In order to answer this question, we must look at the role of a key player in the plot, the KGB, and examine its complex relationship with the political leadership both before and after August 1991.

GORBACHEV AND THE KGB

The KGB presented Soviet President Gorbachev with one of his biggest political challenges when he embarked on his program of political and economic reform in 1987. However democratic his intentions, Gorbachev knew that he could not risk confronting the KGB head-on. So he maintained a tight balancing act during the period from 1987 to mid-1991, an act which often resulted in contradictory policies. On the one hand, he introduced glasnost, a policy of unprecedented freedom of expression in the Soviet Union; he initiated semi-democratic electoral procedures for the parliament; he allowed for the emergence of a de facto multiparty system; and he embarked on a dramatic new foreign policy, which involved a complete reassessment of Russia's relations with the West and Eastern Europe. Gorbachev's "new thinking" put an end to the militant anti-Westernism that had justified a continuous military buildup for forty years. And it set the stage for the dismantling of the Berlin Wall and the collapse of communism in Eastern Europe.

These reformist policies were highly threatening to the KGB, which had relied on strict censorship, a closed political system, an extensive spy network in Eastern Europe, and a virulently anti-Western foreign policy to maintain its power and influence. But Gorbachev offset these changes by other measures, which reinforced a strong KGB. He appointed Vladimir Kriuchkov, a long-time KGB professional, to head the KGB in September 1988 and made him a leading adviser; he did not fire members of the KGB's old guard from the organization's leadership or subject the KGB to legal controls; and he authorized the KGB, along with the regular police and the army, to use brute force in combatting nationalist unrest in places like Georgia, where Russian troops killed twenty-nine civilians in the infamous "Tbilisi massacre" of April 1989.[6]

Gorbachev's ambivalence toward the KGB was a reflection of two underlying problems. First, the reform of the socialist system that Gorbachev started with perestroika had quickly escalated beyond his control. The system was being undermined rather than reformed. Second, Gorbachev was not strong enough politically to rein in the KGB even if he had wanted to. By late 1990 he had suffered a serious decline in popularity and in political authority. Growing ethnic unrest, a deepening economic crisis, demands for independence from the Baltic states, and opposition from within his own leadership were eroding his powers. He could not run the risk of antagonizing the KGB by giving in to democratic calls for a reform of that organization because he needed its coercive forces as a bulwark for his rule. This was a problem that Gorbachev's successor, Boris Yeltsin, was also to encounter.

As for the KGB leadership, publicly Kriuchkov and his deputies declared themselves strong supporters of Gorbachev's reforms. Kriuchkov, who had worked under Iurii Andropov as head of the KGB's First Chief Directorate (foreign espionage), came across as smooth and sophisticated in his initial media interviews as the new KGB chief, supporting the need for a complete restructuring of Soviet foreign policy. He also welcomed the creation of a parliamentary committee to oversee the KGB and stressed the importance of rehabilitating the victims of Stalin's purges. On the basis of his public statements (Kriuchkov gave no fewer than eighteen press interviews during the first two years of his tenure as KGB chief) and his association with the "liberal" Andropov, some Western analysts even assumed that Kriuchkov's appointment was a positive sign for perestroika.[7]

Try as they did to promote a new image for the KGB and to convince the world that their organization was drastically reforming itself, KGB officials had trouble containing their anxiety about perestroika, especially by mid-1990. They had good reason to be nervous. After all, their counterparts in eastern Europe, where communism had already collapsed, had lost their jobs overnight, and some were even facing criminal prosecution. In the non-Russian republics, nationalist groups, who saw the KGB as the ultimate symbol of Russian domination, were threatening it with force, in some cases even storming their buildings. There was also the growing phenomenon of "whistle-blowing" by disaffected KGB staffers. As a result of glasnost, these critics became increasingly vocal, revealing to the press shocking stories of the KGB's arrogant disregard for legality. This public scrutiny was unbearable for such a secretive organization.[8]

Although KGB officials fought back by creating a public relations center (which even sponsored a beauty contest with the winner crowned "Miss KGB"), their ultimate response was frustration and alarm. In March 1990, a group of KGB staffers at the headquarters in Moscow appealed to the USSR Supreme Soviet (the parliament), urging deputies to stop the growing crime and instability in the country by adopting laws to strengthen the KGB's power. Kriuchkov and his deputies began complaining loudly about nationalist aspirations among non-Russians in the Soviet Union, as well as about the dangers of a free market economy. In a speech at the Twenty-eighth CPSU Congress in July 1990, Kriuchkov warned that it would be "a ruinous mistake to throw the country into the arms of the elemental forces of the market."[9]

Gorbachev answered the KGB's appeals by expanding police powers to ensure public order and to combat economic crime and ethnic unrest. He also increased his own authority by persuading the Congress of People's Deputies to pass a new "Law on a State of Emergency" in March 1990. The law established a constitutional basis for the president of the USSR to invoke extraordinary centralized powers. Later Gorbachev gave his outspoken support to a new "Law on the KGB," which was ratified by the Supreme Soviet in May 1991 and gave the KGB sweeping new powers.[10] The warnings of dire consequences from ethnic unrest and the decline of law and order had clearly struck a cord in Gorbachev and his advisers. They could not afford to take these dangers lightly.

THE CONSERVATIVES COALESCE

Behind the scenes, KGB and military leaders began, in the autumn of 1990, to make contingency plans for the imposition of martial law by means of declaring a state of emergency.[11] They put their plans to the test in Lithuania in January 1991, when Soviet security and military troops marched into Vilnius and attacked the television station. Contrary to the impression he gave publicly, Gorbachev was not an innocent bystander in these events. The commander of the Russian Airborne Forces stated unequivocally in a later interview that Gorbachev personally ordered all the various "crackdowns" implemented by the KGB and military and was lying when he denied knowledge of them.[12] Indeed, documents from the KGB archives show that Gorbachev was fully aware of the KGB's plans for imposing a state of emergency and weighed this option on numerous occasions. The Communist Party's Politburo seriously considered evoking emergency measures in March 1991, when thousands of Muscovites took to the streets to voice their support for Boris Yeltsin.[13]

Other archival documents—unearthed by the parliamentary commission to investigate the August coup—also showed that Gorbachev frequently enlisted the KGB to carry out "undemocratic" operations such as secret surveillance and wiretapping of his political opponents (in some cases even his colleagues). Gorbachev not only read the KGB's reports, he made handwritten remarks in the margins.[14] Gorbachev's defenders later argued that he did all this because he was being misinformed by the KGB. According to them, the KGB deluged Gorbachev with exaggerated reports that created a false impression of the political situation. The reports persuaded Gorbachev that things had deteriorated to such an extent and his own position was so precarious that these extra-legal measures, including a state of emergency, could not be avoided.[15]

It is doubtful that Gorbachev was so naive that he believed everything the KGB told him, but that is beside the point, because the KGB's assessments were probably not far off the mark. By the spring of 1991, Gorbachev was losing ground so quickly that a siege mentality on his part would have been entirely understandable. Yeltsin, who had been elected president of the Russian republic in June and thereby had gained legitimate political authority, was pressuring Gorbachev to relinquish much of his power base. Not only did Yeltsin call for an end to the Communist Party's leading role in politics, he also demanded unprecedented independence for the republics of the USSR. Under pressure from Yeltsin, Gorbachev had agreed in late April 1991 to transfer certain functions of the central government to the republics, thus surrendering substantial powers. But this was not enough. Russia and other republics began demanding nothing less than a new federal structure.

While negotiations with republican and regional leaders continued throughout the summer, without resolution, Gorbachev began meeting secretly with Yeltsin and Kazakh party leader Nursultan Nazarbaev to hammer out details of an agreement. It was formalized on 23 July at Novo-Ogarevo as the so-called Union Treaty, which was set for signing on 20 August 1991. The treaty relegated Gorbachev and all members of the central government to secondary political roles, a prospect Gorbachev can hardly have relished.[16] He thus had good reason to avoid signing it. As for his immediate subordinates, Gorbachev's chief of staff, Valerii Boldin, recalls: "They were convinced that such an outcome would cause economic and financial bankruptcy, and wreck the armed forces and all other economic and political structures, while decimating our common culture and aggravating ethnic tensions."[17]

THE ATTEMPT TO TAKE POWER

The initial version of the August 1991 crisis, generally accepted in Russia and in the West, was straightforward: the KGB leadership had been planning to oust Gorbachev for several months and was carefully preparing for the big moment. Kriuchkov and his colleagues believed that Gorbachev had gone too far in changing the system and thus wanted him out. They staged a preemptive coup d'état, surprising Gorbachev completely by placing him under house arrest at Foros, his vacation villa in the Crimea, on 18 August. Their attempt to seize power was a failure because of the courageous resistance of Yeltsin and his followers.[18]

It did not take long for this portrayal of the coup to lose credence in Russia. As unanswered questions and contradictory stories piled up, many Russians began to scoff at the idea that Gorbachev was an innocent victim of the coup plotters and assumed instead that he was deeply implicated. How, they asked, could Gorbachev have been betrayed by men he knew so well? KGB chief Kriuchkov was a trusted colleague. He was at Gorbachev's side on his first visit to the United States in late 1988 and was a key member of his brain trust. Gorbachev had known Anatolii Lukianov, who supported the SCSE after it was formed, since their law school days at Moscow University. Even the pathetic Gennadii Ianaev, sneered at by the media for his drunkenness and ineptitude, enjoyed Gorbachev's unwavering confidence. When parliamentary deputies objected to Ianaev's candidacy for Soviet vice-president in late 1990 on the grounds that he opposed reform, Gorbachev pushed them into accepting him, insisting: "I want to have a person whom I trust completely at my side during this most difficult turning point in life."[19]

That Gorbachev, an astute politician, could have so grossly miscalculated the intentions of his colleagues is puzzling, to say the least, particularly since he was warned repeatedly by various sources that the hardliners wanted a "crackdown." The telephone logs reveal that he spoke at great length with Kriuchkov and other members of the future SCSE the morning of his alleged house arrest.[20] Yet, like a sitting duck, he remained down at Foros. Did he really miscalculate? Or was he well aware of their plans?

The evidence suggests that Gorbachev was not an innocent victim of the coup plotters, but rather backed the idea of introducing a state of emergency in the country all along. Gavril Popov, the former Moscow mayor who warned the American ambassador, Jack Matlock, of a plan to introduce emergency powers in June 1991, said later that he was convinced that Gorbachev was encouraging the hard-line members of his government to push for these measures in order to offset Yeltsin's growing political strength. Only after Matlock misinterpreted Popov's warning and told Gorbachev instead of Yeltsin about the proposed crackdown did Gorbachev drop the idea of declaring a state of emergency in June.[21] Two months later, faced with the imminent signing of the Union Treaty, Gorbachev's colleagues again set plans in motion for a state of emergency, which would put the signing of the treaty on hold. Gorbachev, they say, was fully aware of their moves. "The organizers of this action notified the president beforehand," Lukianov later stated. "And he did not take a single step to prevent it."[22]

The accused coup plotters all insisted that Gorbachev gave them the go-ahead to make preparations and then, instead of coming up to Moscow to take charge, he suddenly backed off, feigning illness and leaving his comrades "holding the bag." (The illness, incidentally, was later revealed as a back problem. One of Gorbachev's physicians reported later that he flew down to Foros on 18 August, the day Gorbachev was reportedly placed under house arrest, and injected Gorbachev with strong pain medications that actually put him to sleep for a while.)[23] This was typical Gorbachevian strategy, which he had employed in earlier situations when it was politically necessary to take coercive measures but he did not want to take responsibility. Although Gorbachev was running the government at the time of the Tbilisi massacre in May 1989 and during the bloody events in the Baltic states in early 1991, he was able to escape blame by claiming ignorance. Indeed, Gorbachev gained a great deal of political mileage from portraying himself as being continually pressured and even deceived by his conservative subordinates. This enabled him to preserve his democratic image with the West while at the same time keeping a lid on reform.

As former prime minister and one of the defendants Valentin Pavlov put it: "Gorbachev decided to play a game that he could not lose. If he stayed there [in his vacation home in the Crimea] and the state of emergency worked, he would come to Moscow later, having recovered from his illness and taken charge. If it didn't work, he could come and arrest everyone, and once again as president he would take charge. In each case he would show the people that his hands were squeaky clean."[24] When four emissaries (Boldin, Varennikov, Oleg Baklanov, first deputy chairman of the Defense Council, and Oleg Shenin, a Central Committee secretary) arrived at Foros on 18 August, expecting to discuss with Gorbachev the arrangements for the state of emergency, they found to their chagrin that his attitude had suddenly changed. He spoke to them sharply and refused to condone publicly the emergency regime, telling them ambiguously to do what they wanted to do.[25]

QUESTIONS ABOUT GORBACHEV'S CAPTIVITY

The claim that there was a KGB-led plot to seize power from the president hinges on Gorbachev's story that he was held in complete isolation at Foros. If he had really been opposed to the introduction of a state of emergency, then presumably he would have tried to convey his views to the outside world if he had been able to. Communications from Foros were allegedly cut off on 18 August, before the arrival at 4:50 of the four emissaries, accompanied by Iurii Plekhanov, chief of the KGB's Guard

TABLE 1
Chronology of the August 1991 Coup

August 18	
4:00 P.M.	Communications at Gorbachev's dacha at Foros are cut off (according to telephonist and Shakhnazarov). Other sources have cutoff at 4:30, 4:32 and 5:50
4:50 P.M.	SCSE emissaries Boldin, Varennikov, Baklanov, and Shenin arrive at Foros.
6:00 P.M.	SCSE emissaries leave.
August 19	
4:00 A.M.	Alpha stormtroopers arrive at Yeltsin's dacha, but make no attempt to arrest him.
6:00 A.M.	SCSE announces state of emergency.
10:30 P.M.	Yeltsin issues decree from Russian White House condemning SCSE.
	Primakov flies back to Moscow.
August 20	Primakov issues statement that Gorbachev is not ill and is a captive.
	Army tanks arrive in Moscow and head for Russian White House.
August 21	
1:00 A.M.	Three young civilians killed in attempt to board tanks.
8:00 A.M.	Ministry of Defense decides to remove forces from capital.
5:00 P.M.	Five putschists, including Kriuchkov, arrive at Foros and are later arrested.
6:38 P.M.	Communications restored at Foros (other sources have this shortly after 5:00 P.M.).
August 22	
2:30 A.M.	Plane carrying Gorbachev and putschists arrives in Moscow.

Directorate. (See table 1.) According to Gorbachev's account, when their unexpected visit was announced, he reached for the telephone to ascertain their purpose only to discover that all lines were dead. Then, he said, he reluctantly received the men, but when he refused to accede to their demands, they left, imprisoning him under heavy guard at his dacha. For the next seventy-two hours, Gorbachev said to newsmen upon his dramatic return to Moscow on the evening of 22 August, he was held incommunicado, unable to make contact with anyone outside of Foros.[26]

The defendants in the coup case later insisted that Gorbachev's communications were not cut off and that he could have flown back to Moscow at any time. Of course, we cannot necessarily trust what they say, since they had strong motives for implicating Gorbachev. But enough evidence has emerged since the coup attempt to substantiate their claims and thereby present a new picture of the KGB's role in these events.

First, the accounts of the alleged cutoff of telephone communications are contradictory. To be sure, different recollections are fairly typical in such cases, but the discrepancies here suggest improvisation after the fact. Presidential aide Georgii Shakhnazarov, who was residing at the Iuzhnyi Sanatorium (12 kilometers from the presidential dacha), reported at a news conference on 22 August that he spoke briefly with the president at 4:00 P.M. on 18 August, after which communications were immediately cut off.[27] The telephonist at the city communications center confirmed that lines were cut immediately after the conversation ended.[28] According to Gorbachev, however, the call to Shakhnazarov, during which he discussed his planned speech to the upcoming session of the Supreme Soviet, was not put through until 4:30.[29] To further complicate the picture, one source says lines were cut at 4:32 P.M., while yet another says it was 5:50.[30] And Colonel Oleg Klimov, a senior officer on the president's personal guard detail, recalled: "The fact is that neither on 18 or 19 August did I know exactly whether or not communications were closed off."[31]

Historian John Dunlop, in his detailed analysis of the coup, noted other inconsistencies in the Gorbachev story. Gorbachev, for example, reportedly made telephone calls to his ally Arkadii Vol'skii during the time when his communications were said to be shut off. Dunlop also mentioned questions that were raised about the telephones in Gorbachev's limousines.[32] This was clarified at Varennikov's trial in July 1994. According to Gorbachev's bodyguards, although some telephones lines were closed, the special telephones in the president's cars were working and the garage was open. Also, the lines in the administration building, a hundred or so yards from Gorbachev's house, were fully operational. Some of Gorbachev's guards called their relatives on these telephones and Gorbachev was aware of these calls. Furthermore, they said, although the gates to Foros were blocked, no efforts were made to remove the obstacles, which would not have been difficult.[33]

Then there is the problem of Gorbachev's alleged illness. Among the flurry of telephone calls he is said to have made at 4 P.M. on the 18th was one to former Ukrainian Communist Party secretary, Stanislav Gurenko. Gurenko testified that Gorbachev called him and said that he was sick, but would nonetheless be flying up to Moscow. Vol'skii, on the other hand, said that Gorbachev called him specifically to tell him that, contrary to what he might hear, he (Gorbachev) was not ill.[34]

If Gorbachev's enemies were really serious about keeping him isolated and in captivity, it is surprising that they would allow Shakhnazarov, along with his wife and son, to join Gorbachev at his dacha, which they reportedly did.[35] Meanwhile Evgenii Primakov, another Gorbachev adviser staying at Iuzhnyi, was permitted to fly back to Moscow on the

19th. On 20 August, Primakov, apparently sensing that the coup was about to fail, issued a statement saying that Gorbachev was in good health and that the committee for the state of emergency was unconstitutional.[36]

Even more difficult to explain is why Gorbachev's guards, thirty-two in all, made no attempt to resist their "captors" (five men armed with Kalishnikov rifles). The head of Gorbachev's bodyguard, Vladimir Medvedev, who was seen whispering furtively with Plekhanov, chief of the KGB Guards, left unexpectedly for Moscow with him and the other SCSE emissaries. But Gorbachev's remaining guards still had their weapons. It is curious that they all sat meekly while their president, by his own account, was trying desperately to leave Foros or, at the very least, to communicate with the outside world.[37] Did it not occur to Gorbachev to ask them for help?

The commander of the Crimean border guards, Colonel Piotr Kharmalov, also behaved rather strangely. A self-professed democrat and Gorbachev loyalist stationed in the nearby town of Foros, Kharmalov admitted to being concerned when he realized communications were cut off: "I had strong fears that the Gorbachev family was in danger," he later said. Instead of calling out his troops to defend the president, however, Kharmalov went to church with his family and prayed.[38] Gorbachev, meanwhile, walked on the beach every day, appearing tanned and relaxed to all who saw him. He later told newsmen that he had been surrounded by border guards who were in league with the plotters, thus contradicting Kharmalov's account. Indeed, Dunlop cites a report from a Ukrainian security official who learned from KGB border guards in the Crimea that they had no role whatsoever in isolating the president.[39]

THE EMERGENCY COMMITTEE IN MOSCOW

Back in Moscow, the members of the SCSE did little better in their roles as usurpers of power than Gorbachev did as a helpless captive. To be sure, the situation grew tense after army tanks appeared on the streets. But no one bothered to prevent Yeltsin from giving a press conference, let alone arrest him. Although the elite "Alpha" stormtroopers unit (which belonged to the KGB) arrived at Yeltsin's dacha at 4 A.M. on the 19th of August, they remained in the woods for hours without making a move, thus allowing Yeltsin to depart for central Moscow. According to Yeltsin, Kriuchkov "decided not to rush developments."[40]

Despite the claims of the Yeltsin camp, the Emergency Committee never planned to storm the Russian White House, where Yeltsin and the other opponents of the coup were headquartered for the duration of the

SCSE's existence. In fact, its members have even denied that they called in the tanks.[41] In an impassioned letter to Yeltsin published in *Pravda* in the summer of 1992, former KGB chairman Vladimir Kriuchkov blamed him for destroying the Soviet Union by exploiting the events of 19–21 August for his own political purposes: "'We succeeded in defending the White House,' you say. Against whom? You yourself know all the circumstances. There was no threat of attack on the White House and you, of all people, were very well aware of that, having received all the necessary assurances to that effect." The purpose of the allegations of storming the White House, Kriuchkov claimed, was simply for Yeltsin to make himself a hero.[42]

Yeltsin himself referred in his memoirs to a telephone conversation he had with Kriuchkov from the Russian White House, during which the latter told him the SCSE would not be using military force. But apparently Yeltsin chose not to believe him and continued to prepare for an attack: "An entire night and then an entire morning passed, and still there was no storming of the White House, nor even a blockade. . . . Was Kriuchkov really so stupid that he didn't understand how dangerous such indecision could be?"[43]

The initial story about the plans to attack came from members of the Alpha troops, who claimed that they had been given orders to storm the White House but had heroically refused. But the unit's commander, General Viktor Karputin, stated emphatically that he had received no such orders.[44] This was borne out during the hearings of the parliamentary commission to investigate the coup. According to Sergei Stepashin, who became a deputy minister of security after the coup, the KGB leadership gave no orders either to arrest Yeltsin or to attack the White House. "Believe me," Stepashin assured those in attendance at the hearings, "'Alpha' was a very well trained unit, it never would have been delayed or have disregarded orders, even at the time when some of us here were defending the White House."[45]

Why did members of the emergency committee not give orders to the troops? Was it because, having assumed they had Gorbachev's backing, they were caught completely off guard and had not prepared for such a contingency? This would also explain why Kriuchkov, Iazov, Baklanov, Tiziakov, and Lukianov flew down to Foros on Wednesday, 21 August, and ended up being arrested. They apparently were making a last-ditch effort to persuade Gorbachev to express his support for them.[46] Yeltsin himself hinted at this when he said: "Unquestionably, yet another reason for the coup plotters' fiasco was their collective responsibility—or irresponsibility for the events occurring. . . . No, there was no 'evil genius' among them. The chief catalyst of the coup was still in Foros."[47]

BACK AT FOROS

The sequence of events that followed the arrival of the five putschists in Foros is unclear from the contradictory accounts that subsequently emerged. Again, particular confusion arises around the issue of Gorbachev's access to lines of communication. According to the initial press accounts, supported vaguely by Gorbachev in his book on the coup, the putschists arrived at the airport in the Crimea at 4:08 P.M. and showed up at Gorbachev's dacha around 5 P.M. Gorbachev reportedly refused to see them until telephone communications were restored, which did not happen until 6:38 P.M. Gorbachev then began making calls to Yeltsin and other republican leaders and then, at 7:19 P.M., to President Bush.[48]

Gorbachev's assistant, Anatolii Chernaev, told things very differently. According to his diary, after he saw the five men arrive at the dacha at 5 P.M., he quickly changed clothes and rushed to Gorbachev's office to tell him that the men were there. Gorbachev was already on the telephone issuing orders and had spoken with Yeltsin and other republican leaders. In Chernaev's presence he called the commandant of the Kremlin in Moscow and later spoke with President Bush.[49] If Chernaev's account is accurate (interestingly, it was later changed in the prosecution's book about the coup to accord with the official version), then communications would have had to have been restored shortly before 5 P.M., not at 6:38.[50]

When Gorbachev spoke to Bush, he reportedly said that he was just finding out what had happened in Moscow, implying that he had not had any information whatsoever for three days.[51] Chernaev, however, repeatedly notes that they had a small Sony television, and one assumes that, since they had electricity, they could turn on radios.[52] Taken together, all these discrepancies suggest strongly that Gorbachev was not a captive and might have easily left Foros or at the very least communicated with the outside world. In fact, this was precisely the conclusion reached by the Military Collegium of the Russian Federation Supreme Court in August 1994 when it acquitted Varennikov of all charges. The court also found that the SCSE had never given orders for a storming of the White House.[53]

However adept Gorbachev had been at fooling the public, he clearly underestimated Yeltsin's ability to gain political capital from the affair. The coup attempt made Yeltsin a hero and a rallying point for the democratic forces in the country. It also gave the final impetus to the breakup of the Soviet Union, which was the only way that Yeltsin could achieve power. As long as the Soviet Union existed, Yeltsin's Russian presidency would take a back seat to the Kremlin. But the collapse of the USSR enabled him to step in and fill the void.

REPERCUSSIONS

The developments that followed the August crisis reinforce the impression that, as an alleged KGB effort to unseat Gorbachev, the so-called coup was largely a farce. To be sure, from the standpoint of those who wanted a democratic political system and independence for the Soviet republics, the motives of the alleged plotters were highly reprehensible. These hardliners wanted to thwart the goals of the democrats by putting a break on reforms and reasserting Moscow's control over the republics. But the assumption that they were operating in opposition to Gorbachev and other members of the leadership was wrong. Not only Gorbachev, but significant numbers of officials from the party, the military, and the KGB were hedging their bets on the outcome of efforts to introduce a state of emergency, hoping that the signing of the Union Treaty could be averted. The men who stuck their necks out by forming the SCSE ended up the scapegoats. Their fate has served as a reminder to their successors in the so-called power ministries of the pitfalls of getting involved in political struggles. Indeed, this may well explain the subsequent reluctance of the army and the police to support Yeltsin when he sought to overstep the Constitution and use force against his opponents in March and again in October 1993.

Only fifteen men altogether were arrested in the coup affair.[54] Immediately problems arose for the prosecution, which charged them under Article 64 of the RSFSR (Russian Republic) Criminal Code, treason against the USSR. But by the end of December the USSR had ceased to exist, so the charges had no legal basis.[55] Furthermore, this crime was defined in part as an act "to the detriment of state independence, the territorial inviolability or the military might of the USSR." Yet the main goal of the accused was to keep the USSR intact. The Procuracy, which was handling the case, finally settled on a single clause in Article 64, charging the defendants with "a conspiracy for the purpose of seizing power." Seizing power from whom? Since the accused themselves were government leaders and had the power in their hands at the time of their alleged crime, the only person that could be was Mikhail Gorbachev. It was thus essential to the procurator's case to show that Gorbachev had known nothing of the plans of the accused and had been held captive by them down at Foros. But this, as demonstrated above, was a highly dubious contention.

Another problem with the case was that many officials had gone along with the SCSE until the final hour, thus making it awkward to single out only a few for prosecution. Why, for example, was Gorbachev's chief bodyguard, Vladimir Medvedev, never arrested? He had, after all, cooperated fully with the emissaries from the SCSE on 18 August, even flying back to Moscow with them. Gorbachev, moreover, claimed that Medvedev had secretly bugged the presidential dacha and passed tapes of conversations on to Kriuchkov.[56] Although he was fired from the KGB, this hardly seems a severe enough punishment for his alleged crimes. And what of the KGB security guards brought to Foros to keep Gorbachev captive at gun point?

Then there were the military officers who participated in planning for the state of emergency, cooperating with the SCSE until its fate was sealed. Chief of Staff of the Soviet Army Mikhail Moiseev sent orders to several regional army commanders telling them to speak in support of the SCSE to their troops and to take decisive steps against coup resisters. Yet Gorbachev actually appointed him minister of defense (replacing Iazov) upon his return to Moscow from the Crimea, only to be forced to fire him two days later.[57]

Army General Pavel Grachev, subsequently Yeltsin's minister of defense, was equally compromised. As commander of the airborne troops in August 1991, he attended meetings of top military, police, and party officials that took place during the planning of the alleged coup. Grachev drew up documents that were used for the implementation of the state of emergency and even dispatched several regiments to Moscow to support the SCSE. By his own admission, he did not give up the idea of storming the White House until 11 P.M. on 20 August.[58] Yet he was never charged with a crime.

Adding to the sense of unreality and confusion that surrounded the alleged coup attempt was the spate of puzzling suicides that occurred when the SCSE failed. First came the announcement that Minister of Internal Affairs Boris Pugo, a member of the SCSE, had shot his wife and himself on the morning of 22 August. Then on 24 August, Army General Sergei Akhromeev was said to have hanged himself in his office, leaving a long suicide note confessing his crimes to Gorbachev and his family. On that same day, a top administrator of the party's Central Committee, N. E. Kruchina, reportedly jumped out of a window to his death. Somewhat later G. S. Pavlov, another party official, defenestrated himself as well.

The official explanation for these reported suicides was that the victims had committed crimes and did not want to face prosecution. But why would Pugo have killed himself, and his wife, before he even knew what was in store for him? He may have assumed he would be arrested, but that was all. He was not the ringleader of the emergency committee. All of his colleagues, including Kriuchkov, were out of prison by early 1993. Was it really worth death to avoid time in prison?[59] Leonid Shebarshin, former head of KGB foreign intelligence, found the Pugo suicide inexplicable: "I knew him." Shebarshin wrote of Pugo: "He was an honest, sober-minded and kind man, dedicated to his work. Why would he shoot himself? Were he and the other members of the Emergency Committee really so sure of the success of the undertaking that failure was tantamount to death?"[60]

As for General Akhromeev, he had not even been a member of the SCSE and, unlike Moiseev and Grachev, had not participated in the military preparations for the state of emergency. He was away from Moscow until 19 August and knew nothing of the plans, although he attended meetings with Iazov and other SCSE members later that day. According to his daughter, Akhromeev was in good spirits on the night before his death. He had written a long speech that he planned to deliver at the Supreme Soviet session scheduled for 26 August. Akhromeev wanted to explain to deputies why he had supported the SCSE and to urge them to take measures to stop the Soviet state from disintegrating. Given the widespread respect Akhromeev enjoyed as a prominent military officer (he had negotiated many of the talks on arms limitations with the United States), his speech might have had a significant impact. But his death deprived him of the opportunity to deliver it. Not only is it hard to come up with a motive for Akhromeev's suicide, it is also difficult to imagine that a Soviet military officer would kill himself in the distinctly nonmilitary manner of hanging.[61]

Several sources have suggested foul play, claiming that these four officials knew too much and could not be counted on to keep quiet.[62] If this was the case, and we will probably never know for sure, it would explain why the procuracy made no effort to bring the case to trial and even prevented the facts from coming to light. The chief investigator in the case, Procurator-General Valentin Stepankov, and his deputy published a sensational book, *Kremlin Conspiracy*, in mid-1992, while the accused were still in prison awaiting trial.[63] The book, which was allegedly based on the evidence and testimony they had gathered, was a blatant attempt to prove the official version of the abortive coup.

After dragging the investigation out further, the Procuracy began releasing the defendants from prison to await trial (primarily on grounds of illness). By early 1993 all the accused, including Kriuchkov, were free. The trial was set to open in mid-April 1993, but was delayed until October (over two years after the alleged coup attempt), only to be postponed again. The government's case against the men was dropped abruptly when the new Russian parliament elected in December 1993 granted them an amnesty, which all except General Varennikov, who wanted to vindicate himself with a trial, accepted.

Why, one might ask, did Yeltsin not put pressure on the prosecution to conduct an objective investigation and bring the case to trial promptly? First, he may have wanted to prevent testimony showing that the accused never threatened to storm the White House, because it tarnished the image of his heroism during the August days. Second, many of the men who became part of Yeltsin's government, including his minister of defense, Grachev, played questionable roles in the alleged coup attempt, which was politically embarrassing to Yeltsin. It has also been suggested that Yeltsin made a deal with Gorbachev, promising to hush up Gorbachev's own involvement in the coup attempt in order to ensure that Gorbachev would leave the political arena quietly at the end of December 1991.[64] Finally, Yeltsin himself began contemplating the imposition of a state of emergency when the opposition to him in parliament became increasingly vociferous in early 1993. And he did just that in October 1993. In order to avoid embarrassing comparisons, Yeltsin may have wanted to steer the public's attention away from the unsuccessful attempt to introduce emergency powers in August 1991.

If indeed the investigation of the August coup was a cover-up, in which the security police became the scapegoat, it would not be without precedent in Soviet history. Both Stalin and Khrushchev turned against their security chiefs and blamed them for repressions that were in fact ordered by the party leadership. As we know now, the security police, however ruthless and evil, were never independent actors in the Soviet system, although they were often portrayed as such. Then, as now, they took their cues from the politicians.

Reforming the KGB

At the risk of pushing historical comparisons too far, it is useful to note that, after every denunciation and purge of the police apparatus in Soviet history, its powers were quickly revived. No Soviet leader could function without a strong and effective political police. Looking at what happened to the KGB after the August coup, we see a similar phenomenon. The KGB was weakened, but not for long. Despite all the lofty talk about a radical reform of the security services, the end result was little more than a "change of the guard" at the top.

To be sure, there was plenty of anti-KGB sentiment on the part of the public. The KGB leadership, blamed for organizing the coup attempt, became the focal point for the popular wrath against the Kremlin regime. On the night of 27 August a large crowd that had gathered outside KGB headquarters, the Lubianka, desecrated the statue of Feliks Dzherzhinskii, first chief of the security police, and threatened to storm the Lubianka itself. Inside, nervous and shaken KGB staffers began furiously destroying documents. Such was their demoralization that, according to Moscow journalist Yevgenia Albats, KGB staffers began drinking vodka openly at their desks, an unprecedented breach of discipline.[65]

Gorbachev cannot have felt much better, given how seriously his authority was weakened by the coup affair. Apparently he had anticipated that only Kriuchkov and those few KGB officials who were directly involved in planning the alleged coup would be blamed and that the rest of the KGB would emerge unscathed. This would explain why, on his return to Moscow, he named Kriuchkov's longtime deputy, foreign intelligence chief Leonid Shebarshin, to take over as acting KGB chairman. Gorbachev soon realized that Shebarshin was unacceptable to the reformers and withdrew the appointment the very next day, replacing Shebarshin with the more palatable Vladimir Bakatin.[66]

Bakatin, a Gorbachev-vintage democrat, had a reputation as a reformer. After a career as a regional party *apparatchik*, he had served as chief of the MVD, or regular police, from October 1988 to December 1990, when he was dismissed under pressure from the hard-liners because he reportedly refused to go along with the planned use of Soviet force in the Baltics.[67] Though the telegenic Bakatin was praised as being untainted by a KGB background, it was not quite accurate to portray him as a complete outsider. His son was a career KGB officer, and, during his tenure as MVD chief, Bakatin had worked closely with the KGB.

Bakatin stepped into the limelight, waxing eloquently in speeches and interviews about the importance of reforming the security services. At a press conference in Moscow on 30 August, Bakatin outlined optimistic plans for revamping and restructuring the KGB.[68] Legality and the protection of individual rights would form the basis for the KGB's operations. The KGB would no longer be a state within a state. There would be "colossal decentralization" of its powers. Already, he said, the special purpose divisions that the KGB had acquired from the army some months earlier had been transferred back to the Ministry of Defense. The Guard Directorate, responsible for the protection of government officials and buildings, had been placed directly under Gorbachev, along with the infamous "Alpha" antiterrorist unit. And the KGB's Eighth Directorate, which controlled government communications and ciphers, was transformed into a separate Agency for Government Communications. Plans were in the works for making the KGB border troops into a separate state agency and also for transferring the Third Directorate (military counterintelligence) to the jurisdiction of the Ministry of Defense.

Bakatin believed, he said, that only a few top leaders of the KGB had supported the coup attempt. Thus he was not about to instigate widespread purges in the KGB. (He allowed, however, that he did fire his son from that organization: "I don't want him working under his father.")[69] In his first address to his employees after taking office, on 27 August, Bakatin assured them that he had no intention of starting a "witch hunt" and would permit most of them to continue in their posts.[70]

Following a brief investigation of who among the members of the KGB Collegium (the top leadership body) was implicated in the coup attempt, Bakatin dismissed fourteen officials. Three of these—Grushko, Ageev, and Plekhanov—were already under arrest, along with their former chief, Kriuchkov. Later, on 25 September, an in-house KGB Commission for Investigating the Role of the KGB in the August coup finished its work and recommended that a large number of KGB officials be dismissed, but Bakatin limited the reprisals to reprimands and allowed most to stay on. He did not touch the middle or lower echelons of the organization.[71]

Bakatin chose experienced KGB officers to serve directly beneath him: Anatolii Oleynikov, who headed the in-house investigatory commission, as first deputy chairman; Fedor Miasnikov, head of the Counterintelligence Directorate, and Nikolai Sham, in charge of the Sixth Directorate, as deputy chairmen. He kept on Leonid Shebarshin as head of the First Chief Directorate (foreign intelligence), but Shebarshin then had a disagreement with Bakatin over who should be his deputy and resigned on 18 September. In his place Bakatin appointed Evgenii Primakov, a well-known academician and longtime member of the foreign policy establishment.[72]

Bakatin later expressed regret that he did not establish a new leadership for the KGB by bringing in new blood. "One of my main mistakes," he later wrote, "was that I arrived at the KGB without my own crew, without a large group of like-minded men dedicated to the cause. I overestimated my own strength. Without my own men, it was almost impossible to shake up this bulky and cumbersome thing called the KGB."[73] As a former party *apparatchik*, Bakatin may have in any case been reluctant to purge KGB officials. "What he found in the KGB," said former KGB official Iaroslav Karpovich, "were essentially his own comrades, his own contemporaries with whom he had studied at one time in party schools and functioned in the same structure. . . . And he could not move against them."[74]

REORGANIZATIONS

In late September, Bakatin turned to the question of structural and organizational change in the KGB. He felt strongly that the security apparatus had to be preserved in some form—"Yes, the USSR KGB was bad, but there was nothing better and the problems of protecting state security . . . would not disappear"—and thus opted for reform rather than abolition. Bakatin was undoubtedly following the wishes of Gorbachev, who clung to the view that the old pillars of the Soviet system had to be kept standing. As one observer put it, Bakatin was a true Gorbachevite—"bobbing, weaving, talking reform, trying to preserve the system for another day by pouring the same amount of old poison into a half dozen new bottles."[75] As a basis for the reform, Bakatin worked out a seven-point general concept of state security, taking into account the new circumstances of the post–cold war world. The principles set forth were lofty and ambitious: division of the KGB into several independent agencies; decentralization of security operations; depoliticizing the KGB; eliminating the mentality of "spy mania" and the focus on fighting dissidents; introducing glasnost into the activities of the services; and ensuring that its actions did not harm the country's security in any way.[76]

Meanwhile, a parliamentary commission had been established to examine the role of the KGB in the coup attempt. The commission, headed by the chairman of the Russian Parliamentary Committee on Defense and Security, Sergei Stepashin, was to work out proposals to restructure KGB agencies and produce drafts for new legislation relating to the security organs. To ensure that the interests of the security services would be protected, Anatolii Oleinikov, first deputy KGB chairman, and Viktor Ivanenko, chief of the Russian security services, were included as members.

In late October 1991, Gorbachev issued a decree abolishing the KGB and creating three separate agencies in its place: an Interrepublican Security Service (for domestic security), a Central Intelligence Service (for foreign intelligence), and a Committee for Protection of the State Border. At the same time, Bakatin was able to report that in just two short months his staff had been reduced from 490,000 to about 40,000. Very little of this reduction was a result of dismissals, however. Some 240,000 employees were moved to the new Border Protection Committee; 90,000 staffers were placed under the authority of the various republican KGB apparatuses; 18,000 were transferred to the Russian KGB; 15,000 went over to the Central Intelligence Service; and 85,000 troops and civilian staffers were moved to the separate communications and guard services.[77] Bakatin revealed that a proposal to transfer the Third Chief Directorate, for military counterintelligence, to the Ministry of Defense was also considered. But it was rejected on the grounds that the situation in the military was so unstable that it was necessary to have an agency independent of the military ensuring its political reliability.[78]

The dissolution of the KGB, formally ratified by the USSR Supreme Soviet on 3 December 1991, was greeted with widespread enthusiasm. The monster had finally been vanquished. Or so it seemed. But some, such as journalist Yevgenia Albats, were skeptical:

> So what has changed besides new signboards being hung up in the "house"? Practically nothing. Just details. . . . whatever people used to do they are still doing, although with considerably less enthusiasm than before in view of the

present-day chaos. Wherever they used to sit, they are still sitting. They are still getting the same paychecks from the same source. The only difference is that the former deputies are sitting in the chairs of their former chiefs.[79]

In Bakatin's own words: "Everyone keeps saying that Bakatin has torn down the KGB structure. For goodness' sake, this is not so. If you come to Kazakhstan, not a single hair has fallen from the head of any official. Or to Kyrgyzstan—I just got back from there, everything is still as it was there. The situation is the same in the Moscow department and in the Kemerovo one. That is, all the branches at the bottom and the structures have remained the same."[80]

Clearly, the motivations for disbanding the KGB stemmed not from a desire to curb its powers but from the realization that it had become the focal point of democratic opposition and the butt of popular discontent. The very name "KGB" symbolized, even more than the name "CPSU," all that was wrong with the Soviet system. Thus, to appease the public and prevent any outbreaks of violence against the security organs, it was decided to split the KGB into independent departments.

There was also the problem of nationalist sentiments in the republics. Once the republics began asserting control over the KGB organizations on their territory, the leadership in Moscow considered it essential to keep the foreign intelligence apparatus out of their grasp by making it a separate, all-union agency. As Bakatin put it: "The main circumstance which led me to hurry with a decision on the 'divorce' [of the foreign intelligence administration from the KGB] was the noticeable effort of several republics, under the guise of discussions on reforming the KGB, to drag intelligence into their corners. Such efforts could lead to only one thing—to a complete collapse of intelligence. We could not permit the First Chief Directorate to be divided into Kyrgyz, Ukrainian, Russian, and other intelligence agencies."[81]

Both Bakatin and Gorbachev were adamantly opposed to the breakup of the Soviet Union and were struggling to preserve some form of union, however loose, among the republics. As part of these efforts they created a new Moscow-based structure—a coordinating council of the Interrepublican Security Service, which included Bakatin, foreign intelligence chief Primakov, and the heads of the security services in the twelve republics. Bakatin had little trouble working out security agreements with the non-Russian republics, because most of their security services, which had the same staff and had changed little in terms of operations, were anxious to cooperate with his service.[82]

The Russian KGB presented an insurmountable obstacle, however. An intense struggle for the KGB's resources ensued between Bakatin and Gorbachev, on the one hand, and Yeltsin, on the other. In early 1991,

Yeltsin, as president of the Russian republic (RSFSR) had had the foresight to lobby for the creation of a separate Russian KGB. (Though the other republics had always had their own state security committees, the Russian republic had been administered by the USSR KGB.) After several months of negotiations with Kriuchkov both directly and through Yeltsin's assistant Iurii Skokov, Yeltsin had gained an agreement establishing a Russian republic KGB in May 1991. He had rightly calculated that this would ensure for Russia a greater share in the spoils of the USSR KGB when the USSR government was eventually dismantled.[83] Indeed, Yeltsin demanded that the Soviet security service be abolished and all its resources and personnel be transferred to the Russian KGB. The Yeltsin camp was supported by Stepashin's Parliamentary Commission for Investigating the KGB, which, according to Bakatin, "blocked every step" toward reform.[84] During November and December 1991 Bakatin tried to defend his turf against the Yeltsin forces, but it was a losing battle, ending with the breakup of the Soviet Union in late December 1991 and the creation of the Russian Federation.

Yeltsin's activity during this period, then, was not directed toward reforming the KGB. He simply wanted to keep it intact long enough to provide him with a viable security apparatus that he could take over once the USSR had disintegrated. As early as 5 October, Yeltsin issued a decree stating that the legal successor to the USSR KGB on Russian territory was the Russian republic KGB.[85] On 26 November, Yeltsin issued another decree, transforming the Russian KGB into the Federal Security Agency (FSA), subordinate to Yeltsin and accountable to the RSFSR Supreme Soviet. The chief of the FSA, Viktor Ivanenko, stated that the name had been changed in order to break once and for all with the KGB. According to Ivanenko the FSA had a broad mandate to ensure the security of the Russian republic.[86]

The FSA was short-lived, however. Once it became clear that the USSR would be disbanded, Yeltsin forged ahead with yet another reform. After calling Bakatin to tell him of his plans, Yeltsin issued a decree on 19 December amalgamating the Interrepublican Security Service, the FSA, and the Soviet and Russian internal affairs ministries (regular police) into a supra-agency, a Russian Ministry of Security and Internal Affairs. All the assets and personnel belonging to the USSR security agencies were now the property of the Russian republic.

Although Yeltsin's takeover of the Soviet security apparatus could hardly be questioned at this stage, there was widespread opposition to the merger of the security organs with the regular police. As Bakatin observed, it was probably the most criticized decree to be signed by Yeltsin. Many democratic reformers saw it as an effort by Yeltsin to create a dangerously powerful security service that he could use to suppress dissent.

Employees of the security services, on the other hand, worried that a merger with the regular police would result in a degradation of their status and a loss of their privileges.[87]

As it turned out, the Russian Supreme Soviet refused to ratify Yeltsin's decree, and the matter was then sent to the Constitutional Court, which voted unanimously to invalidate it. Yeltsin was forced to back down and repeal the merger. His haphazard efforts to create a supraministry of internal and security affairs can hardly have endeared him to members of the security services. The overall impression was that he was ill-advised and impetuous when it came to the security apparatus, an impression that was to be reinforced in the next two years, when the security services were subjected to continuous turmoil as a result of Yeltsin's struggles with his political enemies. Nonetheless, amid his seemingly erratic policies, one could discern a distinct purpose—that of asserting his own personal control over the security bodies.

RUSSIA'S NEW SECURITY STRUCTURE

After four months, during which the security services, both Soviet and Russian, were caught up in the struggle over what would happen to the Soviet Union, the union was dissolved on 25 December and the Russian Federation was formed.[88] Yeltsin wasted no time in setting up Russia's new security structure. By the end of January 1992, the Russian Federation had five separate agencies performing the functions of the former KGB. Largest was the Ministry of Security (Ministerstvo Bezopasnosti), or MB, which numbered some 137,000 employees and was designated a counterintelligence agency. It inherited the tasks of the former Second Chief Directorate (counterintelligence against foreigners), the Third Chief Directorate (military counterintelligence), the Fourth Directorate (transportation security), the Directorate for Protecting the Constitution (domestic security, including operations against terrorism, separatist movements, etc.), the Sixth Directorate (for economic crime and official corruption), and the Seventh Directorate (surveillance, wiretapping, etc.). (See table 2.)

Not surprisingly, given his close association with Gorbachev, Bakatin was not kept on to head the newly formed MB.[89] Instead, Yeltsin chose Colonel General Viktor Barannikov, who had served as chief of the Russian internal affairs apparatus before the coup and then as head of the Soviet Ministry of Internal Affairs (MVD) until the Soviet state was disbanded. A career MVD official, Barannikov had been a longtime supporter of Yeltsin and was so close to the president that he even enjoyed the privilege of attending the sauna with him.[90]

TABLE 2
Organization of the Soviet/Russian Security Services, 1991–September 1995

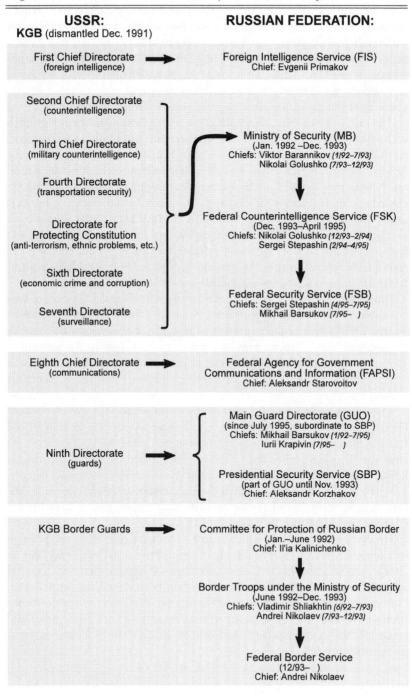

USSR:
KGB (dismantled Dec. 1991)

RUSSIAN FEDERATION:

First Chief Directorate
(foreign intelligence) ➡ Foreign Intelligence Service (FIS)
Chief: Evgenii Primakov

Second Chief Directorate
(counterintelligence)

Third Chief Directorate
(military counterintelligence)

Fourth Directorate
(transportation security)

Ministry of Security (MB)
(Jan. 1992 –Dec. 1993)
Chiefs: Viktor Barannikov *(1/92–7/93)*
Nikolai Golushko *(7/93–12/93)*

Directorate for
Protecting Constitution
(anti-terrorism, ethnic problems, etc.)

Federal Counterintelligence Service (FSK)
(Dec. 1993–April 1995)
Chiefs: Nikolai Golushko *(12/93–2/94)*
Sergei Stepashin *(2/94–4/95)*

Sixth Directorate
(economic crime and corruption)

Seventh Directorate
(surveillance)

Federal Security Service (FSB)
Chiefs: Sergei Stepashin *(4/95–7/95)*
Mikhail Barsukov *(7/95–)*

Eighth Chief Directorate
(communications) ➡ Federal Agency for Government
Communications and Information (FAPSI)
Chief: Aleksandr Starovoitov

Ninth Directorate
(guards) ➡ Main Guard Directorate (GUO)
(since July 1995, subordinate to SBP)
Chiefs: Mikhail Barsukov *(1/92–7/95)*
Iurii Krapivin *(7/95–)*

Presidential Security Service (SBP)
(part of GUO until Nov. 1993)
Chief: Aleksandr Korzhakov

KGB Border Guards ➡ Committee for Protection of Russian Border
(Jan.–June 1992)
Chief: Il'ia Kalinichenko

Border Troops under the Ministry of Security
(June 1992–Dec. 1993)
Chiefs: Vladimir Shliakhtin *(6/92–7/93)*
Andrei Nikolaev *(7/93–12/93)*

Federal Border Service
(12/93–)
Chief: Andrei Nikolaev

The KGB's Eighth Chief Directorate, which oversaw government communications and cipher systems, became the Federal Agency for Government Communications and Information (Federal'noe agentstvo pravitel'stvennoi sviazi i informatsii—FAPSI), headed by Lieutenant General Aleksandr Starovoitov. Starovoitov, a professional Chekist, had been a deputy chief of the KGB's Eighth Chief Directorate. As the Russian counterpart to the U.S. National Security Agency, FAPSI's job was to secure and service government communication lines and also conduct intelligence by technical means, intercepting and decoding information.[91]

The KGB's Ninth Directorate, charged with guarding government leaders and key buildings and installations, became the Main Guard Directorate (Glavnoe upravlenie okhrany—GUO), headed by Lieutenant General Mikhail Barsukov, who also was designated Commandant of the Kremlin. Numbering some eight thousand men, the guard administration included an autonomous subdivision, the Presidential Security Service, under the leadership of Major General Aleksandr Korzhakov, Barsukov's first deputy. Korzhakov had served as Yeltsin's personal bodyguard and was one of his closest and most reliable friends.[92] Within this service, responsible for protecting the president, was the famous Alpha antiterrorist force, numbering several hundred highly trained crack troops.

Directly subordinate to President Yeltsin, the Guard Directorate was not subject to oversight by legislative or judicial bodies. From the time of its creation, Yeltsin began to gradually augment the powers of this agency so he could have a strong arm of support at his disposal. By September 1993 it had acquired the elite Vympel troop unit from the MB. In KGB times Vympel had been a special purpose unit for sabotage and combat abroad.[93]

The fourth agency to emerge from the dismantled KGB was the Border Guard Service, which became the Committee for the Protection of the Russian Border, said at this point to number some 180,000 troops. Its chief was Il'ia Kalinichenko, a career border guards officer and formerly head of the KGB border guards. By early June 1992, Yeltsin had decided against keeping the border guards a separate service, placing it under the jurisdiction of the Ministry of Security and appointing a new border guards chief, Vladimir Shliaktin.[94]

Finally, the KGB's First Chief Directorate (FCD) was now the Foreign Intelligence Service (FIS), headed by Evgenii Primakov, who had been in charge of the short-lived Central Intelligence Service that was created after the coup. Like Bakatin, Primakov had been closely associated with Gorbachev. But, as an experienced foreign policy adviser, with close connections to the former KGB, he transcended ties with any individual leader. And his expertise and prestige were assets that the Yeltsin government badly needed.

The creation of a separate agency for foreign intelligence was generally interpreted as a further weakening of the security apparatus, but this was not necessarily so. The FCD had always been a distinct entity, staffed by elite, highly educated intelligence officers who tended to follow career tracks that were separate from those of domestic KGB staffers. The headquarters of the First Chief Directorate were located at Iasenevo (known as "the forest"), which was on the outskirts of Moscow, far from the Lubianka. Although all the KGB directorates cooperated with each other, there had always been competition—even animosity—between the domestic and foreign branches.[95] So, in a sense, the designation of the First Chief Directorate as a separate agency formalized a situation that had already existed. The main difference was that Primakov reported directly to Yeltsin rather than to the security chief.

The dispersal of the KGB's functions into several agencies dispelled the public image of the security services as a mighty, all-powerful entity. The fact that Yeltsin went out of his way to speak of a fundamental reconstruction of the security apparatus reinforced the perception of the KGB as a vanquished monster. In September 1991 Yeltsin had stated emphatically: "Perhaps we should leave, let's say, the intelligence and counterintelligence service, as in other countries, but all the rest of the tale-telling services—surveillance, eavesdropping, informers, and so on—needs to be abolished, beyond any shadow of a doubt."[96]

Yeltsin never followed through with such reform. With several agencies reporting directly to him, he now had considerable hands-on authority over security and intelligence matters, authority increased by his close personal connections with men like Barannikov and Korzhakov. He was reaping the fruits of the failed August coup attempt, which featured him as the hero, who had vanquished the KGB once and for all. For all his democratic leanings, Yeltsin was not prepared to relinquish this potentially powerful political weapon that was now in his hands. During the next four years of his tenure as Russian president, Yeltsin was to become increasingly dependent on the security services to fend off opposition and carry through with his programs. Instead of restricting the powers of his security apparatus, he would do just the opposite.

Chapter Two

BUILDING RUSSIA'S SECURITY APPARATUS

> I should like to see the power which in our country would
> dare to open the doors of the Lubianka and say: "Thank
> you for your work, boys. You are free. We do not need
> specialists of your kind anymore since we shall change
> the nature of that specialty."
> *(Nataliia Gevorkian, Izvestiia, February 1993)*

IN MID-1992, a former KGB counterintelligence officer lamented the demise of the KGB in an article that appeared in the ultra-right newspaper *Den'*, which Yeltsin later banned. Characterizing the relationship that existed between the KGB and the party in Soviet days, the author made the point that the KGB had always been an instrument of the party leadership, from the Central Committee down to the regional party committees: "The supervisors [of the KGB] were the 'number-one people,' that is, the first secretaries of the party organizations. This job was held for many years by M. Gorbachev in Stavropol, B. Yeltsin in Sverdlovsk and then in Moscow. It was to them and not to anyone else that the KGB reported important information. And it was they who gave orders and who approved or disapproved the operations of KGB organs."[1] This observation is entirely accurate. However much party leaders tried to blame the KGB for unsavory operations that came to light publicly, the KGB was not an independent actor. With rare exceptions, the KGB followed party orders.[2]

Now, however, there was no party leadership to give the security services their marching orders. There was no established structure at the top through which decision making on security matters would be translated into concrete policy formulations. It was unlikely, given their disgraced status and splintered organization, that the new security services would seize the initiative and engage in bold actions on their own. Who would take charge? Clearly Yeltsin intended to step into the void left by the party leadership. But there was also the Russian parliament, whose deputies wanted a say in the workings of the security bodies. As the events of 1992 showed, their agenda was very different from Yeltsin's.

Although Yeltsin never made a clear statement of his plans for the security services, beyond the occasional rhetoric about how different they would be from the KGB, within a few months certain trends could be discerned. Yeltsin had four main aims. First and foremost he wanted to use the services, particularly the MB (Ministry of Security), FAPSI (Communications and Information), and the Main Guard Directorate—to support him in his battles with the political opposition at the top. Second, he wanted the security apparatus to struggle against broader domestic threats—ethnic separatism, terrorism, labor unrest, drug trafficking, and organized crime. Third, he intended the security apparatus, in particular the border troops and the Foreign Intelligence Service (FIS), to enhance the power and influence of the Russian Federation over the CIS (Commonwealth of Independent States). And finally, the security services had the more traditional purpose of counterintelligence against foreign spies and intelligence gathering and "active measures" abroad.

Because the top priority for Yeltsin was defeating his political enemies and consolidating his power, the more straightforward security functions were relegated to a secondary role, while secret surveillance, wiretapping and other covert methods were employed against those whom Yeltsin viewed as political threats.

PARLIAMENT AND THE SECURITY SERVICES

Although the Russian parliament, the Supreme Soviet, also sought control over the security services, the views of its deputies were so diverse that it is impossible to speak of a parliamentary agenda regarding these bodies. The democrats, led by human rights activists like Lev Ponomarev, Father Gleb Yakunin, and Sergei Kovalev, were concerned above all with circumscribing the powers of the security services so that they would not be used arbitrarily against individual citizens. They wanted to place legal limitations on the security police and ensure protection of individual rights in the legal structure. They also wanted to create a system of public oversight.

At the other end of the spectrum were the more conservative parliamentary deputies, who were not interested in furthering democratic reforms of the security services. Rather, they wanted to assert their influence over them in order to compete successfully against Yeltsin for political power. Parliamentary speaker Ruslan Khasbulatov and Russian vice-president Aleksandr Rutskoi, who had increasingly dissociated themselves from Yeltsin's policies, were the most prominent representatives of this group.[3]

However different they were, these deputies were united in one aim—that of imposing parliamentary control over the bodies of the former KGB. On 21 February 1992, the Supreme Soviet passed a resolution, signed by Khasbulatov, stating that it had the right to oversee the planning and implementation of domestic security and foreign intelligence operations, as well as to control budgetary and personnel matters. The resolution also "recommended" that the president of Russia refrain from any further reorganizations of the security and intelligence services until the Supreme Soviet had discussed the findings of its Committee on Defense and Security on this question.[4]

Not surprisingly, the resolution did not go over well with Yeltsin. Four days later, on 25 February, he issued a decree asserting his right as president to control directly the Ministries of Security, Internal Affairs, Foreign Affairs, and Justice and to appoint their leading personnel. Operational control over the Ministries of Security and Internal Affairs, the decree said, would be carried by Sergei Shakhrai, a Russian Federation deputy prime minister.[5]

Meanwhile parliamentary deputies who were members of the Supreme Soviet Committee on Human Rights persevered in their efforts to establish effective parliamentary control over the security services. By late 1992 they had drafted a law "On Control by the Russian Federation Supreme Soviet over the Activities of the Special Services."[6] The purpose of such control, the draft stated, was to safeguard the rights of citizens against arbitrary government actions and to prevent the special services from violating individual rights. The mechanism for parliamentary control was to be a select committee, composed of members of parliament, for oversight of the security services.

Unfortunately, the law on oversight was never passed and no select committee was created. In the summer of 1993, a group of deputies from the Human Rights Committee traveled to Washington, D.C. (at the expense of the U.S. Information Agency), to study the American system for monitoring the intelligence services. The parliamentarians told their American hosts that they were kept completely in the dark about the Russian security services. The size of their budget and staff, as well as information on their operations, was a closely guarded secret.[7]

Ironically, the main obstacle to establishing effective parliamentary control over the security services was the Supreme Soviet Committee on Defense and Security, which consisted of around fifteen parliamentary deputies and had its own subcommittee for dealing with the state security services. This committee was drafting its own version of a law on parliamentary oversight, which conflicted with the draft proposed by the Human Rights Committee. The Committee on Defense and Security was not interested in *democratic* controls over the security services. Indeed, it turned out to be little more than a cheering block for the interests of the MB and the other security agencies.

The reason for its partiality lay in the composition of its membership. As of early 1993, four of its fifteen members were simultaneously officials of the Ministry of Security and one of these four, Boris Bol'shakov, was chairman of the subcommittee on security and intelligence.[8] In addition, Sergei Stepashin, the committee chairman, had only recently, in October 1992, retired from his post as a deputy minister of security (because of pressure from democratic parliamentarians). Thus, for close to a year, the parliamentary committee monitoring the security services was headed by a leading security official.

Stephashin, who was to return to the MB as first deputy minister in mid-1993 and later become head of the MB's successor organization, the Federal Counterintelligence Service (FSK), showed little inclination to strengthen parliamentary control over the security services. From the outset he acted more as a spokesman for the security services than as a representative of the people. As parliamentary deputy Gleb Yakunin put it, "It's difficult for him to work effectively—how can he be expected to supervise his own boss?"[9] When asked about reforming the former KGB in the spring of 1992, Stepashin stressed that it would be a grave error to carry this too far:

> The experience of Eastern Europe shows how useless and dangerous for the state is the overly hasty destruction of the old intelligence services and what irreversible mistakes this can lead to. Countries pay dearly for such an impulsive and unwise decision, however understandable it may be in human terms. . . . A democratic state needs strong and effective security services, especially during the period when it is becoming established.[10]

By 1993 Stepashin's committee had become the focal point of the parliamentary opposition to Yeltsin. Khasbulatov and his supporters were critical of how it handled both the military and the security services and wanted more control for themselves. In late April 1993 the Supreme Soviet, at Khasbulatov's instigation, passed a decree setting up a commission to investigate the Committee on Defense and Security. Stephashin told the press that his committee might be dissolved.[11] Later, however, Khasbulatov backed down, apparently because he did not think it expedient to force a confrontation with the committee at that time.

YELTSIN'S LEGISLATIVE INITIATIVES

In what was to become his typical pattern of governing, Yeltsin set about implementing his agenda for the former KGB with a flurry of decrees and laws, most of which were devised by Stepashin's committee. The laws served three purposes. First, they created the impression that the Yeltsin administration was doing something concrete to regularize and control the activities of the security services and thus align them with his avowed goals of democratic reform. Second, they legalized substantial powers for the services in terms of their operative work. And third, they relegated the main control over these bodies to the Russian president.

However influenced he was by democratic ideas, Yeltsin's instincts reflected his long career as an *apparatchik* in the party bureaucracy, where the interests of the state always prevailed over those of the individual. One of his first decrees concerned state secrets. The decree instructed the security organs to coordinate the work of protecting secrets and to set up "special departments" in institutions and enterprises for this purpose. In enforcing this regime of secrecy, the staff of these departments was to be guided by "previously adopted normative acts" (i.e., the old secrecy regulations under which the KGB operated).[12] This meant that the Ministry of Security would send (or, more accurately, retain) its emissaries to all state agencies in order to prevent certain types of information from being leaked to the public. In other words, Yeltsin wanted to protect his government from the excesses of glasnost.

Next came a Law on Operational-Investigative Activity, passed in late April 1992, which set forth the procedure for the first stage of criminal investigations, including those by the state security organs.[13] It is not without significance that this was one of Yeltsin's first laws. Having an effective investigative service was clearly a top priority for him. The law authorized five agencies to conduct investigative operations: the Ministry of Internal Affairs, or regular police; the Ministry of Security; the Border Troops; the Foreign Intelligence Service; and "operational subunits" of the Main Guard Directorate. The law granted investigators broad leeway in their work. Rather amazingly, they gained the right to conduct secret surveillance, install bugging devices, and open mail and tap telephones, although only in cases of "serious crimes." The permission of the procurator had to be obtained to carry out these measures, with some exceptions. In "urgent cases which could lead to an act of terrorism or sabotage," the only requirement was that the procurator be notified and his sanction obtained within twenty-four hours. There was little to prevent investigators from justifying the use of exceptional measures by seeing a threat of terrorism or sabotage in any case they pleased. Furthermore, in the past it was always a mere formality for the security organs to gain a sanction from the Procuracy. The latter was a weak, corrupt, and inefficient bureaucracy that had always taken orders from the KGB rather than vice versa, and there was no indication that things had changed in the post-Soviet period.

For former dissidents who had experienced firsthand the KGB's intrusive methods of spying and surveillance, the fact that Russia's new security services had the legal right to use the same methods was disconcerting, to say the least. As human rights activist Sergei Kovalev put it: "This law has serious deficiencies. Let us remember that the requested procurator's sanction to conduct operative-search activities is nothing other than the denial of a citizen's constitutional right to judicial protection."[14]

The investigation law was followed by a Law on Security, signed by Yeltsin in May 1992.[15] The most remarkable thing about this law, which set forth the broad concepts underlying the security policies of the Russian Federation, was the powerful role that it ascribed to the Russian president. It acknowledged some authority for the parliament, stating that the Supreme Soviet was to set budget appropriations for the security and intelligence organs, to control their personnel policy, and to determine priorities in security policy.[16] But the language was vague and the mechanisms for such parliamentary involvement were not specified. Moreover, the law charged the president with the overall leadership of the organs of state security, with "monitoring and coordinating their activity," making "operational decisions," and so on. Because Yeltsin passed this law at a time when he was able to issue decrees with little challenge from the parliament, it is not surprising that it would enhance his powers over the security organs.

In July 1992 President Yeltsin signed—and the Supreme Soviet ratified—laws governing the two main security agencies, the Ministry of Security (MB) and the Foreign Intelligence Service (FIS). The Law on the Federal Organs of State Security, which pertained to the Ministry of Security, aroused considerable concern among democrats.[17] What was most disconcerting to them was the similarity of the new law to that passed on the KGB just fourteen months earlier. Indeed, the law conferred basically the same mission and powers on the MB that the earlier law had granted to the KGB, in some cases almost verbatim.[18] Clearly, the authors of the law, among whom were members of the parliamentary Committee on Defense and Security, had not had the inclination to "go back to the drawing board" and had chosen instead to use the law on the KGB as a blueprint.

As noted above, Yeltsin moved the border guards back under control of the MB in June 1992. The new law reflected this change, tasking the MB with managing the border troops. The border force had always been a key element of security and defense in Soviet days, and it was now crucially important to Russia's government, with the situation along its borders so volatile. But the role of border units went beyond that of protecting the border from armed attack. As the new law stated, they were to carry on reconnaissance and to conduct "operational investigations." Thus much of the intelligence gathering directed at CIS states would be implemented or supported by the border guards.

What about restrictions on the MB to prevent it from infringing on individual rights? The law stipulated that MB investigators could, for example, "enter unimpeded into housing and other premises belonging to citizens" but they had to "inform the procurator of such cases within twenty-four hours, with subsequent granting of his permission." What time period did "subsequent" represent? What if the procurator's office did not give its sanction? None of this was made clear in the new laws.

The law (Article 11) also stated that, in order "to ensure security," agents could be detached to other organizations and enterprises, presumably in order to keep an eye on things for the Ministry of Security. A subsequent presidential decree authorized so-called operational reserve officers to be seconded to outside agencies without being demobilized.[19] These watchdogs reportedly were even sent to newspapers to work under cover as journalists. In return for the cooperation of the newspaper, the MB would provide much-needed funds to help defray printing and publishing costs.[20] And Article 17 enshrined another traditional KGB practice into law, that of maintaining a network of secret informers to spy on Russian citizens. Under the new law, "persons helping the federal organs of state security" could enter into a contract with the MB, which would allow them certain protections and give them remuneration.

CONFRONTATIONS ON THE FAR RIGHT

In and of themselves, these laws did not appear particularly draconian or undemocratic. Indeed, the extensive detail and the numerous references to human rights and freedoms gave the overall impression of an effort to create a law-based state. But those who read the fine print had the opposite impression, claiming that the new laws opened up the way for human rights violations.[21] What was to prevent the new security services from taking advantage of the loopholes to abuse their powers, as the KGB had done? Why, they asked, was Yeltsin, a self-proclaimed democrat, putting so much effort into laws relating to security? Why was he not instead fulfilling the promises made by Gorbachev of introducing new legal codes to replace the old ones, which dated back to the early sixties? After all, at that time legal concepts were based on the idea of "class struggle" and the "dictatorship of the proletariat."

The answer to their questions became increasingly clear as Yeltsin began to face strong opposition from the parliament and an erosion of support from the public as a whole. Thus, for example, from the far right came challenges by the National Salvation Front, a neo-fascist political group consisting largely of former communists, along with some retired military and police officers. In October 1992 the Salvation Front, which had strong links to the largest parliamentary bloc, Russian Unity, began issuing public appeals for the resignation of Yeltsin and the reestablishment of the Soviet state.[22]

Yeltsin's response was to get tough by directly confronting this opposition. But first he laid the groundwork, introducing amendments to the legal codes, with the stated purpose of "protecting the constitutional organs of power." The law now made it illegal to call publicly for a change in the constitutional system by force.[23]

Citing these amendments to the law, Yeltsin then proceeded, on 28 October, to issue a decree banning the National Salvation Front for contravening the Russian constitutional system.[24] He ordered the Ministries of Security and Internal Affairs to implement the decree. In response, members of the new front claimed that they had never advocated the use of force in any of their public statements and hence that Yeltsin's ban was illegal. They declared their intention to ignore it.[25]

In the face of this open defiance, Yeltsin's only recourse was to use police coercion to disband the Salvation Front, and this was apparently what he intended to do. But he failed to get the full cooperation of the Ministries of Security and Internal Affairs, which opted to stay out of the fray, declaring that they would act strictly within the framework of the law. The matter was deferred to the Constitutional Court, which subsequently refused to uphold the ban. It was not until a year later, after Yeltsin's violent struggle with the parliament, that he managed to outlaw the Salvation Front.

Why did these two "power ministries" let Yeltsin down? Although it is difficult to know for sure, it is doubtful that MB Chief Barannikov or MVD (regular police) Chief Viktor Erin actually refused to support Yeltsin. A more likely scenario is that they surveyed the sentiment in their respective organizations and found that there was little enthusiasm for a confrontation with this group, whose right-wing views were shared by many MB and MVD officers. (Indeed, one of its leaders was former KGB Major General Aleksandr Sterligov, an outspoken Russian nationalist.) Then Barannikov and Erin probably told Yeltsin that he could not count on the support of security and police troops if the confrontation led to violence. Supporting this hypothesis is the fact that on 28 October, the very day that Yeltsin issued his ban, it was announced in the press that a meeting of the Collegium (the minister and his deputies) of the Ministry of Security had just taken place. The meeting discussed the "dangerous trends toward the creation of unconstitutional power structures which threaten to erode or destroy the embryonic Russian state." But in the press report the Collegium was also quoted as saying that it "resolutely rejected attempts to use the system of the federal state security organs as an instrument in political battles."[26] In other words, the MB refused to get involved.

INSIDE THE MINISTRY OF SECURITY

The spate of reorganizations, personnel changes, negative publicity, and other upheavals that the security services were subjected to after August 1991 took its toll on staffers. It was not business as usual at the Lubianka. Not surprisingly, one of the biggest problems was demoralization. A journalist (with obvious sympathy for the security services) who attended a May 1992 meeting held by MB Chief Barannikov for young counterintelligence officers described the "psychological crisis" that the MB had been going through:

> Today, in addition to economic difficulties, internal factors, so to speak, have had a strong impact on the work of security staffers. There is the campaign to discredit the organs, even including attempts to destroy them completely, there is the desire to regard the work of agents as operatives as unlawful and immoral, there is unwarranted exposure of agents. . . . In addition, employees of the Ministry of Security have experienced a long period of reorganization—as a result of which certain subunits have been eliminated, sometimes thoughtlessly—faced instability and lacked clear-cut guidelines in their work.[27]

The journalist went on to discuss the "decline in efficiency" among security staffers and the fact that they had lost their pride and were afraid even to tell people where they worked. As a result, he said, "Some staffers have begun to seek employment in profitable commercial structures, others are playing a waiting game, and yet others have retreated into a world of personal interests and cares." Nonetheless, he went on, the outlook was not completely hopeless. A poll taken at the Moscow branch of the MB revealed that, despite the general anxiety and concern, 47 percent of the officers expressed optimism and confidence about the future, and 49 percent derived full satisfaction from their work.[28]

Another source, who had recently retired from the counterintelligence service, saw the problem in more dire terms. In his view counterintelligence was in serious decline. The ferment that had arisen in the minds of KGB staffers and secret agents as a result of perestroika had reached a fever pitch after August 1991. Soviet patriotism had been replaced by nationalism and the entire system of values had been turned upside down: "The betrayal of former friends and allies at the highest level is no longer a disgrace, but normal behavior; those sentenced for treason and espionage have traded their camp cots for comfortable apartments and begun to appear on television screens."[29]

According to this ex-officer, the biggest tragedy was the collapse of the agent network, which had formed the backbone of counterintelligence work. Now that the Soviet Union had fallen apart and the free market had taken over, agents had nothing to swear their allegiance to or fight for, and no one to protect them or guarantee their honor. "The sole basis for secret collaboration today," he observed bitterly, "is thirty silver coins at the going exchange rate."[30]

Although accurate in his description of the current situation, the author was looking at the past through rose-colored glasses. By all accounts, the kind of lofty idealism and dedicated patriotism that the author said motivated KGB staffers and agents was rare. According to numerous sources there was in fact plenty of corruption, bribery, and other types of "wheeling and dealing" in the old KGB.[31] In the absence of glasnost, however, all this went unreported and the official image of the KGB as an honorable organization was maintained. As one observer put it: "In former times anything that happened there never filtered out. When Academician [Andrei] Sakharov once stated that the KGB is the least corrupt organization, he probably meant that, by comparison with the lawlessness that reigned during the time of Nikolai Shchelokov [Brezhnev's notoriously corrupt crony, who headed the regular police] in the MVD, the KGB really did appear to be quite a decent organization."[32]

Now, however, the security organs were fair game for attacks and exposés in the press. With salary cuts and the loss of perquisites and privileges as a result of the government's economic woes, MB employees had more reason than ever to engage in illicit entrepreneurial activities—and there was plenty of opportunity. But they ran a greater risk of public exposure than they did in KGB days.

In an apparent effort to restore the image of the security organs and to curtail some of the more blatant illegalities, MB chief Barannikov initiated an in-house campaign against corruption. As a result, several top MB officers were removed from their posts in early June 1992. According to MB accounts, these officers had misappropriated apartments that were designated for official use and had obtained other valuables illegally.[33] Barannikov's first deputy, Anatolii Oleynikov, was among those who lost their jobs. Oleynikov, who had served in the KGB since 1968, resigned "for reasons of health," but one of his closest aides was charged with abuses, so it was generally assumed that Oleynikov had been tainted by the affair. Barannikov's dramatic announcement of the scandal created a media stir, leading some observers to speculate that the dismissed officers were scapegoats and that Barannikov, a former MVD chief, had simply wanted an excuse to get rid of some of the KGB old guard.[34]

But some housekeeping was in order because cases of the MB's complicity in illegalities continued to come to light. In one incident, which occurred in Yeltsin's hometown of Ekaterinburg (formerly Sverdlovsk), MB operatives were accused of putting pressure on the local police to expedite exit visas on behalf of their clients, from whom they then elicited a charge.[35] In early June 1993, a high-ranking officer of the Russian MB was arrested for taking part in illegal sales of munitions and other military property in the Moscow District. To make matters worse, certain unnamed but influential government officials then put pressure on the Moscow branch of the MB to drop the investigation, which it refused to do.[36] Even more serious was the arrest in June 1993 of Deputy Minister of Security N. Lisovoi, who had been appointed by Barannikov and was responsible for the financial, economic, construction, and medical units of the ministry. Lisovoi was charged along with several military officials in connection with the so-called "Arkhangelsk case." He had allegedly embezzled state property, taken bribes, and abused his official position.[37]

While publicized cases of MB illegalities were still relatively rare, the MB's image as honest and incorruptible had been deeply tarnished. Naturally, people began asking, for every reported case of wrongdoing, how many were covered up? Many former and current security officers were engaging in free-market activities, taking advantage of their unique training and access to information as well as their vast ties in government and military circles. Not surprisingly, such activities raised serious questions about conflict of interest, particularly since economic success often involved illegalities. As it turned out, Barannikov himself soon became involved an economic scandal.

The Ministry of Security at Work

Traditionally a great deal of rivalry and antagonism had existed between the MVD, where Barannikov had made his career, and the KGB. Therefore it stands to reason that, when Barannikov arrived to take over the counterintelligence service, bringing with him several MVD subordinates, there would be some resentment. Barannikov, however close he was to Yeltsin, did not have a completely free hand. The old KGB officers could still make their influence felt. This may explain why Oleynikov's replacement as first deputy MB chief was Nikolai Golushko, who had a long and successful career as a KGB counterintelligence officer.[38] Golushko, a Ukrainian, began his security work in 1963 in the Kemerovo Region of the Russian republic. By 1974 he was in Moscow, heading the department for inter-ethnic relations of the USSR KGB's notorious Fifth Chief Directorate.[39] It was this directorate, later renamed the Directorate for Protecting the Constitution, that persecuted dissidents, religious activists, and non-Russian nationalists. After later serving as chief of the USSR KGB's Secretariat, Golushko became chairman of the Ukrainian KGB in 1987, remaining there until the Soviet Union broke up.

Golushko's ties to the KGB old guard, to men like Iurii Andropov and former Fifth Directorate chief Filipp Bobkov, the bête noire of human rights activists, and his own well-earned reputation for being ruthless against dissenters, made him a repugnant figure among Russian democrats. How could the security service be reformed with someone like Golushko in a leading post there? Some Ukrainian patriots, moreover, considered him an agent of Moscow who had implemented repressive Soviet policies against Ukrainians on behalf of the Kremlin, and some said that Golushko had taken key files with him from the Ukrainian KGB when he moved to Moscow in late 1991.[40]

The presence of someone like Golushko in the MB did not mesh with the new image this agency was trying to project, although Golushko himself later said that he had little problem getting along with Barannikov.[41] Judging from the public statements emanating from the MB, its purpose— at least with regard to domestic operations—was completely different from that of the KGB. At a press conference in April 1992, Barannikov stated flatly: "Above all, we have rejected the concept of ideological subversion. That is what the activities of the fifth service [Fifth Chief Directorate] used to entail."[42] The main focus of the MB's efforts, he said, was on counterintelligence to combat foreign spies. In reference to other domestic problems, Barannikov cited terrorism as a major threat, along with economic crime, which involved "high echelons of power and international links."

All this sounded reasonable. The MB's stated goals differed little from those of Western counterintelligence services. Why, then, did Barannikov need a staff of 137,000 (as compared with around 24,000 full-time FBI employees)? During 1992 alone, according to MB spokesmen, the MB had encountered more than 240 terrorist explosions and numerous hijacking attempts. There were up to 1.5 million illegal firearms in Russia. There was a growing danger of acts of nuclear, biological, chemical, and industrial terrorism.[43] Much of the terrorism was inspired by ethnic separatists. According to the head of the MB's Public Relations Department, General Andrei Chernenko, "persons of Caucasian nationality" posed an especially great problem. Extremist groups in the service of "certain political movements beyond the boundaries of Russia" had penetrated into Russia and were committing violent acts.[44] This marked the beginning of a steady campaign of words against people from the Caucasus, Chechens in particular.

A growing challenge, according to the MB, was that posed by Western "special services." In an October 1992 interview, Chernenko said that spying by foreign intelligence services had doubled and trebled in certain areas over the past year. "Our adversary," he went on, "prefers a very simple and old-fashioned method—the recruitment of agents from among Russian citizens. Unfortunately, it succeeds." Chernenko revealed that in early 1992 the MB caught a group of agents "belonging to a powerful intelligence service" who "tried to get on the heels of our retreating army." (The implication was that these agents were conducting subversion among Russian army troops abroad.) He also noted that the MB had arrested a Russian colonel, a high-ranking specialist, who had an active criminal association with the CIA.[45]

Barannikov echoed this note of alarm in his speech to the December 1992 Congress of People's Deputies, pointing out that the transparency of Russia's borders with the new CIS states allowed foreign spies to escape the scrutiny of the security organs.[46] At a January 1993 media briefing, a group of MB officials urged journalists to draw public attention to "unprecedented interference" by Western special services in all spheres of Russian life. Foreign intelligence agents, they said, had virtually unlimited opportunities to gain access to the organs of state power at all levels, as well as to places where Russian state and military secrets were concentrated. At least ten international agencies with branches in Russia and other CIS states were coordinated by foreign special services, they said. During 1992 the MB exposed no less than twenty foreign agents. They had also uncovered attempts to smuggle abroad significant amounts of oil, precious metals, and weapons.[47]

The MB's statements about Western subversion, while bland in comparison with what KGB officials used to say, were nonetheless out of keeping with the general tenor of relations between Russia and the West. Russian Foreign Minister Andrei Kozyrev, after all, was at this time urging Russia to draw closer to the West and to stop being suspicious of Western intentions toward Russia. He also warned Russians against efforts to reestablish the Soviet empire.[48] Presumably, Kozyrev had the backing of Yeltsin, who expressed friendliness toward the United States and its allies and support for the independence of the former Soviet states. Was the MB leadership falling under the influence of the conservative Russian nationalists in the parliament, or was it simply trying to drum up public support for its operations by emphasizing the threats to Russia's security? If the latter was true, then Yeltsin may well have had no objections to the seemly belligerent line the MB was taking. Like Gorbachev before him, he was able to distance himself publicly from these statements and appear conciliatory toward the West. At the same time, if he decided to take a tougher approach, he could always fall back on the excuse that he was being pressured by the security services.

In fact, the concerns voiced by the MB on the growing threats of Western subversion did not fall on deaf ears. Many Russians, it seems, took these threats seriously. According to an opinion poll taken in early 1992, despite the end of the cold war a significant proportion of the population supported the efforts of the Russian security services. The poll revealed that over one-third of the respondents believed that Western foreign intelligence services were working to undermine Russia and the CIS.[49]

Fighting Corruption

An even greater proportion of the Russian public, according to this opinion poll, were deeply worried about organized crime and considered the security services to be the only force capable of grappling with this problem. Corruption was not a new problem. Bribe taking and behind-the-scenes deals had been accepted practice for officialdom already in Soviet days. By the late Brezhnev period, "mafias," or organized criminal groups, pervaded the Soviet republics, providing illicit goods and services by stealing state property, and by smuggling and bribery. Mafia bosses were sometimes high party or state officials who used their positions to squander state funds. As one Western source expressed it: "The economy in the former USSR was controlled by what was in essence an organized criminal syndicate: the Communist Party. The bribes that flowed up the party hierarchy formed the tribute, the protection money or the informal taxes, that were a necessary part of conducting business in the USSR."[50] With few exceptions, neither the regular police, the MVD, nor the KGB did much to stop this flourishing illegal economy. Indeed, most regular policemen were "on the take" themselves. According to one MVD spokesman, in 1991 a third of the mafia's profits went to bribe MVD staffers.[51]

After the Soviet Union collapsed, government officials, with few restraints to prevent them from abusing their positions, were able to use the process of privatization of state property for their own gain. The overlap between government-controlled economic enterprises and private entrepreneurial ventures created vast opportunities for illegal economic activity at the highest levels.[52] Although these activities could not necessarily be termed "organized crime," the absence of a legal means of enforcing contracts and the more general breakdown of law and order often brought corrupt officials, as well as legitimate entrepreneurs, into contact with the mafia.[53]

Yeltsin placed the struggle against corruption high on his agenda. Here he had to have the MB's cooperation, not only because he wanted to rid the system of economic abuses, but also because he was using the anti-corruption drive to move against his political opponents. With official corruption so ubiquitous, attempts to curb it opened up a Pandora's box and set the stage for an intense political struggle. Yeltsin's tendency to bypass the regular legal channels and to create extra-judicial administrative bodies to expose corrupt officials further politicized the anticorruption campaign. One of the first such bodies was an ad hoc working group to combat crime, headed by Prime Minister Egor Gaidar and formed in the spring of 1992, to prevent the expropriation of state property during the process of privatization. Though the group's leaders took credit for saving the state millions of rubles, they acknowledged that, since they did not have the services of the MB or the regular police at their disposal, their effectiveness was limited.[54]

In October 1992, Yeltsin created a new, more authoritative body, the Interdepartmental Commission for Combatting Crime and Corruption, which included the ministers of security and internal affairs, the chief of the Foreign Intelligence Service, and the heads of various economic ministries and the customs service. The commission, headed by Vice-President Aleksandr Rutskoi of Russia, was to coordinate the work of the law enforcement agencies in the struggle against crime. The focus would be on preventing Russian bureaucrats from selling state property, economic secrets, and raw materials to domestic or foreign firms for personal gains, as well as to prevent currency and banking crimes.

From its inception the commission had a highly political role. Rutskoi, who drew up the statute on the new commission, said it would deal with conflicts between ministries and departments concerned with law enforcement and would "examine cases of interference by the organs of state power and management in the operational activity of law enforcement agencies." Though Rutskoi's stated goal was to prevent politicians from influencing criminal investigations, both the MB and the MVD resented outside involvement in their operations.[55]

By this time the MB was already actively engaged in fighting organized crime and official corruption. Not surprisingly, given its active public relations department, the MB made a point of publicizing its role as the guardian of Russia's assets and the leader of the struggle against dishonest entrepreneurs. Although stories of corruption at the very top dominated the news, there were plenty of reports about the MB's successes in struggling against illegal arms dealers, members of the mafia, and the like. In one case, that of a group of gangsters from St. Petersburg who had committed armed robberies, the MB had arrested seventeen persons and implicated several hundred others.[56] Then there was the so-called Operation Trawl, orchestrated by the MB to stop the illegal export of timber, metals, and ammunition from Russia that was reportedly valued at 6.6 billion rubles. According to the MB's Chief Barannikov, the MB had, by December 1992, opened up 217 criminal cases in connection with this operation.[57]

In May 1993 news appeared of the MB's capture of a group of officers and soldiers exchanged in arms trading in the city of Rostov.[58] The MB also achieved a major victory against a large number of businessmen in

St. Petersburg and Pskov who were smuggling precious raw materials and industrial goods across Russian borders to sell abroad.[59]

Meanwhile in September 1992 Yeltsin had posted state security employees (part of the "operational reserve") to government institutions as watchdogs against corruption.[60] According to General Aleksandr Gurov, deputy chief of the MB's Directorate for Combatting Corruption, by December 1992 the MB had a card file of over three thousand persons suspected of economic crimes, although only a small portion had been arrested.[61]

Gurov's boss in the anticorruption directorate, General Anatolii Trofimov, a veteran KGB official, asserted in a January 1993 interview that corruption among those holding government positions was reaching epidemic proportions. "Legal nihilism," he said, "is taking root in the public mind and an attitude of self-protection and survival, of acquiring the means of survival by any available means, including unlawful methods, is emerging."[62] Trofimov cited several cases where Russian officials had used their positions for personal gain and urged the government to pass laws to regulate the activity of government employees to prevent them from defrauding the state.

Barannikov spoke in more alarmist terms at a two-day conference on crime convened by Yeltsin in February 1993. "Organized crime in conjunction with corruption has reached such a level that it has begun to pose a real threat to the state's ability to ensure the safety of both society and the individual," he said. Referring to the thousands of cases of corruption by government officials, Barannikov placed a good portion of the blame on "foreign special services," which he claimed recruited people in organized crime and helped them build relations with international criminal organizations. He also blamed the unstable economic situation caused by chaotic privatization. It was not that the MB was opposed to economic reform, he said—"please do not number our department among the diehard conservatives"—but that the process should be more carefully regulated.[63]

Yeltsin also spoke at the conference, agreeing with Barannikov's assessment of the grave threat posed by organized crime: "Corruption in the organs of power and administration are literally eating away the body of the Russian state from top to bottom." Noting that the state had lost billions of rubles in 1992 as a result of corruption, Yeltsin voiced impatience with the efforts of the MB and the MVD to deal with this problem: "It is high time to sort out what is taking place at the Ministry of Internal Affairs, the Ministry of Security, and the Defense Ministry. In particular, entire ammunition dumps are being stolen from the Defense Ministry and no one says a thing. This is going beyond the limit." By contrast, Yeltsin gave a strong endorsement to Rutskoi's Interdepartmental Commission for Combatting Crime: "We count on its efficient work. It can do everything, it can find anyone who steals or takes bribes."[64] It was decided at the conference to add to the commission's manpower by transferring to it thirty specialists from the MB, the MVD, and the Ministry of Defense.[65]

CORRUPTION AND POLITICS

The anticorruption drive soon turned into a spectacle of accusations and counteraccusations among Russia's political leaders, with the MB in the middle. The Russian media, fed by a constant stream of revelations, was having a heyday. But there were few prosecutions. As former KGB staffer Vladimir Rubanov observed: "The problem of exposing corruption is turning from a legal into a political one. As soon as the law enforcement agencies begin to take measures in regard to some corrupt individual, immediately some highly placed patron arises behind his back."[66]

Yeltsin's own entourage was soon hit with charges of covering up illegalities. Iurii Boldyrev, head of the Control Administration of the President's Office, announced in early March 1993, shortly before he was fired, that he had discovered illegalities in the privatization process in Moscow back in the summer of 1992 but had been told by Yeltsin to stop the investigation. Boldyrev claimed that members of Yeltsin's administration were using his office to collect incriminating information against Yeltsin's enemies but at the same time were suppressing investigations against his supporters. He also mentioned widespread corruption among Russian military commanders in the Western Group of Forces, about to withdraw from East Germany. Boldyrev's Control Administration had prepared a report, with help of the MB and other legal agencies, documenting numerous instances of theft of government property, money laundering, and other crimes among Russian officers, but Boldyrev's successor at the Control Administration promptly issued a statement denying the charges against the military officers.[67]

A month later Yeltsin received a bigger blow. His erstwhile ally Rutskoi made a sensational announcement to the Russian parliament on 16 April, claiming that economic "shock therapy" had caused an intolerable rise in economic crime and accusing several officials close to Yeltsin of criminal activities. Among them was Egor Gaidar, the former acting prime minister (replaced by Viktor Chernomyrdin in late 1992), who, Rutskoi alleged, sold the country's gold reserves and permitted foreign firms to export valuable natural resources, and First Deputy Prime Minister Vladimir Shumeiko, who abused his position in granting monopoly import rights to certain foreign firms. In addition, Rutskoi implicated

Deputy Prime Minister Mikhail Poltoranin in the illegal sale of Russian property in Berlin.[68]

Another scandal that touched Yeltsin directly was the "Red Mercury" case, dubbed in the Russian press as "Eltsingate." Rutskoi claimed that Yeltsin and his aide Gennadii Burbulis gave monopoly rights to a firm in their native city of Ekaterinburg on the production and sale for export of a strategically important raw material given the name "red mercury." The day after Rutskoi delivered his speech, the procommunist paper *Pravda* published several secret documents relating to the "Red Mercury" case and confirming the allegations that Yeltsin and his close aides were involved in the manufacture and sale of this material. Significantly, the secret production and export of red mercury dated back to KGB days, when the Sixth Directorate oversaw the venture. The documents indicated that both the Foreign Intelligence Service (FIS) and the MB were still connected with the venture.[69]

Damage control and aggressive counteraction became the order of the day for Yeltsin and his colleagues. They accused Rutskoi of disclosing state secrets, claiming that he was privy to all the information on red mercury and had deliberately distorted the facts to incriminate his political opponents. A few days after the appearance of the *Pravda* article, the FIS issued a statement claiming that the compound "red mercury" did not exist and that it was being used as a cover for the export of valuable strategic materials, including gold, plutonium, and uranium. The FIS denied any involvement in these commercial ventures.[70] The next day the president of Promekologiia, the Ekaterinburg firm in question, appeared on television. While acknowledging that his firm had worked in the "closest collaboration" with the Ministry of Security and with the president's administration to organize the production and export of a product they called "red mercury," he denied any wrongdoing. They were, he said, engaging in normal commercial activity on behalf of the country's interests, and Rutskoi's disclosures had now undermined this activity.[71]

COMMERCIAL VENTURES FOR THE FORMER KGB

The flurry of allegations and counterallegations regarding the "Red Mercury" case, and the complicated maneuevers of those involved, were difficult to follow. But one thing was clear: not only politicians but also members of the security services were actively engaging in commercial ventures, just as their KGB predecessors had done. The MB was responsible for enforcing a wide range of laws affecting business transactions with the West, particularly those laws governing exports of raw materials and advanced technology. This gave its staffers access to information that was of use to business people, including data on their competitors and on government regulatory policies.

The MB's role as arbitrator of transactions involving foreign exports thus offered it unique opportunities to participate in these ventures. Or, at the very least, the fact that it was privy to most of the information regarding these transactions gave it considerable influence. As Yevgenia Albats put it: "The KGB's [sic] involvement in a company apparently instills confidence in foreign investors. With so vast an institution backing it, a new venture seems less likely to vanish into thin air. Clearly, moral considerations aside, the foreign businessmen are right—these partners do know their business."[72]

The first reports of commercial activities by members of the security services appeared as far back as 1990, when several KGB staffers turned up on the board of the ANT Company. ANT was a semiprivate cooperative that was allegedly engaged in secret exports of Soviet weapons and was subsequently shut down.[73] Then there was the "Santa" foreign economic association, created in the autumn of 1990 by officers of the KGB's Third Chief Directorate (for military counterintelligence). Santa allegedly had branches in several cities and was engaged in selling military goods abroad.[74] In November 1991 *Stolitsa* magazine reported that the heads of the all-Russian stock exchange center and two-thirds of its staff were officers of the KGB. The article claimed that the center had a network of institutions for channeling and laundering money for the KGB, the military, and the Communist Party.[75]

After the dissolution of the Soviet Union and the demise of the Communist Party, commercial operations became an even greater attraction for security professionals. Without the constraint of party control, MB officers, anxious to supplement their regular salaries, became entrepreneurs on the side. Often they worked with former colleagues who had left the KGB to engage in full-time business.

One organization that became actively involved in commercial operations was the Federal Agency for Government Communications and Information (FAPSI). The law governing FAPSI, enacted in February 1993, specifically granted it the right to lease government communications lines to commercial banks and other enterprises for confidential transactions such as fund transfers and credit charges.[76] This provided FAPSI with a rich source of income for the much-needed upgrading of its communications technology. The agency also began leasing radio frequency bands and even selling certain types of equipment to foreign firms.[77] The Main Guard Directorate also sought money on the side. In February 1992 its chief, Mikhail Barsukov, signed a lucrative, three-year agreement with a private company, which was granted exclusive photo and film rights within the Kremlin in exchange for a substantial sum of money.[78]

Ex-Chekisty

Retired or dismissed KGB officials also became entrepreneurs, moving into business in droves. The Institute of Sociology of the Russian Academy of Sciences polled some thirty former KGB officers who had quit their jobs to engage in commerce and found that, while only one in three was financially successful, the majority were happy with their current work. Most of those polled said that they relied on assistance from "colleagues who still work at the old place" to further their commercial ventures.[79] Often these "ex-Chekisty" would act as facilitators in arranging Western investments in Russian enterprises. In these cases they were not reluctant to reveal their backgrounds. "Look," they would say to Western businessmen, "we know how to keep you out of the hands of the KGB because we used to be in it."

Another popular activity was private security and investigation, services for which there was such demand in Russia that the government passed a law in 1992 regulating such work and setting conditions for obtaining licenses to operate.[80] Moscow's Stolichnyi Bank, for example, hired former members of the KGB's elite Alpha unit. According to one source, "The 'Stolichny KGB' eavesdropped on clients, as well as employees, with top-of-the-line equipment imported from Europe."[81] The Russian press reported in early 1993 that the Moscow-based Most construction and financial company, which employed large numbers of former KGB officers, had a security force of 450 men to guard its three thousand employees. Another firm, Menatop, had a five hundred-man security guard.[82] The Moscow guard agency Baiard, created in 1990, had by 1994 over one thousand employees. By December 1994 more than one hundred private guard and investigative agencies were registered officially, while around nine hundred were operating without licenses. [83]

Sergei Stepashin observed after he became head of counterintelligence in 1994: "Our professionals are highly sought after everywhere and offered salaries that sometimes are ten times higher than what they were paid in the government service."[84] By 1995, according to the executive director of the Association of Russian Banks on Security Questions, 50 percent of the managers of independent security services consisted of former KGB employees, while about 25 percent were from the MVD and the rest from the military. These private security personnel were well armed: in Moscow alone over 7,000 regular pistols, 4,600 gas pistols, and almost 4,000 rifles had been issued to them.[85] Although in most cases they worked well with their former colleagues from the law enforcement agencies, there were clashes, such as the one that occurred in December

1994, discussed below, between the Most security guard's and Yeltsin's Security Service.

Former intelligence officers were particularly sought after because of their education and knowledge of foreign languages and international affairs. A leading FIS official acknowledged in late 1993 that commercial enterprises and banks were hiring his former staffers to work in their own in-house intelligence services.[86] Some retired officers started their own firms. Leonid Shebarshin, who headed KGB foreign intelligence operations, founded the Russian Economic National Security Service, which employed around twenty ex-Chekisty and provided a variety of services to private companies and joint ventures. Among his employees was an old friend and colleague, Nikolai Leonov, who had been in charge of spy operations in the Western Hemisphere during the 1980s. Shebarshin's group carried out checks on the financial standing of foreign partners, offered analytical support to businesses and also provided physical security.[87]

Aleksei Kisilev, another former intelligence officer, started the Commercial Security Service, which protected the financial secrets of businesses and provided market research and economic analysis to foreign firms. His service gained long-term contracts with several leading Japanese companies.[88] Another firm, NAMAKOM, was doing private security, consulting, and background checks for Western companies, advising these companies on the reliability of investments in Russia. Its chief, Iurii Ivanovich Drozhdov, had headed the KGB's Department S, which dealt with illegals (KGB agents abroad under cover). Drozhdov had organized the exchange of KGB spy Rudolph Abel, managed the famous terrorist Carlos, and trained Palestinian terrorists. In his seventies, Drozdov retired from the KGB in 1990 because he did not get along with his boss, Shebarshin.[89]

Former foreign intelligence officers appeared much better off financially than their counterparts who had worked in domestic operations. Leonov, for example, was living like an English gentleman in a lavish (by Russian standards) apartment, with all the amenities. Judging from a few direct contacts with ex-KGB domestic staffers, their means were more modest. This is not surprising, since those who worked abroad enjoyed perks and material benefits that were not available to KGB officers at home. And men like Shebarshin and Leonov continued to have good relations with the foreign intelligence service, so they probably still enjoyed some of their old privileges.[90]

According to a retired counterintelligence officer, some of his former colleagues were so poor that they were forced to move into the criminal world, where they stood to gain substantial material benefits. With their knowledge of police methods, their access, through connections with friends still employed in the service, to political and economic information, and their ability to identify counterintelligence agents who had infiltrated criminal groups, these men were sought after by criminals. And the numerous reorganizations in the counterintelligence service, according to this source, were driving some current officers into the mafia.[91]

It is difficult to assess the extent of the KGB-mafia connection. Some Western sources have also reported that many ex-Chekisty now work for the criminal underground, but much of the evidence is anecdotal.[92] Former KGB chairman Kriuchkov, as might be expected, expressed indignation over these claims, calling them slanderous. KGB employees, he said, were always honest and honorable and still are.[93] If there is any truth in Kriuchkov's words, then it applies to the particular Soviet context. This basically meant that the ruling elite, including KGB bureaucrats, could help themselves to large pieces of the state pie because they were the ones who controlled the economy and made the rules. KGB officers did not have to engage in racketeering and underground smuggling rings because they could do well enough as part of the *nomenklatura*, particularly if they worked for foreign intelligence. After 1991 the situation changed. In order to get rich quick in free-market circumstances, more and more government bureaucrats began to disobey the law, and the line between "mafia" and official corruption in Russia became blurred.

RETURN OF "BIG BROTHER"?

The line separating Chekisty and ex-Chekisty was also hard to draw, because some officers continued to work for their former employer as consultants or maintained business ties with old colleagues. Whatever the case, security personnel, past and present, became heavily involved in commercial ventures. Naturally, people began to wonder where the money from those business deals was going and who had authorized them. Why was Yeltsin allowing this sort of thing to go on, particularly in the Guard Directorate and FAPSI, which were directly under the president? When the above-mentioned Law on the Federal Organs of Government Communication and Information was published, it met with loud protest from the liberal press. *Nezavisimaia gazeta* dubbed it the "law of the Big Brother," pointing out that it not only gave the executive organs of government a monopoly over government communications and information, but also permitted unwarranted interference in the communications networks of private banks and firms.[94]

The law authorized FAPSI to issue licenses for the export and import of information technology, as well as for the telecommunications of all private financial institutions. FAPSI, which was equipped with a body of special communications troops, was given the right to monitor enciphered communications of both government agencies and those of nonstate enterprises. In other words, it could penetrate all private information systems. The law gave lip service to parliamentary supervision of FAPSI (Article 21 stated vaguely that officials from this agency were to give reports to the Supreme Soviet). The president, by contrast, "monitors the execution of basic tasks entrusted to FAPSI," and "sanctions their operations."

Apparently Yeltsin was giving these executive security agencies broad latitude, both commercially and otherwise, because he wanted them to be both powerful and loyal to him. Yeltsin's decisions on the security services had appeared haphazard and reactive when he began his tenure as president of the new Russian Federation in late 1991. In retrospect, however, his policies seem more calculated. One Russian legal expert, Viktor Suslov, suggested that Yeltsin's ill-fated attempt to merge the ministries of internal affairs and security in late December 1991 was a smoke screen to deflect attention from his real moves to reconstitute the KGB's successors under his own authority.[95] As Suslov pointed out, during the furor over the proposed merger, the Russian Federation Main Guard Directorate (GUO) was being established. No one seemed to notice that Yeltsin was building up a substantial security force that was answerable only to him. As Suslov put it: "While the public was keeping an eye on the 'purity of morals' in the Russian Ministry of Security and the Ministry of Internal Affairs, the presidential secret guard committee gained force and acquired additional powers. . . . In a word, tens of thousands of servicemen who in theory are protecting and maintaining three dozen presidential residences day and night. But in practice?"[96]

The functions of this agency were set forth in a Law on State Protection of Government Bodies and Their Officials, passed in April 1993.[97] The GUO was placed on the same footing as a state committee, but in fact neither the Law on the Government nor the Law on the President made provision for such a structure. Suslov had assumed therefore that the Constitutional Court would examine the legality of Yeltsin's new creation, especially since a group of parliamentary deputies had petitioned it to do so. But this did not happen. In terms of its concern over the powers of the former KGB, public attention continued to be focused on the highly visible Ministry of Security.

It is not difficult to understand why the president would establish his own elite troop formations and a powerful communications agency. He was faced with opposition from many quarters, and by 1993 a confrontation with parliamentary opponents was looming. As events would show, it was essential to Yeltsin to have reliable troops at his disposal. And control over the channels of information, both public and secret, was a crucial strategic resource. Nonetheless, the establishment of such bodies set a dangerous precedent and did little to further the cause of democracy in Russia.

The broad, intrusive powers that had been granted to agencies like the GUO, FAPSI, and MB aroused concern about a possible return to the past, when secret surveillance and illegal political investigations were the order of the day. And not without reason. Although MB officials complained that they no longer had the resources and staff to carry out telephone taps on a widespread basis, Deputy Minister of Security Andrei Bykov allowed that his staff of 1,000 could monitor the telephones of 2,500 persons in Russia simultaneously. This amounted, he said, to monitoring up to 30,000 persons annually.[98] These figures excluded the wiretaps carried out by FAPSI and the Main Guard Directorate, which reportedly monitored government officials, politicians, and other agencies.[99]

What protection did Russians have against such practices? As mentioned above, the procurator's office was the guardian against police abuses. But the Procuracy never said no to the security services. As one Russian journalist expressed it: "If you decide to 'complain' about the secret services to the Procuracy, the procurator will simply direct your statement to the same counterintelligence people and duplicate their response to you. The procurator himself does not even have access to secret documents."[100] Although this situation was worrisome to human rights activists, it suited Yeltsin's purposes. By early 1993 Yeltsin began to enlist his security police in the secret surveillance of his political opponents. Drawing the police into his political struggles, Yeltsin was heading for confrontation with his rivals.

Chapter Three

SECURITY SERVICES PUT TO THE TEST:

THE POLITICAL CRISES OF 1993

> Many of my contacts told me that he [Yeltsin] was a victim
> of that old delusion of new regimes: under the old regime—
> the bad guys, Gorbachev, Brezhnev, Andropov and all
> the rest—the KGB was bad; but under the new (good)
> guy, Yeltsin, the KGB would be good. He'd be able to
> keep them in line; he'd take care of it personally.
> What a tragic mistake of judgment that was.
> *(Yevgenia Albats,* The State within a State, *1994)*

LOOKING BACK at the events of August 1991, Elena Bonner, human rights activist and the widow of Andrei Sakharov, criticized Yeltsin for not acting more boldly. At that time, according to Bonner, Yeltsin should have discarded democratic principles for the sake of expediency, dissolved the Russian parliament, and held new elections. Had he done this, then he could have achieved economic reform and a constitutional government. "We lost our August victory," Bonner said. "The hope that it could be built on and developed by parliamentary means was Yeltsin's main historic error."[1] One of the unfortunate consequences of this error, Bonner added, was that the KGB had "taken heart again." In other words, if Yeltsin had acted resolutely, albeit undemocratically, he could have established a new political and economic system before the former KGB had a chance to recoup the losses inflicted by the August putsch attempt.

From the standpoint of Yeltsin's personal power and his planned reform program for Russia, it is of course true that he would have furthered his aims to a much greater extent if he had been more decisive early on. But the readiness with which he employed the undemocratic services of the former KGB in all his subsequent political battles raises doubts about how democratic his goals were to begin with. As one political commentator observed in May 1993, "Yeltsin is a symbol of democracy in the eyes of those who support him. They forgive him for violations of the Constitution, or simply do not notice them, because they consider his opponents nondemocrats. Well, these opponents think otherwise. Since there are tens of millions of people on each side, this indicates how great the danger of a schism still is. After all, a schism is a situation whereby each of the sides is guided by the truth which is above the law."[2]

This is not to underestimate the severe constraints under which Yeltsin was operating. Even in democratic states, authorities have trouble resisting the temptation to resort to strong-arm tactics when faced with threats to stability. Yeltsin was being challenged from several directions. And increasingly, as positive performance indicators proved lacking, he was functioning on "negative legitimacy." The main elements of his program were "anti"—anticorruption, anticommunism, antiseparatism, and, by the spring of 1993, antiparliament. In all his struggles Yeltsin needed the backing of the so-called power ministries—the Ministry of Defense, the Ministry of Internal Affairs, and the Ministry of Security. Without a show of force behind him, Yeltsin could not wage a determined fight against his enemies. But did he have this support?

THE MARCH CRISIS

The first test came in the spring of 1993, when the uneasy truce between Yeltsin and the parliament was broken. After the Eighth Congress of People's Deputies voted in mid-March to deprive Yeltsin of his extraordinary presidential powers, Yeltsin went on television on 20 March to declare the imposition of "special rule," giving him veto powers over the congress until new elections were held.[3] He also announced a referendum on 25 April, when citizens would vote on a new constitution and on confidence in the president. Yeltsin made it clear that the "power ministries" had been instructed to enforce his decree.

During the next few days, however, it became less and less certain that Yeltsin's instructions would be carried out. Minister of Defense Pavel Grachev insisted that the army would "mind its own business" and alluded to dissension with the ranks over Yeltsin's decree.[4] Barannikov, chief of the Ministry of Security (MB), said in a speech to the 21 March session of the Supreme Soviet, that his ministry would not get involved in the political confrontation and urged that a compromise be found.[5] Spokespersons for the MB reportedly denied that Barannikov had approved Yeltsin's decree beforehand and said no discussion of implementing the decree had taken place among their leaders.[6] On 24 March, four days after Yeltsin's television address, the press reported that the power ministries were observing strict neutrality, which meant that, should Yeltsin provoke a confrontation with parliament, they might not back him.[7]

Given such a lukewarm reaction from the defense and security ministries, it is not surprising that, when Yeltsin's decree was finally published on 24 March, it contained no reference to a "special regime." Indeed, although he stuck to his decision to hold a referendum in April, Yeltsin retreated from his confrontational stance. As he himself later wrote: "Now that I was so close to decreeing restrictions on the rights of Congress through an act of will, once again I backed off."[8]

Meanwhile the Russian press was speculating about which way the army and the police would lean if the political struggle reached an impasse. "Close attention to the men with the guns is quite justifiable today," observed one journalist, who claimed that, despite the army's declared neutrality, Defense Minister Grachev was in the Yeltsin camp and that he had supported the edict on "special rule."[9] Yeltsin had reportedly made a special point of keeping on good terms with the top military leadership, offering them perquisites such as state dachas and pay raises, while at the same time turning a blind eye to the rampant corruption within the armed forces (the case of the Western Group of Forces being a good example). In return, Grachev was said to have promised the support of certain army units, including the troops of the Moscow Garrison, in the event of a crisis. But he hoped to avoid this eventuality because anti-Yeltsin sentiment ran high among the officers of the armed forces and Grachev worried about provoking a split within his forces.[10]

Barannikov was not planning for a similar show of force by the MB on behalf of Yeltsin. He and Minister of Interior Viktor Erin were said to be "sitting the fence," waiting to see what would happen. Although Barannikov was close to Yeltsin and sympathetic to his policies, he did not feel confident enough of his control over the MB to enlist its support on behalf of Yeltsin.[11] Also, he may have doubted Yeltsin's staying power and did not want to link himself irrevocably to the president. The days of August 1991 offered a stark reminder of the vulnerability of the security services when drawn into power struggles. If Yeltsin were defeated in a violent showdown with his parliamentary enemies, those who backed him would face reprisals. Both Barannikov and Erin did make an appearance with Yeltsin at a rally of 100,000 of his supporters near the Kremlin on 28 March. But, as *Rossiiskaia gazeta* (Russian Gazette) put it: "The generals were hardly likely to have attended the rally out of their own free will. In all probability, they were persuaded to attend by the Russian president standing alongside them."[12] Asked in a subsequent interview about his presence at the rally, Barannikov explained: "I act, not out of political partiality but from my official duties as laid down by law. These provide for certain officials [i.e., Yeltsin] to be protected with all measures of security."[13]

The MB was clearly in no mood to crack down on Yeltsin's enemies. On 1 May some two thousand procommunist, anti-Yeltsin demonstrators marched on Red Square in violation of a decree issued by Yeltsin two days earlier, banning demonstrations near government buildings. Over five hundred people were injured and one militia member was killed during clashes between the demonstrators and police. In the aftermath, the MB took an uncharacteristically detached stance, declaring that it had no information on who had incited the disturbances and refraining from an investigation. According to an MB spokesperson, the MB would not interfere in the activities of political parties and public associations.[14]

BARANNIKOV'S DOUBLE GAME

Barannikov had stated in this above-mentioned interview that "while I am minister, the security organs will not let themselves be drawn into political games, whoever would like this and however."[15] But reports were already circulating that Barannikov's ministry was gathering compromising information about members of Yeltsin's entourage, along with information on his enemies, "to remain afloat in the event of victory by either side."[16] And rumors were rife that Yeltsin was about to dismiss Barannikov.

Although Yeltsin won a victory against his opponents in the 25 April referendum (which endorsed Yeltsin and his policies), he still faced challenges, not the least of which were the escalating charges of corruption against key members of his government. Judging from the intense preoccupation with the corruption issue on all sides of the political spectrum, it was explosive and he could ill-afford to have a minister of security who was not wholeheartedly on his side. The MB, after all, had "the goods" on thousands of corrupt officials, as well as broad authority—conferred by Yeltsin's decrees—to conduct searches and interrogations.[17] Yeltsin did not want the MB's investigative powers to be unleashed on his men.

As discussed above, Vice-President Alexander Rutskoi was one of the first to make allegations of corruption against specific members of Yeltsin's government. Having opposed Yeltsin's attempt to declare special rule in March 1993, Rutskoi was outspoken in his opposition to the 25 April referendum and was apparently using the charges to deprive Yeltsin of a victory. He managed to gain the support of Procurator-General Stepankov, whose office announced that it had initiated proceedings in the "Red Mercury" case and planned to question several members of the presidential staff. In addition, the procurator's office claimed to have new evidence of embezzlement by high-ranking military officers, including Grachev.[18] In retaliation, Yeltsin stripped Rutskoi of key responsibilities, and on 28 April dismissed him from the leadership of the Interdepartmental Commission on Crime and Corruption, putting himself in charge.

This did not put an end to the corruption allegations, however. Rutskoi insisted that he had documentation to back up his claims, some of which was already in the hands of the procurator. In late June the deputy procurator-general, Nikolai Makarov, delivered a lengthy report to the Russian parliament in which he said that, although his investigation was ongoing, many of Rutskoi's charges had already been confirmed by a special investigation. Yeltsin's deputy minister Mikhail Poltoranin had, he said, concluded an illegal deal with a German businessman and his first deputy minister, Vladimir Shumeiko, had signed several directives transferring Russian government property, including an apartment in Monaco worth 29 million French francs, to private Russian and Western firms. Makarov recommended specifically that Shumeiko and Poltoranin be removed from their jobs, a step that the parliament approved. He also implicated a number of military commanders in the misappropriation of state property and claimed that two Mercedes automobiles had been purchased in Germany for Defense Minister Grachev under a fictitious name.[19]

Where did the procurator's office get the documentation for all these allegations? According to Makarov, they were "demanded and obtained from the Ministry of Security and the Ministry of Internal Affairs (MVD) of Russia in a volume of over 3,000 sheets." He also said that the MB had participated in the investigation that formed the foundation of his report.[20]

Not surprisingly, rumors about Barannikov's impending dismissal mounted. Yeltsin kept quiet, however. He had in fact categorically rejected the possibility of Barannikov's forced departure on 15 May, when he addressed a group of senior MB officials at a closed meeting. Nonetheless, he made it clear in this address, parts of which found their way into the press, that he would not countenance any dissent within MB ranks. After thanking MB leaders for their help in getting rid of some fifty-seven government officials who had opposed him, he went on to quote former CIA director, Allen Dulles: "Politics must be based on the correct analysis of those facts which can be gathered together. This analysis must be given to an institution that is not pursuing mercenary [korystnye] aims and is not tied to any political line."[21]

Was this a direct message to Barannikov and those who had helped gather the documents for the procurator's office? To make his point, Yeltsin went on to say that he knew many in the MB supported his reforms, but he also knew that some were following a different path:

> I am not calling for some sort of a purge and so on. But if someone—and we have the facts—works outside the program of the ministers, the president, and such cases as I have already cited in the presidential structure and the

government, we have to get rid of him. It is very dangerous to have people in this agency who do not support the general policy. There are, to be sure, only a few, maybe ten, if you include the local organs. Of course, they don't make waves, but in principle, there is no place for them in these organs.[22]

Some security officials remained unconvinced by Yeltsin's appeals for unconditional support. *Literaturnaia Rossiia* (Literary Russia), which published excerpts from his secret address, quoted one member of the audience as saying: "How can the position Yeltsin took in his address be reconciled with his calls for real, constitutional democracy?"[23]

BARANNIKOV'S DISMISSAL

Barannikov's response, according to subsequent press reports, was to continue providing Yeltsin's enemies with materials to back up their corruption charges against the Yeltsin camp. On 22 July 1993 the Procuracy, with the assistance of the MB, searched Poltoranin's apartment and called him in for a three-hour interrogation. Three days later Procurator-General Stepankov indicated that he was planning to arrest Shumeiko. Within the week Yeltsin had fired Barannikov.

The official reason given for Barannikov's dismissal was an incident that took place on the border between Tadzhikistan and Afghanistan on 13 July 1993. A group of four hundred Afghan soldiers and Tadzhik rebels opposed to their government attacked a border post guarded by Russian border troops, who, caught completely by surprise, sustained heavy losses. Twenty-four Russians were killed and eighteen wounded during an eleven-hour battle. It later was claimed that the MB and its border guard headquartered in Moscow had known that the posts along the border with Afghanistan were likely to be attacked, but made no effort to prepare. The warning of an impending attack was reportedly never communicated to the border post in question. Furthermore, no reinforcements were sent after the attack had begun.[24]

Responding to the tragedy, Yeltsin not only dismissed Barannikov, but also Vladimir Shliakhtin, chief of the border guards. He placed overall responsibility for coordinating forces along the border in the hands of Defense Minister Grachev and appointed Grachev's subordinate, First Deputy Chief of the General Staff Andrei Nikolaev, as Shliakhtin's replacement. All this was a clear signal that Yeltsin was unhappy with the MB leadership, which heretofore had sole authority for border protection.

Yeltsin stated publicly that he had dismissed Barannikov "for violating ethical norms," as well as for mishandling the border crisis. It was not immediately clear what the ethical violations were, but, shortly before Barannikov's dismissal, a Moscow paper had claimed that Yeltsin had come across some "explosive" documents linking Barannikov to corrupt activities: "Clouds are beginning to gather over the head of Russian security service chief V. Barannikov. The accusations leveled at his agency are that, while having enormous legislative and technical resources, it does little to prevent gigantic international swindles, the flight of capital from the country, etc."[25] The implication was that somehow Barannikov and his colleagues were profiting from these "international swindles" themselves.

Then came reports that Barannikov's wife had traveled to Switzerland with the wife of Deputy MVD Chief Andrei Dunaev in the summer of 1992. The ladies allegedly purchased some 300,000 dollars worth of luxury items, paid for by a foreign firm, Seabeco, connected with a Russian businessman named Dmitrii Iakubovskii.[26] As it turns out, these reports were just the tip of the iceberg. The Barannikov scandal was part of a much larger scandal involving several members of Yeltsin's administration.

Iakubovskii's name had been cropping up frequently in press disclosures about the international mafia. He had at one time headed a joint enterprise, Agropromkhin, set up by the Russian government in Zurich and had also been involved with the sale of Russian Army property in Germany. In June 1992 First Deputy Prime Minister Shumeiko of Russia appointed Iakubovskii an adviser to the Russian government and a month later he became a deputy chief, with the rank of colonel, of FAPSI (Federal Agency for Government Communications and Information). Just as he was about to take up the post of the president's special coordinator of the security services, a controversy arose and Iakubovksii flew off quickly to Switzerland.[27]

Iakubovskii, who had compromising information on Barannikov, soon became indispensable to the Yeltsin administration. Two members of Yeltsin's anticrime commission even made a special trip to Zurich, returning with evidence showing that Barannikov had been bribed by Seabeco's chief, a Russian emigré named Boris Birshtein.[28] On 23 July, just days before Barannikov's ouster, Iakubovskii returned to Moscow to help with the case. Barannikov reportedly sought unsuccessfully to have Iakubovskii arrested at the airport.[29]

A subsequent account of Iakubovskii's secret visit to Moscow, based on testimony from Yeltsin's chief legal adviser, Aleksandr Kotenkov, and on interviews with Iakubovskii himself, revealed that he was part of a high-stakes effort to discredit not only Barannikov, but also Rutskoi, Khasbulatov, and Procurator-General Stepankov. Iakubovskii claimed that he had documents proving the involvement of these officials in bribery and stealing money from the state. Iakubovskii was so essential to the success of the corruption cases against Yeltsin's enemies that Yeltsin and his aides kept him hidden in the Kremlin and then smuggled him out the country.[30]

REACTIONS TO BARANNIKOV'S OUSTER

Despite the illegal and unscrupulous activities in which Barannikov was involved, corruption was not the main reason why Yeltsin dismissed him. After all, corruption was rampant throughout the government and, according to one former member of Yeltsin's administration, it was common knowledge that Barannikov had been involved in illegalities when he served in the MVD in Azerbaidzhan in the 1980s, yet Yeltsin had still appointed him to head the MB.[31] Furthermore, judging from the myriad reports in the Russian press, several other members of Yeltsin's circle, such as Shumeiko and possibly Grachev, were implicated in the Iakubovskii scandal.[32]

Yeltsin, in his memoirs, attempts to portray himself as an innocent party who was shocked to learn about Barannikov's criminal dealings. In fact, he appears nervous about his own involvement in the scandal when he admits that he attended a secret dinner with Boris Birshtein at Barannikov's dacha in May 1993: "The meeting with Boris Birshtein had forced me to do some serious thinking. I was to learn much more about him and Seabeco, his ill-reputed firm. At first this somewhat unpleasant introduction to him seemed accidental to me, and I tried to chase away any bad thoughts of a setup. However, these thoughts were to come back to haunt me with a vengeance."[33]

For Yeltsin, political loyalty was what mattered. Barannikov's sin was that he accommodated Yeltsin's enemies in their campaign to pin corruption charges on Poltoranin, Shumeiko and others. As former KGB general Oleg Kalugin put it: "Where did Rutskoi's eleven suitcases come from? Who filled them with secret documents and gave the opposition the opportunity to make use of sensational, unverified materials?"[34]

Barannikov's ouster aroused considerable controversy in the media, controversy that reflected the deep divisions within the Russian government and the impending confrontation between Yeltsin and his parliamentary foes. The conservative press saw Barannikov as a scapegoat who had been unfairly blamed for the border incident and who was being punished for his unwillingness to support Yeltsin in unseemly partisan political struggles. According to this view, Barannikov had merely tried to stay politically neutral and adhere to the Constitution.[35] *Pravda* even hypothesized that Barannikov was brought down by competing members of Yeltsin's security apparatus: Mikhail Barsukov, head of the Main Guard Directorate, and Aleksandr Korzhakov, the chief of Yeltsin's personal security detail, who resented Barannikov's direct access to the president and wanted to weaken the MB's influence. To support this hypothesis, *Pravda* reported that the elite Vympel troop unit was transferred from the MB to Barsukov's Guard Directorate.[36] The pro-Yeltsin media, on the other hand, portrayed Barannikov as a weak-willed turncoat who had obstructed Yeltsin's attempts at political reform and at the same had failed to use his agency effectively in crime and lawlessness.[37]

In the wake of all the controversy, Barannikov himself finally came forward, taking the unprecedented step of publishing an open letter to Yeltsin, dated 23 August 1993. Barannikov's tone was defensive and unrepentant: "I have never concealed anything from you, although I was aware that my reports were not always a source of positive emotions to you. But that could not be helped: You placed me in charge of a fairly 'uncomfortable' agency."[38] Barannikov went on to say that certain members of Yeltsin's entourage, in an effort to get rid of him, had persuaded Yeltsin that Barannikov was giving him "filtered" information. But this was not true.

Barannikov claimed that the border incident had little, if anything, to do with his dismissal, since the blame lay on the shoulders of the Ministry of Defense, whose duty it was to repel an attack by armed aggressors. The real reason for his ouster, Barannikov claimed, was that he did not support the plan concocted by the "ultra-radicals" around Yeltsin for a confrontation with Yeltsin's opponents. Furthermore, Barannikov said, his agency began to expose members of the government who were involved in mafia-type activities. The Ministry of Security was seen as a dangerous threat to these officials, who then lobbied against him. Barannikov discussed the pressures to which he had been subjected since he took over as MB chief and the "bucketfuls of mud" that had been thrown at his agency. "You, the president," he wrote, "are obligated to defend the ministry and its honest officers from the tough pressure."

Barannikov ended his letter on a bitter note:

I am the last minister, or rather former minister, from the government that you formed and on which the Russian people pinned so many hopes. Maybe there is a certain logic, a certain finality in the fact that the last to be dismissed was the security minister who had been with the president from the outset and thought that he would go with him to the end. It must be that the entourage that deals neither with economics nor defense, and that apparently cannot do anything except indulge in political intrigues, has turned out to be stronger and more cunning than the professionals.[39]

With this letter, Barannikov cut himself off completely from the Yeltsin camp. Indeed, he had by this time allied himself firmly with Yeltsin's enemies. Supreme Soviet President Khasbulatov had even gone so far as to declare Yeltsin's decree dismissing Barannikov null and void.[40]

SIGNS OF CONFRONTATION

By August 1993 the battle lines between Yeltsin and his parliamentary opponents had been drawn and a confrontation was looming. The liberal press drew attention to this, repeatedly urging Yeltsin to reach a compromise. Vladimir Tret'iakov, editor of *Nezavisimaia gazeta*, warned Yeltsin in a mid-August editorial that he should not allow the situation to reach a point where he had to resort to bloodshed to save his political position. Tret'iakov advised the president to accommodate the parliament by getting rid of subordinates like Poltoranin and Shumeiko and announcing new elections to both the parliament and the presidency.[41]

This suggestion fell on deaf ears. Yeltsin was already working out a strategy to defeat Rutskoi, Khasbulataov, et al. At a 12 August news conference he declared that elections to the new parliament "must take place without fail in the fall of this year," with no mention of a presidential election. He predicted that "a crucial battle" would take place in September and added ominously that "various options for resolute action on our part have been prepared."[42] A few days later he dismayed democrats when he announced the creation of a Federation Council, consisting of representatives appointed by the president from the various regions and republics of the Russian Federation. This council would ultimately be the upper house of a new parliament, thus diluting the parliament's democratic nature.

Yeltsin also continued his effort to discredit his opponents by charges of corruption. He assured those in attendance at the August press conference that he intended to punish everyone, no matter what his position, whose guilt had been established. His new anticrime commission, he said, was dealing with all those officials who had embarked on cover-ups. A few days later, four members of the commission, an ad hoc body with no formal authority under the law to institute criminal charges, announced their findings at a news conference, broadcast live on Russian television. They exonerated Poltoranin and Shumeiko completely, saying they had found no evidence of wrongdoing in either case. But, they went on, Rutskoi had committed terrible crimes, including the theft of millions of rubles of state money through a parliamentary charity called the Renaissance Foundation. The case had been referred to the Moscow Procuracy because, they said, the procurator-general, Valentin Stepankov, could not be trusted. Indeed, the four commission members accused Stepankov of planning the assassination of Dmitrii Iakubovskii.[43]

Accusations and counteraccusations continued for the next few weeks. At one point, Poltoranin was called in for three hours of questioning at the headquarters of Stepankov, but nothing came of the case against him. Rutskoi supporters, meanwhile, claimed that the documents incriminating him had been fabricated by members of Yeltsin's entourage.[44]

Yeltsin escalated the conflict on 1 September when he issued a decree suspending both Rutskoi and Shumeiko from their posts, allegedly because of the corruption charges against them and the need to have "objective investigations" of the charges. Shumeiko himself, it turned out, had requested his dismissal from the post of first deputy prime minister, but the vice-president was fired against his will. Many questioned the legality of Yeltsin's action, seeing it as a deliberate attempt to provoke his opponents. As one observer put it: "In order to lure the 'enemy' out of his den, Yeltsin has 'exposed' himself. Now even the cold-blooded Khasbulatov will hardly be able to restrain the hot-tempered deputies."[45] Both Khasbulatov and Rutskoi labeled Yeltsin's decree a blatant violation of the Constitution and made it clear that they would challenge it.

COURTING THE POWER MINISTRIES

In preparation for a violent showdown with the parliament, Yeltsin had been courting the "power ministries"—the Ministries of Internal Affairs, Defense, and Security. In June, after raising salaries and benefits for the military, Yeltsin addressed a gathering of the army high command. He praised the officers for their achievements and announced the promotion of eighty of them to the ranks of general and admiral.[46] In September, Yeltsin paid a visit to the Taman Division, the Kantemir Division, and the airborne troops, apparently to prepare them for the possibility of a decisive confrontation with his enemies. Yeltsin had also steadfastly kept his anticorruption commission from investigating charges of bribery and corruption among high-ranking military officers, including Defense Minister Grachev. These efforts by no means ensured the firm support of the armed forces for Yeltsin, however. There was tremendous discontent with Yeltsin's political reforms at all levels of the military, and Rutskoi, as a former military commander during the war in Afghanistan, was popular among officers and rank-and-file alike. In appealing for the army's support in his upcoming confrontation with Rutskoi and Khasbulatov, Yeltsin was clearly taking a gamble.[47]

Realizing that he might be on weak ground with the regular military, Yeltsin also cultivated the MVD, or regular police. He had fired First Deputy MVD Chief Dunaev (whose wife was involved in the scandal with Barannikov's wife), and Dunaev had made a public fuss, protesting to the parliament that the removal of both him and Barannikov was unfounded and illegal.[48] Perhaps to compensate for this blow to the MVD, Yeltsin made overtures to MVD Chief Erin. "The one to be seen more and more frequently around B. Yeltsin," the conservative paper *Pravda* observed, was Erin, who "generally speaking, is mediocre but ready to obey any order—even a criminal order—of his 'patron.' "[49] In mid-August, Erin was reportedly availing himself of the presidential dacha at Sochi, a privilege not usually given to an ordinary minister.[50] In mid-September, Yeltsin, accompanied by Erin, visited the MVD's renowned Dzerzhinskii Division, the elite, special purpose troops trained to combat internal unrest, which were stationed close to Moscow. The visit was seen by the media as an effort by Yeltsin to shore up support among these troops.[51] Later, on 1 October, Yeltsin issued a presidential edict awarding Erin the rank of army general, presumably a payment in advance for pledged loyalty.[52]

The Ministry of Security, whose support was also crucial, posed more of a problem for Yeltsin. The ouster of Barannikov and top aides such as Vladimir Bondarenko and Andrei Chernenko caused disarray and uncertainty in the ranks of the MB, which had already been subjected to personnel changes at the top after the KGB had been dissolved.[53] As acting security minister, Yeltsin appointed Barannikov's first deputy, Golushko, presumably to provide some continuity within the MB leadership.[54] But, as he reveals in his memoirs, Yeltsin was unsure of Golushko's loyalty: "I had my doubts about him. I did not know him very well. . . . I did not know how he would react. At the same time, perhaps it was a good thing I was getting the opportunity to test him in an extremely grave situation. Soon it would be clear to me if we had a new security minister or whether I would have to look for another candidate."[55] Yeltsin had named a more reliable supporter, his parliamentary advocate, Sergei Stepashin, to be Golushko's second-in-command. But decisions concerning the MB's role during the crisis would be in the hands of Golushko.

In the event that the MB would prove unreliable, Yeltsin could turn to the Main Guard Directorate (GUO), which was firmly under his control. The GUO not only controlled the troops of the former Ninth Directorate of the KGB; it had also acquired the elite Alpha and Vympel troop units. So it was well equipped to come to the president's defense.

THE CRISIS BEGINS

Having made these preparations and sounded out his power ministers, Yeltsin made the sensational announcement on 21 September that he had dissolved the parliament. The immediate response from parliamentary leaders was to declare Yeltsin's order null and void and to "elect" Rutskoi as president of the Russian Federation. Rutskoi then appointed his own heads of the "power ministries": Barannikov as minister of security, Dunaev as minister of internal affairs, and Colonel General Vladislav Achalov as minister of defense. Achalov, who was associated with the extreme right wing of the political spectrum, did not enjoy broad support within the military. His appeal to troops around Moscow to come to the parliament building with their weapons met with no response, even when buttressed with the promises by Khasbulatov and Rutskoi of pay raises and better housing conditions.

Although Yeltsin's ministers declared their support for his decision to dismiss the legislature and rule by presidential decree, they showed little enthusiasm. Golushko was especially guarded. On 22 September he appeared on television to announce that the members of the MB leadership had agreed to "implement" Yeltsin's decree, but he hastened to point out that the decree did not give the MB emergency powers, "especially not the authority to carry out forceful action." He went on to warn against the confrontation getting out of hand because "if one or another politician allows this to happen, it could have serious consequences."[56]

Golushko seemed to be saying that his ministry would go along with Yeltsin's decree dissolving the parliament as long it did not entail enforcement by security troops. In a subsequent personal interview, Golushko confirmed that he had disapproved of using force, adding that his ministry was not in a good position to do so anyway, because Yeltsin had taken away its two main troop units (Alpha and Vympel).[57] Nonetheless, as Yeltsin realized, force (or the real threat of force) was the only means by which he could get his opponents to capitulate. So Golushko's qualified endorsement was of little use to him. The problem, it turned out, was that there was considerable disagreement within the MB over Yeltsin's decree, which meant that the MB could not be counted upon to back it up in the case of violence, no matter what Golushko wanted them to do. On 23 September a Moscow paper reported that at least twenty high-ranking MB officers had stated that they would not act against the parliament should they be called upon.[58] A few days later, MB General Anatolii Pronin, head of the ministry's internal security operations, suddenly resigned, reportedly because he was a supporter of Barannikov.[59] Barannikov himself claimed that some seven thousand state security officers supported the parliament against Yeltsin, a figure that was verified by Moscow security chief Evgenii Savostianov.[60] Even if these figures were exaggerated, there was clearly enough dissent within the MB to justify Golushko's hesitation.

As for the MVD, its forces would be in the front line of any confrontation. The MVD's militia was already out on the streets, responsible for ensuring public order, so it would be the first to be involved in any violence. Although he said that the MVD would "carry out its professional duties" on behalf of Yeltsin, Erin was justifiably cautious in his public comments, doing his best to downplay the possible use of force. Within a few days there were reports that members of the MVD staff had refused to support Erin's stance.[61] In fact, Erin did call internal troops, including the Dzerzhinskii Division and OMON units (troops of special designation), into Moscow to reinforce the regular militia, which numbered around 100,000 in Moscow alone.[62]

THE SHOWDOWN

The situation grew increasingly tense in the next few days. Rutskoi, Khasbulatov, Barannikov, and others remained holed up in the Russian White House (where the parliament met), heavily armed and issuing appeals for support to the army and to the public at large. Yeltsin's Main Guard Directorate reinforced security around the Kremlin and other government buildings, while the White House itself was surrounded by the militia. The showdown escalated to violence on Sunday, 3 October, when thousands of proparliament demonstrators, urged on by Rutskoi and Barannikov, marched on the Moscow mayor's office and on the Ostankino television station. The latter was guarded by MVD special purpose militia and some five hundred internal troops, but they proved helpless in the face of the crowd and did nothing to prevent them from storming Ostankino. In fact, around two hundred of them reportedly defected to the side of the defenders of the White House. The attack on Ostankino left more than sixty dead and hundreds wounded.[63]

Yeltsin responded by declaring a state of emergency, a move Gorbachev had contemplated on several occasions, but never could bring himself to do. This motivated Grachev finally to issue orders for certain of his army units to come into Moscow (the Taman and Katemirov divisions, along with the 119th Paratroopers and 27th Motorized Infantry), but they did not arrive until the next day. According to Moscow security chief Savostianov: "There were no operational plans for enlisting the army. The question had to be resolved from scratch."[64]

Yeltsin acknowledged in a subsequent interview that the military had arrived too late. It was, he said, "a psychological problem for the leadership of the defense ministry. . . . You know, the defense minister should have decided for himself. After all, that was his job, to react appropriately in such cases. But he did not do so." Yeltsin went on to suggest that Grachev may have had doubts about whether his senior military officers would obey him.[65] For his part, Grachev blamed MVD Chief Erin for the fact that no army troops were present to defend Ostankino. He said that Erin had convinced everyone at a government session that he could cope using just his own forces.[66]

The MB, meanwhile, maintained a low profile, despite the fact that it was responsible by law for suppressing "mass disorders" and assisting the MVD in enforcing a state of emergency.[67] When later asked about the MB's passivity in responding to the violence, Savostianov claimed that his agency was caught completely by surprise and had not expected that Rutskoi and his allies would urge their supporters to take up arms. Pressed by his interviewer, Savostianov admitted that "we and the militia forces are not geared to working in combat conditions, more precisely to civil war. . . . To be frank, the Ministry of Security did not play its role in averting the events. The fact that we were prevented from doing so—legal bans, lack of power structures—is another matter. Possibly the most important thing is the operational personnel's intrinsic reluctance 'to get into politics.' "[68]

It has been suggested that Yeltsin allowed the crowd to attack Ostankino so that he would then have an excuse to storm the White House. Although this may not be so, it is true that the attack on Ostankino provided the necessary impetus for the use of force. In the words of Egor Iakovlev, editor of Obshchaia gazeta: "When the decision was made to surround the White House, Yeltsin and the government found themselves in a very awkward position: people increasingly disliked their attitude. If it had not been for the attack on the TV tower, if there had not been any bloodshed, it is difficult to see how they could have gotten out of that impasse."[69]

In the end it was a combination of army troops and MVD troops that mounted the initial attack. A few hours later a detachment of 180 or so men from the Alpha and Vympel units penetrated the White House and negotiated the surrender of Khasbulatov, Rutskoi, Barannikov, and Achalov. (As Yeltsin later revealed, he had trouble persuading the Alpha and Vympel units to back him, even though they were subordinate to his guards rather than to the MB.) Some MB special troops were in evidence during these events, but their role was minimal.[70]

The violence of 3–4 October left a total of 144 persons dead and hundreds wounded.[71] This was the first time in Russia's post-1917 history that troops, either army or police, had been called out in full force and actually used in a domestic power struggle. In the past, when Khrushchev defeated Beria in 1953, for example, or in 1957, when he successfully ousted his rivals Malenkov and Molotov, troops had been put on alert but had never been used. Even during the August 1991 coup attempt, troops never engaged in armed struggle against civilians. Put to the test on Yeltsin's behalf, the performance of the power ministries was weak, to say the least. Had these ministries committed themselves firmly to back Yeltsin's 21 September decree with force, the long standoff and the bloodshed would probably have been avoided. Yeltsin's opponents put up resistance precisely because they knew that the army and police were ambivalent. As Yeltsin learned, having the support of the ministers did not mean having the support of their forces.

AFTERMATH OF THE CRISIS

There were no public recriminations following the violence. At a session of Yeltsin's security council on 6 October, attended by Prime Minister Viktor Chernomyrdin and his two deputies, Egor Gaidar and Sergei Shakhrai, all the power ministers were present. It was expected that events of recent days would be discussed, but "the president immediately made it clear that life goes on and that we should not look back." The discussion turned to Russia's new military doctrine.[72] Yeltsin not only refrained from reprimanding his police and military chiefs, he gave them awards. Erin received a "hero of the Russian Federation" title, while Grachev and Golushko, along with Deputy Defense Minister Konstantin Kobets, received the lesser "order for personal courage." (No reason was given for the discrepancy, but it may have been because the militia suffered more losses.) The irony was not lost on political observers. In the absence of reliable protection from the police and the army, Gaidar had, on 3 October, urged unarmed residents of Moscow to defend democracy against the parliamentary oppositionists. As a result, innocent civilians lost their lives. Yet Yeltsin was rewarding the military and police leaders. "When a mass of people dies in the front line during peacetime," asked *Izvestiia* indignantly, "is this a result of personal heroism in high office or of a marshal's strategy?"[73]

In fact, Yeltsin was hardly in a position to blame the military. Its officers had been placed in a difficult situation by the whole affair and could not be held responsible for the mood of their troops. It was not the job of the army to restore public order and suppress internal unrest. In an apparent effort to change this situation, Yeltsin's security council unveiled a new Russian military doctrine on 2 November 1993, which authorized the use of army troops for curbing civil disorder.[74] This innovation was to prove highly significant: at the end of the next year, the military would be employed in a bloody internal conflict in Chechnia.

In October, however, the main responsibility for suppressing civil violence lay with the MVD and MB. Although MVD Chief Erin had been willing, his troops were not up to the task. The MB, whose forces were much better trained, was an even greater failure. Golushko later tried to defend his employees, claiming that many had been wounded and that they behaved courageously.[75] But Yeltsin was unconvinced and started making plans to revamp the security service and reorganize its forces so that he could ensure their support and loyalty to him. By mid-October rumors about a purge and reorganization of the MB were rife. Major structures from the MB were to be transferred to other agencies and Golushko was to be fired.[76] Although the president's office and the MB denied the rumors, Yeltsin's close adviser Mikhail Poltoranin stated in an interview that the Ministries of Defense, Interior, and Security should be purged and reorganized because they had not done enough to support the president during the October crisis.[77]

Another hint of an impending shakeup came from Moscow's security chief, Savostianov, who said in November that it was imperative that MB employees take an oath of allegiance. Arguing that the MB should be reorganized, Savostianov stressed that its functions should be more clearly delineated. Either it should be a special service or a law enforcement organ, not both.[78] In fact, plans for reorganizing the security services, which were underway, would reflect these very points. Golushko was far from happy about the changes. He reportedly objected to a proposal by Yeltsin's aides to place the MB's telephone monitoring unit under FAPSI and tried to get a meeting with Yeltsin. He ended up talking to Sergei Filatov, head of the president's administration, who told him that the matter had been decided.[79] On 5 November Golushko met with Yeltsin to discuss reforms of his ministry, including measures to forecast more effectively potential internal threats to the government. One MB proposal was to organize a special section of the Directorate for Combatting Terrorism to deal with extremist groups that had organized into political parties.[80]

Meanwhile, Yeltsin had suffered a political setback on 12 December 1993, when elections to the new parliament gave the ultra-nationalist, right-wing Liberal Democratic Party (LDPR) of Vladimir Zhirinovskii an unexpectedly large vote. As the elections showed, the mood of the Russian population was far from overwhelming in its support of Yeltsin's reform policies. The voters did approve the new Consitution, however, which gave the president extensive powers vis-à-vis the legislature.[81] Indeed, many liberals worried that it would result in an authoritarian government.

The new Constitution granted the president the authority to dissolve the state Duma (the lower house of the legislature) if it rejected his nominee for prime minister or voted no-confidence in the government. The president also could appoint and remove from office cabinet ministers, call extraordinary elections, announce referenda, nominate the military high command and personal representatives in the provinces, and introduce nationwide states of emergency. These constitutional powers enabled Yeltsin, who in early November had backed off his promise to hold presidential elections in June 1994, to bypass the legislature to some extent and thus avoid a new confrontation. In retaining Viktor Chernomyrdin as prime minister, however, Yeltsin decreased the likelihood of such a confrontation. Chernomyrdin was regarded as far less radical than Gaidar (who resigned as deputy prime minister after the elections) and enjoyed considerable appeal among the more conservative parliamentarians.

DISSOLUTION OF THE MINISTRY OF SECURITY

However disquieting, Zhirinovksii's strong showing at the polls had its advantages for Yeltsin. It meant that Yeltsin could employ authoritarian tactics without arousing too much criticism from Russian reformers and from the West. Faced with the possibility of Zhirinovskii as an alternative, Yeltsin's democratic critics were less vocal and more willing to give him the benefit of the doubt than they had been before. Yeltsin's reorganization of the security services was a case in point. Although it was portrayed as an unprecedented democratic reform, it in fact placed the security services even more firmly under his direct control, enhancing his powers considerably. And the reorganization did little to change things at Lubianka. History was repeating itself.

On 21 December 1993, the seventy-sixth anniversary of the founding of the Soviet security police, Lenin's infamous Cheka, Yeltsin issued a decree announcing that he had disbanded the Ministry of Security. According to the decree, the security system that had existed from the Cheka days up to the present had proved "unreformable" and "attempts at reorganization that have been made in recent years were basically superficial and cosmetic." As a result, the decree went on, the existing system "has outlived itself; it is ineffective, burdensome for the state budget, and a restraining factor in the implementation of political and economic re-forms."[82] At a news conference on 22 December Yeltsin claimed that he had abolished the "last bulwark of the totalitarian system." Political sur-veillance of the people would cease and only straightforward counterin-telligence operations would be conducted.[83]

That the security services had only been superficially reformed up to this point was no news to the liberal critics of Yeltsin's regime. This had been their constant refrain ever since the dissolution of the KGB in 1991.[84] But Yeltsin's admission of such was a new twist. In lumping the MB to-gether with the KGB and its predecessors, he was casting aspersions at current MB leaders who had been calling themselves reformers. But, after all, Yeltsin had been ultimately responsible for these bodies for almost two years. Did he not also bear some of the blame for failing to reform the former KGB?

Yeltsin's solution to the problem, as announced in his decree, was to repeat the pattern of his predecessors and create yet another security ser-vice under a new name. This time it would be called the "Federal Coun-terintelligence Service" (Federal'naia Sluzhba Kontrrazvedki, or FSK). Golushko, who was appointed director of the FSK, was ordered to draw up regulations for the new service within two weeks and submit them to Yeltsin for approval.

Yeltsin's decree caused considerable consternation at the Lubianka. Not only rank-and-file officers, but also senior MB officials had learned about the dissolution of their organization only from news reports. They were especially disturbed about the clause in Yeltsin's edict that said they were to be considered only temporary employees of the new counterintel-ligence service until they were "recertified." No one seemed to know what this recertification entailed. Would it be used to settle old scores, to pun-ish people who had not followed Yeltsin's political line? In a subsequent interview, Golushko's first deputy Stepashin said that the MB had been disbanded because of "the growing corruption within power structures, the stepped-up activity of foreign special services from both nearby and distant foreign countries, and their attempts to recruit government offi-cials." He added, ominously, that twenty people had been sentenced for espionage during the past year alone.[85] So the MB's problem was not only corruption, but possible treason within its ranks. Were these the traitors that CIA agent Aldrich Ames, who would be arrested as a spy for Russia in just a few short weeks, had informed the Russians about? If this was the case, it was not clear why the Yeltsin administration waited until this time to crack down on the MB.

The regional offices of the counterintelligence service were also experi-encing disquiet. An *Izvestiia* correspondent reported that the mood was somber; security employees were worried about their jobs. There was also bitterness. One older security professional resented the fact that his agency was "blamed for everything." Another went so far as to say that Yeltsin's edict had driven him into Zhirinovskii's camp. If he was dismissed, he said, "one thing would be left—to offer my services to the power structures of Zhirinovskii's party. This politician inspires hope that, if his party becomes the ruling party, then the state will treat people of our profession with greater respect than it does today."[86]

Security staffers at all levels voiced concern that their agency could not function without the ability to use covert surveillance. How were they expected to fight terrorism and subversion without employing these techniques, which were the accepted practice of all normal governments? MB leaders were at a loss as to how to respond. In meetings held with the staff, they had to admit that there was "no basis for explaining the president's edict." But some MB officers expressed the view that the president's statement about stopping political surveillance was simply rhetoric and that things would continue as usual.[87] As it turns out, they were right. When asked some weeks later whether or not his agency would continue conducting secret surveillance and telephone monitoring, Stepashin responded defensively: "A counterintelligence service without operational and technical underpinning does not make any sense. So we are going to keep all these."[88]

Golushko refused to comment publicly on the changes until 29 December, when he gave an interview to *Izvestiia*, making it clear that he was not pleased: "You are probably familiar with the saying 'if you want to reduce efficiency, launch a reorganization.' This is what is happening in this case." He then observed that "at the very least, I personally would not have made such sharp changes in the wake of the October events. I am not condemning the president, I obey him and we are doing everything to implement the edict. But in this case I am talking about the purely human feelings of honest staffers."[89] Golushko denied that the Ministry of Security had not been reformed after 1991: "The Ministry of Security started for the first time to operate on the basis of the law. . . . Therefore the image of our operational staffers changed psychologically, methodologically, and professionally." He also played down the significance of what Yeltsin had portrayed as an unprecedented reform. He acknowledged that the staff would be reduced by 30 percent and that the functions of his new agency would be restricted to counterintelligence. But he added that the redundant staffers would not be fired; they would simply be moved to other agencies, such as the MVD or the Procuracy. And he claimed that in fact most of his staff had been engaged strictly in counterintelligence work all along. All in all, it was clear that for Golushko, a loyal Chekist of many years, Yeltsin's seemingly impetuous attack on the Ministry of Security was hard to swallow.

REORGANIZATION OF SECURITY

The statute (*polozhenie*) on the Federal Counterintelligence Service (FSK), signed by Yeltsin on 5 January 1994, was not published until three months later. Nonetheless, some details of the reorganization were provided by Golushko's first deputy, Stepashin. He announced that the number of employees in the new FSK would be 75,000, 46 percent less than the number of MB personnel. This was a considerably greater cut than that projected by Golushko. The central management of the FSK would be reduced from 3,500 to 1,500 officials. According to Stepashin's initial statements, which he later contradicted, the new service would bear no resemblance to its predecessor agency. The FSK would only combat foreign espionage (political, military and economic), terrorism, and drug and weapons trafficking. It would no longer fight economic corruption, which would be transferred to the MVD. The latter would also acquire the former KGB investigation prison in Lefortovo, where the organizers of the October insurrection were languishing.[90]

The question of investigative powers for the new agency remained unclear, despite the fact that it was pivotal to its functioning effectively. How could security officers operate without being able to arrest people and investigate crimes? FSK public relations chief Aleksei Kondaurov stated flatly that the FSK would no longer conduct investigations, which would be transferred to the Procuracy.[91] Another FSK official explained that, instead of investigations, they would only do "inquiries" (*doznaniia*), which in Russian law form the initial stage of a criminal case. Yet another spokesman said its officers still had the power of arrest and would help the Procuracy with investigations if necessary.[92] Stepashin created a more ambiguous picture, saying that the FSK would not conduct political investigations, "except, of course, for those cases when we are talking about illegally formed or prohibited associations of an extremist nature setting up armed formations and attacking the Russian constitutional system."[93]

Another ambiguity emerged with the border guards. They were to be formally separated from the counterintelligence service and made into an independent Federal Border Service (Federal'naia Pogranichnaia Sluzhba), with the status of a federal ministry, subordinate directly to Yeltsin. Colonel General Andrei Nikolaev remained on as border troops chief.[94] Golushko, however, said that the border troops commander would be subordinate to the chief of the FSK "whenever operational tasks to protect the border are being performed."[95] Stepashin too said that, while the border troops had evolved into an autonomous service, "the FSK will continue to provide counterintelligence backup for the effective protection of Russia's state borders."[96] Thus the ties between the border troops and the counterintelligence service were by no means severed.

Some of the inconsistencies probably resulted from disagreements between the former MB leadership, which wanted to retain as much as possible of their organization in the new agency, and members of the Yeltsin administration. The latter's main goal was to preserve the power of the security services to fight political opposition, by whatever means necessary, while at the same time ensuring that Yeltsin had the ultimate control. Thus, for example, "certain units" were reportedly transferred from the old MB to FAPSI, Yeltsin's own creation.[97] While the loss of these units might weaken the MB's reincarnation, the FSK, it did not detract from Yeltsin's power. Indeed, it gave him an advantage to have the security services dispersed, as long as they were in his hands.

FAPSI also gained a monopoly on government information systems. Yeltsin signed a decree on the formation of a "single informational-legal space" for the CIS (Commonwealth of Independent States), which gave FAPSI responsibility for coordinating data banks and telecommunications links between Russian and CIS security and law enforcement agencies.[98] As Russian journalists had noted, FAPSI was winning out in the battle to control telecommunications in Russia by bringing computer systems of state and commercial enterprises into line with its communications systems, giving FAPSI access to key economic information on private Russian and foreign firms.[99]

Shortly before the December reorganizations, the Presidential Security Service was split off from the Main Guard Directorate (GUO) and made a separate Presidential Security Service (Sluzhba Bezopasnosti Presidenta, or SBP). Yeltsin's decree on the SBP, which would remain under Aleksandr Korzhakov, enacted on 13 November 1993, was never published. Its precise functions and responsibilities remained a secret.[100] A Yeltsin adviser observed at that time that the SBP had recently expanded its activity beyond that of guarding the president to establishing its own analytical staff.[101] Given the close relationship between Yeltsin and Korzhakov, it might have been expected that Yeltsin would build up Korzhakov's power by enhancing the status of his guards. Naturally, Yeltsin felt more secure relying on Korzhakov's men than those of a more independent agency.[102]

The liberal press was quick to draw conclusions about what the reorganizations really meant. *Komsomol'skaia pravda* observed: "It is obvious that, by setting up the FSK in direct subordination to the head of state, the president has taken charge of virtually all Russia's special services. . . . Everything is under the president's exclusive control."[103] According to *Nezavisimaia gazeta*: "[Golushko] has been tasked with developing a new concept for the security service and the maintenance of its personnel. But the reform really involves old staffers and cosmetic manipulations, and also, possibly, the growing influence of General Korzhakov, who not only heads the president's guards, but several 'supplementary' structures, including military formations."[104] Events would prove this observation about Korzhakov's power to be accurate.

CONTROLLING THE SECURITY SERVICES

Of course it would have been difficult for Yeltsin himself to oversee the security services directly, particularly given their proliferation into several bodies. There was no single official to report to him, as there had been in KGB days, when Kriuchkov and his predecessors were in charge. And there was no Communist party apparatus to monitor the security agencies. How then were security matters to be administered?

In early January 1994 Yeltsin appointed his special assistant for legal affairs, Iurii Baturin, to take direct charge of this area, as the president's national security aide. Baturin, at age 44, was portrayed in the media as an "outsider," someone who was not part of the apparatus. But he had good credentials for overseeing the security apparatus. A graduate of the Institute of State and Law, Baturin had worked there under Georgii Shakhnazarov, a longtime Andropov aide, for ten years. He also acquired a degree in journalism from Moscow State University and was proficient in several foreign languages. His training and career experience would have put him into close contact with the KGB.[105]

In 1990–91 Baturin served on Gorbachev's staff (working under Shakhnazarov) and later, in the spring of 1993, joined Yeltsin's administration. He reportedly won Yeltsin's confidence when he helped to draft the president's September 1993 decree dissolving the Russian parliament.[106] Baturin's duties were to involve "coordinating the activities of special services and supervision and decision-making on everyday matters which must not encumber the president."[107] One of his first tasks was to work out the new statutes of the FSK, together with Golushko and Stepashin.[108]

Another official with oversight for the security services was Oleg Lobov, secretary of Yeltsin's security council. Lobov was a longtime associate of Yeltsin's from the president's hometown of Ekaterinburg. He headed the Certification Commission, which vetted security officers for service in the new FSK. Approximately 250 officers went through the recertification process, which involved an assessment of their loyalty to Yeltsin. All but fourteen passed the test. Lobov made it clear that the FSK would be expected to support the president and defend his policies against all opposition.[109]

Also serving on the commission was Vladimir Rubanov, former chief of the KGB analysis department and creator of the KGB's Institute for the Study of Security Problems, which lived on under the MB and FSK. Rubanov, who joined the KGB in 1971, left the security services in 1992. In August 1993, he became deputy secretary of the Security Council and hence Lobov's assistant.[110]

Although Yeltsin's new security team consisted of relatively young, progressive officials who seemed to want reform, they did not start out by drastically curtailing the powers of the security services. Indeed, some of Baturin's statements suggested that he was not in favor of any new restrictions.[111] Most former MB officials passed the recertification process with ease and the new statute on the FSK, which appeared in late March 1994, differed little from earlier laws governing the security organs. The only significant structural change, aside from the deemphasis on investigatory functions, was that the FSK was subordinated only to the president, with no mention of legislative oversight.[112]

The creation of the Federal Counterintelligence Service marked yet another chapter in Yeltsin's struggle to hold on to the reins of power while at the same time espousing democratic principles. The October 1993 crisis was a close call for him, in large part because he had overestimated the willingness of his power ministries to back him up with force. At the crucial moment, when the confrontation with his opponents had brought violence, Yeltsin found himself a supplicant to those in charge of the troops. In order to avoid such a situation in the future, he had to ensure, insofar as was possible, that he could depend on the men and the institutions that were charged with maintaining internal security and suppressing political opposition. This entailed reorganizing the security services yet again and placing them more firmly under the president's control.

Chapter Four

1994: AN EXPANDING ROLE FOR
DOMESTIC SECURITY

> A strong Russia needs strong special services.
> *(Boris Yeltsin, May 1994)*

THE OCTOBER 1993 crisis and the subsequent December elections changed the constellation of political forces in Russia—and Yeltsin's position within that constellation—dramatically. Both events served to drive a wedge between Yeltsin and the group of reformers who had been allied with him since he became Russia's president in June 1991. The bloody confrontation with the parliament in October not only hardened Yeltsin's resolve to create a power structure that he could depend on to support his presidency; it also distanced him from democratic supporters who questioned his handling of the crisis. The strong showing of Zhirinovskii's ultra-conservative Liberal Democratic Party in December—and the weak performance of the proreform Russia's Choice electoral bloc—pushed Yeltsin even farther away from reformers like Gaidar, who resigned from Yeltsin's government after the elections. As political scientist Michael McFaul pointed out, Yeltsin and his circle of advisers concluded that the mood of the country had changed: "If Yeltsin was going to win reelection in June 1996 he had to act and talk more like Zhirinovsky and less like the 'democrats.'"[1]

Yeltsin did just that, adopting a "get-tough" stance that was characterized by a crackdown on crime and a new emphasis on a strong Russian state. In doing so, Yeltsin was embarking on an uncharted and perilous road. In hindsight, it is now clear that this shift to the right led directly toward the invasion of Chechnia in December 1994, which destroyed the uneasy alliance between Yeltsin and the reformers once and for all.[2] The security services, in particular the domestic agencies, were a key element of Yeltsin's new strategy. Indeed, the new Federal Counterintelligence Service (FSK), established from the Ministry of Security, was pushed to the forefront of the intensified struggle against crime and the aggressive policy toward Chechnia. Korzhakov and the Kremlin guards were less visible but no less influential supporters of this hard line.

THE FEDERAL COUNTERINTELLIGENCE SERVICE

The FSK had existed for only a little over a year before it was again re-named, in April 1995, and given a new law to describe its functions and authority. This was a crucial period for the security services and for the fate of democratic rights in general. From the moment of the FSK's creation, it was clear that, contrary to what Yeltsin had said in his December 1993 decree about reforming the security organs once and for all, the FSK would play an increasingly powerful role on the domestic scene. Indeed, the year 1994 witnessed the resurgence of a security apparatus whose legal powers more than matched those of the KGB.

It is not clear why the statute (*polozhenie*) setting forth the functions of the FSK, signed by Yeltsin in January, was not published until the end of March. Probably the Yeltsin administration thought it would be prudent to have some breathing space between the initial announcements about the creation of the FSK and the appearance of its statute. Or perhaps some internal disputes over the contents needed to be resolved. Whatever the reason for the delay, it is significant that the collective authors of the statute—Golushko, Stepashin, Baturin, and Lobov—chose not simply to amend the 1992 law on the Ministry of Security, but rather to start from scratch. In producing a new statute, they were attempting to break with the past and legitimize the FSK in the eyes of the public. But this was difficult to do, since the statute (as opposed to a law (*zakon*), which had to be passed by the parliament), was not the product of democratic deliberations of elected representatives of the people. It embodied the ideas and plans of a small group of men close to Yeltsin. The Russian parliament was at some point supposed to enact a law based on this statute, but its deputies had no say in the creation of the FSK.

Although in some respects quite similar to the earlier law on the Ministry of Security, the statute reflected significant differences.[3] Whereas the 1992 law had stipulated a monitoring role for the parliament, the president, and the judiciary (which proved completely ineffective), Article 9 of the FSK statute stated emphatically that "monitoring the activity of the Russian FSK and counterintelligence organs is carried out by the Russian Federation president." According to Article 3, "the Russian FSK is subordinated directly to the Russian Federation president." There was no mention whatsoever of the parliament or the judiciary.

The new statute elaborated the functions of the FSK in unprecedented detail. For the most part they were similar to those of the Ministry of Security, except that there was more emphasis on following the internal political and economic situation and making forecasts and analyses for the president. The statute also specified that the FSK was to combat "illegally created or prohibited public associations encroaching on the Russian Federation's constitutional system," as well as terrorism and illegal arms formations. The drafters thus removed any ambiguity about the responsibility of the new service to keep the president informed of internal political threats and to support him in crises, such as the one in October 1993. Indeed, the term "counterintelligence" was inappropriate for a security organ whose tasks extended far beyond this area. As one of the authors, Baturin, expressed it: "Strictly speaking, some of the functions included in the statute are not really counterintelligence, but rather belong in the sphere of domestic intelligence, but all of them are part of the sphere of state security."[4] What Baturin failed to say was that these security functions were to be carried out on behalf of the president, rather than the state as a whole.

According to its statute, the FSK had eighteen directorates, or departments, plus a secretariat and a public relations center. Among the more important directorates were: Counterintelligence, Military Counterintelligence, Operative Surveillance, Directorate to Protect Strategic (mainly nuclear) Facilities, Economic Counterintelligence, and Counterterrorism. Although the original number of FSK officers was set at 75,000, by early July 1994 authorities were referring to a staff of 100,000 (not including workers in scientific research, in personnel, and in security and maintenance of official premises).[5] The FSK staff continued to grow. In the autumn of 1994, a Special Operations Directorate was set up at the FSK, headed by former Vympel commander Dmitrii Gerasimov. One of its tasks was to combat air terrorism and hijacking.[6]

The statute left the crucial question of investigatory powers vague, assigning to the FSK the task of "carrying out technical-operational measures, criminological and other expert assessments and investigations." As it turned out, the FSK regained its criminal investigation functions and Lefortovo Prison several months later. On 23 November 1994, President Yeltsin signed an edict authorizing the restoration of investigative bodies within the FSK and specifying for this purpose an additional one thousand staffers.[7] Explaining this reversal, Sergei Stepashin said: "Time has shown that the decision adopted in December of last year to the effect that the FSK should be 'purely a special service' has turned out to be premature." In fact, as Stepashin himself acknowledged, Yeltsin had made plans to return investigative functions to the FSK way back in May of 1994. The need to intensify the fight against crime and terrorism was such that the FSK's investigatory work was necessary. The Procuracy and the MVD (Ministry of Internal Affairs), Stepashin said, could not handle the job alone.[8]

Director of the FSK

The statute concentrated all FSK decisions in the hands of the director, including veto power over members of the FSK Collegium, consisting of the director, deputy directors, and leading personnel. The director could also determine, with the approval of the president, the size of the FSK staff and make proposals for legislation relating to security. Given Yeltsin's aim of keeping the security services under his tight control, it was surprising that he would confer such powers on his security chief, especially someone like Nikolai Golushko, a career Chekist with his own network of supporters in the FSK. As it turned out, Yeltsin abruptly dismissed Golushko as head of the FSK at the end of February 1994, replacing him with Golushko's more trustworthy first deputy, Sergei Stepashin.

According to the FSK public relations office, Golushko resigned because of "family circumstances," a version he adhered to in a personal interview. But most people believed that he had been forced out. Some claimed it was because he had done nothing to prevent the release from Lefortovo Prison of the leaders of the October rebellion—Khasbulatov, Rutskoi, et al.—who had been granted an amnesty by the new Duma. Golushko himself acknowledged that he and Yeltsin had disagreed about this. Another theory was that his dismissal was somehow connected with the arrest of CIA officer Aldrich Ames a few days before on charges of spying for Russia. The most likely explanation, given that rumors of Golushko's impending dismissal had been circulating for several months, was that Yeltsin had never forgiven him for his lack of support during the October crisis.[9]

As Yeltsin says in his memoirs, he had had his doubts about Golushko from the beginning, keeping his appointment provisional as only "acting" security minister. Stepashin, who was brought back into the counterintelligence apparatus in the summer of 1993 as Golushko's first deputy, had been waiting in the wings to take over. Stepashin was much more reliable, from Yeltsin's point of view, because he had entered the security services under Yeltsin's auspices. And he had a more moderate image. Indeed, some people, such as Yevgenia Albats, who had served with Stepashin on the Parliamentary Commission to Investigate the KGB's Role in the August coup, had for a long time considered him a reformer. It was Stepashin who said in August 1991 that "the KGB must be liquidated." Later, according to Albats, he "preferred to forget that quote."[10] When he became a security official himself he began to change, losing his inclination to introduce democratic reforms. By 1994, in Albats's view, he was completely in the other camp.[11]

Stepashin, who was only forty-two years old when Yeltsin appointed him director of the FSK, had risen in the government remarkably quickly. Before 1990, when he entered politics by running for the post of people's deputy, Stepashin had taught political history at the MVD's Higher Political School. He had written his dissertation in 1986 on the rather uninspiring subject of "Party Direction of Fire-Fighting Formations." Now he was a major national figure who appeared frequently before the media, and a key member of Yeltsin's administration. Many longtime security officers scoffed at the idea of a nonprofessional like Stepashin taking over this important job. But Golushko claimed that Stepashin was highly intelligent and capable. And in some respects, he was suited for the post. Aside from his proven loyalty to Yeltsin, Stepashin had valuable experience working with the parliament. Also, he had served during the 1980s as a political commissar in the special forces of the MVD in various "hot spots" in the Caucasus. Because the Yeltsin administration considered ethnic separatism to be one of the greatest threats to Russia's security, this problem would be a high priority for the FSK and would occupy much of Stepashin's time.[12]

However powerful his post, Stepashin would be watched by Iurii Baturin, who, as Yeltsin's "point man" on security matters, would make sure that all FSK policies were in the president's interest. Baturin reportedly had gained a firm spot in Yeltsin's inner circle by this time. According to one assessment: "Iu. Baturin's 'brilliant' resourcefulness, which enabled him to acquire colossal influence over Yeltsin, who is becoming decrepit, was in linking the concept of 'national security' with the concept of Yeltsin's 'security.'"[13] Significantly, Yeltsin brought Baturin along with him to Washington, D.C., when he made his visit in September 1994.

NEW TASKS FOR THE COUNTERINTELLIGENCE SERVICE

Both Stepashin and Baturin tried to justify the new service to its critics and explain the significance of its statute. Baturin, in one lengthy article, touched upon the question of parliamentary oversight, which the statute completely ignored. He pointed out defensively that in Britain, oversight of the special services was very limited and the prime minister had the real control. Furthermore, he went on, "We should not blindly copy any democratic experience, though it makes sense to study it. . . . Therefore I would like to warn those who advocate comprehensive deputy oversight: a special service that is under public oversight is finished."[14]

With regard to balancing human rights with the need for an effective security service, Baturin made it clear that, in his view, the latter took precedence. He noted disapprovingly that in Russia the center of gravity had shifted toward the interest of the individual at the expense of the state, "without taking into account concrete realities in the life of our society." This, he warned, could end up "jeopardizing the security of the individual as well."[15] In other words, if the state was unable to ensure domestic stability and order, this would have an adverse impact on everyone.

Baturin went on to complain of the difficulties security officers faced when they had to comply with procedural laws, such as those that protected individuals from unlawful searches and surveillance, in exposing spies and criminals. No one objects, he pointed out, when the foreign intelligence service violates people's rights, because their operations are not aimed at Russian citizens. But heated criticism is aimed at those engaged in domestic counterintelligence. "What our counterintelligence lacks," he said, "is not a civilized demeanor, but rather aggressiveness, initiative, and concentration on the greatest threats to the state."[16]

Baturin's arguments would be put forth repeatedly in the coming months to justify laws that expanded police powers. They were important because Baturin was Yeltsin's main legal adviser and they reflected the general shift within the Yeltsin administration toward authoritarianism. In the eyes of many observers, Baturin had represented the new generation of well-educated experts who favored reforms and would advise Yeltsin in that direction. But the attitude of the Kremlin had changed. Talk of democracy was being superseded by talk of law and order and the fight against spies.

Stepashin was equally emphatic when it came to the need for a stronger counterintelligence service, but this might be expected, given his new position. Speaking at a three-day conference in early April 1994 on "Security of the Individual, Society, State and Russian Special Services," he warned, in language reminiscent of KGB days, that the threat from spies had increased considerably and could inflict major damage on the defense and economic potential of Russia. He went on to say that "a strong democratic Russia should have strong security bodies. As any other state, it has the right to resort to adequate measures to protect its national interests."[17] This was a far cry from Stepashin's euphoric call in August 1991 for the liquidation of the KGB.

CHANGING CONCEPTS OF RUSSIAN SECURITY

A key development at this conference, which was sponsored by the FSK and was attended by more than eight hundred participants, including members of the press, was the attention to developing a new concept of national security. As part of this process, FSK officials said that they would place more emphasis on economic security. The FSK would expand its role in combatting organized crime, as well as in protecting commercial secrets and monitoring the activities of free-market enterprises. Stepashin explained the significance of economic security in an interview with *Komsomol'skaia pravda*.[18] In the past, he said, such security was linked solely to external factors. Now, the main threat was internal—the black market, official corruption, organized crime, illegal exports of strategic materials, and so on. The job of the FSK was to provide the government leadership with information on these negative phenomena and to combat corruption in financial, lending, and banking structures, as well as in investment funds. The FSK was also helping business enterprises conclude contracts with foreign firms, carrying out credit checks and protecting computer data for commercial and state enterprises.

Stepashin provided further details about the FSK's new role in a lengthy interview on 25 May, the day before Yeltsin was to visit Lubianka for a conference.[19] Noting that a new economic counterintelligence directorate had been set up within the FSK, he cited examples of their successes in instituting criminal proceedings against officials involved in economic malfeasance and noted that laws (including a new law on the FSK to supplement its statute) were being developed that would improve their ability to fight corruption. Those who thought that black markets and "shadow capital" would stimulate the national economy were wrong, he said. And he defended the FSK against critics who accused them of persecuting private entrepreneurs.

Like Baturin, Stepashin argued that the FSK could not be effective in protecting society from crime if it had to deal with procedural laws protecting the individual: "We . . . talk about expanding the rights of individuals without understanding that today, in the environment of the disintegration of the USSR and the growing criminal element that is encroaching on political power, we must to some extent give up the standard concept of human rights. I am not calling for a return to the 1930s, but the survival of our society is at stake."[20]

Yeltsin's speech to the FSK the next day endorsed the new line taken by Baturin and FSK officials wholeheartedly.[21] "Whatever changes may occur in Russia and the world," he said, "we are still a long way from the day when the counterintelligence services will have nothing to do." He stressed that, because the paramount task for Russia was to surmount the economic crisis, he wanted the FSK to devote special attention to economic counterintelligence. Organized crime, in his words, was not limited to ordinary criminals, but had links with statesmen and politicians. It was up to the FSK to expose them, using "original, decisive, and at times even bold measures." Yeltsin assured FSK employees that if they achieved results in the struggle against crime the public would be so grateful that its innate fear and distrust of the security services would go away. In other words, the fight against crime would give them a new legitimacy.

After presenting his report, Yeltsin held a closed discussion with top FSK officials. According to St. Petersburg FSK chief Viktor Cherkasov, Yeltsin assured them that, with the exception of restoring the investigative apparatus, which included special subdivisions to fight crime, there would be no more extensive reorganizations of counterintelligence. A law on the organs of the federal counterintelligence service was already in draft form.[22] Yeltsin's words must have been reassuring to security officials. Finally, after almost three years of turmoil within their organization, the president was coming down on their side, giving them a firm mandate to do their jobs as they had to be done. But Yeltsin was also reflecting the mood of the public, which had expressed itself strongly in favor of law and order in the December elections.

THE ISSUE OF CRIME

A few days later, a presidential decree on "Urgent Measures to Implement the Program to Step Up the Fight against Crime" was published.[23] The decree announced major steps to raise the efficiency of the law enforcement organs, including material incentives for the staff and better equipment and resources. It also called for a substantial increase in the strength of the MVD internal troops (an additional 52,000) and for greater coordination in the operations of the FSK, MVD, and other law enforcement bodies.[24] Control over the issuing of entry visas was to be tightened and, as of 1 July 1994, all copying and printing machines acquired by individual citizens had to be registered with the government. The decree also ordered the preparation of laws broadening the rights of the police to conduct searches and to carry weapons.

Crime had become the number one domestic issue—aside from the state of the Russian economy—by early 1994. In January the Analytical Center for Social and Economic Policies, part of Yeltsin's administration, prepared a report on the crime situation for the president. The report, summarized in *Izvestiia*, presented a grave picture.[25] Seventy to eighty percent of private enterprises and commercial banks, it said, were forced to pay tributes to organized crime. Unlike mafias in other countries, which controlled only such criminal activities as drugs and gambling, the Russian mafia controlled all types of economic activity. The report described the collusion between criminal gangs and local law enforcement officials, which made it especially difficult to crack down on crime. Overtaxation, unclear, complex regulations, and the absence of an effective court system contributed to the problem, which had become acute since mid-1993. Criminal groups had moved forcefully into commercial ventures, using racketeering, kidnapping, and murder to intimidate competition. The report's author recommended that a special anticrime unit be created and that it exclude anyone who had worked in either the MVD or the Ministry of Security (MB) because of the complicity of both these agencies in illegal activities. Yeltsin, needless to say, did not take this advice.[26]

Meanwhile officials in the Yeltsin administration were launching a media campaign designed to persuade people of the need for strong anticrime legislation and a consequent broadening of police powers. At a news conference in Moscow on 11 June, Vladimir Rubanov, deputy secretary of the Security Council, said that the new measures would save the state 10 trillion rubles. Stepashin, Erin, and the newly appointed acting procurator-general Aleksei Iliushenko all voiced their strong support for legislation to strengthen the fight against crime. Stepashin announced that eight hundred investigators had already been brought back to the FSK for the anticrime crusade.[27]

The next day, Stepashin and FSK public relations chief Aleksandr Mikhailov made an unusual appearance on the television program *Itogi*. Mikhailov took the audience back into history, citing the success of the Cheka's infamous 1918 "Red Terror" in combatting widespread crime. Within a year after the Cheka's "extraordinary measures" were introduced, he said, all criminals had been arrested and shot. Ignoring the fact that the Cheka's Red Terror killed one and a half million people, including many innocent victims, Mikhailov put it forth as an example Russia should follow: "I am sure that society supports the fiercest measures in the struggle against crime."[28] Then Stepashin, asked if stronger laws would violate individual rights, responded: "Of course, but in the interests of 99 percent of the population."[29] With this kind of thinking influencing the Yeltsin administration, an erosion of democratic freedoms seemed inevitable.

YELTSIN'S ANTICRIME DECREE

On 15 June, when the press published Yeltsin's anticrime decree, it became clear what the media campaign had been leading up to.[30] With the stated purpose of preserving the security of society and state, the decree introduced a system of *urgent* (as opposed to *extraordinary*) measures to struggle against crime. Those suspected of grave crimes could be detained for up to thirty days without being formally charged. During that time suspects could be interrogated and their financial affairs examined, along with the affairs of their relatives or persons who had lived with them for more than five years. Secrecy regulations of banks and commercial enterprises would not protect suspects in these cases. FSK and MVD employees had the authority, without a warrant, to enter any premises, to examine private documents, and to inspect automobiles together with their drivers and passengers.

The decree evoked a storm of protest from the liberal press and human rights activists, as well as from some conservative members of the state Duma. As democratic critics saw it, the decree revoked all the hard-won individual rights that were ingrained in the Constitution for the purpose of protecting people from arbitrary police power. Journalist and legal expert Iurii Feofanov, among others, complained that Yeltsin did not understand that procedural guarantees are the essence of the law. Once they are eroded, human rights are no longer protected. Stalin's mass repressions, Feofanov pointed out, began with the simplification of judicial procedure in certain cases. Before long, court trials were eliminated altogether.[31]

The human rights group "Memorial" issued a statement saying that Yeltsin's decree put the possibility of building a law-based state into serious doubt. Acknowledging their impotence to cope with crime using legal methods, the statement said, the authors of the edict sacrificed the Constitution: "The authorities in every country are tempted to achieve stability and order by using dictatorial and illegal methods. We know from history that totalitarian regimes—Soviet Russia, fascist Italy—coped with crime. But at what price?"[32] Yeltsin's former economic adviser Grigorii Iavlinskii also came out strongly against the new measures, observing that they were reminiscent of the old Politburo decrees, passed by a narrow group of rulers with no consideration for democratic procedures. With crime now being fought by unconstitutional and unlawful methods, the perfect opportunity existed "for settling scores with rivals and for staging intergroup political showdowns."[33]

Ridiculing the decree, *Nezavisimaia gazeta* published a cartoon showing crowds surrounding a loudspeaker out of which came the words: "Attention! All bandits—step forward!" In an accompanying article, journalist Ivan Rodin predicted that the new regulations would be applied selectively. It was doubtful, for example, that information on the unethical activities of Yeltsin's personal security chief Korzhakov, which had been reported to *Nezavisimaia gazeta*, would result in a check of his private finances. The motivation for the decree, Rodin wrote, was above all political: Yeltsin was using the fight against crime as a propaganda ploy to prolong his tenure as president.[34]

Chairman of the Duma Committee on Legislation Vladimir Isakov, a member of the conservative Agrarian Party, also claimed that the edict had primarily political aims. First, Yeltsin wanted to provoke a confrontation with the Duma, which opposed the decree; second, he wanted to accustom people to the idea that presidential edicts can replace the law; and third, Yeltsin foresaw possible popular unrest over the economic decline and wanted to have strong police detachments to back him up.[35] However political his motives may have been, however, Yeltsin was clearly responding to the general cry of alarm over rising crime. The problem was to follow through by effectively countering the wave of lawlessness.

Isakov claimed that there was no legal mechanism to implement the edict since it did not have the same force as a law (*zakon*) or the Constitution: "Any lawyer will tell you that in a situation where he has to choose between a law and an edict, a judge, prosecutor, or investigator must unfailingly *Follow the Law*." Thus, he said, inveterate criminals will have the perfect opportunity to get off the hook by hiring a lawyer to defend them on the grounds that their rights have been violated. In Isakov's view, the edict effectively removed the distinction between the law enforcement agencies and criminal gangs: "Law enforcement organs that do not base their activity on the law are transformed from a tool in the struggle against crime into the largest mafioso gang backing up the power and interests of their 'godfather.'"[36]

The Duma Committee on Defense and Security, whose members were mainly conservative and communists, unanimously condemned Yeltsin's edict as a gross violation of the Constitution, and committee chairman Viktor Iliukhin criticized Yeltsin for not asking the Duma to produce anticrime legislation.[37] Duma members urged Yeltsin to suspend the edict and then produced their own decree, "On Protecting the Constitutional Rights and Freedoms of Citizens when Implementing Measures in the Struggle against Crime."[38] The decree instructed the Duma's committees on security and on legislation to prepare drafts of anticrime legislation within two weeks and ordered President Yeltsin to refrain from implementing his edict of 14 June.

THE YELTSIN ADMINISTRATION ON THE DEFENSIVE

Yeltsin's decree, then, was arousing criticism from all sides of the political spectrum. Sergei Kovalev, the highly respected chairman of Yeltsin's Human Rights Commission, sent a letter to Yeltsin requesting him to rescind it. If implemented, Kovalev warned, the decree would result in unjustified arrests, interference in people's private and commercial activities and a growth in corruption among officials. To assume that some citizens can be protected by violating the rights of others, he said, is to ignore the lessons of the past: "The edict you have signed is also dangerous because, by pursuing short-term political advantage, it essentially undermines respect for the law."[39]

Yeltsin refused to back down, but he did respond to Kovalev. On 22 June he sent a letter asking him to understand the circumstances that forced him to sign the decree and saying that he shared Kovalev's concerns about violations of human rights. He requested that Kovalev monitor the implementation of the decree to prevent such violations. The head of the president's administration, Sergei Filatov, meanwhile, allowed that the decree was not dogma and could be altered if people's rights were being abused.[40]

Law enforcement officials defended the decree in the media, but not with great success. Stepashin, for example, asserted: "I am in favor of the violation of human rights if the person involved is a bandit and criminal."[41] Apparently forgetting the principle of "presumption of innocence," he did not explain how the police would distinguish between innocent and guilty suspects when they applied "urgent measures" that violated constitutional rights. His statement aroused widespread indignation, leading the party Russia's Choice to call upon Yeltsin to dismiss him. Later Stepashin tried to back off his statement, explaining that he was merely referring to "restrictions on a criminal's right to commit a crime."[42]

Whatever Stepashin had meant to say, he clearly missed the point. This was reflected in the directive he wrote, along with MVD Chief Viktor Erin and acting Procurator Aleksei Iliushenko, giving instructions to the law enforcement organs on how to implement the decree. The fact that this detailed directive was published in the press suggested it was intended, in part at least, to placate concerns about arbitrary police methods.[43] Indeed, procurators, who were the designated watchdogs over police operations, were instructed "to reveal promptly and to halt cases of the illegal arrest of citizens" and to stop "insufficiently justified" inspections of finances and personal property. But the idea that procedural guarantees would be denied when the authorities were dealing with presumed criminals remained. According to the instructions: "The additional powers granted by the decree to the law enforcement organs [are to be] implemented only with regard to persons suspected of gangsterism or participation in some organized criminal group."

Both Yeltsin's decree and these instructions were disturbing to democrats, not only because they might have been motivated by political concerns, but also because they suggested that the Yeltsin administration attached little importance to legal principles. The vague, ambiguous phrasing of the documents, recalling the legal jargon of the Soviet period, allowed the police broad leeway in their investigative operations. As was the case under Soviet rule, protections against arbitrary police persecution were not ingrained in the law, but were left up to the procurator.

In view of the intense criticism of the decree, the Yeltsin administration naturally sought to persuade the public that the sacrifices of democratic rights were justified by the overwhelming need to fight crime. Thus the law enforcement agencies barraged the media with statistics about rapidly rising crime rates. Deputy Procurator-General Oleg Gaidanov reported in early July that the number of serious crimes committed in the first six months of 1994 was 30 percent higher than it was for the same period in 1993.[44] Writing in *Rossiiskaia gazeta*, FSK intelligence staffers pointed out that the incidence of terrorist bombings had risen rapidly since 1991. Whereas in that year only 50 such acts had occurred, in 1992 it was 240 and in 1993, 350.[45] An MVD official estimated that there were 5,700 criminal gangs in Russia, totalling 100,000 members. In the first quarter of 1994, he said, Russia averaged 84 murders a day. Many of these were contract killings tied to the mafia.[46]

At a press conference in Moscow on 20 June, several conservative journalists, including Artem Borovik, editor of *Sovershenno sekretno* (Top Secret), a monthly edited by former KGB officials, urged their colleagues to stage protests against rampant crime in the country. For the purpose of drawing attention to the problem of crime, they proposed that all newspapers simultaneously carry on their front pages in early July stories about crimes committed by organized gangs.[47] The press needed no prodding when it came to reporting about crime, especially violent crime. The coverage it gave to violent acts reinforced the impression that Russia, Moscow in particular, was besieged by crime.

What emerged from this heated debate over crime and Yeltsin's decree, which preoccupied the Russian media for almost two months, was that the issue had important implications for Russia's political development. The argument was not just about police powers and legal protections for individual citizens; it was about people's attitudes toward government in general and their concepts of democracy. Some commentators demonstrated a keen grasp of the legal principles underlying the issues being discussed and what they would mean in practice. But, judging from their statements, members of the Yeltsin administration had little understanding of the legal nuances considered so important in Western democracies. They were still in the era of socialist legality. As for the Russian people as a whole, they doubtless considered their security from criminals to be far more important than their procedural rights.

CRIME AND PUNISHMENT

Yeltsin got a significant public relations boost from the endorsement of FBI Director Louis Freeh, who arrived in Moscow for an official visit on 2 July. Freeh's visit, the first of an FBI director to Moscow in the history of the Bureau, received considerable media attention. The day before his arrival, *Nezavisimaia gazeta* published a lengthy article on the FBI, describing in detail the organization and operations of what it called "one of the most powerful special services in the world."[48] (Interestingly, the article reported that the FBI had approximately 22,000 employees—less than a quarter of the FSK staff). Freeh met with MVD Chief Erin, signing an agreement on cooperation between the FBI and the MVD, and also spoke with Stepashin, at the Lubianka, and Baturin. When asked what he thought about Yeltsin's anticrime decree, Freeh was reported as saying that, in his opinion, it was justified because it maintained a reasonable balance of police powers and individual rights.[49]

Meanwhile, the Russian police had already acted on their broad mandate to fight crime. On 21 June 1994, the Moscow MVD carried out a citywide operation, code-named Hurricane. Within two hours, investigators, with the support of 20,000 troops from the crack Dzerzhinskii Division, had visited 689 sites and detained 2,251 people. Administrative proceedings were instituted against 759 detainees.[50] In early July the FSK press center reported that its staffers had arrested members of a right-wing extremist group, the so-called Werewolf Legion, who had tried to burn down the Moscow sports complex "Olympia" and were planning a series of bombings of movie theaters in Moscow.[51]

Opponents of the anticrime measures remained unpersuaded, however. *Moskovskie novosti* (Moscow News) claimed in late July that criminal terror was continuing unabated and that the police were so ineffective that they made it easy for hired killers to do their work.[52] The murder of parliamentarian Otar Kvantrishvili, for example, had occurred four months earlier and the police had come up with no clues. The investigator in the case was off on a vacation. An even greater problem, said the paper, was that of collusion between police and criminals: businessmen were afraid to give evidence to the police against criminals because they could not be assured of confidentiality and thus could be victims of reprisals.

On 23 July 1994, a group of directors of large Russian firms sent an open letter to President Yeltsin, complaining that his June decree had not protected them against crime. In fact, the letter said, it had made the situation worse by lulling the public into complacency and preventing the authorities from realistically assessing the state of law and order in the

country. According to the letter, when "hitmen" went into business offices and demanded money, the law enforcement organs often took their
side, rather than that of the legitimate businessmen. Worse still, the police
used information from banks (often controlled by criminals) to undermine confidence in companies and break up business partnerships. "In
our view," they went on, "such actions discredit your decree, undermine
confidence in your government and the ability of the state to protect the
interests of honest people. We ask you, who is protecting whom? Whose
interests do the law enforcement agencies represent?[53]

Clearly, corruption in the law enforcement agencies had become so
widespread that it seriously threatened efforts to fight organized crime.
Not only the MVD, the regular police, but also the FSK, had corruption
problems, not the least of which was the high-profile case of former security chief Barannikov. Although he had been amnestied by the Duma for
his role in the October crisis, the Procuracy had started criminal proceedings in April 1994 against Barannikov and former MVD deputy minister
Dunaev on charges of bribery and abuse of authority. (Their wives were
charged with smuggling contraband.) After Procurator-General Aleksei
Kazannik had resigned in a dispute with Yeltsin, his replacement, Aleksei
Iliushenko, announced that he was prepared to "go for blood" on
Yeltsin's behalf.[54] *Pravda* speculated that the object was to keep Barannikov from talking too much publicly by offering him freedom in exchange for silence: "It is no secret that Viktor Pavlovich knows a very
great deal about the 'secrets of the Kremlin court.' For instance, which
dollar incomes are used to educate the sons of certain highly placed gran-
dees in prestigious foreign colleges, which of them have accounts in what
bank, or which of them are involved in corruption or the trade in natural
resources."[55] In fact, the case was eventually dropped and Barannikov
kept his silence, but the rumors about corruption in high places persisted
and did little for the image of the FSK.[56]

THE KHOLODOV MURDER

Perhaps the most serious criminal case involving the security services was
the murder of a prominent investigative reporter, Dmitrii Kholodov, on 17
October 1994. Kholodov, who wrote for the paper *Moskovskii komsomolets* (Moscow Komsomolite) had been investigating corruption among top
military officers in the Western Group of Forces (Germany). He had also
been reporting on the activities of the FSK in Chechnia, where security
officers had been covertly trying to undermine the rebel government of
Dudaev (see below). Kholodov reportedly received a telephone call from
an FSK employee telling him to pick up a suitcase left in a locker at a

Moscow railway station. The suitcase was supposed to contain important documents on military corruption, but when Kholodov opened it at his office a bomb inside exploded and Kholodov was critically wounded.[57]

Kholodov's murder caused outrage and indignation, particularly among journalists and newspaper editors, who saw it as an attempt to intimidate the press. Some blamed the FSK directly for the murder, while others claimed it was the work of Defense Minister Pavel Grachev and his subordinates who were implicated in the corruption scandal.[58] One of these subordinates was Colonel General Matvei Burlakov, former commander in chief of the Western Group of Forces. He was under investigation for the sale of Russian military property for his own personal gain and a host of other corrupt deals. And, it will be recalled, Grachev himself had allegedly received two Mercedes automobiles as a result of a scam. (Hence he was dubbed by the press "Pasha Mercedes".) In August 1994 Grachev had created a stir by appointing Burlakov a deputy defense minister even though his name was under a cloud. Yeltsin, responding to public pressure, dismissed Burlakov from his new post in early November, pending the corruption investigation.

Both Grachev and Burlakov vigorously denied the corruption charges and maintained their innocence with regard to the Kholodov murder. Appearing before the Duma on 18 November, Grachev declared emphatically: "I am clean before the army."[59] But Iurii Boldyrev, the former Yeltsin administration official who had exposed the military corruption scandal back in 1992, continued to insist that evidence of corruption was overwhelming and that it was being covered up by the president. Yeltsin's hand-picked acting procurator-general, Iliushenko, strengthened this impression when he announced in November that there were no facts to back up the charges against Grachev and Burlakov.[60] Iliushenko's remarks prompted the Russian paper *Rossiia* to question Yeltsin's motives in appointing him: "If it turns out . . . that Burlakov is guilty of something, a question arises as to why the president has been so insistent about Iliushenko's candidacy. After all, Iliushenko is the person who two years ago was used to create the appearance that all was well in the Western Group of Forces."[61]

What was the role of the FSK in all this? First, the FSK was responsible, along with the Procuracy, for fighting corruption within the military. So presumably it had access to the documents on the case involving the Western Group of Forces. If there was a cover-up, Stepashin and his agency would almost certainly have been a part of it. Second, as the main organization in charge of fighting terrorism, the FSK was investigating the murder of Kholodov, but did not appear to be doing much. In an apparent effort at damage control, Stepashin met with members of the "Russia's Choice" Duma faction in mid-November to announce that the killers had been exposed and their names would be revealed at the end of the year. Because he did not actually say that they had been apprehended, Stepashin's announcement was rather unusual to say the least.[62] Two weeks later he backtracked slightly, saying: "I realize that I took a pretty big risk when I announced the date by which the killers would be found. But on the other hand we have a very serious approach, and here we are also cooperating with the prosecutor's office and the MVD."[63]

It is not difficult to see why Stepashin would cover up a case of high-level military corruption and even, possibly, a murder. He was, after all, a Yeltsin loyalist and his first duty was to support the Yeltsin administration. In the past the security organs had never hesitated to investigate and report cases of crime within the military, particularly because there was competition between the two power structures for influence and for resources. But by late 1994 the Yeltsin government was besieged with critical problems and was losing credibility. If corruption allegations against Grachev and his officers were shown to be true, this would seriously damage the president, who had insisted on Grachev's innocence. With the Chechnia crisis looming on the horizon, such a development would be disastrous. The power ministers had to stick together.

NUCLEAR SMUGGLING

As noted earlier, it is difficult to estimate the extent of the involvement of counterintelligence officers (either former or current) in organized crime. Although there were criminal indictments—that of Barannikov being the most prominent—evidence linking the FSK and its predecessors to the mafia was, not surprisingly, difficult to pin down. And the media, especially in the West, has tended to exaggerate such connections.[64] On the other hand, it is unlikely that criminals would be able to thrive if there were not some collusion with counterintelligence officers.

Take, for example, reported cases of smuggling of nuclear materials across Russia's borders. The smuggling and possible sale of such material to terrorists or to developing countries seeking nuclear-weapons capability has aroused growing concern in the West. Arrests for trafficking in illegal nuclear substances in Germany and other west European countries led Western officials to the conclusion that the nuclear materials, including weapons-grade plutonium and uranium, came from Russia. Furthermore, following two seizures—one of highly enriched uranium and the other of plutonium—in the summer of 1994, police officials in Germany said they suspected that former Russian counterintelligence officers were procuring the materials for illegal sale abroad.[65]

It was the job of the counterintelligence service, as spelled out clearly in its statute, to prevent such cases, with help from the MVD, whose internal troops guard nuclear installations. Although no longer formally in charge of the border guards, the FSK still had the authority to conduct criminal investigations dealing with border violations, including the smuggling of nuclear material. More important, its Directorate for Counterintelligence Support to Strategic Facilities and its Military Counterintelligence Directorate were responsible for protecting both nuclear weapons and nuclear power facilities and preventing the theft of weapons, nuclear materials, and technological secrets dealing with strategic weaponry.[66]

Russian security officials have on occasion acknowledged that nuclear smuggling posed a serious threat. Early in 1993 Golushko, as first deputy minister of security, expressed concern about the safety of nuclear weapons facilities, including depots where weapons to be eliminated in accordance with international agreements were stored.[67] At this same time, Gennadii Evstaf'ev, chief of the Foreign Intelligence Services Administration for the Control of Weapons of Mass Destruction, told the press of efforts by individuals and groups to smuggle nuclear materials out of Russia. "This is mainly done at the amateur level," he said, "but there were attempts to organize channels for smuggling them out of the country."[68] In the spring of 1994, the commander of the Russian internal troops, Colonel General Anatolii Kulikov, complained that those guarding nuclear installations were not sufficiently trained to fight organized criminals and that they lacked necessary technical equipment. This implied that the mafia was a potential threat to nuclear installations.[69]

Once Western government officials began pressing the issue of nuclear smuggling with the Russians, as a result of the spate of exposures in Germany, security officials took a different stance. When FBI Director Louis Freeh broached the question during his July 1994 visit to Moscow, they vehemently denied that any nuclear materials had been stolen from their country. MVD Chief Yerin insisted that the security system for nuclear facilities was totally reliable. And Stepashin commented later that he was requesting from Freeh information substantiating his worries. Otherwise, he said, opposition groups might interpret the FBI's concern as an excuse to interfere with Russian nuclear facilities.[70]

This response was to be expected. Even if Stepashin and Erin were aware of thefts of Russian nuclear material, they would not make any public acknowledgment of it. First of all, it would have been an admission of the failure of their own protection systems. Second, many Russians saw the West's concern over nuclear security in Russia as an attempt to exert foreign control over Russia's primary asset—its nuclear capability. When the FBI and the German counterintelligence service expressed a desire to assist Russia in preventing thefts and smuggling of these substances, Russians interpreted this as a demand that Russia give up its

nuclear independence. Thus, FSK officials not only denied that the plutonium discovered in Germany came from Russia; they also accused Germany of orchestrating a propaganda campaign in order to persuade the
public of the need for foreign supervision of Russian nuclear facilities
and to squeeze Russia out of the market as a major producer of nuclear
materials.[71]

Although the FSK and other government officials continued to insist
that Russia had no problems with nuclear security, they did agree to discuss the issue with representatives from the government of Germany.
Stepashin had three days of talks with Germany's minister of state, Bernd
Schmidbauer, in August 1994, which culminated in an agreement on cooperation between Russia and Germany in combatting illegal trade in
nuclear materials. And Stepashin made a return visit to Bonn a month
later.[72] Yeltsin meanwhile had appointed Stepashin head of a commission
to monitor the nonproliferation of nuclear materials. In this capacity
Stepashin visited some Russian nuclear facilities on 23 August, presumably to investigate security problems.[73] Shortly thereafter, the FSK announced arrests in two separate incidents of several people suspected of
stealing radioactive material, thus giving credence to the numerous media
stories about illicit nuclear trade.[74] Yeltsin, however, on the eve of a state
visit to Bonn, persisted in the stance that German concerns about stolen
plutonium from Russia were all a "fuss."[75]

Following Stepashin's visit to Bonn, the FSK and the MVD stepped up
efforts to increase nuclear security. Mikhail Dediuchin, chief of the FSK
Directorate for Counterintelligence Support to Strategic Facilities, observed that his service was studying closely a list of persons possibly involved in nuclear smuggling that had been provided by the Germans and
had concluded that at least one of the persons had worked at a Russian
nuclear plant. He added, however, that most of the material involved was
not suitable for the manufacture of nuclear weapons.[76]

Whatever their private views, Russian officials were forced by the spate
of nuclear smuggling exposures to demonstrate heightened attention to
the problem. They introduced measures for tighter controls on institutions using nuclear materials and reinforced the MVD's guard at nuclear
centers.[77] Whether these measures would prove effective was unclear, especially because conflicting reports on the extent of the problem made it
difficult to assess. *Moscow News*, for example, reported at the end of
1994 that the number of cases of attempted smuggling of nuclear materials had risen markedly. The paper attributed the problem to low pay for
those working in nuclear installations and to insufficient controls.[78] But a
senior security official later said that, despite the cases of attempted thefts
(nineteen Russians sentenced in the second half of 1994, and sixteen ar-

rests), "Russian nuclear objects are reliably guarded and there are no grounds for imposing international control on them."[79]

Given the potential for a disaster should the security around nuclear facilities be threatened in a major way, the FSK and related agencies could no longer ignore the problem of nuclear thefts. Although they were hesitant to publicize serious lapses in their system of nuclear safeguards, Russian security officials had strong domestic reasons for keeping their nuclear facilities closely guarded.

ETHNIC CONFLICTS: TROUBLE IN CHECHNIA

One worry for the FSK was the possibility of terrorism on the part of dissident non-Russian nationalities within the Russian Federation. Approximately one-fifth of Russia's population is non-Russian, comprising over one hundred nationalities and divided into thirty-two ethnic federal territorial units. Tension over unresolved ethnic issues had been mounting steadily since 1991, with non-Russian minorities becoming increasingly belligerent in their demands for autonomy from Moscow. Monitoring ethnic issues along with other departments in the Yeltsin administration, suppressing separatist unrest, and preventing violent conflict or terrorism was the job of the FSK.

The most volatile and troublesome area within the Russian Federation was the North Caucasus, where the former Chechen-Ingush Autonomous Republic, inhabited by 1.3 million Muslims, is located. A crisis had been building there for some time. In October 1991, a Chechen nationalist movement headed by Major General Dzhokar Dudaev overthrew the existing government and elected Dudaev president. In November 1991, the local Supreme Soviet declared the region's independence, creating a purely Chechen republic, separate from Ingushetiia. Yeltsin responded by announcing a state of emergency and deploying MVD troops to the region. But the troops were disarmed by Chechen militiamen and forced to withdraw. And the Russian Supreme Soviet declared Yeltsin's state of emergency invalid, ordering him to settle the conflict peacefully. Since that time Chechen nationalists had resolutely pursued their demands for complete political independence and the conclusion of a treaty with Russia recognizing them as a separate state. The Ingush republic, meanwhile, was reconstituted in June 1992 as part of the Russian Federation.

The Yeltsin administration consistently refused negotiations with Dudaev until he recognized that his republic was a part of the Russian Federation. But Dudaev, despite the increasing opposition to him from his own people (he narrowly escaped an assassination attempt in May

1994), stood firm.[80] Violence erupted in Chechnia on numerous occasions in 1993–1994, spilling over into other areas of the North Caucasus. At the end of July 1994, for example, at the airport of Mineralnye Vody a group of Chechens took several hostages, who then perished when the Russian MVD tried to rescue them.

Stepashin visited the North Caucasus in May and again in early July 1994 in order to assess the situation at first hand. And one of his deputies, Moscow FSK Chief Evgenii Savostianov, made a trip to Chechnia right after the hostage crisis at Mineralnye Vody. Both said that stabilization of the situation in Chechnia was a top priority because it threatened the security of the North Caucasus as a whole. But Stepashin adamantly reiterated Yeltsin's stance that no negotiations were feasible until Chechnia agreed to join the Russian Federation.[81]

Dudaev's defenders, who included the chief of the Chechen National Security Service, Sultan Geliskhanov, claimed that the FSK was deliberately fomenting tensions in Chechnia in order to undermine Dudaev and thus have an excuse to send in troops. According to Geliskhanov, the FSK had been spending billions of rubles on organizing subversive operations—terror, sabotage, propaganda, disinformation—aimed at toppling the Dudaev government. As one piece of evidence, they cited the capture of a FSK lieutenant colonel in Chechnia in late April 1994. The officer reportedly admitted his involvement in FSK special operations there.[82] Not surprisingly, FSK officials denied these claims, but the evidence was not in their favor. Another FSK officer was captured in Grozny, the capital, in late August and charged with espionage.[83] The FSK, it turns out, was doing all it could to undermine Dudaev and replace him with someone more responsive to the Yeltsin administration.[84]

Chechen opposition forces, armed by the FSK, launched several attacks against the Dudaev government in September and October 1994 but did not succeed in exerting their control over the government. Interviewed on television in late September, Stepashin said that Chechnia was in the grips of a grave crisis. He insisted again that the only solution was for the Dudaev government to agree to join the Russian Federation.[85] Much to the embarrassment of the Yeltsin government, FSK efforts in Chechnia continued to backfire. In late November several dozen Russian soldiers were captured there and revealed to be under contract with the FSK. Yeltsin responded to this incident by abruptly firing Savostianov, who had helped to devise the operation. (Savostianov's dismissal was also connected with the raid on the Most Bank, discussed below.) Stepashin was spared, but he was clearly "on the hot seat." As one Moscow paper put it, "The latest goings-on in Grozny cannot be assessed other than as a dismal failure of the Russian Counterintelligence Service."[86]

THE RUSSIANS INVADE

It was at this point that the Yeltsin administration decided on military action to overthrow Dudaev and subdue Chechnia. In preparation for the invasion, Stepashin, Grachev, and MVD Chief Erin flew to nearby North Ossetia on 5 December. Two days later Stepashin issued a statement saying that Russia had to restore constitutional order in Chechnia.[87] Shortly thereafter, on 11 December 1994, Russian troops began their fateful attack on Chechnia. Stepashin, headquartered in North Ossetia, insisted that this was no war, but that Russian troops were simply "disarming" bandit gangs on Chechen territory.[88] Stepashin was overseeing the invasion along with military leaders, but his agency also had a separate task. The FSK had reportedly formed two special military groups, whose purpose it was to "neutralize" Dudaev.[89]

Who made the decision to invade Chechnia? According to Stepashin, the Security Council was unanimous in deciding to "establish constitutional order in Chechnia."[90] In addition to Yeltsin, the council included the ministers of defense, internal affairs, and foreign affairs, along with council secretary Oleg Lobov, Prime Minister Viktor Chernomyrdin, FIS Chief Primakov and FSK Chief Stepashin. All these officials together made the final decision on the invasion. But, according to an FSK spokesman interviewed in Moscow, their policy was based on information provided largely by Stepashin, whose agency had been monitoring developments in Chechnia closely.[91]

Minister of Defense Grachev, who had under him the Military Intelligence Agency (GRU), would of course have had an important input. Given the notorious deficiencies in the fighting capacity of the Russian Army, said to be poorly equipped, apathetic, and plagued with desertions, and the fact that several of Grachev's leading generals were outspoken in their opposition to military action in Chechnia, Grachev might have been expected to oppose the invasion. But he was under a shadow because of the corruption charges and may have hoped that a military success would restore his credibility. (He reportedly said that the whole operation could be accomplished in a couple of hours by a single paratrooper regiment.)[92]

Baturin, on the other hand, was against the invasion. But he was out of town at the time the decision was made and later claimed to have had no involvement in the process.[93] He must have seen it coming, however. Stepashin had been talking tough about Chechnia for several months, implying that force might eventually be employed. Interviewed in late November 1994, Stepashin said that he thought the current policy of nonmilitary involvement in Chechnia was the correct one. But he allowed that "there is no problem from the military viewpoint with bringing troops in there."[94] What was perhaps most significant about Stepashin's comments was his insistence that, as an integral part of Russia, Chechnia was violating Russia's internal constitutional order. Any violent actions by Chechens were considered terrorism and the FSK, he said, was establishing new forces to deal with this. In Stepashin's view, the Chechens were political renegades, little different from any oppositionists who violated Moscow's laws.

Stepashin's justification for pushing the invasion, then, was that the Russian government had to deal ruthlessly with political opposition, just as it did in October 1993. This stance recalled KGB days, when the idea of compromise or negotiation with those of opposing political views was not countenanced. That Yeltsin and the Security Council went along with him suggests that Stepashin's views enjoyed support. As one former KGB general, Oleg Kalugin, observed of the Chechnia policy: "It's a clear sign of the growing, if not overwhelming influence of the security people on Mr. Yeltsin."[95]

The Rise of Korzhakov

Of course, "security people" did not mean only those in the FSK. Yeltsin also depended heavily on his other security agencies, particularly the Presidential Security Service (SBP), led by General Aleksandr Korzhakov. Korzhakov had been a loyal member of Yeltsin's entourage for over nine years. Before that he had served in the KGB's Ninth Directorate, which he joined in 1970 at the age of 20. This directorate, it will be recalled, was responsible for guarding the Soviet leadership and key government buildings. In order to serve in this elite guard, it was necessary to go through a rigorous screening process. Not only physical strength, but strict discipline and the ability to "keep one's mouth shut" were among the prerequisites for service in the "deviata" (ninth).

In December 1985 Korzhakov had been assigned to the group guarding Yeltsin, who had just become the Moscow Communist Party chief. After Yeltsin lost his Moscow post in late 1987 (as a result of a falling-out with Gorbachev) and was demoted to a minor job as first deputy chairman of the State Construction Trust, Korzhakov disobeyed the rules of the "ninth" and maintained close ties with Yeltsin, a practice that led to his dismissal from the KGB in 1989. When Yeltsin made a political comeback and was elected chairman of the Russian parliament the next year, Korzhakov became the head of the security detail that was formed to guard him. From that time onward, Korzhakov was at Yeltsin's side twenty-four hours a day. He grew to be indispensable to Yeltsin. According to Russian journalist Andrei Zhdankinin: "After breaking with the 'Kremlin herd,' Yeltsin experienced isolation and strong pressure from the KGB . . . it was Yeltsin's good fortune that his [guard] service was headed by a professional who was familiar with the enemy."[96]

Korzhakov became much more than a bodyguard and tennis partner for Yeltsin. In addition to overseeing four thousand presidential guards, he supervised all the services that provided for the president's operations—communications, presidential airplanes, and the secret bunker in case of war. As Zhdankinin put it: "From the president's standpoint, who can be entrusted with this life-guaranteeing sphere if not a person who has repeatedly confirmed not only his fidelity, but also his professionalism? The number of people like this near the president can be counted on the fingers of one hand."[97]

Korzhakov reportedly monitored everything that flowed in and out of Yeltsin's office, including his private telephone conversations. "It's simple," observed Yevgenia Albats. "He's the one who spends every day and every night with the President."[98] Already in May 1994, Korzhakov had managed to arrange an official agreement with Stepashin on cooperation between his SBP and the FSK. The agreement compelled the FSK to make its secret information available to the SBP, as well as to put its investigators and technical resources at the disposal of the SBP upon request.[99]

Korzhakov, it turns out, made use of his security forces for a seemingly independent initiative on Yeltsin's behalf. On 2 December 1994 a group of his men burst into the offices of the Most Bank in Moscow, headed by Moscow businessman Vladimir Gusinskii, and tried to arrest several of the bank's drivers and bodyguards. Taking advantage of the June anticrime decree, which permitted the police to search and seizure without warrants, they claimed they were investigating the role of this bank in the abrupt fall of the ruble several weeks earlier and were also searching for illegal weapons. To complicate matters, the security staff of the Moscow FSK branch was called on the scene to protect the Most group, and gunfire broke out.[100]

The incident reportedly led to the dismissal of Moscow FSK chief Savostianov, who was already in trouble over Chechnia. Savostianov was not a career Chekist and he enjoyed a reputation among democrats for being a reform-minded official.[101] His replacement, Lieutenant General Anatolii Trofimov, by contrast, had served in the KGB for years, most recently heading the FSK's Anticorruption Directorate. He was well known among former dissidents, many of whose cases he had handled during the Soviet period. In fact, it was Trofimov who investigated the case against Yeltsin's human rights commissioner Sergei Kovalev, which resulted in a lengthy prison-camp term for him. (Coincidentally, Yeltsin dismissed Kovalev from the post of human rights commissioner shortly after Trofimov's appointment.)[102]

Political observers saw the raid on Most Bank as a sign that Korzhakov was using his privileged position with Yeltsin to branch out and engage in dangerous initiatives.[103] The real target of the raid, they said, was Yeltsin's political rival, Moscow mayor Iurii Luzhkov, whose office was in the same building as the Most Bank. The bank served as the authorized agent of the Moscow city government. In a subsequent interview, Korzhakov defended his actions by claiming that the security staff of Most chief Gusinskii had carried illegal weapons and was using scanners to listen in on the communications of Yeltsin's special services. He portrayed the Most group as a mafia organization "under the nose of the Moscow mayor's office" and declared that the job of his service included fighting corruption.[104]

Korzhakov's defiant interview caused a storm of indignation. Moscow's Mayor Luzhkov denied the charges that he was giving special favors to Gusinskii, and the *Moscow News* claimed that Korzhakov was after Luzhkov because he was a possible contender to Yeltsin in the presidential elections.[105] There was doubtless some truth in these accusations. Korzhakov had a large stake in keeping Yeltsin in power, and Yeltsin, for his part, had little reason to discourage the independent initiatives of his loyal bodyguard. Indeed, as subsequent developments showed, Korzhakov was well rewarded for his efforts on Yeltsin's behalf.

With the Most raid and the operation in Chechnia, the Yeltsin administration had committed itself to a confrontational course against internal opposition. The mood in the Kremlin was markedly different from what it had been when Yeltsin embarked on his tenure as president of the new Russian Federation in late 1991. Indeed the new, more aggressive approach to fighting crime and ensuring the security of the Russian state, at whatever cost to individual rights and freedoms, made many observers question whether the label "democrat" could still be applied to Yeltsin. He seemed to be much more receptive to the ideas of security officials and bodyguards than to the recommendations of his dwindling number of reform-minded advisers. This was to become all the more apparent in 1995.

Chapter Five

FOREIGN INTELLIGENCE:

THE EMPIRE AT IASENEVO

> Russian intelligence was and remains one of the most
> important instruments in ensuring the state's security
> and conducting its foreign policy.
> *(Tatiana Samolis, press secretary for*
> *Evgenii Primakov, February 1995)*

T HE DISCUSSION thus far has focused on the domestic branches
of the KGB's successor services. But foreign operations are still a
crucial part of the picture, although they do not receive as much
attention in the Russian media as those of the domestic side. Also, of
course, foreign operations are affected by, and have an impact on, internal political developments in Russia.

All states require a system of intelligence gathering beyond their borders in order to implement their foreign policy goals. That Russia had to
retain an effective foreign intelligence apparatus after the Soviet Union
unraveled and the KGB was disbanded was never questioned, even by the
most ardent Russian democrats. The domestic operations of the KGB were
those that had aroused protest among human rights activists in the past,
because they were directed primarily against Soviet citizens and were used
to repress internal political dissent. The KGB's foreign operations,
shrouded in secrecy, were never the object of criticism in the Soviet Union
that they were in the West. This continued to be the case after 1991. In
the eyes of most Russians, the new Foreign Intelligence Service (FIS), created from the KGB's former First Chief Directorate and headquartered on
the outskirts of Moscow at Iasenevo, has a legitimacy that its domestic
counterparts, the multifarious police and security bodies created by
Yeltsin, lack.

This attitude may explain why Russian reformers do not judge former
KGB foreign intelligence operatives as critically as they do those who
worked on internal security. Take General Oleg Kalugin, for example,
who had years of service as a top KGB spy before he gained instant
fame in June 1990 with his highly publicized denunciation of the KGB. He
was accepted into the democratic movement, despite his KGB past, be-

cause he had spied on foreigners abroad, rather than on Russians at home.[1] Although some democrats were suspicious of Kalugin—Elena Bonner, for example, who commented that "it is very strange when KGB generals join the democratic movement"—they did not associate him with the KGB's domestic repression and did not call him to account for his past actions.[2]

For the West the issue is different. Although it may have been more legitimate than other branches of the KGB, the First Chief Directorate was an arm of an aggressive, totalitarian regime. It did more than gather intelligence; it also implemented a broad range of "active measures," designed to further Soviet foreign policy goals and hence to undermine Western democracies. Such measures included disinformation, forgeries, and other "dirty tricks," as well as support for international terrorists and political murders. (This is not to deny that the CIA also engaged in its share of "covert actions.") Kalugin himself openly admitted that he helped to organize the 1978 murder (with the poisoned tip of an umbrella) of Bulgarian dissident Georgi Markov.[3] Markov, who had a wife and small children, had committed no crimes, except to defect to England and to be outspokenly critical of the Bulgarian regime.

British writer John le Carré asked Kalugin about the Markov murder while visiting him at his Moscow apartment in 1993. His response is worth quoting in full because it tells us a great deal about how former KGB intelligence officers rationalize their unsavory operations:

> People ask me, "Did you have anything to do with Georgi Markov's assassination?" "Listen," I tell them, "we're not children. I was the head man for all that stuff, for Christ's sake! Nothing operational could be done unless it went across my desk. O.K.? Markov had already been sentenced to death in his absence by a Bulgarian court, but the Bulgarians were terrible. They couldn't do a damn thing. We had to do it all for them: train the guy, make the umbrella, fix the poison." Listen, all we did was carry out the sentence. It was completely legal, O.K.?[4]

Kalugin and his colleagues were the arch enemies of the West. They devoted their careers to destroying democratic principles and they committed real crimes. Kalugin no longer works for the FIS—at least not directly—but many of his former colleagues do. Can we trust these men when they claim that they have no hostile intentions toward the West and that they have eschewed their past methods of operation? As discussed above, Russian counterintelligence officials—and many ordinary Russians—still take the view that Western intelligence services are a threat to Russia. Is their own intelligence service, the FIS, really as benign as it purports to be?

A New Image

After the FIS was created in late 1991, Iurii Kobaladze, head of FIS public relations, launched a campaign to create a new image for his organization. He wanted to assure audiences both at home and abroad that the purpose and functions of the FIS were very different from those of its predecessor, the KGB's First Chief Directorate. With the cold war over, Russian intelligence services were more interested in cooperating with the West than in spying on it. As evidence of this, Kobaladze claimed that the FIS had reduced its staff abroad by 50 percent and closed thirty overseas stations during 1992. It was no longer engaging in the activities that gave the KGB a bad name.[5] Clearly, Kobaladze had a message to deliver and he did not like being side-tracked. Asked at a Moscow conference in May 1994 why the FIS had retained so many KGB officers in its central administration, Kobaladze snapped: "We couldn't fire everyone. What were we supposed to do with these people? Send them to the moon?"[6]

In his campaign to persuade the outside world that the FIS was a benign organization, Kobaladze was assisted by a coterie of PR experts, most of whom, like him, were trained as journalists and served abroad for the KGB disseminating disinformation to the West. Tatiana Samolis, the press secretary for Primakov, was for eighteen years on the editorial staff of *Pravda*, the Communist Party's daily paper, before joining the FIS.[7] Working closely with Kobaladze, often making joint appearances with him, she echoed his statements about the new role of Russian foreign intelligence. Interviewed in late December 1993, Samolis spoke about the changes that had taken place over the past two years: "Presently, our intelligence service has foregone its former 'appetites' and it operates where we have real, not imaginary interests. . . . As it stopped being a weapon of confrontation, the FIS has become a tool of control that has a stabilizing role to play."[8]

Another key member of the FIS public relations team has been Lieutenant General Vadim Kirpichenko, head of a group of consultants serving Primakov. Kirpichenko joined the foreign intelligence service in 1952, when Stalin was still alive. He had been a classmate of Primakov in the Arabic Department of the Institute of Oriental Studies, whose graduates were often earmarked for a career in foreign intelligence. Kirpichenko rose to become head of Department S (responsible for illegal agents) in the seventies and by 1979 was first deputy chairman of the KGB's First Chief Directorate, a post he held until the August coup.[9] Despite his advanced age, Kirpichenko has played an active role in the efforts to promote a favorable image for the FIS in the West.

In countless interviews and public appearances, Kirpichenko has talked openly about his past career in the KGB, conveying the impression that this is of purely historical interest, because of the changes in Russia's foreign intelligence operations. "Russia is not building up its intelligence potential," he said in mid-1992. "Today we do not have the kind of global approach we had before."[10] In October 1993 he gave a detailed outline of Russia's new approach to foreign intelligence.[11] First and foremost, he said, the FIS had renounced the concept of an "enemy." A transition from confrontation to collaboration had taken place, and the FIS's main role was that of stabilizing world tensions by working for nuclear nonproliferation and exchanging information with other countries on conflicts in various parts of the world, such as the former Yugoslavia. "Uncivilized methods" of recruiting agents were no longer permitted in the FIS. Recruitment had been reduced to "finding people who themselves want to help us voluntarily, whether for money or out of love for Russia." In April 1992 Kirpichenko announced that the FIS had appealed to its counterparts in the United States to reach a cooperative agreement rejecting recruitment of agents by coercive means, including the use of drugs.[12]

Kirpichenko reiterated some of his ideas about the role of foreign intelligence in an article that appeared at the end of December 1993.[13] He again stressed that in this new, postconfrontational world, his agency was primarily an instrument for ensuring stability. And he spoke optimistically about extending collaboration with Western intelligence services: "In our opinion the strengthening of the international legal base and the increasing role of international organizations uniting most of the world's countries on a non-bloc basis are creating pre-conditions for the formation and development of a world intelligence community." But in almost the same breath Kirpichenko stressed that Russia would need a foreign intelligence service for a long time to come. "We regard it as utopian," he went on, "for some enthusiasts to propose the mutual abandonment of intelligence operations between Russia and another specific state."[14]

As part of their effort to change the image of the FIS in the eyes of the West, Kirpichenko and public relations officer Kobaladze traveled to the United States in January 1993. Although they were not invited to the CIA, they did manage to visit the House Select Committee on Intelligence and the FBI. As Radio Rossii expressed it, "The animals talked with the hunters about cooperation."[15] FBI and FIS officials reportedly agreed in broad terms on some form of collaboration to fight nuclear proliferation, drug trafficking, and terrorism, but no specifics were given. For the FIS, the main value of the visit was that it furthered its public relations campaign. "We are telling people here what the Russian intelligence service is like," Kirpichenko responded when asked about the purpose of his visit. "We are telling them about the new face of intelligence in a democratic society."[16]

At home, meanwhile, Kobaladze's office had helped Ostankino Television produce a two-part documentary on the Foreign Intelligence Service, designed to explain the mission of the FIS to the Russian public and to give some of their former spies favorable publicity.[17] Other films followed. In February 1994, Russian Television presented a documentary series on Soviet intelligence agents abroad. The program featured interviews with a host of former KGB officers who had been involved in the recruitment and handling of agents.[18] Ironically the series, which glorified the work of KGB agents, began right after the arrest of CIA operative Aldrich Ames on charges of spying for the Russians. The public relations efforts paid off. Whereas the Russian press published several articles critical of the FIS in 1991–1993, by 1994–1995 the criticisms had decreased considerably.[19]

EVGENII PRIMAKOV

FIS Chief Evgenii Primakov also helped to promote the FIS's new image. Having worked, directly or indirectly, for the KGB's foreign intelligence administration since at least the 1960s, Primakov was adept at presenting himself as a progressive, sophisticated administrator who had long since discarded communism. The fact that he was an "academician" with a higher degree bolstered this impression. Primakov, who was born in 1929, grew up in Tbilisi and speaks fluent Georgian. He graduated from Moscow's Institute of Oriental Studies in 1953 and then did postgraduate work at Moscow State University. In 1956, having mastered both Arabic and English, he began working as a correspondent in the Middle East for the State Committee for Television and Radio. During the sixties Primakov served as Middle East correspondent for *Pravda*. According to journalist Yevgenia Albats, by this time he had acquired a code name, "Maxim," and was cooperating actively with the KGB—a virtual requirement for any Soviet journalist abroad. Primakov, not surprisingly, publicly denied his past connections with the KGB. But privately he reproved Albats for breaking the story about his KGB connections: "You really are naive, Zhenya. No one who wanted to work abroad got away without some contact with the organs."[20]

In 1970 Primakov became deputy director of the Institute for World Economy and International Relations (IMEMO), a subsidiary of the International Department of the Communist Party's Central Committee. He then headed the Institute of Oriental Studies from 1979 to 1985, when he returned to IMEMO to become its director. (Both institutes carried out research for the KGB and the party leadership.) At the same time Primakov was first deputy chairman of the Soviet Peace Committee, a KGB front organization, whose goal was to disseminate propaganda and disinformation abroad.[21]

By 1989 Primakov had become one of Gorbachev's top foreign policy advisers, specializing on the Middle East. He served as Gorbachev's emissary to Saddam Hussein, visiting Baghdad on several occasions during the Gulf War.[22] According to one observer, "Shevardnadze [then minister of foreign affairs] was voting for military action against Hussein in the United Nations, while Primakov—smiling good-naturedly—was patting Saddam on the back during a peace mission to Baghdad."[23] Primakov also was supervising Soviet policy toward Azerbaidzhan in January 1990, when Soviet troops invaded Baku to suppress, with considerable bloodshed, the independence movement there.[24]

As his career suggests, Primakov was not an outsider when he took over the foreign intelligence apparatus, although he did his best to portray himself as such. Having been part of that old-boy network of journalists, international affairs specialists, and party bureaucrats who had extensive ties with the KGB, he must have felt comfortable at Iasenevo, especially with some of his former classmates around. To hear him talk, however, Primakov was a seasoned democrat. Not long after taking up his new post, he stated categorically that the FIS would not continue the KGB's practice of using journalists as a cover for KGB officers abroad (a promise on which he soon reneged). He assured people that the FIS would not spy against Russia's neighbors in the CIS (another unfulfilled promise). He welcomed parliamentary supervision over the intelligence service. And he declared that the main trait of Russian foreign policy in the future would be a "rejection of confrontation."[25]

What about his past writings as a journalist and academician in the pre-perestroika days, writings rich with communist ideological content and echoes of the imperialistic Soviet worldview? Primakov brushed them off: "Now those articles that I wrote at one time, of course do not sound quite right. But when I was writing them, believe me, I was convinced that I was writing the truth."[26] He presented himself as a completely changed person, a democrat and a believer in friendship with the West. As one journalist observed: "Academician Primakov is familiar with the Western standards of an intelligence chief's behavior. He misses no opportunity to tell newsmen about the sweeping reforms at "The Forest" (Iasenevo).[27] In June 1993, Primakov embarked on his own diplomatic mission to the United States. He met with CIA Director James Woolsey to discuss cooperation between Russia and the United States on such problems as nuclear proliferation, terrorism and drug trafficking.[28]

Woolsey returned the visit in August 1993, meeting in Moscow with leaders of both the FIS and Ministry of Security.[29]

Primakov's first deputy, Viacheslav Trubnikov, has been no less adept at projecting the image of a moderate, humane, and reform-minded bureaucrat, despite—or perhaps because of—his many years in the KGB. Trubnikov's KGB career began in the sixties, after he graduated from the Moscow State Institute of International Relations. Fluent in both English and Hindi, he spent fifteen years in South Asia, working part of the time under cover as a journalist. In his new job at the FIS, Trubnikov was quick to disclaim traditional KGB tenets. Making numerous media appearances, he spoke of the importance of developing contacts with Western secret services and of shifting the emphasis from political to economic intelligence gathering. The main principles in determining the "rules of the game" in mutual relations between the special services, Trubnikov told a journalist, should be "respect for the honor and dignity of the intelligence operative and the members of his family."[30]

MYTHS AND REALITIES

These statements from the FIS were a far cry from what the KGB was saying in the 1970s and 1980s. Were they just a public relations gambit or did they have some truth? Despite dismissals and departures of leading personnel (five of the seven top foreign intelligence officials had reportedly been replaced by August of 1993), the old guard remained at the helm.[31] Could they have changed their ways so drastically?

To be sure, the dissolution of the USSR and the end of the cold war had a substantial impact on the foreign intelligence apparatus and led to a serious rethinking of priorities. It could not have been otherwise. The changed international climate, together with the fact that the vast network of agents in eastern Europe had collapsed, meant that the FIS was operating in a different context than it did when the KGB still existed. The days of psychological warfare against the West were over. And, like other former Soviet agencies, it had to be downsized, given the dire financial straits of the new Russian government which forced budgetary constraints on the entire government. The FIS was not immune from budget cuts.[32]

But the FIS still had an important job to perform for the Russian government. The Russian Federation continued to be a superpower, and to remain so it had to have an effective intelligence-gathering service, just as it needed a strong military. For the FIS, new challenges arose to replace old ones. Whereas in the past it had focused on the West, it now had a host of new states along the Russian border to watch over. High-tech industrial and economic intelligence, especially computer software with military applications, had assumed a greater importance. And with scores of Western businessmen pouring into Russia and the other CIS states, greater opportunities presented themselves for recruiting agents and gathering intelligence.

How could these tasks be accomplished with a substantially reduced staff? This was an important question for Western governments, which needed to know what kind of an espionage threat they were dealing with. As it happened, the FIS found a way to solve its manpower problem. Although a fair number of foreign intelligence officers (there are no exact figures) left their jobs to engage in business, politics, diplomacy, and journalism, many of those who took early retirement continued to work unofficially for the FIS, or at least maintained enough contact with their former employers to earn the occasional "consulting fee." According to Yevgenia Albats, for example, the retirees "swelled the ranks of agents who continued to toil away in the *rezidentury* (residences) of the Russian embassies abroad under cover of the more respectable titles of diplomat, journalist, trade official, or tourist."[33] So, although the foreign intelligence staff was reduced significantly on paper, the FIS still had substantial human resources at its disposal.

As mentioned, Primakov promised upon taking up his intelligence post that he would stop the KGB practice of having intelligence officers pose as journalists abroad.[34] But Albats says that this promise was not kept: "Who were the 'civilians' who immediately began showing up at newspaper offices, claiming that intelligence was being 'downsized' and offering their aid as press consultants? . . . Primakov, forced by budget cuts to reduce his staff, assiduously searched out such berths for them."[35] In early 1994, the issue arose again. *Nezavisimaia gazeta* reported that Primakov had ordered the financing of foreign offices of several Russian newspapers used by FIS staffers as covers to be stopped. A decision had been made to "phase out" journalistic cover.[36] No explanation was offered as to why this was not done two years earlier.

As it turned out, the period of phasing out was to last a long time. In early 1995, British authorities expelled an Ostankino Television correspondent from their country because he had been exposed as an FIS officer. Questioned about this, an FIS official responded that, indeed, journalistic cover was still used, but only to the extent that it was "dictated by need."[37]

As for the diplomatic corps, in September 1991 Minister of Foreign Affairs Boris Pankin (who later became Russian ambassador to Britain) declared that intelligence personnel would no longer be part of the staff of Russian embassies abroad. Apparently there were considerable cutbacks of such personnel at the beginning. But, not surprisingly, given that this is standard practice for most countries, the FIS continued to send agents abroad under cover as diplomats, as part of the staff of the Ministry of Foreign Affairs.[38]

KGB defector Stanislav Levchenko predicted in 1992 that a reduction of FIS staffers under diplomatic cover would not necessarily mean a cutback in intelligence gathering abroad. What would happen, he said, was that the FIS would "develop hundreds of new 'covers' under the guise of 'joint ventures.'" This would present problems for agencies like the FBI, Levchenko said, which in the past had always had a pretty good idea of which "slots" at Russian embassies and trade missions were reserved for the KGB. Now, with an unprecedented number of Russians engaging in commerce abroad, it would be difficult to single out the spies from the legitimate entrepreneurs.[39] In fact the FBI was already complaining about an influx of FIS spies, disguised as businessmen and tourists, into the United States.[40] In response to an FBI statement that the FIS and GRU (military intelligence) had increased their spying activity in the United States by 12 percent in 1992, an FIS spokesman claimed that the FBI and CIA were making exaggerated claims about Russian espionage in order to prevent reductions in their own budgets.[41]

THE LAW ON FOREIGN INTELLIGENCE

The Law on Foreign Intelligence, passed in August 1992, made it clear that economic and technological information from the West was a top priority for the FIS.[42] Section 5 of the law stated explicitly that the FIS was to "promote the economic development and scientific-technical progress of the country by means of the acquistion of economic and scientific-technical information . . . and the provision of government bodies with this information." The law also stated that "career personnel may occupy positions in ministries, departments, establishments, enterprises and organizations in accordance with the requirements of this law without compromising their association with foreign intelligence agencies." Furthermore, it said that "career personnel of foreign intelligence agencies may not occupy other salaried positions *unless this is a professional necessity*" (author's italics). Another part of law (Section 15) specifically mentioned the cooperation between the FIS and other government bodies: "Ministries and departments of the Russian Federation will assist the foreign intelligence agencies of the Russian Federation in their intelligence activity" (Section 15).

Interestingly, the law referred not only to the FIS but to two other foreign intelligence agencies: that of the Ministry of Defense, the GRU, and also one belonging to the Federal Agency for Government Communications and Information (FAPSI). The GRU, which collects intelligence for the Soviet military, has existed ever since the Stalin era and is well known to counterintelligence services in the West. Because it has always been smaller and had a much narrower function than that of the KGB, it never attracted a great deal of attention. The KGB and the GRU were sometimes portrayed as competitors, but, whatever antagonism existed between the two organizations, the KGB always was supreme. And this is doubtless true of the FIS as well.

The fact that FAPSI had its own intelligence agency—operating "in the sphere of coded, classified and other types of special communications"— is significant. As mentioned earlier, FAPSI was an offshoot of the former Eighth Chief Directorate of the KGB, and thus one of its key functions was gathering intelligence by technical means. But in KGB days, when all the directorates were under the same roof, such intelligence was presumably integrated with the other information flowing into the KGB before it was passed on to the party leadership. Now it appeared that FAPSI was handling its intelligence separately from the "human intelligence" that FIS gathered and was transmitting it to the president directly.

According to the Law on Foreign Intelligence, the president of the Russian Federation had direct control of the intelligence agencies. He was to appoint their leaders, supervise their activities, determine their strategy, and make all the major decisions (Section 12). Although the parliament was also to participate in decisions, there is little evidence that it played a role either before or after the December 1993 elections. Section 24 paid lip service to parliamentary supervision of the activities of foreign intelligence agencies, stating only the heads of these agencies must report on their activities and expenditures to standing commissions. It did not make clear what sort of control, if any, the parliament had. FIS officials claimed in late 1992 that a law on parliamentary control over foreign intelligence agencies was being prepared in the Supreme Soviet, but it never materialized.[43] In July 1993, the Supreme Soviet Subcommittee on International Security and Intelligence made a perfunctory visit to Iasenevo (for the first time) and inquired about the budget and operations of the FIS. Judging from press accounts, the visit produced nothing other than a brief report to the Supreme Soviet presidium.[44]

FIS officials were proud of the Law on Foreign Intelligence, which, as it turned out, they themselves wrote. They hailed it as a landmark piece of legislation because it provided a legal basis for intelligence operations for the first time ever. As Valerii Kantorov, chief of the FIS legal department and one of the law's authors, put it: "The need for a such a law is obvious. Intelligence is too sharp a tool of the state to be allowed free rein.

Earlier, when there was no such law, upon what basis did intelligence operate? On the basis of arbitrary decisions. . . . There were no guarantees that some government figure would not use intelligence for personal aims. With the passage of this law, such guarantees now exist."[45] Kantorov went on to point out that now FIS officers would be able to feel morally sure of themselves, because everything they did would be legal and above board. He referred to Section 4 of the law, which stipulated that respect for individual rights and freedoms was a principle of intelligence activity, and Section 5, which said that "intelligence activity may not be conducted for antihumanitarian purposes."

Although this law espoused democratic principles, it did not offer concrete means of implementing them. In this sense, it reflected the Soviet legal tradition. From the point of view of seasoned intelligence professionals, who were used to operating without regard to anything except orders from KGB headquarters, the law served a useful purpose. It provided them with an aura of legitimacy and purposefulness without hampering their ability to carry out their tasks.

DEFECTIONS

The FIS was by no means immune from the political and economic crises that beset the Russian Federation from its inception. By all accounts, the collapse of the Soviet Union and the end of the cold war created a morale problem among foreign intelligence operatives. Whatever sense of mission they had had before was gone. The loss of an ideological basis for intelligence operations and the overriding problem of determining Russia's security interests—now that the enemy was no longer clearly defined—fostered an atmosphere of disquiet. A former high-ranking intelligence officer, Nikolai Leonov, observed: "It is a bitter realization that our Russian society, having been deprived of a constraining system of ideological fetters, as of today has in practice been left devoid of any kind of national idea as its own concept. Where are the ideas about a great Russia, superpower status and statehood, its role and place in this changing world? They do not exist."[46] Russia's continuing economic decline and the constraints on the FIS budget doubtless contributed to the discontent at Iasenevo.

Defections rose sharply. In March 1992, FIS Colonel Vladimir Konoplev, who was operating under the cover of first secretary of the Russian Embassy in Brussels, defected to the Americans with his family. He had been responsible for scientific-technical espionage. Konoplev, who reportedly had top contacts inside the EEC (European Economic Commu-

nity) Commission, the Belgian Defense Ministry, and possibly NATO, revealed the names of several Belgians who were providing Russia with
secret military and economic information. Among them were Gvido
Kindt, the scientific correspondent for a leading Belgian newspaper, and
Emil Eliar, a businessman with broad ties to companies engaged in foreign trade. Konoplev's defection also led to the exposure of Russian "diplomats" in Denmark, France, and Italy.[47] FIS public relations chief Iurii
Kobaladze tried to downplay the significance of the defection, pointing
out that Konoplev had been engaged in industrial, rather than political
espionage, which "all the major powers are engaged in."[48] But this was a
clear setback, and an embarrassment, for the FIS.

The defection of Konoplev came as a deep shock for his Russian comrades, because he had a reputation for taking great pride in his work as a
spy. As it turns out, Konoplev had been on the payroll of the Americans
and the Belgians for quite a while. But, according to one analysis, it was
not only money that led him to betray his country (although this was
clearly a consideration). It was also that his former organization as a
whole had become the object of such public criticism that even its intelligence officers began to feel ashamed of their work there. And, with the
government increasingly unsure of its national interests, it became difficult for KGB employees to feel a sense of purpose. The campaign in the
Russian press to rehabilitate traitors like Oleg Gordievskii, and the amnesty granted to a former KGB officer in San Francisco who had been
serving a fifteen-year prison term for collaboration with the CIA, compounded their disillusionment with the former KGB.[49]

Budget cuts may have been another factor in Konoplev's decision. According to one source, the Brussels contingent did not even have enough
money to pay for transporting documents by diplomatic pouch to Moscow. When they did manage to send photonegatives of documents to the
center, there was not sufficient paper to print them. The films would lie
around Iasenevo for months.[50]

Five months later, in August 1992, the Russian press reported that
Viktor Oshchenko, counsellor at the Russian Embassy in Paris and an FIS
employee, had been granted asylum in England. In the wake of his defection, several French citizens were charged with passing secret scientific
information to the Russians.[51] Oshchenko also exposed a British engi-
neer, Michael Smith, whom Oshchenko had recruited when he was working under cover as a Russian diplomat in London in the 1970s. Smith had
received 20,000 pounds sterling from the KGB and the FIS for the secret
military and technological information he provided.[52]

The problem of defectors was not new to the Russian foreign intelligence apparatus. Between 1975 and 1990, according to former First

Chief Directorate (FCD) chief Leonid Shebarshin, fifteen KGB agents were exposed as traitors, with six arrested in Russia and the other nine defecting abroad.[53] The latter group included Oleg Gordievskii, a high-ranking KGB officer stationed in London, who went over to the British in 1985 and has since come out with two books on the KGB. In May 1991, just a few months before the KGB was disbanded, KGB major Mikhail Butkov, under cover as a journalist for *Rabochaia tribuna* (Worker's Tribune) in Oslo, Norway, also defected to the British.

But by 1991 the betrayal rate was much higher. According to FIS First Deputy Chairman Trubnikov, ten intelligence staffers "went over to the West" between March 1991 and September 1992.[54] At the beginning of 1994 FSK Chief Stepashin reported that twenty people had been arrested on espionage charges in 1993, while several dozen more espionage cases were under investigation.[55] As one press commentator put it: "The Russian special services' catch of spies for the West in 1993 was worthy of being registered in the *Guinness Book of World Records*."[56]

What were the implications of this spate of exposures? On the one hand, they suggested a real problem with loyalty and morale in the foreign intelligence apparatus (including the GRU, where at least some of these traitors had come from). But many cases dated back several years. Though the discovery was made in 1992 or 1993, the initial recruitment had been much earlier. According to Trubnikov, for example, "the traitors . . . were the end result of efforts directed against us by the Western intelligence services over a long period of time. . . . These were people who had been in our ranks and who were recruited a long time ago."[57] The morale problem could thus be viewed as a long-standing one.

More significant, the exposures and arrests indicated that the counter-intelligence apparatus was doing a remarkably efficient job. This was surprising. How could an organization that had been beset by restructuring, dismissals, defections, and budget cuts—not to mention continuous attacks in the press—perform so effectively? A year before the August coup, in September 1990, an anonymous KGB colonel gave an interview in which he was highly critical of the KGB's foreign intelligence administration, describing it as a degenerate and corrupt bureaucracy, filled with indifferent staffers who thought only of their own well-being and who constantly covered up the shortcomings and mistakes of those below them. After mentioning some of those who had been caught betraying their country, the colonel said: "The point is that we have only been able to find these agents out thanks to other traitors, defectors from the West."[58] One such traitor, it appears, was CIA officer Aldrich Ames.

THE AMES AFFAIR

Aldrich Ames, who began working for the KGB in the spring of 1985, was without doubt the highest-placed traitor ever to operate in the United States. As Soviet branch chief of counterintelligence for the CIA from 1983 to 1986, and later in other key counterintelligence posts, Ames knew the names of all agents that the CIA had recruited in Russia and virtually all CIA intelligence-gathering operations that were carried out against the Soviets and Russians in recent years.[59] The announcement of his arrest, along with that of his Colombian-born wife, Rosario, in late February 1994 caused a sensation in the United States. Although the FBI had suspected Ames's treachery for some months and had been gathering evidence against him, the revelations of his spying for the Russians came as a surprise to the general public, especially given the climate of friendly relations between Russia and the United States.

People were even more shocked when they learned that the Russians had paid Ames millions of dollars for his services over the years. How could Russia's foreign intelligence service (KGB and FIS) afford to be so lavish? What about the budget cuts and belt tightening since 1991? The lesson, it seems, was that the Russians were willing to pay a lot when the returns were great, and this was certainly so with Ames. Western experts estimate that Ames revealed the names of at least ten Russians working for the CIA from 1984 or 1985 onwards. Among them were Major General Dmitrii Poliakov, whose code name was "Top Hat" and who worked for the GRU (military intelligence). Poliakov was tried and shot in 1988, but this was not announced until 1990.

Other victims were Valerii Martynov and Sergei Motorin, who had been recruited by the CIA in Washington in 1980 and were executed in 1985; an agent code named "Donald," recruited by the FBI while working for the Soviet mission at the United Nations, and V. Potashev, an employee at the Soviet Embassy in Washington who agreed to collaborate with the CIA in 1981. "Donald" was executed in 1990 and Potashev received thirteen years in prison.[60] The biggest loss was that of a high-ranking officer in the North American section of the KGB's Second Chief Directorate (counterintelligence), code named "G. T. Prologue," executed in 1990. The FBI found evidence on Ames's home computer (which he used to type messages to the KGB) that it was he who betrayed "Prologue."[61]

Why had the CIA not been more vigilant? Its staff had learned from earlier espionage cases, such as that of the Walker family, whose navy spy ring resulted in vast damage to U.S. security interests before it was discovered in 1975, that greed, rather than ideological conviction, was usually the motivation in betrayals. And the Ameses, inexplicably, had done nothing to hide their wealth. According to FBI spokesmen, it was their lavish spending that finally put the FBI on their trail. But this was after they had already deposited substantial sums of money in their bank accounts. As a Russian observer put it: "The Ameses apparently did everything in their power to ensure that the FBI found them out. They bought a house in a luxurious suburb of Washington and paid for it with a lump sum rather than in installments. They bought a very expensive sports car. And most surprising of all, they spent an enormous quantity of money, which far exceeded their salaries."[62]

Quite clearly Ames, while not wanting to get caught, had been careless. But Russians questioned whether this had been the only reason that he was exposed. One theory that circulated widely in Moscow after Ames's arrest was that the FBI, in drawing public attention to its failure to take note of Ames's wealthy spending habits, was in fact attempting to cover up the real cause of his exposure as a spy—a mole in the Russian Foreign Intelligence Service. According to the Russian paper Kommersant-Daily: "The atmosphere of shock and despondency [at the FIS] over the loss of a very valuable agent has been compounded by a suspicion, which has already evolved into a firm conviction, that Aldrich Ames was given up to the Americans by an as yet unidentified official of the FIS itself."[63] This mole, moreover, was said to be very high up—at the level of a deputy to Primakov—because of the restricted access to information about Ames. Former intelligence officer Mikhail Liubimov voiced the same opinion: "Aldrich Ames was not exposed in Washington, he was betrayed from Moscow. The fuss that is being raised now in the U.S. is only a smoke screen to cover an American agent in the highest levels of the government in Russia."[64]

General Oleg Kalugin, now retired but remaining an insider in foreign intelligence circles, also did not discount the possibility of a traitor from within, someone close to Primakov.[65] But he could not be considered a completely reliable source, since he had been assuring the Americans that there were no moles in the CIA during his countless interviews and media appearances.[66] Was this just another propaganda ploy? Kalugin was, after all, a friend of Primakov and other leading FIS officials and, although he was moved to counterintelligence in 1980, he still had close connections with foreign intelligence officials when Ames was allegedly recruited in 1985.

The Ames affair raised a host of other questions about recent episodes in the espionage war between the West and the former Soviet Union. There was, for example, the role of Ames in the case of Vitalii Iurchenko, who had served as a KGB officer in Washington in the early 1980s and had later been responsible for placing agents in the West. In the summer of 1985 Iurchenko defected to the United States from Rome. He was one of the most important KGB officials to defect in years and, during extensive debriefing by the CIA and the FBI, he exposed two American spies: Ronald Pelton, who worked for the National Security Agency; and Lee Howard, a CIA employee. Pelton was arrested, but Howard, who had apparently been tipped off, escaped to Moscow. In early November, Iurchenko slipped away from his handlers and fled to the Russian Embassy in Washington. Upon his return to Moscow, the KGB claimed that he had never defected, but had been abducted by the CIA, and awarded him a medal for bravery.[67]

Although American intelligence officials took the stance that Iurchenko was a genuine defector who changed his mind, the exposure of Ames raised the possibility that Iurchenko's defection was part of a KGB plot.[68] By claiming that there were no other KGB moles in the CIA, Iurchenko might have been trying to lull the Americans into complacency and hence provide a cover for the recruitment of Ames. Adding to this speculation was the fact that Iurchenko had recently been made deputy chief of the First Department of the KGB's First Chief Directorate, in charge of residencies in the United States and Canada, and should have known about Ames, but he did not mention Ames to the CIA. (Ironically, Ames helped to debrief Iurchenko, sometimes alone, and was thus in a position to report to the Soviets everything Iurchenko said.) As for the exposure of Pelton and Howard, the theory went, the KGB had already gotten everything they could from them, so it was no great loss. And the Americans were led to believe that the subsequent spate of arrests of their agents in the Soviet Union resulted from information passed on by Howard, rather than any mole in the CIA.[69]

Former KGB spy Mikhail Liubimov stated unequivocally that Iurchenko was a KGB plant and that his betrayal of Howard and Pelton was considered a necessary sacrifice by the KGB for the sake of providing a cover for Ames. (By exposing these two, Iurchenko was able to convince the CIA of his authenticity.) Liubimov also claimed that Ames exposed Oleg Gordievsky, the KGB officer who was working for the British and who defected in May 1985. Rather than to arrest Gordievsky and thus lead the Americans to look for the source of his exposure, the KGB called him back to Moscow and tried to "crack" him with the help of drugs. But Gordievsky suspected trouble and managed to escape from the Soviet Union with the help of the British.[70]

Another question concerned the possible connection of Ames to the murder of CIA officer Fred Woodruff, which occurred in the former Soviet republic of Georgia on 8 August 1993. Woodruff was reportedly on a mission to lend assistance to the security forces of Georgia's President Shevardnadze's when he was shot while riding in the back seat of a car driven by Georgia's security chief. It was later learned that Ames had visited Georgia just a few weeks earlier. Some speculated that Woodruff was killed by the FIS because he had stumbled upon evidence that Ames was a spy.[71] But the connection was tenuous. Why would the Russians risk an international incident when they probably knew that American authorities were already on Ames's trail?

Moscow's Response

For all the furor that the exposure of Ames caused in Washington, the official reaction in Moscow was mild. FIS spokesman Iurii Kobaladze neither confirmed nor denied that Ames had been a Russian agent: "It is unclear for what reason the Russian foreign intelligence is believed to be involved in that affair. This question should be addressed to the Americans, those who made the arrest, those who formulated the charges, U.S. administration officials. This is not our business. We never comment on such issues."[72] But Mr. Kobaladze was soon undercut by the chief of the Russian General Staff, Lieutenant General Mikhail Kolesnikov, who said at a press conference on 26 February that Ames "defended our interests because he exposed spies who were pumping Russian secrets to the United States."[73] Kolesnikov's admission that Ames had been very useful to Russia was unusual, to say the least. One Russian commentator suggested that this was a ploy to throw the Americans off-track by implying that Ames had been working for the GRU (military intelligence) rather than the FIS. But two days later Kolesnikov stated that Ames had never worked for the GRU, thus confusing matters further.[74]

Despite this inconsistency in the official line, the basic message from Moscow was that Washington should not "politicize" the Ames case. Kobaladze insisted that Russia had never promised to curtail intelligence activity, especially since the United States had continued an active program of espionage against Russia. "Individual episodes should not be used to build up tensions in Russian-U.S. relations," he said.[75] As if to make the point that both Russia and the West were still engaged in clandestine intelligence gathering, the Russian Counterintelligence Service (FSK) announced the arrest on 15 January of a high-ranking defense official on charges of spying for Britain.[76] When the U.S. government, as a protest against the discovery of Ames, ordered an FIS officer in Washington, Aleksandr Lysenko, to leave for Moscow, the Russians were quick to retaliate. A few days later they expelled the CIA representative in Moscow, James L. Morris.

Unfortunate as the loss of Ames was for the FIS, at least its officials could be proud of their past achievement. Clearly Aldrich Ames had been one of the best assets an intelligence service could have.[77] One FIS staffer observed: "The intelligence service recruited practically the head of the agency. What do you call that, a setback?! . . . Of course, the fact that he has been arrested is not a good thing. The intelligence service certainly can't rejoice about it. But it is completely wrong to state unequivocally that it is a setback."[78] As retired KGB general Boris Solomatin put it: "When Russia itself looks into the mirror of this story it will suddenly see that big bucks which are being spent on intelligence are 'working.' And we will realize the importance of intelligence work to the state and will begin to organize it properly."[79]

Indeed, the FIS had already affirmed in December 1993 that there would be no further cutbacks in its staff and that it had "preserved its fighting trim."[80] The FIS awarded ten of its highest awards to intelligence officers for their achievements in 1993 and announced that it was building a new, supermodern training and technical base outside Moscow.[81] In June 1994, FIS First Deputy Chief Trubnikov stated proudly that, despite all the reshuffling and financial difficulties, the Russian intelligence service remained among the top four services in the world, sharing that honor with the CIA, the Israeli Mossad, and the British secret service.[82] The Ames affair was well behind them.

YELTSIN'S ENDORSEMENT

Yeltsin himself, having the ultimate authority over the FIS, gave this agency a strong mandate to pursue Russia's broad foreign policy objectives. In late April 1994 Yeltsin visited FIS headquarters at Iasenevo for the first time since December of 1991 and delivered a thirty-minute speech to some eight hundred staffers, after which he met with the senior FIS management for over two hours. The speech, by all accounts, met with enthusiastic approval from members of the audience.[83] This is not surprising, given Yeltsin's promise to them: "We will be strengthening the service and enhancing the prestige of those who work for it. This is not only the president's principled view, it is my policy." Yeltsin told his listeners that, at a time when the military budget was being cut, foreign intelligence had become the most important guarantee of Russia's security. This means, he went on, that the role of foreign intelligence should and would increase. "We expect," Yeltsin said, "that foreign intelligence will produce the information needed for the adoption of fundamental state decisions on the issues of Russia's foreign and domestic policy, the implementation of our economic policy and the securing of scientific and technical progress."

Although he welcomed Russia's improved relations with the West, Yeltsin warned against attempts by the West to dominate Russia and to impose actions that ran counter to Russia's interests. That, he said, was unacceptable. He criticized the United States for its political campaign over the Ames affair: "U.S. intelligence is stepping up its efforts to acquire agents in Russia. But the U.S. special services believe that the FIS and its military counterparts have no right to act in the same way. I assure you that Russia does not intend to put up with this kind of discrimination any more."[84] And Yeltsin also made it clear that, despite Western concerns about Russia's imperialist ambitions, his government would assert its interests in the CIS states and work for a stronger integration of these states with Russia.

Among the objectives Yeltsin set forth for the FIS was to acquire "preemptive information" on the plans and intentions of the West toward the other CIS states and to "systematically monitor" the situation along Russia's borders. Also, he said, they needed accurate and thorough assessments of how other states viewed Russia in order to thwart any attempts at influencing Russia's domestic politics. Yeltsin went on to stress the importance of intelligence for Russia's economic security and for the prevention of organized crime. And, finally, he talked about the role of the FIS in the struggle against terrorism, drug trafficking and nuclear proliferation, which should be carried out in cooperation with foreign special services.

Yeltsin's speech was a strong endorsement for the FIS; he made it clear that the FIS would play a pivotal role in designing and implementing foreign policy. In fact, this was already the case. Primakov himself had been conducting "shuttle diplomacy" on Yeltsin's behalf, making frequent trips to both Europe and the Middle East, as well as to other CIS states. In July 1993 Primakov traveled to Iran and Afghanistan as the special envoy of President Yeltsin. He met with the Iranian foreign minister in Teheran and with the Afghan president in Kabul, primarily to discuss the conflict on the Tadzhik-Afghan border. Following his return to Moscow in early August, Primakov headed off directly to see Yeltsin and report on the visit.[85]

Earlier, in February 1993, Primakov had traveled to Bonn for consultations with leaders of the German special services. They discussed cooperation in combatting the drug trade, international terrorism, and nuclear proliferation, as well as the problem of radioactive contamination of the Baltic and North Seas.[86] After Bonn, Primakov visited Budapest, where he had talks with Hungarian security leaders about forms of cooperation and about means of stabilizing the situation in Yugoslavia. Then in May he made a four-day visit to Prague for discussions on the usual issues of international terrorism and nuclear proliferation. Among Primakov's travels the next year was a June tour of North Africa, where he had a meeting with his old acquaintance Yasir Arafat in Tunis and talked with other leaders about the Middle East peace process.[87] Such foreign diplomacy was unprecedented—KGB chiefs and the heads of their foreign intelligence had always maintained a low profile—and suggested that Primakov's role was much more influential than that of earlier intelligence chiefs.

FORMULATING POLICY

This hypothesis is supported by the fact that, under Primakov's auspices, the FIS has published three major foreign policy assessments. In January 1993 Primakov wrote a report for the Russian government in which he said that the spread of nuclear weapons had undermined hopes for a stable world order. He pointed out that several former Soviet states bordering Russia had nuclear weapons and at the same time were torn by ethnic strife and political instability. This created a highly volatile and dangerous situation.[88] That the report was leaked to the U.S. government suggests that Primakov wanted to prepare Washington for possible strongarm tactics against the other CIS states.

In November 1993 Primakov came out with a lengthy statement on NATO and its proposed expansion.[89] The basic premise of the report was that the incorporation of the central and eastern European states into NATO directly affected Russia's security interests and hence required thorough evaluation. After laying out the positions of current NATO countries and those of the proposed members, the report elaborated Russia's perspective. Russia was concerned that NATO would not be able to transform itself quickly from a military and political alliance oriented against Russia to an instrument for ensuring peace and stability. This would be a problem if NATO included east European countries.

NATO's expansion, according to Primakov, would place a large military force with offensive potential in immediate proximity to Russia's borders. This would make Russia rethink all its defense concepts and restructure its defense forces. Another problem was that the Russian public considered NATO a hostile force and was thus not prepared to look upon its expansion with equanimity. This would strengthen the reactionary, anti-Western groups in Russia and create a "siege mentality." The report ended by stressing that the entry of the countries of Central and Eastern Europe into NATO—the time frame and the terms of membership—must take into account the interests of Russia.

It was unprecedented for the foreign intelligence apparatus to issue policy statements publicly. The KGB, during its entire history, never publicized its views as an independent entity. The views expressed in the FIS NATO report, moreover, diverged sharply from those of the Russian Foreign Ministry, which at this time had voiced a more favorable opinion of NATO's proposed expansion. Even more surprising was that the FIS presumed to speak for the Russian military, warning that NATO's expansion would put pressure on its resources and give rise to political discontent in the armed forces. As First Deputy FIS Chairman Trubnikov explained after the second FIS report was issued: "The fact that the intelligence service has made two public reports is an indication that we want to be heard. Both on the issue of the spread of weapons of mass destruction and on the issue of NATO expansion, and what that could mean to Russia. We express our point of view as we deem necessary."[90]

Primakov issued a third FIS report on the eve of Yeltsin's trip to Washington, D.C., in late September 1994. The report, entitled "Russia-CIS: Does the West's Position Need Modification?" warned the West not to oppose the economic and political reintegration of the CIS states.[91] This trend, the report said, was inevitable and did not represent a resurgence of Russian imperialism, as some Western observers claimed. The West was unwilling to accept that Russia was growing stronger as a world power. If Western governments attempted to interfere in the process of reintegration, the report went on, it would cause a cooling of relations with Russia. In presenting his report before Yeltsin had had the opportunity to make a statement on the Western position toward the CIS, Primakov had upstaged the president. When he spoke on the subject at the United Nations, Yeltsin endorsed the FIS line unequivocally, so perhaps Primakov's statement was a trial balloon. In any case, the FIS clearly had moved beyond the function of information gathering and analysis and was attempting to influence policy.

The active involvement of the FIS in the nuclear nonproliferation issue was another illustration of this trend. The FIS had established a Directorate for Control of Armaments and the Spread of Weapons of Mass Destruction, which was following the nonproliferation issue carefully. Its chief, Lieutenant General Gennadii Evstaf'ev, had voiced concern about the development of nuclear weapons in North Korea, Israel, India, and Pakistan. But, in an interview given in January 1994, he sought to allay immediate concerns about North Korea by claiming that it had frozen its nuclear program and should not be pressured by the West—in the form of U.N. sanctions—to comply with demands for an inspection of nuclear sites. Asked how close North Korea was to developing a nuclear weapon, he said that it had developed the means for making a bomb but was in a transitional phase.[92]

A 1990 document unearthed by journalist Yevgenia Albats in the KGB archives painted a different picture of North Korea's progress in developing the bomb. Written by KGB Chief Kriuchkov, the document said that North Korea had completed the development of its first nuclear explosive device at a research center in the town of Yonghyong. If this report was accurate, then the North Koreans were much farther along by 1994 than either the FIS or the Russian Ministry of Foreign Affairs was willing to admit to the West.[93] In June 1994, Primakov himself met with President Kim of South Korea and later with Hans Blix, director of the International Atomic Energy Agency, but the meetings did not result in a change of policy by Russia, which continued opposition to U.N. sanctions against North Korea.[94]

How did the Russian military view the active role that the FIS was playing in foreign policy? There was little sign of disagreement with the FIS on most key issues. Indeed, the Russian military was just as explicit as the FIS in its opposition to the inclusion of east European states in NATO.[95] Both the FIS and the military also were calling for further integration of CIS states with Russia in the area of security and defense. The Russian Defense Ministry had successfully negotiated agreements to retain a substantial Russian troop presence in the CIS. The FIS did not comment publicly on the issue of Russian troops, but this clearly suited FIS purposes. Although the FIS might have been competing with the military for budgetary resources, it shared with the military a desire to maintain Russia's status as a great power and to retain or reassert some form of sovereignty over the states that were earlier part of the Soviet Union.

THE FIS IN THE "NEAR ABROAD"

By early 1993 Russian foreign policy had become noticeably more aggressive than it had been in the early days of the Russian Federation, particularly with regard to the other CIS states and the Baltic countries, the "near abroad." Officials from the Russian Ministry of Foreign Affairs, and Yeltsin himself, shifted to what has been called a Russian "Monroe Doctrine" in their statements about Russia's relationship with the countries that were once Soviet republics. Russia presented itself as being first among equals in the CIS, voicing a strong determination to protect the rights of ethnic Russians in the CIS and Baltic states.[96]

The Russian military asserted Russian sovereignty primarily by arming the forces it favored in ethnic and political conflicts in the various CIS states (the procommunist leaders in Tadzhikistan, the Abkhazians in Georgia, Gaidar Aliev in Azerbaidzhan, Russian separatists in the Trans-Dniester region of Moldova) and by retaining many of the Russian troops that were stationed in the republics of the former Soviet Union. As one Western source concluded in 1993: "Russia has done nothing to help achieve an equitable and peaceful resolution in any of the conflicts. In Azerbaidzhan, Georgia and Moldova, Russian troops have colluded in the de facto dismemberment of the republics. In regions where there is, as yet, no sign of violent conflict, inflammatory statements by Russian politicians and punitive actions by Moscow have served to increase tensions."[97]

The FIS has played a more subtle, but no less important role in Russian policy toward the near abroad. First of all, it has provided the Russian government with information and analyses on the political situation in these countries. In the case of the Central Asian states and Belorussia, whose political leaders for the most part follow the dictates of Moscow, this has been a straightforward task. In the spring of 1992 the FIS signed agreements with these states on cooperation in exchanging intelligence, joint operations, and training. A council, comprising leaders of each state's intelligence agencies, was to meet every three months.[98] Ukraine and Armenia were not parties to this agreement, but Armenia reached similar cooperative arrangements with the FIS later in 1992, and in March 1993 the Ukrainian Security Service (SBU) signed an agreement with the FIS pledging cooperation and agreeing not to work against each other.[99] In April 1994 Primakov and President Mircea Snegur of Moldova reached an agreement on intelligence cooperation.[100]

FIS officials have asserted time and again that their agency does not spy on other CIS states, which may well be true, with some exceptions. As long as it has close cooperation with the security services of these states and can obtain all the information it needs from them, there is little reason for the FIS to devote its own resources to spying. Also, the FIS can fill in the gaps through back channels. By all accounts, the security and intelligence services of all the CIS states are staffed with former KGB operatives, who slavishly followed Moscow's orders in the Soviet period. Although many Russian KGB officials left their posts in the former republics and returned to Moscow after the collapse of the Soviet Union, most native KGB staffers stayed on to work in the new security structures.[101] Whatever information the FIS does not obtain from its formal contacts with CIS agencies it probably gets through this "old-boy network." Ukraine is a good example. Its current intelligence officers graduated from the same training centers as Russian officers and worked with the Russians in Moscow and abroad.[102]

For their part, the CIS states, other than Russia, do not have effective intelligence-gathering organizations of their own because the Russian Federation inherited much of the staff and resources of the USSR KGB's First Chief Directorate. In Ukraine, for example, most of the security personnel are experienced in counterintelligence and domestic security, rather than foreign intelligence. In the latter area they always operated at Moscow's initiative. Also, the sudden influx of foreigners into Ukraine and other CIS countries and the problems of ethnic conflicts, crime, and terrorism has greatly increased the responsibilities of their counterintelligence personnel and strained the resources of their security services.[103]

It might be assumed, therefore, that intelligence gathering in countries bordering the CIS—China, Afghanistan, Iran, Turkey—would be conducted mainly by the FIS, with the cooperation of the security services of the adjoining CIS states. In addition, the Russian border troops, which are stationed along the borders with these countries, also have intelligence units.[104] Of course, with the continued political and economic turmoil in the CIS states and the fluidity of borders with Russia, the functions of counterintelligence and intelligence often overlap. This calls for close coordination of the operations of the FIS with the counterintelligence services of Russia and the CIS states.

ACTIVE MEASURES

There have been numerous reports that the FIS engages in "active measures" in the near abroad, attempting to influence political events to suit Moscow's purposes. Although the Russian military has taken the most visible role in exerting Moscow's will over the former republics and involving Russia in regional conflicts, the FIS provides the unpinning for this involvement. In Georgia, for example, the FIS is said to have conducted an extensive disinformation campaign to discredit Zviad Gamsakhurdia, who was elected chairman of the Georgian parliament in 1990 and then became the first president of independent Georgia. After civil conflict forced Gamsakhurdia to flee Tbilisi, the capital of Georgia, in early 1992, the FIS then sought to buttress support for Eduard Shevardnadze, who had been party leader of the Georgian republic under the Soviets and later had served as Soviet foreign minister. Shevardnadze is reported to have a close relationship with FIS Chief Primakov, and some Georgians believe that he cooperates with the Russian intelligence service in exchange for their support. To complicate the picture, however, the former head of Georgia's security service, Igor Giorgadze (dismissed in August 1995 for alleged involvement in a plot against Shevardnadze), was also said to be a protégé of Primakov, who offered Georgian security officers free training in Moscow.[105]

In Armenia, it was rumored that the FIS had a role in the March 1994 defection of Vahan Avakian, the first deputy chief of Armenia's Administration of National Security, to Moscow and then to Bulgaria. His defection was prompted by the arrest of his wife at Erevan Airport as she tried to smuggle secret documents out of the republic.[106] The FIS was also blamed for the 1993 murder of the former republic KGB chairman, Marius Iuzbashian. According to the Armenian minister of internal affairs,

Vano Siragedian, Iuzbashian had become undesirable to Moscow because he knew too much about Moscow's behind-the-scenes role in the conflict over the disputed territory of Nagornyi-Karabakh.[107]

The close ties between officials of the FIS and the Ukrainian SBU have led to considerable speculation about their collusion. *Argumenty i fakty* (Arguments and Facts), for example, issued a report in the spring of 1993 claiming that the two services were deliberately trying to foment tensions between the governments of Ukraine and Russia in order to undermine their relationship.[108] Not surprisingly, the claim was immediately denied by both the FIS and the SBU.

As for Latvia, Lithuania, and Estonia, which are not part of the CIS, the FIS has made it clear that it spies on these countries in the same manner that it spies on the West, using secret agents and recruiting "illegals" from the local population.[109] Of course, the FIS is helped by the fact that thousands of former KGB employees and informers are still living in the Baltic states, some occupying important government positions. They have reportedly continued to provide information to the Russians, often out of fear that they would be exposed if they did not.[110] The controversy over KGB informers in the Baltics and the scandals that have ensued over revelations of KGB connections among prominent public figures also has offered the Russian security services the opportunity to manipulate politics in these states, since they have files on former agents and can use them to their advantage.

Another means through which the FIS collected intelligence in the Baltics was the Northwest Group of Forces of the Russian Army, which had troops in Latvia and Estonia until 1994. This military group had intelligence and counterintelligence units operating at several locations in Latvia and Estonia. Their staff recruited agents from all spheres of government and public life, and they also had special units for conducting radio intercepts. According to Latvian sources, the intelligence was used by both the FIS and the GRU.[111] This may be one reason why the Russian government was reluctant to remove its troops from the Baltic states.

The FIS and Eastern Europe

Ever since the East European countries were made satellite states of the Soviet Union in the aftermath of World War II, their security and intelligence services had served as adjuncts for the Soviet security services. The KGB had permanent representatives in all the East European states to carry out liaison functions with Moscow and to ensure that the satellite states did their bidding. Training of key personnel was carried out in the Soviet Union, and Moscow approved all major operational decisions.

The East German, Czechoslovak, Polish, Hungarian, and Bulgarian security services collected intelligence and conducted "active measures" for the KGB, while the latter, for its part, provided the satellite services with advisers and resources. Thus, for example, when the Bulgarians decided that they wanted to get rid of the troublesome dissident Georgi Markov, the Soviets willingly provided them with the means to do so. As Oleg Kalugin expressed it: "The Bulgarians never hid anything from us. They turned to us with all their questions. . . . We never refused them assistance."[112]

The collapse of communism in eastern Europe led to the dismantling of the secret police in these countries and, to an even greater extent than with the Baltic countries, a witch hunt for former secret police employees and collaborators. In Germany, for example, counterintelligence officials used the files of the STASI (East German secret police) to track down hundreds of former agents. They also arrested Marcus Wolf, former chief of East German foreign intelligence, who worked closely with the KGB, on charges of treason and bribery.[113]

These developments, of course, were a severe blow to the KGB, which had depended on its East European counterparts for spying operations, particularly against the NATO countries. But, according to numerous reports, the KGB, and more recently the FIS, maintained contact with many of their former spies and agents, establishing an underground network throughout Eastern Europe. In Germany, for example, Russia allegedly kept a fully staffed spy residency in its embassy, in order to run illegal agents. Their efforts were directed at collecting economic and technical secrets, as well as keeping Russia apprised of economic conditions and political developments in Germany.[114] This has not prevented Germany's security services from establishing formal ties with the FIS. Primakov created a stir in Bonn when he visited the headquarters of the German intelligence service in early 1993 to discuss a range of areas for cooperation.[115]

Rumors of uncontrolled KGB activities and the existence of an international communist underground mafia persisted in Poland long after the first Solidarity-led government took office in 1989. Although the KGB formally moved its staff to the Soviet Embassy in Warsaw, KGB and GRU units remained in the Soviet armed forces that were still stationed in Poland and presumably continued their intelligence-gathering efforts. Polish counterintelligence officials, however, claimed that they had things "under control" and that their relations with the KGB were based on the principle of equality.[116]

Amid reports that Russian intelligence was still active in the Czech republic, Evgenii Primakov made a visit to Prague in May 1993 to reestablish relations between the FIS and the Czech security services on an official level. Primakov and Interior Minister Jan Ruml of Czechoslovakia agreed to share information on organized crime, including drugs and arms trafficking. The Czech press claimed that Czech officials demanded a list of Czech KGB collaborators and Primakov refused. Primakov's press secretary, however, denied that such requests were made.[117] Later in 1993 Ruml made a return trip to Moscow, where he and Primakov agreed that their agencies would not operate against one another. Writing in *Izvestiia*, journalist Leonid Mlechin was skeptical about Russian promises not to spy on the Czech Republic: "It would take a naive person to assume that Russian intelligence will ignore Eastern Europe."[118] Moreover, he pointed out, East European counterintelligence services do not have the experience, personnel, or technical resources to counteract Russian spying effectively.

The lack of experienced, well-trained personnel, along with other considerations, has in fact meant that the security services in several states—Poland, the Czech and Slovak republics, Bulgaria—continue to employ considerable numbers of career officers from the days of the Soviet empire.[119] Though these officers have sworn allegiance to their countries and have in many cases gone through a screening process, their ties with Moscow may not be easy to erase, particularly if the FIS is able to entice them with money. On the other hand, these officers are, at the least, a known quantity, familiar to the counterintelligence services. This probably makes them less of a threat than the underground agents and the ex-spies who have gone into private enterprise but still maintain their contacts with Russia.

The political and economic upheavals that have occurred in what was formerly the Soviet bloc have changed the landscape for espionage dramatically. These changes have doubtless called for a complete reassessment of the priorities and methods of operations in Eastern Europe. But this has not prevented the Russian Foreign Intelligence Service from pursuing its mission—furthering the goals of Russian foreign policy through intelligence gathering and active measures. The post–cold war environment now requires the Russian Foreign Intelligence Service to use subtler and less overtly aggressive methods, and economic circumstances act as an additional constraint. But Russian intelligence officers operate in a more politically favorable climate than they did in Soviet days, which makes their tasks of spying and active measures easier. Although in some ways the FIS is a less threatening adversary to the West than the KGB was, it inherited the KGB's staff of experienced foreign intelligence operatives, who know their job and are continuing to do it well.

Chapter Six

RUSSIA'S BORDERS AND BEYOND

> I would be very cautious in speaking of state borders with
> the former Soviet Union republics. I am deeply convinced
> that sooner or later we will be together.
> *(Russian Counterintelligence Chief*
> *Sergei Stepashin, June 1994)*

T HE STORY of the KGB's successors is not just about Russia. It is also the story of what happened to the states that were part of the Soviet Union until 1991 and now form part of the CIS. Prior to 1991 there were no state borders between Russia and the other Soviet republics; their security services were part of a whole, the Moscow-controlled KGB. The dissolution of the Soviet Union resulted in the creation of fifteen new and independent states, twelve of which joined the Commonwealth of Independent States (CIS).[1] How is the new border regime—in Soviet days controlled by the KGB—administered? What are the security services of the new CIS states like, and what are their relations with Moscow?

RUSSIA'S NEW BORDERS

The status of Russia's borders and the problems of administering its border regime epitomize the complex security issues that have arisen in the wake of the dissolution of the Soviet Union. The creation of the newly independent states with concomitant ethnic and territorial problems has forced the Russian government to focus increasing attention on its border policy. However improvised and ambiguous this policy appears, its ultimate goal, pursued on several fronts, is straightforward. Russia is attempting to use border politics to integrate the CIS into a tight military, economic, and political union. This task is made easier by the fact that most CIS states have retained close ties to Moscow, ties reinforced by the common bonds of their security services.

In Soviet days border troops and the protection of the empire's 67,000 kilometer state border were the responsibility of the KGB, which oversaw both internal security and foreign intelligence. This arrangement was appropriate because administering the border regime—a top priority for the xenophobic Soviet government—involved both these functions. Not only did border guards enforce an impenetrable *cordon sanitaire*, keeping foreigners from sneaking into the country and their own citizens from sneaking out (under the Soviet regime it was a state crime, punishable by up to three years imprisonment, to cross the border illegally); they also assisted the foreign intelligence branch in cross-border operations and in spying.[2]

Now the Russian border guards, which became the independent Federal Border Service in late 1993 after being part of the MB (Ministry of Security), face different challenges. The dissolution of the Soviet Union and the subsequent creation of the Commonwealth of Independent States altered Russia's borders dramatically. (See map.) Russia no longer has an empire directly along the boundaries of east European states such as the Czech and Slovak republics, Poland, Hungary, and Romania, or, to the south, Turkey, Iran, Afghanistan, and Pakistan. These borders now belong to the newly independent states that were once part of the Soviet Union. But Russia still shares borders with eighteen different countries (five of which are CIS states) and has over 60,000 kilometers of border to protect.

In initial months after the dissolution of the Soviet Union, the Russian government took the public stance that its interests in the CIS extended only as far as its new borders, which correspond to the old administrative divisions between Russia and the other former Soviet republics. But it soon became clear that this was not a viable approach. First of all, Russia did not have the resources to establish a border regime—with border posts, fortifications, etc.—along the vast areas of these new boundaries (stretching over 11,000 of Russia's total 14,000 land kilometers of border).[3] Take Kazakhstan, for example, which shares the longest border with Russia of any of the CIS countries. As the current chief of the Federal Border Service, General Andrei Nikolaev, expressed it:

> What image of the state border have we become accustomed to? Barbed wire, soldiers, dogs. . . . If we try to reestablish this kind of border, first of all, people will tear it down and, second, we will lose not only our shirts but our underwear as well. For example, the length of Russia's border with Kazakhstan is 7,559 km. One kilometer costs one billion rubles. Merely to build the border itself—without any infrastructure, housing and so forth—we would require 7.6 trillion rubles, which is 150 percent more than all our current expenditure on maintaining the border guards.[4]

By 1993 the pretense of independent state borders for the other CIS states had been abandoned. The Russian government was stating openly

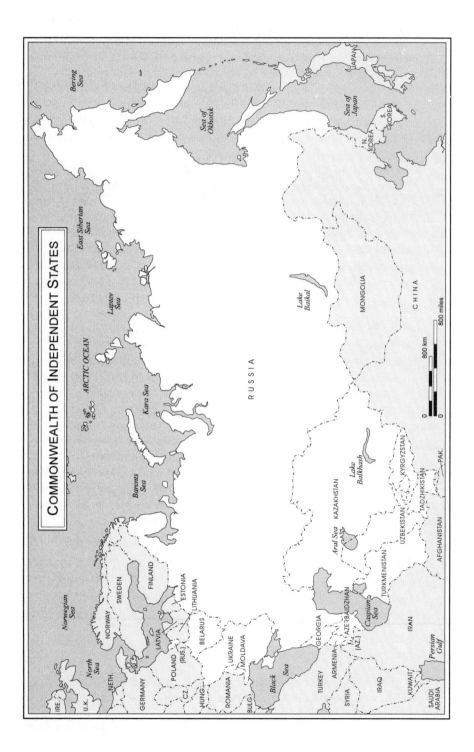

COMMONWEALTH OF INDEPENDENT STATES

that its top priority was to guard the outside borders of the CIS rather than the borders it shared with CIS countries. Furthermore, as Moscow began to tighten its grip on the former Soviet republics, it began to advocate "transparent borders" with the conterminous CIS states: Belarus, Ukraine, Georgia, Azerbaidzhan, and Kazakhstan. This meant that the borders would remain open for unrestricted passage of people, goods, and means of transport. The only places where strict border regimes would be established would be in zones of acute conflict, such as in the North Caucasus. The Law of April 1993 on the State Border of the Russian Federation reflected this policy. It abolished the border zones, so that only border strips 5 kilometers wide remained, and it stipulated the goal of establishing a reduced and simplified border regime with all CIS states.[5]

This policy has proved successful with Kazakhstan as well as with Belarus, which has always advocated transparent borders with Russia. In January 1995 Russia and Kazakhstan signed a formal agreement on cooperation along their mutual border, pledging to simplify customs procedures and remove border posts.[6]

Ukraine, on the other hand, presented Russia with problems. First, the 2,245-kilometer border between Russia and Ukraine has yet to be defined, let alone demarcated. Second, the two countries have disagreed on how much cross-border integration there should be and on the extent of security on their common border. Although they installed some border control points along their border with Ukraine in 1993–1994, the Russians said all along that they preferred an open border with Ukraine. But the Ukrainians took the view that, as an independent state, they needed a controlled border with Russia. As early as November 1991 Ukraine had already created its own border troops and had adopted a special law to govern them.[7]

Extensive negotiations finally produced an agreement, signed on 3 August 1994, between Russia and Ukraine on border issues. The agreement loosened up custom and trade regulations so that economic cooperation between the two countries would be facilitated. The two sides also agreed to cooperate in fighting criminals who attempted to cross the border. But the chief of the Ukrainian border troops, Colonel General Viktor Bannykh, continued to insist on an official state border between his country and Russia.[8]

For the purpose of protecting its new frontier with Azerbaidzhan and Georgia, Russia has a Caucasus Special Border District, headquartered in Stavropol.[9] As a result of the Chechnia conflict, this district was placed on heightened alert and reinforced with more troops in early December 1994. Russia then closed its border with Azerbaidzhan, on the grounds that commandos were moving into Chechnia from Azerbaidzhan to fight the Russian Army. Air and sea communications between Azerbaidzhan and Russia were also shut down, causing significant economic hardships for Azerbaidzhan, which receives half of its imports through Russia. Azeris speculated that the real reason for the blockade was Russia's intention to pressure Azerbaidzhan to abandon a lucrative oil contract it had signed in September 1994 with a Western consortium. This contract called for oil from the Caspian region to be pumped out through Iran and Turkey rather than Russia.[10] Russia was not prepared to allow Azerbaidzhan to make its own economic agreements without considering Russian interests.

In late December 1994 Nikolaev announced that he had installed more border guards along the border between Georgia and Chechnia in order to prevent the flow of arms and mercenaries into Chechnia. A temporary ban was placed on the transport of goods from Georgia into Russia.[11] Within a few days the Russian government announced exceptions to the ban, presumably because it had to keep supplies going to Russian troops stationed in Georgia, and a partial lifting of restrictions along its border with both Georgia and Azerbaidzhan.[12]

THE OUTER BORDERS OF THE CIS

In Russia's view, leaving security along the outer border of the CIS up to the individual CIS states jeopardizes Russia's strategic interests. The other CIS states, in turn, do not have the manpower or resources to secure their outer boundaries. A good example is the border between Tadzhikistan and Afghanistan, where there has been continuous conflict since the Soviet Union broke up. As the former Russian border troop chief Vladimir Shliakhtin pointed out, the Tadzhiks could not stop the flow of illegal drugs, armaments, and Afghan militants across their border. In Soviet days, the border had been defended largely by Slavs (a deliberate policy on the part of the KGB, which considered Tadzhik nationals to be unreliable because of their ethnic ties with Afghanistan). After they achieved independence, the Tadzhiks were not able to establish a viable border service of their own so they had to rely on the Russians, whom they requested to take over jurisdiction of the former Soviet border troops along their borders with Afghanistan and China.[13]

The Russians needed no persuading; loose borders with Afghanistan and China were a threat to them too. In Shliakhtin's words: "On Tadzhikistan's external borders we defend Russia's interests."[14] A similar situation existed with Turkmenistan, which is coterminous with both Afghanistan and Iran. In August 1992, Russia and Turkmenistan signed an agreement on cooperation between the two states in guarding Turkmenistan's southern borders. A joint Russian-Turkmen command took charge of the border that Turkmenistan shares with Afghanistan and Iran.[15] In late 1993 and early 1994 the Council of CIS Border Troops Commanders met on three occasions to discuss border issues. The result was a series of general documents on the protection of CIS external borders, signed in St. Petersburg in July 1994 by all eleven full CIS members. (Moldova was not yet a full member.)[16]

Meanwhile Russia continued negotiating on a bilateral basis with individual CIS states. In October 1992, Kyrgyzstan signed an accord relegating the protection of its border with China to Russia.[17] Russia has also had contingents from its Federal Border Service helping local troops along the outer borders of Uzbekistan, Armenia, Georgia, and Kazakhstan.[18] The border between Georgia and Turkey, for example, was in 1995 controlled by four detachments of Russian border guards and a squadron of patrol ships. And Russia had four border detachments along Armenia's borders with Turkey and Iran.[19] Although in most cases the agreements stipulated an eventual withdrawal of Russian troops, pressure from Moscow, combined with scarce resources and lack of trained personnel in the newly independent states, would doubtless prolong the Russian presence.

Belarus, with a sizable border guard force of its own, has worked amicably with Russia on border issues. Not only does it have an uncontrolled border with Russia, it takes responsibility for protecting its border with Latvia, Lithuania, and Poland (with Russian financial assistance). In late August 1994 the president of Belarus, Aliaksandr Lukashenka, dismissed the commander of the border forces, on the grounds that he was not doing an effective job of guarding the border with Poland. Lukashenka himself took over direct control of Belarus's border guards.[20]

Azerbaidzhan and Ukraine have been less cooperative. Azerbaidzhan has resisted pressure to allow Russian border troops, which were withdrawn in late 1992, to help in protecting its outer frontiers, despite Russian complaints that arms, drugs, and illegal immigrants are coming into their country via Azerbaidzhan. In May 1994 Russian border troops commander Nikolaev revealed that Russia had given Azerbaidzhan an ultimatum. If Azerbaidzhan wanted to prevent Russia from closing the border between the two states, which it had already begun to do, it would have to protect its outer border (with Iran and Turkey) more effectively by having joint patrols with the Russians.[21] But Azerbaidzhan did not cave in and the issue remained unresolved. As for Ukraine, its border chief, Colonel General Bannykh, has said repeatedly that his government opposes joint border forces.[22]

The Russian Federal Border Service

As noted above, Russian border guards were placed under the jurisdiction of the Russian Ministry of Security when they were officially formed in June 1992. This meant that states allowing Russian border guards to patrol their outer borders were subjected to the watchful presence of the Russian security services—a situation that probably created difficulties for the Russian side in their negotiations. This might have been a factor in the decision of the Yeltsin administration in late 1993 to make the border service a separate agency. The Federal Border Service was placed directly under President Yeltsin, with the status of a federal ministry.[23] The FSK (and then the FSB) still had operational responsibility for counterintelligence along the borders, however, so it continued to play a role in border security.

No precise figures on border guard strength have appeared since the reorganization. But border guards chief Nikolaev said in May 1994 that the agency had 75 generals, and if current plans to expand the border troops were carried out, this number would rise to 145. He added that the ratio of one general to 1,800 troops was the norm. This meant around 135,000 troops with a possible expansion to over 250,000 (more than the number of its border guards in Soviet days).[24] In June 1994 the Russian press reported that five new antiterrorist units, numbering fifteen to twenty men, were being added to the border service stationed at "hot spots."[25] And in the spring of 1995, Nikolaev announced an ambitious program for building up and improving the Federal Border Service in the years 1996–2000.[26]

Coming up with the manpower to meet border troop requirements and with money for their upkeep and for the construction of border posts has been a challenge for the financially strapped Russian government. In early 1995 Nikolaev went before a parliamentary group and spoke at great length about the insufficient resources for his troops.[27] Of the 3.2 trillion rubles requested by the Federal Border Service for its annual 1995 budget, the government and parliament had allocated only 2.2 trillion.[28] Equipment is hopelessly outdated and in need of repair. Forty percent of the signaling and communications systems along the border have served out their operating lives and require replacement. In the area of Pskov, which is near the Russian border with Estonia, border guards went on strike (which is illegal) in 1993 because they had no residences and had not received wages. And the border checkpoints lacked such basic necessities as telephones.[29] By early 1995, Russia had built a new, modern control point near Pskov, equipped with technology for effective screening of goods and people, but such problems persist elsewhere.[30]

Why does Russia need such a substantial border troop force? First of all, although Russia has managed to establish open borders with some neighboring CIS states, it still must have border guards along portions of its new boundaries, those shared with Ukraine, Georgia, and Azerbaidzhan, for example, and also those shared with Latvia and Estonia. Second, certain outer boundaries of the CIS, such as the Tadzhik border with Afghanistan, have seen so much armed conflict that they require extra troop strength. During 1994 Russia doubled its border force in Tadzhikistan to reach 15,000 men.[31] Clearly Russia's borders and those of the CIS are highly unstable. The Yeltsin government wants to be able to act resolutely in the case of conflict and to protect its frontiers from the illegal flow of contraband, people and armaments. But also, as in the case of Tadzhikistan and Georgia, border troops are performing "peacekeeping" functions within the country on behalf of Moscow. Increasingly, then, border troops are being used as an extension of Russia's military might in the CIS.

This new role of enforcing Russia's dominance over the CIS involves border troops in the kind of armed combat that was traditionally reserved for the regular military. To be sure, border troops were drawn into fighting along the Chinese border during the Soviet period. But this occurred rarely and on a small scale. Today, along the Tadzhik-Afghan border Russian troops regularly engage in violent skirmishes, which frequently result in casualties, as in July 1993, when Afghan rebels staged a surprise attack on a Russian border post.

BORDER SERVICE CHIEF ANDREI NIKOLAEV

As mentioned earlier, Yeltsin fired Shliaktin, his border guards chief, because of this incident and appointed Colonel General Andrei Nikolaev. Born in 1949, Nikolaev was graduated from the Frunze Military Academy in 1976 and then from the Military Academy of the General Staff in 1988. In June 1992 he became first deputy chief of the Main Operations Directorate of the General Staff of the Russian Federation Armed Forces, rising to become first deputy chief in December 1992.[32]

Nikolaev's appointment marked a sharp departure from the usual practice of naming a career border guards official to the top post. Given that Nikolaev was a deputy of Minister of Defense Grachev, some observers concluded that his appointment meant an assertion of military control over the border troops. The fact that Russian army troops were sent to the Tadzhik border to take part in the defense strengthened this impression. But this proved not to be the case. Before long Nikolaev, who had the status of a minister and was made a full member of the Russian Security Council in April 1994, was asserting the independence of his agency against efforts of Grachev to integrate it with the Ministry of Defense.

In mid-1994 a dispute arose between Nikolaev and Grachev over the policy of transferring resources from the regular military to the border guards, a policy that aroused the ire of the army's generals. At a meeting of the Security Council on 13 July, Grachev angrily expressed his dissatisfaction with the government's border policy, in particular the trend toward building up the border guards' manpower and materials at the expense of the regular army. He noted that "a state cannot have two armies," especially when the shortfall in the draft intake for the armed forces was almost 50 percent.[33] Grachev had earlier proposed to the Russian parliament that the border troops be subordinated to the Ministry of Defense, a proposal that Nikolaev rejected outright.[34] Yeltsin ended the dispute by supporting Nikolaev: "There are military forces and there are border troops. That's how it was and that's how it will stay."[35] Not only did Nikolaev succeed in defending the autonomy of his Federal Border Service; he managed, by the end of 1994, to have two thousand army and navy officers transferred to the border troops and to set up border units on the basis of several disbanded Ministry of Defense units.[36]

Nikolaev has been an outspoken advocate of integrating the CIS into one military and economic unit and returning to the border regime of the former Soviet Union (minus the Baltic states). "I am happy to say that the ideology of the first days of independence is on the way out," he stated in an interview given at the end of 1994. "Russia's president has often noted: the CIS countries have no alternative to integration."[37]

Nikolaev has been working hard to establish a unified CIS border command for guarding the external borders of the CIS, with open borders among all its states. For this purpose, Russia convened a meeting of the border troop commanders of all the CIS states in Moscow in mid-January 1995 to discuss a draft agreement to this effect. But Ukraine and Azerbaidzhan were not in favor of the agreement, especially in light of what was taking place in Chechnia, where five thousand men from the Caucasus Special Border District troops, reinforced by ten motorized maneuver groups from other border areas, were supporting Russia's military troops.[38] At a meeting of CIS heads of state in Almaty, the capital of Kazakhstan, in February 1995, Azerbaidzhan and Ukraine again rejected the terms of an agreement on guarding the external CIS border.[39]

Beyond Russia's Borders: Security Services of the CIS

Border issues involving CIS states are closely intertwined with the activities of their security services. Indeed, a look at what has happened to the former KGB organizations in the CIS states sheds light on Russia's overall policy of trying to reintegrate these states into a strong, Russia-dominated structure. (See Table 3.) When we considered, in the last chapter, what Russia's Foreign Intelligence Service (FIS) was up to in the CIS, we saw a murky picture. This is not simply because the FIS, quite naturally, has not revealed its aims. More important is the fact that, at heart, Russia still considers these newly independent states part of its domestic domain. So Moscow is to a great extent pursuing its policy through traditional means, the internal security apparatus of the former KGB.

For all the talk about independence and democratic change, the security services in the CIS countries have changed little since 1991. Most KGB staffers were kept on, and their functions continued as before, except that suppressing political dissent was no longer openly on the agenda. Most important, ties with Moscow remained strong. The old-boy KGB network stretched across state borders. Why, it might be asked, would the political leadership in the new states allow these ties to continue, thus undermining their independence? First of all, the majority of CIS leaders were former communists who rose to powerful positions in the Soviet days. Whatever their commitment to their own nation states, they still had loyalties to Moscow. Second, most of the CIS states were heavily dependent on Russia economically and thus had strong motivations to preserve close economic ties with Russia. Finally, there was the issue of political and military security, which could not be achieved without help from Moscow.

Ukraine's New National Security Service

In Ukraine, balancing the pressures from Moscow with nationalist sentiment at home has proved a difficult challenge. As the third largest in territory of the CIS states, after Russia and Kazakhstan, Ukraine, with a full-fledged army and strategic nuclear weapons, has been a key player in the near abroad, and its security services are of particular interest. Even before the Soviet Union was disbanded, the Ukrainian Supreme Soviet, on 20 September 1991, issued a special resolution creating a new agency to replace the Ukrainian branch of the KGB. The purpose of the new organization, the Ukrainian Security Service (SBU), was straightforward—pro-

TABLE 3

Security Services of Non-Russian CIS States, September 1995

Armenia	State Administration for National Security
	Chief: Serzh Sargisian
	Appt. May 1995
Azerbaidzhan	Ministry of National Security
	Chief: Namik Abbasov
	Appt. March 1995
Belarus	Committee for State Security (KGB)
	Chief: Vladimir Egorov
	Appt. July 1994
Georgia	Ministry of State Security
	Chief: Adtandil Ioseliani (acting minister)
	Appt. September 1995
Kazakhstan	Committee for National Security
	Chief: Maj. Gen. Sat Tokpakbaev
	Appt. December 1993
Kyrgyzstan	State Committee for National Security
	Chief: Maj. Gen. Anarbek Bakaev
	Appt. February 1992
Moldova	Ministry of National Security
	Chief: Maj. Gen. Vasile Calmoi
	Appt. July 1992
Tadzhikistan	Ministry of Security
	Chief: Lt. Col. Saidanwar Kamolov
	Appt. August 1992
Turkmenistan	Committee of National Security
	Chief: Maj. Gen. Saparmurad Seidov
	Appt. May 1992
Ukraine	Ukrainian Security Service
	Chief: Maj. Gen. Volodymyr Radchenko
	Appt. July 1995
Uzbekistan	National Security Service
	Chief: Maj. Gen. Rustam Inoyatov
	Appt. June 1995

tecting the state's sovereignty, constitutional structure, and territorial integrity, and warding off the subversive activity of foreign states.[40] The resolution was intended to express Ukraine's new security goals as an independent country, but it had a familiar ring. The old KGB had almost identical publicly declared goals.

In terms of organization, the new service also kept up with tradition. Like its KGB predecessor, the SBU included directorates for intelligence, counterintelligence, and military counterintelligence, as well as those for combatting corruption, functional and technological maintenance and documentation, analysis, personnel, and others. SBU branches replaced the KGB territorial branches.[41] As with the new security structure in Moscow, some functions of the former KGB were not included in the new Ukrainain agency: communications security, electronic intelligence gathering, and the guards service were subordinated to other state bodies or made separate agencies. The staff of 18,000 was reduced by half.[42]

According to official statements, SBU operations were to be completely different from those of the KGB. It could not be otherwise, given the strong desire of Ukrainians to assert their independence from Russia and the almost universal hatred of the KGB. The service would not employ informers or persecute dissidents. Instead, it would concentrate on gathering information, protecting the environment, and fighting terrorism, drug trafficking, and corruption.[43] But Ukrainian human rights activists were suspicious of the new security agency, given the policy of keeping KGB professionals on to serve in the SBU. At one point they even picketed the SBU offices in Lvov, demanding that a former political prisoner rather than a career KGB official be the new SBU chief there.[44]

Their protests fell on deaf ears. Although SBU spokesmen claimed in early 1992 that sixteen KGB generals had been sent into retirement, all those who surfaced in leading SBU posts were career KGB officials.[45] Ukraine's political leadership, itself full of former communists, opted for experience over democratic credentials. As one SBU official put it: "Of course, at present we are using the services of the old experienced personnel. Certainly professionalism is attained only by years of the hardest work, by the most difficult rough work, and it would be the greatest stupidity to give up their services. Even the Bolsheviks did not refuse the tsarist special agents."[46] Nationalist credentials were not a priority for the SBU either. A surprisingly large proportion of employees in the new service (35 percent) were Russians rather than Ukrainians.[47]

Continuity with the old KGB was exemplified in the appointment of Evhen Marchuk to head the new Ukrainian service. Marchuk had been in the KGB for years, rising from junior officer to first deputy chairman under Nikolai Golushko in 1990. Undoubtedly aware that his past was a liability, Marchuk devoted considerable effort to enhancing the image of the SBU, emphasizing in speeches and interviews how different it was from the former KGB: "The current course of the Ukrainian Security Service has taken a 180-degree turn. . . . Today we do not have a priori enemies; that is, any special service is not hostile unless we receive concrete data that it is engaged in subversive work."[48]

Marchuk stressed that the top priority of the SBU was to protect the interests of independent Ukraine, not those of Moscow. But his close association with Golushko (who was despised by Ukrainian democrats and was now first deputy chairman of the Russian Ministry of Security), and his long tenure in the KGB, made people worry that Marchuk was still under the thumb of his former bosses. The Ukrainian KGB had been Moscow's chief vehicle for maintaining political control over Ukraine and for suppressing Ukrainian nationalism. Marchuk himself had been a KGB investigator in cases against Ukrainian dissidents in the Soviet period.[49] Would Marchuk and other officials now be able to defend an independent, democratic Ukraine?

As in Russia, one of the first items on the agenda of the new Ukrainian government was a Law on the Security Service of Ukraine, intended to provide a basis for its operations.[50] Passed by the Ukrainian parliament in March 1992, the law stipulated that the Ukrainian security service (the SBU) was subordinate both to the president of Ukraine and to the Supreme Soviet (parliament) of Ukraine. This was an encouraging sign from the point of view of the reformers, who were anxious to establish a system of parliamentary oversight. The parliament, after all, included several prominent human rights activists. In the words of one commentator: "People the former KGB once worked against, carrying out operations in which Golushko took pride . . . had now become legislators."[51] According to the law, the SBU had to respond to questioning by committees of the parliament and regularly inform deputies about their activities. Presumably the security services were to provide information on financial questions, which the parliament then would act upon. But, as in the case of Russia, the actual divisions of responsibility between the president and the parliament and the means of parliamentary control were not spelled out.

What was most striking about the Ukrainian Law on the Security Service, given that it was passed by the parliament, was its similarity to the Russian Law on the Federal Organs of State Security, passed in July 1992.[52] The wording and sequence of the articles were practically identical. This is because in both the Russian and the Ukrainian cases, the new laws derived directly from the earlier laws on the KGB. Given that the KGB, both USSR and Ukrainian, was a symbol of Russian repression against national minorities, it is somewhat surprising that the new Ukrainian government would make no effort to distance itself from this organization. Did Kiev simply not have the legal resources to come up with an original law of its own? Perhaps. Nonetheless, if the new government really intended the SBU to be completely different from its predecessor—as well as independent from Moscow—it would not have put forth a law that was a carbon copy of the Soviet one.

Operations of Ukrainian Security Services

Marchuk said that his organization would focus operations on "upholding the constitutional order and Ukraine's territorial integrity." This was a difficult task, given such problems as that of Crimea, whose predominantly Russian population was demanding independence from Ukraine. Crimea was also the home of the Black Sea fleet, the object of intense dispute for control between Kiev and Moscow. Marchuk warned those who supported an independent Crimea against breaking the law. But his stance was distinctly mild in comparison to some Ukrainian politicians who wanted their government to crack down on the Crimea and who blamed Moscow for encouraging the demands for independence.[53] Marchuk was aware of the need to balance the interests of Russians (22 percent of Ukraine's population) with those of Ukrainians, and the SBU was vigilant in suppressing anti-Russian sentiments in Ukraine. Its leaders announced in July 1992, for example, that they had arrested members of the nationalist organization "Popular Rukh" for writing anti-Russian slogans on the walls of houses.[54]

With regard to the threat to Ukraine's security posed by foreigners, Marchuk was initially cautious, saying only that certain foreign organizations tried to influence public opinion in Ukraine in a negative way. Later, however, he began alluding to the "harmful designs" of foreign businessmen in Ukraine, claiming that Western entrepreneurs were interfering in Ukrainian politics.[55] Local SBU officials adopted similar tones. One official said that foreign businessmen were stealing Ukraine's technological secrets and suggested that foreigners be monitored more carefully. By early 1995, the note of alarm was heightened, as it was in Russia. Even supposedly benevolent Western sponsors of research in Ukraine became suspect in SBU eyes.[56]

As with the Russian security services, the SBU had a special subdivision, the "T" Administration, established in August 1992, for the purpose of protecting Ukraine against "anticonstitutional" activities. According to the chief of this administration, Lieutenant Colonel Viktor Burlakov, it focused on a wide range of threats to the political stability of Ukraine and worked in cooperation with other law enforcement agencies, such as the regular police, the Ministry of Interior. Burlakov took a dim view of the Westerners who came freely into Ukraine after 1991 and who gave assistance and financial backing to research. He was also opposed to foreign religious groups, who he claimed were enticing Ukrainian citizens to gather secret information about the Ukrainian military and the security services.[57] In mid-1994, he stated that the "T" Administration had uncovered numerous foreign anti-Ukrainian organizations that were working to undermine Ukraine's territorial integrity and political stability. Their criminal actions, he said, ranged from "inflaming" ethnic prejudices to planning terrorist attacks.[58]

What about foreign intelligence gathering? As noted earlier, the CIS states, other than Russia, were left with a shortage of personnel and resources for intelligence gathering. This has been a problem for the SBU's directorate for foreign intelligence. As one source put it: "Gathering intelligence on its own is a completely new job for the SBU; the Ukrainian KGB's intelligence department operated at Moscow's command and did not conduct any independent projects."[59]

As to the kind of intelligence Ukraine is seeking, industrial espionage is a top priority. According to one source, the agency's operations in this area saved the government the equivalent of $250 million from 1992 to 1994.[60] The SBU also keeps a close watch on Ukraine's neighbors, including Russia. Since Ukraine has had difficulty building up an effective foreign intelligence apparatus of its own, gathering intelligence in the West is probably a limited venture. But Ukraine does have some agents in eastern Europe. In August 1993, SBU officer Anatolii Lysenko was arrested in Poland on charges of espionage for Ukraine and sentenced to two years in prison.[61]

Another key SBU agency is the military counterintelligence administration, which provides counterintelligence support against espionage in the Ukrainian armed forces, ensures the political loyalty of the officers and troops, and protects nuclear and other military facilities.[62] The issue of political loyalty in the Ukrainian armed forces is a complex one, given the fact that a significant proportion of officers (well over 50 percent) and troops are Russian. The Ukrainian government did require an "oath of allegiance" for all members of the military, but there is still cause for concern about their reliability. The conflict with Russia over ownership of nuclear weapons on Ukrainian soil and over the Black Sea fleet complicates the issue even further.[63] Although nationalist groups like the Union of Ukrainian Officers have reportedly pressed the SBU to take decisive action against pro-Russian tendencies in the armed forces, it is unlikely, given the close ties between the SBU and Moscow, that this will happen.[64]

CRIME, SECURITY, AND POLITICS IN UKRAINE

The SBU has fought hard against organized crime within the armed forces and against illegal sales of military property and technology. Judging from statements in the press, corruption in the Ukrainian armed forces is widespread and hence a focal point for the military counterintelligence department. In late 1993, for example, the sbu announced that its military counterintelligence directorate had stopped the illegal sale of two Ukrainian MIG 25 bombers to one of the other cis countries. A number of high military officials were implicated in the deal.[65]

As with the Russian security services, the sbu assumed a leading role in the fight against all forms of official corruption. The new president of Ukraine, Leonid Kuchma, who was elected in July 1994, continued former President Leonid Kravchuk's policy of support for a strong security service, putting special emphasis on the struggle against economic crime. In a speech to security personnel delivered not long after his election, Kuchma urged the sbu to step up its efforts: "We must give Ukraine's security service every support in the moral, material and financial aspects. I promise you such support."[66] Later, in February 1995, Kuchma announced that he was reorganizing the security service and increasing its powers in order to make it more effective in the struggle against crime.[67] To those following developments in Russia this had a familiar ring.

Shortly before he was defeated by Kuchma in the presidential elections, Kravchuk had appointed Marchuk to the post of deputy prime minister for national security. This meant that Marchuk oversaw a broad range of security operations, not just those of the sbu. Marchuk's replacement as head of the sbu was Valeriy Malikov, formerly his first deputy and a Russian native, who had been with the kgb since 1970.[68] Within a little over a year, Malikov was replaced by yet another kgb professional, General Volodymyr Radchenko. Radchenko had a notorious reputation for suppressing dissidents when he served in the kgb in 1970s and 1980s, and his appointment the year before as head of the Ministry of Internal Affairs had been met with dismay by democrats. As one observer expressed it: "It is difficult to imagine that in a democratic country, for example in present-day Germany, a former Gestapo functionary who struggled against antifascists, or a stasi [East German secret police] officer who persecuted dissidents, might be appointed to the post of internal affairs minister."[69] But, as usual, expediency prevailed and such protests went unheeded. When Radchenko was appointed sbu chief it became clear that outsiders would not be given top sbu posts.

With men like Marchuk, who in February 1995 was made acting prime minister and was given a permanent position in early June, and Radchenko in charge of Ukraine's national security policy, a trend toward a more powerful security service and closer ties with Russia seemed likely. Indeed, it is through organizations like the sbu and its counterpart in Moscow that such ties have been promoted. In addition to the accord reached with the Russian fis, the sbu signed agreements with the Russian counterintelligence service (at the time, the Ministry of Security) in 1992–

93, which served as the basis for extensive cooperation.[70] In a statement made not long before he left his post as SBU chief, Marchuk described this cooperation:

> We have an agreement with the Russian special service. In those cases when there is mutual interest, we go to them and they come to us. Incidentally, a group from the Russian Federal Counterintelligence Service [FSK] is presently in Kiev, and we are jointly planning a complicated operation. We did not have to deal with cases of anybody from the Russian Federal Counterintelligence engaging in some secret subversive activity here.[71]

Ironically, despite his KGB past, Marchuk seems to enjoy wide respect among Ukrainians. He is generally viewed as a pragmatist, even a liberal, who acts with resolve in difficult situations and is able to negotiate successfully with the Russians. Many consider his experience in the security services as an asset, which offers him an insider's perspective and enables him to maneuver through the chaos of Ukraine's political and economic problems.[72] In this sense, Marchuk symbolizes the ambiguities of politics in the former Soviet Union, which are hovering between democracy and authoritarianism.

SECURITY SERVICES OF BELARUS AND MOLDOVA

Belarus has made much less progress than Ukraine in reforming its security service. The post-Soviet political leadership did not even bother to change the name, which remains the KGB. When Belarus became an independent state in 1991, General Eduard Shirkousky, who had occupied the post of KGB chairman since October 1990, stayed on, despite the fact that he had signed the Communist Party's appeal supporting the coup. The majority of his staff remained with him. Indeed, some of those brought in by the Communist Party to work in the KGB as far back as the 1950s are still serving. Outside KGB headquarters in Minsk the statue of Feliks Dzerzhinskii, first chief of the Soviet security police, still stands, although his statue has long since disappeared in Moscow.[73]

The failure to reform the Belarussian KGB stems largely from the fact that communists continue to dominate the government and they have had little interest in curbing the powers of the organization they traditionally relied upon. The government of Belarus does not want to break its ties with Russia, so its KGB has continued to take its cues from Moscow.[74] In January 1992, the Belarussian parliament approved a temporary statute on the KGB, which gave it similar functions to those of the old KGB, as well as the same organizational structure. The only significant change from the past was that the communist-dominated parliament, rather than the party Politburo, had control of the KGB.[75]

The KGB leadership had few objections to being under parliamentary control. In practice, this meant only that KGB chairman Shirkousky had to report to the chairman of the parliament, Stanislav Skushkevich. By 1992 the latter was already engaged in a bitter power struggle with Prime Minister Vyacheslav Kebich of Belarus, and the KGB provided him with a powerful weapon—evidence of official corruption.[76]

As in Russia and Ukraine, the corruption issue became the cause célèbre of the KGB. In late 1992 Shirkousky announced that his organization was investigating two hundred high-level cases of embezzlement and corruption.[77] Strengthened by investigative powers granted in a new Law on Operational-Investigative Activity (almost identical to the Russian law), the KGB began zeroing in on top Belarussian officials. By the end of 1993, Shirkousky reported to the parliament that a web of corruption covered the entire government. A month later parliamentary deputy Aleksandr Lukashenka, chief of the parliamentary commission for fighting corruption, was calling for the resignation of Kebich.[78]

Shirkousky himself was dismissed from his post in the fray, to be replaced briefly by Henadz Lavitski in early 1994. Following his election to the newly created post of president of Belarus in July 1994, Aleksandr Lukashenka fired Lavitski and several of his deputes, naming a new KGB chairman, former head of the Ministry of Internal affairs (MVD) Vladimir Yegorov. As a president with broad powers, Lukashenka, a former political commissar in the KGB border guards, has shown little inclination to rein in the KGB, especially after placing his own appointees in top KGB posts. In the words of one critic: "The president of Belarus has made the power structures his chief favorites. They are the Ministry of Internal Affairs, the KGB, and the army. . . . It is no accident that the budget of the KGB for this year [1995] matches all the outlays needed for the government, the Supreme Soviet, the procurator's office, and the president's administration, taken together."[79]

In August 1994 Lukashenka issued a decree creating a new temporary statute to govern the KGB, which reportedly provided a wider legal basis for it to pursue political investigations. The statute was not made public.[80] Like Yeltsin, Lukashenka also has his own presidential security service, which works in close collaboration with the KGB.[81]

Ever since Belarus became an independent state, its KGB has maintained close ties with Russia's security services. Belarussian KGB officials said at the outset that the CIS security services were so deeply connected it would be impossible for them to function independently of one another.[82] Lukashenka, who has asserted strong control over the KGB, has continued this policy. He has been an outspoken advocate of unification with Russia, but in this respect he is reflecting popular sentiment. In a May 1995 referendum, Belarussians voted for integration with Russia and for making Russian an official language.[83]

With regard to neighboring Moldova, the fact that Russia's Fourteenth Army, led until the summer of 1995 by Lieutenant General Aleksandr Lebed, is still in occupation in the Trans-Dniester region of the country (which has been trying to break away from Moldova) has given Russia considerable leverage. After Moldova achieved independence, the Moldovan government initially refused to ratify the accords on the creation of the CIS and announced its intention to reunify with Romania. But then Russia used military intervention on behalf of the ethnic Russians in Trans-Dniester, along with economic blackmail, to pressure the Moldovan leadership. This strategy worked and gradually Moldova began to consider Russia's demands.[84]

Moldova's president, Mircea Snegur, has taken a favorable stance toward economic integration with the CIS, but he has resisted political and military integration, especially given the considerable public opposition to closer ties with the CIS. According to one analyst: "Rather than either uniting with Romania or subordinating themselves to the CIS, Moldovans have managed the difficult task of asserting their independence and are beginning to express their own unique identity."[85]

It is not clear what role the security services have had in this process. Moldova has a Ministry of National Security, headed by Major General Vasile Calmoi, but it has received little attention in the media, so it might be assumed that its political influence is limited. As for relations with the Russian services, in June 1994 Calmoi signed an agreement with FSK Chief Stepashin, pledging, in the usual manner, cooperation on a broad range of security problems. The two services agreed to exchange information and work together in fighting terrorism, drug trafficking, and illegal arms sales.[86] Whatever additional opportunity this presents to Russia for influencing politics in Moldova, the presence of the Russian Army there and the economic constraints should be enough to ensure that Moldova responds to Russian concerns.

TRANSCAUCASIA

In Armenia and Azerbaidzhan, old Communist Party elites have survived to dominate politics and for the most part these elites are sympathetic toward some sort of a CIS union. Despite strong nationalist sentiment and deep resentment against Russian interference among the people of these states, their political leaders cooperate with Moscow. It could hardly be otherwise, given that Moscow has been actively involved with politics at the top in both countries. In 1993 Moscow backed the overthrow of Azerbaidzhan's independent president, Abulfez Elchibey, bringing about the installation of the more compliant Gaidar Aliev, former Communist Party boss in the republic and before that chairman of the republican KGB, as president. In Georgia, Moscow had a hand in the ouster of democratically elected Zviad Gamsakhurdia and the return to power of Eduard Shevardnazde, former head of the republic's regular police and then Communist Party chief of Georgia until the late 1980s.[87]

Having backed both leaders, Moscow has since pressured them to follow its dictates. Shevardnadze was forced in October 1993 to cave in to Russian demands and allow Russian troops in his country because of the conflict in Abkhazia (a region of Georgia that has demanded independence), which was threatening to bring down his leadership. And Moscow dissuaded Aliev from following through on Azerbaidzhan's oil contract with the West (which excluded a pipeline through Russia) by continuing military support to the Armenians. There are even rumors that Russian security services have had a role in some of the coup attempts against the governments of Aliev and Shevardnadze. It has been suggested that Aliev's pro-Moscow rival, former Azeri Prime Minister Surat Guseinov, is being covertly encouraged by the Kremlin. More recently, Russian security services have been linked to the terrorist act aimed at Shevardnadze in August 1995.[88]

As a result of the political instability, crime, and violence in Georgia and Azerbaidzhan, the security services of these states have been deeply involved in both republican politics and CIS affairs. Georgia's Ministry of State Security was established by Shevardnadze in October 1993, replacing the earlier Information and Intelligence Service that had been set up under former president Gamsakhurdia. Its chief until late August 1995, Major General Igor Giorgadze, joined the KGB in the early 1970s, rising to a leading post in counterintelligence by 1990. He later served as Georgia's minister of internal affairs, before resigning in early 1992.[89]

Giorgadze was known as "Moscow's man." The Russian Ministry of Security had pressed hard to have him head the security apparatus under Shevardnadze. After assuming his post, Giorgadze set forth a clear agenda. Drug smuggling, terrorism, and organized crime were the most serious threats to Georgian security, he said. In order to give his organization the power to struggle against such phenomena, he created a special task force of highly trained elite troops. The first challenge came from within the government. Giorgadze soon became embroiled in a conflict with the minister of defense, which led to the bombing of the headquarters of the Ministry of State Security in late December 1993. The internecine violence continued. By July 1994, ten high-ranking officials from the "power ministries" had been assassinated.[90]

Security officials have played a major role in trying to neutralize the armed opposition to the government, composed mainly of supporters of the deceased President Gamsakhurdia in western Georgia.[91] This opposition has become an increasing threat to Shevardnadze, who in late August 1995 came close to being assassinated in a terrorist attack.[92]

What about the connections between Georgia's security staffers and their counterparts in Moscow? Filled with Chekists from the KGB period, the Georgian Ministry of State Security has little inclination to promote the interests of Georgia against those of Moscow. Giorgadze declared his strong support for Georgia's membership in the CIS and his determination to work closely with his Russian colleagues.[93] The idea of turning to the West for help in solving some of Georgia's problems was not acceptable to him: "Our opposition desires an orientation toward the West, which is not a sinful desire in itself, but under the present circumstances Georgia's path to the West lies via Russia."[94] This of course was in keeping with Shevardnadze's strategy of close cooperation with the Yeltsin administration, drawing criticism from many Georgians, who see him as Moscow's puppet.

The irony is that Giorgadze himself seems to have turned against Shevardnadze, or least to have ended up highly compromised in Shevardnadze's eyes. The Georgian procurator accused him of complicity in the August attempt on Shevardnadze's life, causing Giorgadze to flee to Moscow, where he faced attempts by Georgia to extradite him. His security post was assumed by his first deputy, Adtandil Ioseliani, in early September 1995. Not surprisingly, there has been considerable speculation about the role of Russia's security services in the affair. Have they been trying to undermine Shevardnadze's position—and thereby gain leverage over him on key issues such as the deployment of Russian troops in Georgia—by encouraging his enemies?[95]

Similar questions have arisen in regard to Azerbaidzhan, where President Aliev faces serious threats from political opposition and has also to deal with the war in Nagornyi-Karabakh and a disintegrating economy. In the initial period of independence, before Aliev came to power, the Elchibey leadership set out to get rid of the vestiges of the KGB's past by instituting new controls and dismissing a number of KGB officials. The former chairman of the Azeri KGB, Vladimir Guseinov, was even arrested in 1992 because of his role in the bloody crackdown against Azeri nationalists by Russian troops in January 1990 in Baku.[96]

But Aliev reversed this trend. Azerbaidzhan's Ministry of National Security, headed since March 1995 by Namik Abbasov, has been a key element of his political leadership. Ties with the Russian security services remain close. In May 1995 Russian security chief Stepashin traveled to Baku, where he met with President Aliev and signed a bilateral agreement with Namik Abbasov on cooperation in fighting terrorism and organized crime. They also agreed on joint training and exchange of personnel. "From now on," Stepashin noted, "the employees of the Federal Security Service will be able to come to serve in Baku without any obstacles."[97] Would this not undermine Azerbaidzhan's independence by providing further opportunities for the Russians to meddle in Baku's politics? Aliev did not give the impression of concern. He was full of praise for the agreement, noting that, in these difficult times, it was important that the CIS security services cooperate closely.[98]

Having spent his entire career in the KGB before becoming party first secretary in Azerbaidzhan in 1969, Aliev knows the rules of the game with Moscow and is an expert at political survival. According to one observer: "The old Bolsheviks recall that Aliev, being practically the only person from the Caucasus in the Kremlin, was one of the most clever and cosmopolitan politicians."[99] "Instead of communism, I came to believe in God," he said after coming back to politics in 1993. But, he said, his loyalty to Moscow was still unwavering: "After all, there is so much that binds me to Russia. I might say that my entire life binds me to it."[100] For Aliev, this is probably the rhetoric of expediency. Faced with constant pressure from Moscow, he finally backed down in October 1995 and agreed to an oil deal with the West that would carry oil from the Caspian shelf through pipelines in both Georgia and Russia, via Chechnia.[101]

Armenia's political transition has taken a different path, in that its popularly elected president, Levon Ter-Petrossian, has managed to stay in power, despite the stresses of Armenia's long conflict with Azerbaidzhan, which has kept the country on a war footing. Ter-Petrossian, a former dissident and longtime democrat, did not have ties to the party-KGB bureaucracy in Armenia or in Moscow. But his government still needed a security service. Armenia's security service, the State Administration for National Security (GUNS), was created in place of the KGB in November 1992. Fourteen months later, Ter-Petrossian decided the agency needed to be overhauled. In January 1994, he signed a decree suspending the operations of its personnel other than border guards and technical staffers. He then appointed Davit Shakhnazarian as acting chief, ordering him to screen agency personnel and draft a new charter within three months, just as Yeltsin did with his security service.[102]

As might have been expected, Ter-Petrossian's actions gave rise to considerable dissatisfaction in security circles, with some saying that Armenia's security interests would be seriously damaged. In the end, however, most of the security personnel survived the screening—just as employees of the Russian FSK did at the same time—and the Administration for National Security remained in tact. Ter-Petrossian has been full of praise for the security administration, reporting in a speech in August 1994 that it had accomplished more in the past six months than in the preceding four years.[103]

Much of the security service's effort has been directed against internal political opposition to the Ter-Petrossian government. In early 1995, security chief Shakhnazarian (who was replaced by Serzh Sargisian in May 1995) gave a televised address devoted to justifying the measures his service had taken against the main oppositional party, on the grounds that it was involved in drug trafficking and political murder. Shakhnazarian revealed that the Russian FSK had helped his agency in its investigations.[104]

One important factor has encouraged close relations between the respective governments and security services of Russia and Armenia, despite the latter's strong sense of national identity and ethnic cohesion. Armenia has depended heavily on Russian military assistance to gain an advantage in its war against Azerbaidzhan, which began several years ago over the disputed territory of Nagornyi-Karabakh. Although relations have not always been smooth, Yerevan cannot risk alienation from Moscow and therefore consistently supports Russian policies toward the CIS.

CENTRAL ASIAN STATES

The five Central Asian states—Kazakhstan, Kyrgyzstan, Tadzhikistan, Turkmenistan, and Uzbekistan—share similar attitudes toward Russia and the CIS. The political leadership is dominated by former communists from the Soviet period, who have deemed it essential to preserve economic and military ties with Russia, as well as close relations with the Russian police and intelligence apparatus. Even Kyrgyzstan's president, Askar Akaev, generally thought of as an independent-minded reformer, has been reluctant to take a strong stance against reintegration with Russia. At the same time, however, Central Asian leaders must deal with the realities of the new post-Soviet political structure and accommodate the strong nationalist sentiments in their states.[105]

Kyrgyzstan has the most enlightened political regime of any of the Central Asian states. President Akaev, although a former member of the Communist Party, is the only Central Asian leader who had not been a high-level party bureaucrat, and he has shown himself open to democratic change.[106] Russia has not put the kind of pressure on Kyrgyzstan that it has on other CIS states, and the Akaev government has not been subjected to coup attempts or ethnic conflicts. Nonetheless, Kyrgyzstan has played by the rules and its leadership has not asserted itself to the point where it can dissolve the old KGB ties.

The presence of the former KGB—the State Committee for National Security of Kyrgyzstan, headed by Major General Anarbek Bakaev—might provide Moscow with a means for exerting its influence on the political scene. But, as it stands now, this service does not play an important political role. President Akaev is secure enough politically that he apparently does not need to rely on his security services to suppress opposition.[107]

As for Kazakhstan, the largest in territory of the Central Asian states, its president, Nursultan Nazarbaev, is the embodiment of an old-style communist ruler. Having won a mandate (in an April 1995 referendum) to remain president until the year 2000, he is firmly in control. Nazarbaev was vehemently opposed to the breakup of the Soviet Union in 1991 and has consequently lobbied hard for the re-creation of central economic and military structures to bind together members of the CIS. In January 1995 he and Yeltsin signed a declaration calling for the creation of a joint Russian-Kazakh army and border guard.[108] The strength of the old, Russified political elite and the presence of a large Russian population in Kazakhstan (over 37 percent of the total) make efforts at establishing real independence from Russia illusory. The status of the Kazakh security service and its ties with Russia reinforce this impression.

In July 1992, the Kazakh Supreme Soviet adopted a law creating a Committee for National Security (Komitet National'noi Bezopasnosti, or KNB) to replace the KGB. Its chairman, Lieutenant General Bulat Baekenov, assured the public that this was not simply a change of name, because the KNB, unlike the KGB, would protect the interests of the individual over those of the state.[109] It turns out, however, that the powers of the new security agency were much the same as those of its predecessor. As was the case with Ukraine, the Law on the Organs of National Security of Kazakhstan was strikingly similar to the Russian law (and hence to the earlier KGB law).

The majority of staffers from the KGB, many with lengthy careers there, were kept on to serve in the KNB. KNB Chairman Baekenov had close to twenty years in the KGB behind him. Baekenov lobbied hard on behalf of his security apparatus, claiming in 1993 that foreign spies had "stepped up their subversive activities" against Kazakhstan and that therefore the KNB needed more personnel and resources.[110] Clearly these spies did not include Russians, whom Baekenov and other Kazakh leaders treat as trusted brothers. In early 1993 Baekenov and the Russian minister of security at the time, Barannikov, signed an agreement on cooperation in a broad range of security matters, including border patrol and counterintelligence. They pledged "to pool their efforts in safeguarding each other's interests and protecting strategic military facilities."[111]

The next year, Russian Security Chief Stepashin visited Almaty to work out concrete details on cooperation between the two security services with the new KNB chief, Major General Sat Tokpakbaev, who had replaced Baekenov in late 1993. They signed several protocols for joint operations on a range of security issues. At a news conference in Almaty, Stepashin justified the agreements by observing that "if Russia did not help set up counterintelligence services in the CIS countries, this would have been done by others."[112]

As for the other three Central Asian republics, they too have followed the pattern of Kazakhstan, retaining the old KGB under new names. Like Kazakhstan and Kyrgyzstan, Turkmenistan has a Committee of National Security (Komitet Natsional'noi Bezopastnosti, or KNB), which replaced the KGB in 1992. Turkmenistan has the most authoritarian political system of all the Central Asian states. All power is in the hands of President Saparmurat Niyazov, whose term of office has been extended to 1999, and the media is fully controlled by the state, which does not permit oppositional views to be expressed.

The KNB is crucial to the survival of the Niyazov government. Headed by Major General Saparmurad Seidov, the KNB uses its sweeping powers primarily to fight members of the political opposition to the government. A tactic used frequently by the KNB is to gather compromising materials on adversaries of Niyazov and then to charge them with corruption.[113] The KNB has a close working relationship with Russia's security services, which have supported the KNB in efforts to suppress opposition to the Niyazov government.[114]

In Uzbekistan, President Islam Karimov rules with an iron fist and the parliament is controlled by members of the old Communist Party *nomenklatura*. In the words of a former Uzbek official: "Independence for us has been a cruel joke. The people have been cheated. The state controls them all in the name of peace and stability—and, of course, in the name of the state."[115]

Uzbekistan's National Security Service, headed since June 1995 by Major General Rustam Inoyatov, has been particularly active in pursuing those engaged in antistate activities and members of the political opposition. This service has also been cracking down severely on economic crime and on foreigners. In a September 1994 interview, the former security chief warned: "If any interference in our internal affairs or breaches of the law come to light, the laws of Eastern hospitality are replaced by the full gravity of the law. In the current year alone administrative sanctions were applied to 910 foreign citizens. One hundred ninety-three of them were deported and three foreigners were charged with criminal offenses."[116] The dissolution of the Soviet Union had little effect on Uzbekistan; it is still living in its Soviet past. As one Uzbek put it: "We live in a police state that would have made the old Bolsheviks proud."[117]

Tadzhikistan's politics have been dominated by violent conflict within the country and along the border with Afghanistan. There has been continuous political opposition to the government, led by President Imomali Rakhmonov. In 1992 the oppositionists briefly usurped power, but by the end of that year—after a civil war in which thousands perished—control had returned to the ex-Communist Party elite. This elite has depended on support from Russian forces, as well as on a Russian-dominated security apparatus, for its survival.[118]

Tadzhikistan's KGB became first a National Security Committee and then, in early 1994, was transformed into a Ministry of Security, now headed by Lieutenant Colonel Saidanwar Kamolov. In response to criticism of its repressive tactics, the Ministry of Security insisted, in a publicly broadcast statement in late 1994, that it has "selflessly defended the constitutional government under the complicated conditions of the civil war."[119] Russia's security services, along with the Russian Army and border guards, are doubtless offering their support in this struggle.

The cooperation between Russian and the other CIS security services has deep roots that go back to Soviet days, when the republic KGB's were extensions of the KGB in Moscow. Then, as now, these KGB branches were key vehicles for implementing Moscow's policies. By 1994 these policies were focused on the reintegration process within the CIS, a process that has accelerated considerably in 1995, mainly because of Moscow's more assertive stance. Why the change in policy from that adopted by the Yeltsin government after the Soviet Union collapsed? It could be that Yeltsin wanted to send a message to the West that if Russia did not receive Western aid it would start to restore its empire. It could also be that Yeltsin was anticipating the 1996 presidential elections and was seeking the support of those who bemoaned the dissolution of the Soviet Union and criticized himself for causing it. Finally, of course, Yeltsin might have simply been reclaiming for Russia its interests in territory it has, for over a century, considered to be its domain.[120]

Chapter Seven

THE SECURITY SERVICES AND

HUMAN RIGHTS

> Society is accustomed to a situation in which everything,
> good or bad, is given to it from above. In particular, this
> applies to human rights, which are still not thought of
> in Russia as inalienable. A view that rights are granted
> remains a part of public attitudes and also a part of
> the self-attitudes of authorities.
> *(Sergei Kovalev, chairman of the Russian Federation
> Human Rights Committee, August 1994)*

NOW THAT RUSSIA and the other former Soviet republics have discarded their communist systems of government, the issue of human rights in the former Soviet Union seems to have lost the urgency that it had in the communist period. Unfortunately, however, although world attention is no longer focused on the problem, it has not disappeared. Indeed, in some CIS states, security police are violating people's rights on a wide scale, just as the KGB did up until the late 1980s. Even in Russia, where the security services have been significantly restrained, they have not discarded their old ways completely and they still employ KGB officers who persecuted political nonconformists in the past.

In March 1995, an opinion poll was taken among 650 Muscovites to assess their views of the results of perestroika after almost a decade. Nearly a third of those polled said that no progress had been made in democratizing the country and protecting human rights, and 26 percent said the situation had worsened.[1] As the pollsters pointed out, this negative assessment may well have simply reflected general dissatisfaction with the Yeltsin government for a range of reasons, including the Chechnia invasion. But it nonetheless suggested that a significant number of Russians do not consider the human rights problem to be solved. What is the human rights record for Russia and the CIS since the KGB was disbanded? To what extent are old KGB practices still being employed?

Human Rights before the Collapse
of the Soviet Union

In the 1970s, when the West first addressed human rights in the Soviet Union as an issue of international concern, a movement to defend these rights was already underway within the country. The goals of the movement, which consisted of a few dozen individuals who protested openly against the abuses of the regime, were modest. These individuals did not have far-reaching, radical political objectives, but sought to promote freedom of expression and the rule of law by exerting pressure on the leadership. They also sought to mobilize Western public opinion to force the Soviet regime to change.[2]

Soviet human rights activists paid dearly for their dissent, which brought them up against one of the world's most repressive political police, the KGB. Operating with the blessing of the Communist Party leadership, the KGB unleashed thousands of domestic officers in a brutal campaign to suppress the incipient movement. As a result, many dissidents lost their jobs and were either exiled or incarcerated in prisons and labor camps, where harsh conditions ruined their health and sometimes even killed them. Some were confined to psychiatric hospitals, which was a favorite punishment of KGB Chairman Iurii Andropov because it avoided the publicity of a court trial.

Although they achieved small successes, particularly in drawing world attention to human rights abuses, real relief did not come until the Gorbachev era, when arrests of dissenters gradually ground to a halt and freedom of expression became a reality for the first time in Soviet history. By the late 1980s protesters could demonstrate without being whisked away by the police, and independent (*samizdat*) publications flourished. The official press soon caught up with the trend, daring to criticize the regime and to report facts honestly.

Meanwhile, the KGB, whose primary job had been to suppress political dissent, found its hands tied. Its activities were confined to behind-the-scenes operations, such as infiltrating the multitude of independent groups that were forming and collecting information to be used in the case of a reversal in the political climate. In fact, such a change was not beyond the realm of possibility. Gorbachev did a great deal to democratize the country and to limit human rights abuses, but he failed to accomplish the one thing that would ensure that the new liberties prevailed in the longer term: he did not guarantee them under the law.

Despite continued promises of major reforms in the criminal codes, which dated back to 1960–61, the old laws, with some exceptions, remained in force. And the judiciary was not granted independence, but continued to be a servant of the regime. Although the authorities did not enforce the old repressive laws, the rights of Soviet citizens continued to be dependent on the will of those in power. In May 1988, a report published by the Commission on Security and Cooperation in Europe made the following assessment: "To gauge the progress the Soviets have made in the field of human rights, it is necessary to look beyond activities they have tolerated under Gorbachev's rule to liberties they have guaranteed. It is a short search that turns up little."[3]

In fact, Gorbachev, despite his democratic image in the West, actually strengthened some laws against dissent, although, as a result of growing anti-Russian nationalism the focus was more on ethnic separatist movements than on individual critics of the regime. In July 1988 the government issued a decree banning unauthorized public demonstrations and making participants liable to punishment. Nine months later, responding to pressure from democrats, the Gorbachev regime amended the draconian Article 70 of the Criminal Code by eliminating the term "anti-Soviet agitation and propaganda," which had offered the KGB an excuse to round up all types of political nonconformists at will. But Gorbachev introduced other amendments to Article 70 that offset this change. As a result, the KGB still had a solid legal basis for suppressing political or nationalist dissent.[4]

The parliament forced Gorbachev to eliminate the most egregious features of these amendments in the summer of 1989. But once he became president in March 1990, he used his broad powers to introduce a sweeping new "USSR Law on Enhanced Responsibility for Encroachment on the National Equality of Citizens and Forcible Violation of the Integrity of USSR Territory." The law added yet another clause to Article 70 and stiffened the criminal sanctions. It also strengthened the 1988 law against demonstrations by prohibiting participation in public associations, movements, or parties that "kindled ethnic hostility or violated the integrity of the USSR's territory." These vague proscriptions were intended to give the regime a legal basis to combat separatist demands by non-Russian nationalists in places like Georgia and the Baltics, where Gorbachev had already sent in troops to suppress nationalist disturbances.[5]

A trained jurist, Gorbachev focused considerable effort on legal policy, redefining the relationship between citizens and the state by means of changes in the law. But, as Robert Sharlet observed, the "ad hoc quality and retrograde motion of Gorbachev's legal reforms" suggested that he had the traditional "Bolshevik ambivalence" toward law.[6] Although he initiated glasnost and democratization, these were reforms from above, on which Gorbachev wanted to keep a lid. He continuously sought to protect his government from the excesses of his reforms by giving the state more legal powers to curb them. The result was a distinctly mixed record for human rights.

HUMAN RIGHTS AND THE LAW UNDER YELTSIN

As a president with broad legislative and executive powers, Yeltsin has had the opportunity to have a significant impact on human rights in Russia since 1991. For the most part, his approach to this issue has been similar to that of Gorbachev. On the surface—until the Chechnia invasion at least—the human rights situation has been favorable. Political prisoners, religious repression, and restrictions on freedom of movement are for the most part phenomena of the past. The Russian media, often harshly critical of the Yeltsin regime, offers a noteworthy example of free expression. But enshrining these rights firmly in the law has been a long, drawn-out process, fraught with contradictions.

This is not to say that the Yeltsin administration has done nothing to make the system of justice more protective of individual rights. In June 1992, the Code of Criminal Procedure was amended to give a detainee the right to legal counsel immediately (rather than, as in the past, after the initial questioning), as well as the right to demand a judicial review of the legality and grounds for his or her detention.[7] A 1992 Law on the Status of Judges was designed to confer greater respect on the profession by raising salaries and benefits, and the new Constitution of Russia, approved in the December 1993 referendum, created an independent judiciary, in which judges cannot be removed and enjoy immunity.[8] Nonetheless, it takes time to train judges who function effectively. And the corrupt and inefficient Procuracy, which is charged with overseeing the criminal justice system, has yet to be reformed. Although a new law on the Procuracy was in the process of being passed in the autumn of 1995, it was by no means clear that it would result in a system of effective oversight to ensure that the security organs and the regular police observe legality.[9]

These positive changes, moreover, have often been offset by other laws, intended to protect the state rather than the individual. Yeltsin's sweeping anticrime decree of June 1994, discussed above, is a good example. In one fell swoop, the decree deprived suspects of protection against secret tapping of telephones, search and seizure without a warrant, and against lengthy detention without charge. Later, in March 1995, Yeltsin issued an edict against fascism, which gave the security police even broader authority to arrest and investigate suspects.[10]

The new draft Code of Criminal Procedure, in the final stages of being adopted by the late summer of 1995, is another example. According to the draft, produced by the president's State-Law Administration, persons under arrest cannot appeal to the courts, but only to the procurator to protest their confinement. Article 203 of the code allows police to tap telephones and also to enter private premises without a warrant "in cases that do not tolerate delay." The draft provides for the appointment of a "special prosecutor" by the president to bring "highly placed individuals" to justice, thus undermining the principle of independent judges. And all detainees, apparently with the exception of those falling under the special categories set forth in Yeltsin's anticrime bill, can be held for up to seven days (as opposed to the previous seventy-two hours) before charges are filed, while the counsel for the defense does not become acquainted with the materials of the criminal case until after the preliminary investigation has been completed.[11]

Like Gorbachev, Yeltsin has also tinkered with the laws on state (political) crimes, which are enforced by the security police. In 1992 Article 70 (the well-worn legal weapon against political opposition) was broadened yet again, and a supplemental clause was added to Article 79 (mass disorders) on "hindering the activity of the constitutional organs of power" by actions of force and failing to comply with resolutions of the Supreme Soviet.[12]

What was the significance of these amendments? They were vague enough so that they could be interpreted broadly by the courts and would provide Yeltsin with a legal basis to move against political opponents and ethnic separatists. Indeed, his bloody confrontation with parliamentary foes in October 1993 was justified by the claim that they were "violating the Constitution." More recently, in their invasion of Chechnia, Yeltsin and his advisers repeatedly referred to what they said were illegal efforts by the Dudaev government to change the Constitution by force. Dudaev was demanding an independent Chechnia and consequently succession from the Russian Federation, whose territory is inviolable under the Constitution.

The Russian parliament, although opposed to many of Yeltsin's policies, has been equally inclined to promote harsh laws granting police broad authority at the expense of individual rights. In July 1995, the Duma passed a new Law on Operational-Investigative Activity, which had been introduced by the Yeltsin administration to replace the 1992 law. It widened the list of agencies entitled to conduct investigative operations to include the Federal Tax Police, the Customs Service, and Korzhakov's Presidential Security Service. It also gave investigative agencies greater powers than those in the earlier law. For example, investigators could wait forty-eight, instead or twenty-four hours before getting approval for such intrusive measures as telephone tapping and searches without warrants. The grounds for carrying out procedures that violated individual rights were broadened, making it easier for investigators to justify the legality of their decisions to conduct such investigations.[13]

In that same month, Duma deputies finally adopted a new draft Russian Federation criminal code which had been undergoing revision for five years.[14] The code broadened the law on violations of national and racial equality, which carries a sentence of up to five years' imprisonment. The ambiguity of this law opened the door for serious abuse of individual rights. Prosecutors and judges would have wide latitude in deciding what constituted "acts directed at incitement of social, national, racial, or religious hostility or discord," a charge that could be leveled easily in a society with so many different ethnic and religious groups.[15]

The general view of the legal experts is that the new criminal code, a synthesis of presidential and Duma versions, is a significant improvement over the old code, which dated back to the early 1960s and lacked effective sanctions against organized crime.[16] This is doubtless true. Moreover, it might be argued, laws in the United States covering certain crimes also give the enforcement agencies considerable flexibility. But, unlike the United States, Russia does not have a tradition of respect for legal rights and a well-established, democratic system of justice to intrepret and administer the laws. So there is a greater danger that criminal laws will be used arbitrarily by security authorities.

The tendency to favor the state over the individual in lawmaking, exhibited by both the Yeltsin administration and the parliament, was especially disturbing since many of the new laws concerned crimes investigated by the security police, which had a history of flagrant abuse of human rights. Even in the atmosphere of political pluralism and freedom of expression under Yeltsin, the security police have not always desisted from using the law to employ KGB-style tactics.

THE MIRZAIANOV CASE AND STATE SECRETS

The Mirzaianov case is a good example. In the Soviet period, secrecy statutes were a key element of the totalitarian legal system. According to one Western source: "The notion of penal repression for the offense in question [disclosing state secrets] rapidly expanded from very modest beginnings into a broad principle of legal policy with varied and multiple uses and became a major weapon of the regime's control mechanism, especially in the post-war years."[17] Not only did secrecy justify the most extreme censorship; it also was used to prevent people from going abroad (on the grounds that they had access to secrets), and from mixing with foreigners.

The fact that the Yeltsin government actually took it upon itself to elaborate a new secrecy law in 1993 meant that it was not ready to discard this powerful weapon.[18] Prohibitions against revealing secrets remained a potential brake on excessive freedoms. The law, harshly criticized by human rights activists, set forth in detail the procedure for establishing what information is secret and how it is protected. The concept of secrecy was given a broad interpretation. According to the law, secret classifications could be assigned to information on foreign policy, economics, defense, intelligence, and counterintelligence. A more specific list of what information was classified as a state secret and which agencies and departments were authorized to classify information, was to be made public at a later date. Although the promised list did not appear, Yeltsin did issue a directive in 1994, authorizing the heads of thirty-eight ministries and departments to decide what material should be classified.[19]

Punishment for revealing a state secret (Article 75 of the Russian Criminal Code, enforced by the security organs) was severe: up to five years of imprisonment. Moreover, the law carried a provision (dating from the Andropov era) making it a crime—punishable by up to three years in prison—to reveal commercial secrets, which were never clearly defined.

In general, the security police under Yeltsin have not used secrecy laws to prosecute individuals, but there have been exceptions. On 22 October 1992, officers from the Russian Security Ministry arrested two chemical scientists, Vil Mirzaianov and Lev Fedorov, authors of a September 1992 *Moscow News* article entitled "Poisoned Politics."[20] Although Fedorov was released the same day, Mirzaianov was charged with disclosing state secrets and detained in Moscow's Lefortovo Prison. Eleven days later, in the wake of mounting public protests against the arrest, Mirzaianov was released, pending trial.[21]

What secrets had Mirzaianov allegedly disclosed? Mirzaianov, an employee at the State Scientific Research Institute for Organic Chemistry and Technology, revealed that Russian scientists at his institute had developed a new chemical weapon more toxic than anything the United States had. Although Russia had not actually violated any international accords (because it had yet to sign the U.N. Convention on Chemical Weapons), the revelation was nonetheless embarrassing. Russia had declared its intention to join the convention (which it did in January 1993) and had claimed that it was no longer conducting research on or producing chemical weapons.[22]

The Security Ministry defended its actions against charges by critics that it was persecuting an innocent person who disagreed with official policy. In the words of its deputy for public relations, A. P. Kondaurov: "The Ministry of Security, in accordance with the Law on Federal Security Organs, is charged with and is responsible for protecting state secrets. Our workers do not have the right—I repeat, do not have the right—to look the other way and not act when a law is broken."[23] The MB forged ahead with its case against Mirzaianov. In April 1993, the chief investigator in the case, Viktor Shkarin, summoned a *Baltimore Sun* reporter to Lefortovo Prison for questioning. The reporter had written a piece for his paper in which he quoted Mirzaianov. This was the first time that a journalist had been called in by the security police to testify on a state secrets case since the collapse of the Soviet Union.[24]

The trial began in January 1994, when Mirzaianov appeared in the Moscow City Court with his lawyer. The defendant had contended all along that he did not divulge any secrets, because the information in his article was of a general nature and did not provide technical details. It was, he said, of no use to foreign spies. Furthermore, although there was a law on state secrets, it was passed after Mirzaianov's arrest, and the promised list of information that was to be classified as secret had never been published. Yeltsin had reportedly signed a "temporary list of information constituting a state secret" shortly after Mirzaianov's article appeared, but no one had seen it. Mirzaianov and his lawyer appealed to the court to have the prosecution produce the list, so they could see exactly what regulations Mirzaianov was accused of violating, but the court refused.[25]

Mirzaianov responded by announcing that he would no longer appear in court. The next day, after he failed to show up at his trial, security police arrested him. The arrest worked in Mirzaianov's favor, because it drew even more public attention to his plight and aroused the protests of numerous human rights groups. With the pressure of increasingly negative publicity, the Yeltsin administration decided that it was time to call a halt to the case. Yeltsin's national security adviser, Iurii Baturin, a lawyer by training, told the press that the president was considering using his powers to have the prosecution drop the case against Mirzaianov on the grounds that it violated the Constitution. (Article 15 of the new Russian Constitution states that all laws and normative legal enactments affecting human rights cannot be applied unless they have been published.) On 11 March 1994, the charges against Mirzaianov were abruptly dismissed and he was freed from prison.[26]

Why did the Yeltsin government allow the case against Mirzaianov to go ahead in the first place? The end result, after all, was to call into question the democratic intentions of the Russian government and give rise to cries that the Ministry of Security was resorting to KGB methods. The answer probably lies in the fact that Mirzaianov was more than a "thorn in the side" of security officials who had caused offense by speaking out. He was a highly placed scientist who knew the latest developments in chemical weapons research and had been lobbying for several years for more awareness of the health dangers involved in chemical weapons production. Mirzaianov had drawn increasing ire from his bosses as he became more and more critical of what was going on in his field. Writing about the secret intentions of the military-chemical complex to circumvent international agreements was the last straw.

According to Mirzaianov, it was the top leadership of this military-chemical bureaucracy that instigated his arrest and trial.[27] But the Yeltsin administration would have had to approve these decisions, especially since the case was bound to receive publicity in the West. And Yeltsin's security ministry showed no lack of zeal in its efforts to punish Mirzaianov for his alleged wrongdoings.[28] The case sent an ominous message to democrats: their rights were not protected by the system. The only recourse against abuses was publicity. But, effective as publicity could be in pressuring the Russian political leadership to back down, it was not a substitute for the rule of law.

WHEN GLASNOST GOES TOO FAR

The Russian government has not resorted again to criminal prosecution for violating "state secrets" in order to silence its critics in the media.[29] But security authorities continue to use the secrets law as a means of intimidating the press. In March 1995, for example, *Moscow News* received notification that journalist Nataliia Gevorkian had published information that was a state secret in an article she wrote about the state company for exporting arms, "Rosvooruzhenie." She was ordered to give her sources to the authorities.[30]

The security services began a campaign in early 1995 to discredit journalists who criticized the government and heighten public concern about violations of secrecy laws. The harsh media reaction to the Chechnia invasion was the immediate impetus for this campaign. Following a televised statement in late December 1994 by President Yeltsin, who accused Russian journalists of accepting payoffs from the Chechens, the Federal Counterintelligence Service (FSK) went on the offensive. FSK officials took credit for supplying Yeltsin with evidence of these payoffs and promised to make it public (which they never did).[31] As an *Izvestiia* commentator observed: "The authorities' actions are understandable: They are irritated by the mass media's rare unanimity in their assessment of the events in Chechnia. Their awkward position has to be explained somehow to the Russians. The methods used here come from the arsenals of a past which is well known to us."[32]

Meanwhile the FSK's brother agency, the Ministry of Internal Affairs (MVD), was warning journalists covering Chechnia that they had to observe the laws on state secrets. The MVD public relations center issued a statement in late December, claiming that Russian journalists were using all possible means to get military personnel in Chechnia to divulge secret information. The MVD proposed that emergency regulations be issued to prevent journalists from committing such violations.[33]

Even more ominous was an FSK report that was leaked to the liberal paper *Independent Gazette* in mid-January.[34] Conjuring up all the images of the cold war days, the report described how the U.S. "special services" (the CIA) allegedly use private foundations and research organizations, including those attached to universities, for conducting espionage and subversion in Russia. Pretending to be independent teachers, businessmen, and researchers, these American visitors were actually paid by the CIA to collect information to subvert the Russian political process and undermine its defense capacity. According to the FSK, uncontrolled contacts between visiting foreigners and secret-possessing Russians, and the exploitation of information revealed in the Russian media gave foreign spies unprecedented access to secret information. The report recommended that stringent measures be taken to counteract this phenomenon and restrict the flow of information to foreigners via the press. Also, it said, there should be more control over travel abroad by people with access to secrets.

At the same time, stories were appearing in the press that the FSK had issued special instructions to several Russian ministries regulating contacts with foreigners.[35] Although the FSK denied the report, its spokesperson did say that "it is strictly within the competence of the federal government to define measures to protect state secrets, as well as it is within the competence of agencies and organizations whose activities are associated with state or commercial secrets."[36]

This was President Yeltsin's view as well. In his address to the FSK delivered in May 1994, he had devoted particular attention to the growing problem of protecting state secrets and stressed that the FSK should step up its efforts in this area: "The collapse of the system of state secrets is causing serious alarm. . . . It is essential to make full use of the powers granted you. First and foremost the right to ensure that the requirements for the protection of state secrets are carried out precisely."[37]

RESTRICTIONS ON FREEDOM
OF MOVEMENT

As in the past, secrecy regulations are sometimes evoked by the security police to prevent Russian citizens from going abroad, either for a visit or permanently. According to the January 1993 Law on Entry Into and Exit From the Russian Federation, certain individuals may be denied permission to leave Russia on the grounds that they have access to state secrets. In such cases, a five-year waiting period, from the time the access has been removed, is imposed. Clearly this restriction is used far less arbitrarily than it was in the past. The new law applies only to those who have had access to the two highest levels of secrets, "top secret" and "information of special importance," and it gives people who have been refused the right to appeal the decision to a special commission, which has in some cases overturned the refusal.[38]

One problem with the law, as pointed out by the human rights organization Helsinki Watch, is that an applicant seeking permission to leave the country presumably has to resign from his or her position if it entails access to high-level secrets and then has to wait for five years.[39] Also, permission to leave when the question of secrecy is involved is ultimately up to the security services, which, judging from their public statements, are not inclined to be flexible. Although the number of "refuseniks" is now quite low, there is little to prevent security officials from changing their policy and using secrecy as an excuse to prevent emigration if they choose to do so.

Restrictions on freedom of movement within Russia pose a greater problem for human rights. The *propiska* (pass) system, which requires individuals to secure residence permits from local authorities in order to reside in most major cities, still operates, despite efforts by democrats to abolish it. During the October 1993 crisis, when Yeltsin declared a state of emergency in Moscow, Mayor Iurii Luzhkov decided to enforce the law by having police expel thousands of Caucasians and Central Asians from the city because they did not have residence permits. This clearly discriminatory action, applied selectively to certain ethnic groups, set an ominous precedent.[40] As one Western expert put it: "This ethnicization of politics is also extremely dangerous in a country which has 30 million people of non-Russian origin and when millions of Russians live in the 14 other former Soviet republics."[41] In January 1995, shortly after the invasion of Chechnia, Moscow police were ordered to search hotels, boardinghouses, and other residences for Caucasians who did not have residence permits. Those without permits were deported.[42]

OTHER FORMS OF REPRESSION

The security services also use extrajudicial means to suppress freedom of speech. During the October 1993 crisis in Moscow, security police reportedly beat up more than twenty journalists trying to cover events, arousing strong protests from human rights groups.[43] The Russian Memorial Society released a statement complaining of cases of "cruel, inhumane, and humiliating treatment" by the security forces during the state of emergency. Even those who accepted Yeltsin's decision to storm the Russian White House found the subsequent crackdown on opposition groups and the media troubling. To be sure, it was a crisis, but the government's heavy reliance on the police, the security forces, and the military made it clear how fragile democracy was in Russia and how easily it could be eroded in the name of restoring order.[44]

A similar crackdown occurred in Chechnia during the invasion that began in December 1994. According to human rights commissioner Sergei Kovalev, who was in Chechnia at the time, the security police "continually hindered the activity of correspondents in the war zone and force has been used to interfere with reporters [including] instances of mistreatment, death threats, and confiscation of material."[45] This continued for the next several months, with journalists being detained for long periods at police checkpoints and often being threatened with violence.[46]

Although nothing has been proven, it is highly probable that the FSK and other police agencies have had a role in the mounting unofficial violence against journalists and human rights activists. Such violence, including murder purportedly perpetrated by unknown thugs, was a standard KGB tactic against troublesome dissidents. In the pre-glasnost days such practices were easy for the KGB to get away with because it controlled all information surrounding the cases and could easily cover up the facts. Although glasnost and investigative reporting have made cover-ups more difficult, the rapid growth of crime and corruption in Russia has provided a convenient backdrop for police-inspired violence. The public is accustomed to the idea that crime is rampant and therefore assumes that these acts of violence are committed by the mafia for its own purposes.

Increasing reports of ties between the security services and the mafia, however, have led to suggestions that the violence is sometimes carried out with the complicity, or even at the behest, of the security services. In such cases the victim has no connection with organized crime, but is an outspoken critic of the government. An early example was back in March 1992, when thugs beat up Memorial Society activist Boris Pustyntsev, who at the time was a member of the movement to disband the Russian security services.[47]

More recently, former dissident Sergei Grigoriants, head of the Glasnost Foundation (another human rights group) and organizer of a series of conferences, "The KGB: Yesterday, Today, and Tomorrow," has been subjected to a series of unexplained misfortunes, the last of which was a personal tragedy. The misfortunes began in early 1994, when his secretary, driving from Moscow to Kaluga to retrieve Grigoriants's archives, which had earlier been confiscated by the KGB, was hit by another car and came close to being killed. In March 1994, unidentified robbers broke into the offices of "Glasnost" and stole documents and materials. Five months later Grigoriants himself was severely beaten by thugs (who were never caught) near the entrance to his apartment in Moscow. And finally, in January 1995, Grigoriants's twenty-year-old son Timofei was killed by a hit-and-run driver as he walked home one evening. In the opinion of many Russian democrats, this string of incidents bore the familiar mark of the security services, which was resorting to the strategies of the KGB in order to intimidate its critics.[48]

Media figures have been frequent victims of such violence. In September 1994, Bella Kurkova, the head of a television and radio company in St. Petersburg, was beaten up outside the entrance to her home. She attributed the attack to political motives.[49] A few weeks later came the murder of journalist Dmitrii Kholodov, discussed earlier. FSK spokespersons continued to insist that their agency had nothing to do with the crime, pointing out that the explosive device used to kill Kholodov was of the type used in the regular army. But they offered no clues as to who was responsible. By January 1995 the FSK stated flatly that the killer's identity had not been ascertained and implied that it never would be.[50]

No sooner had the Kholodov case begun to fade away, than another media figure was suddenly killed. On 1 March 1995, Vladislav Listev, a prominent television journalist, was gunned down by an unknown assassin at the entrance to his home in Moscow. Although FSK spokespersons maintained from the outset that all signs pointed to the mafia, the mafia had little apparent motive. FSK officials were called in on the case, giving the impression that the investigation had top priority. As usual, nothing came of it. In the words of one journalist, "One can now say that the investigation into the Listyev case has finally slipped into the normal and usual groove, where the murderers are unknown and there is no knowing if they will ever be found."[51] The FSK, meanwhile, used the occasion to make a pitch for more powers and resources to fight crimes. Whoever committed the murder of Listev, the FSK clearly stood to gain.[52]

Harassment of journalists on a lesser scale has been an everyday phenomenon. Telephone tapping, surveillance, and threats are still in the arsenal of the security services when dealing with members of the media. Journalist Yevgenia Albats recounted how a colleague was summoned, against her will, for a "chat" with security police in the summer of 1993: "What did the Chekists want from her? Nothing in particular. To have the opportunity to telephone her, to obtain information which stayed outside a newspaper interview or article, to learn some details. . . . They wanted to know what the political police in our fatherland—the KGB— have always wanted to know from time immemorial."[53]

Albats and other critics of the Russian security services interpreted these actions as both a sign that the service was up to its old tricks and evidence of its autonomous power. But the two do not necessarily go together. To be sure, the security police still could violate people's rights. But this does not mean that they acted completely on their own. They would not have been able to use KGB methods if the Yeltsin administration had taken steps to circumscribe their powers and make them accountable for their actions. The Kremlin bore the ultimate responsibility.

HUMAN RIGHTS AND THE INVASION OF CHECHNIA

Russia's assault on Chechnia in December 1994 illustrates this point well. Although the media, both Russian and Western, initially portrayed Yeltsin as unwitting, in fact he fully endorsed this military operation. As far back as May 1994, Yeltsin had stressed the need for the use of force in Chechnia in his speech to the FSK: "The conflicts in Chechnia, North Ossetia, and Ingushetiia are assuming a protracted nature, and are throwing the country into a ferment. Enormous resources are being diverted in order to settle them and to eliminate the consequences. The intervention of the armed forces, law enforcement bodies, and other departments is needed. . . . Inaction and irresolution are fraught with the most serious consequences."[54] After his initial absence from public view when the invasion began (because of a nose operation), Yeltsin emerged to give his wholehearted support, even dismissing several military generals who voiced their opposition to the campaign.[55]

At the same time, however, the assault on Chechnia represented a gain for the security services, the FSK in particular, because, as noted earlier, they were the mastermind behind it.[56] It was no coincidence that FSK Chief Stepashin became the main spokesperson on Russian policy toward Chechnia at this time. Stationed at Mozdok, near the Chechen border, during most of December and January, he and his colleagues were deeply engaged in the strategic planning of the operation, despite the fact that it was carried out by the Russian military under the command of Minister of Defense Grachev.

Why was the FSK such a prominent player in these events, given that this was a military operation? Because this was an internal conflict that arose on the territory of the Russian Federation. The FSK was doing its job of "restoring constitutional order." But, since this involved subduing an entire people, occupying an entire republic within the Russian Federation, it required military forces. Herein lies the deep contradiction of Moscow's policy toward non-Russian nationalities, a policy that is fraught with serious implications for internationally recognized human rights.

The events leading up to the assault on Chechnia have already been described. Moscow failed in its efforts, led by the FSK, to subvert the Dudaev government by nonmilitary means and install a leadership that would bend to its will. The only choice, in the view of the Yeltsin administration, was to employ force. But, as might have been expected, given the determination of the Chechens to fight to the death against their Russian oppressors, the assault turned into a full-scale war that was to drag on indefinitely. The war was not a just war against the recalcitrant Dudaev government and its army, but against more than a million innocent civilians.

The Yeltsin administration stated unequivocally that Russia was justified in sending regular military troops to Chechnia because the new military doctrine, ratified by Yeltsin in November 1993, allowed for the employment of such troops to eliminate internal threats. Minister of Justice Valentin Kovalev of Russia enumerated what these threats were: "Illegal activity by nationalist, separatist, and other organizations aimed at destabilizing the country and violating its territorial integrity and carried out with the use of armed coercion. The creation of illegal armed formations. The growth in organized crime and smuggling activity on a scale threatening the security of citizens and society."[57]

Critics of the invasion, both in Russia and the West, saw things differently, however. On the question of Russia's territorial integrity, they pointed out that the Chechens, an ancient ethnic group with a unique language and Muslim culture, had lived on their territory for thousands of years. They had fought bitterly against the occupation of their land by the forces of tsarist Russia in 1864. After the Bolshevik Revolution, they had united with other Caucasian groups to form an independent North Caucasian Federation in 1918. But the Bolshevik Red Army invaded North Caucasia in 1921 and annexed it to Russia. Chechnia was later combined with the territory of Ingushetiia to become in 1936 the Chechen-Ingush Autonomous Soviet Socialist republic, part of the Russian republic.[58]

As the American expert Paul Goble expressed it: "The Russian Federation and its borders are the most artificial of the post-Soviet states. Drawn by negation and with explicit political goals by Stalin, the specific features of these borders, not to speak of Moscow's violations of its CSCE [Commission on Security and Cooperation in Europe] undertakings and of generally accepted human rights principles, undercut the argument of those who want to dismiss the Chechens as simply an 'internal affair' of the Russian state."[59]

The Chechens never accepted their subjugation to the Russians, and Stalin was so fearful of their disloyalty (and possible sympathy for the Germans) that in 1944 he had security troops round them up en masse and deport them in cattle cars to Central Asia. Thousands perished in the process. It was not until 1957 that the Soviet government allowed the Chechens to return to their homeland. Given their history of suffering at the hands of the Russians, it is not surprising that the Chechens strove for independence after the Soviet Union disbanded. It is even less surprising that they demonstrated such fierce resistance to the Russian invasion of December 1994.

LONG-TERM IMPLICATIONS OF THE CHECHNIA WAR

As part of their justification for the invasion, Russian authorities repeatedly pointed to the widespread criminal activities of the Chechens—terrorism, drug smuggling, and trade in illegal weapons. In the words of American scholar Robert Sharlet: "From the outset of the crisis, Yeltsin and his ministers declared the entire Chechen people pariahs in Russian society, labelling them a nation of criminals who posed a serious threat to the integrity of the Russian state. . . . a number of other 'ethnic' mafias are active in Moscow, including Georgians, Azeris, various Central Asian gangs and of course, the omnipresent Russian mobs. Nonetheless, it has been a state policy to use the Chechens as a scapegoat for the epidemic of crime in the Russian Federation."[60]

In a January 1995 interview, Vladimir Tomarovskii, deputy chief of public relations for the FSK, explained that it was not enough just to go after President Dudaev of Chechnia and his associates. Russia was dealing, he said, with a "vast criminal mafia."[61] What would become of all these "criminals" once the Russians were firmly entrenched in Chechnia? They would be arrested and prosecuted, according to Russian Federation Deputy Procurator Oleg Gaidanov: "And if the law determines their actions to be crimes against the individual, against property, against constitutional order, or as armed resistance to the representatives of federal power, then we must grade them according to the relevant articles of the Russian Federation Criminal Code."[62]

Considering the large numbers of Chechens who participated in the "armed resistance," the Russian criminal justice system would have its hands full.[63] Furthermore, FSK Chief Stepashin estimated that about 8 percent of the Chechen population would continue to resist once the military operation was over. This would require a substantial police presence. In addition to the MVD, whose troops were to maintain order after the regular army left, the FSK opened a major department in Chechnia with a staff of almost eight hundred men.

Stepashin said in one of his many media interviews that the mission of the FSK was "similar to the way in which security officers disarmed bandit formations in the Western Ukraine and the Baltics" (when they resisted Soviet occupation after World War II).[64] Apparently realizing that he had made another one of his gaffes, he was quick to qualify his statement: "It is not a question of a historical analogy, but of the tactics of operations." In fact, the analogy was more than apt. The situation in Chechnia required precisely the kind of brutal and indiscriminate "mopping-up operations" that the Soviet NKVD (predecessor to the KGB) conducted in newly occupied border regions of the Soviet Union after 1945. In those areas the security police viewed the entire local population as suspect and never hesitated to shoot on the spot or arrest individuals who might have supported the resistance to Soviet rule.

The Russian attitude may explain their indiscriminate bombing and apparent disregard for noncombatants in Chechnia. Without doubt the most deplorable consequence of the invasion from the point of view of human rights has been the large numbers of civilian casualties and the physical devastation of the Chechen capital, Grozny. By mid-January 1995 an estimated 18,000 civilians had perished and hundreds of thousands were homeless. In late March 1995, the U.N. High Commissioner for Refugees reported that the number of refugees from the Chechnia conflict had reached 220,000. Their conditions were miserable; most had inadequate food, water, and medical supplies.[65]

There have been countless reports of deliberate attacks by Russian troops on unarmed civilians. In one case they opened fire on a convoy of vehicles containing people fleeing the fighting. They attacked without warning and continued firing on those trying to escape. Ten people were killed.[66] A much worse slaughter occurred in early April 1995 in the Chechen village of Samashki, where special police troops massacred between one hundred and three hundred residents.[67] According to observers in Chechnia, Chechen prisoners are regularly beaten and tortured in holding cells called "filtration points." Western journalist David Remnick, for example, met many people who had been "tortured in ways worthy of the old KGB."[68]

Sergei Kovalev and the Memorial Society denounced such acts, and the invasion as a whole, as major human rights violations. Another prominent human rights organization, Helsinki Watch, which sent observers to Chechnia, accused Russian troops of violating the Geneva Convention on conduct in war by looting and targeting civilians with artillery fire. Numerous other national and international human rights organizations denounced the Russian operation, but to no avail.[69]

The Chechnia invasion and the Russian justification for it had implications that went far beyond this region. Efforts to keep the Russian Federation together by force rather than conciliation and compromise threatened to turn the country back toward authoritarianism. The war and the military occupation, deplored by the Russian public, seemed only to reinforce hard-line tendencies in the leadership, tendencies that placed individual rights far down on the list of priorities.

Human Rights in the CIS: The Western States

With Russia and issues like Chechnia in the spotlight, the human rights situation in the other CIS states has drawn little attention in the West. But human rights is not an issue that is exclusive to Russia. The KGB left its legacy in all the CIS states (as well as in the Baltic countries). Indeed, the KGB was often more ruthless with non-Russian nationalists than it was with Russians. The record since 1991 presents a mixed picture, with considerable differences among the former republics.

Ukraine was admitted to the Conference on Security and Cooperation in Europe in January 1992 and has made considerable progress in meeting commitments to international norms. Almost immediately after declaring independence, the new Ukrainian government began to reform its legal system, which, like those of other republics, had been a carbon copy of the Russian model. But, as mentioned earlier, the fact that the power structures are filled with former communists and KGB officials has impeded efforts at lasting democratic legal reforms. As a 1993 report by the U.S. Commission on Security and Cooperation in Europe observed: "Simply put, democracy remains a foreign concept to a substantial portion of the population. It did not emerge from experience, it was simply declared. Hence, even under optimal circumstances, it will take time to develop a 'culture' of democracy. While the form of the totalitarian state has disappeared, the substance has not."[70]

Ukraine has issued a flurry of declarative laws asserting the government's commitment to human rights. But what about the "nitty-gritty" procedural and criminal codes that in the past allowed the KGB to persecute dissent? In this regard, Ukraine has shown a pattern similar to that of Russia. Indeed, when the Kiev government introduced changes in the legal codes that had to do with crimes investigated by the security service, it took its cues directly from Moscow. Like Yeltsin, President Kravchuk signed a law in late 1993 strengthening criminal sanctions for "crimes against the state," which are under the purview of Ukraine's Security Service (SBU).[71]

The Ukrainian Law on State Secrets, passed in January 1994, was almost a duplicate of the Russian law, enacted six months earlier.[72] Both states adopted the traditional Soviet policy of having state secrets cover a wide range of information, which is zealously protected. In 1993 President Kravchuk even set up a Committee for Protection of State Secrets in the Media, which had broad powers of censorship, but it was later dissolved.[73]

As in Russia, the fight against crime has eroded important procedural rights and made citizens vulnerable to possible abuse by the security police. In August 1994 the newly elected president, Leonid Kuchma, issued a decree designed to combat corruption, which allows for those arrested to be held without charge for up to thirty days, just as in Russia. Within three months, according to the Ministry of Internal Affairs, 1,680 people had been subjected to preventative detention under the new law. Also, with the permission of the procurator, detainees can be held for up to one and a half years after charges have been filed. Although search warrants are required in most cases, security police are authorized to enter private premises without a warrant on grounds of national security, notifying the procurator within twenty-four hours.[74]

Ukraine has a vocal political opposition and several active political parties, the most important of which is Rukh (the Ukrainian Popular Front for Perestroika), which took a leading role in promoting an independent, democratic Ukraine. In general, the Ukrainian government has been tolerant toward this opposition and has permitted an uncensored and often highly critical media to develop. There have been exceptions, however, particularly in the case of journalists. In 1992 a criminal investigation was instigated against a journalist for alleged slander of the leadership. The case was dropped two months later.[75] More recently, in February 1995, SBU officials in the city of Lvov initiated criminal proceedings against a correspondent for a local paper, on charges of "divulging a state secret." The correspondent had written an article in which he had cited an SBU document on recruiting secret agents from the local population. He faced up to eight years in prison if convicted.[76]

There have also been isolated reports of harassment and violence attributed to the SBU. In May 1994, Roman Koval, head of the political group "Ukraine's State Independence," sent an open letter to Marchuk, chief of the SBU at the time, asserting that the SBU was carrying out secret surveillance of his organization.[77] Volodia Kuleba, the editor of a leading opposition newspaper that was highly critical of the government, had his apartment burned down and later, in October 1993, was beaten up at the entrance to his home. He interpreted the attacks as a warning to him about the limits of glasnost.[78] In early 1994, Mikhalyo Boychyshyn, a prominent member of Rukh, disappeared suddenly without explanation, arousing speculation that his disappearance was politically motivated.[79] A well-known television journalist, Liudmilla Lysenko, was severely beaten in March 1995 by thugs in the center of Kiev. There were other similar examples.[80]

But these incidents are relatively isolated, so it can still be said that Ukraine has made appreciable strides in terms of human rights since it achieved independence. The problem, as in Russia, is that these rights are not fully enshrined in the law and therefore can be abused, a particular danger because of the broad authority that Ukraine's security service enjoys.

In Belarus the government has ceased overt persecution of political dissidents. But its laws are still filled with the kind of loopholes that permit abuse by the security police, and security authorities regularly harass the independent media. In December 1994, the Executive Committee of the International Confederation of Journalists' Unions reported several attacks on freedom of speech. The editor of *Sovetskaia Belorussia*, for example, was fired without apparent justification, and certain opposition newspapers were not allowed to print their articles.[81]

The pattern continued in 1995. Newspapers have been censored when they have planned to print articles about corruption in the government leadership. In April KGB officers visited a printing house and demanded to see the contents of the next edition of a leading opposition paper, *Svoboda*. They also advised the director of the printing house to cease publication of the paper. A month earlier the deputy director of a major nongovernment television station was beaten up by unknown assailants.[82] President Lukashenka seems determined to use the KGB to ensure that his strong powers are not challenged in any way.

As for Moldova, much of the human rights debate centers on the conflict over the breakaway republic of Trans-Dniester and other ethnic problems, which have made the development of a rule of law in the country difficult. Nonetheless, the Moldovan government under President Snegur has tolerated a sharply critical independent press, with some exceptions, and has allowed freedom of religion and movement.[83] Despite its economic and political problems, Moldova has made considerable progress toward establishing a democratic state. A new constitution was enacted in 1994, with provisions to protect individual rights and ensure the separation of powers, drawing on a newly established constitutional court.

President Snegur also accepted the plan of the CSCE (Commission on Security and Cooperation in Europe) as a basis for ending the conflict in the Transdniester region. In the words of one analyst: "Moldova is better positioned now than at any time since independence to overcome that deadlock that characterized its early political life and to bring the separatist crisis to an end. If these twin tasks can be accomplished, the government could then focus on carrying through the economic and political reforms the new nation so desperately requires if it is to thrive."[84] Hopefully Moldova's security services will not thwart this process.

HUMAN RIGHTS IN TRANSCAUCASIA

Here we are dealing with an area where civil strife and interethnic warfare make concepts of human rights difficult to put into perspective. In Georgia, for example, the fierce hostilities between the Abkhazians and the Georgians and the violent opposition to the Shevardnadze government have put the institution of democracy and the rule of law on hold. Terrorism abounds throughout Georgia, where mafias often carry out their own forms of justice. President Shevardnadze of Georgia, in an effort to stabilize the situation in his country and reinstate some form of law and order, instituted a state of emergency in September 1993. Emergency rule has given Shevardnadze's government sweeping powers, including the authority to order summary executions, which have aroused deep concern among human rights activists.[85]

Shevardnadze has defended his authoritarian practices by citing the need to restore civil peace in Georgia, a job which is largely up to the security police: "We are facing unruly banditry. These are acts of banditry, acts of subversion . . . now it is time for a decisive say from the Ministry of Security, and the whole system of the ministry has to demonstrate its professional skills in fighting terrorists acts."[86] Not surprisingly, there have been numerous reports of police abuses, particularly against those who were allied with the late Georgian president, Zviad Gamsakhurdia.

In August 1994, Helsinki Watch representatives stated that several political oppositionists had been shot or beaten while incarcerated.[87] The Federation of Georgian Journalists and other press organizations sent a letter of protest to the Georgian parliament in February 1995, calling for a halt to police persecution of the independent media. The letter claimed that newspapers were being confiscated and distributors beaten up or imprisoned.[88]

Given the continued terrorism, the Georgian government probably has little choice right now but to rule with authoritarian methods. Indeed,

Shevardnadze has been urging the Georgian Security Service to act more resolutely in the fight against terrorism, a fight now complicated by the recent accusations against Security Chief Giorgadze of involvement in the attempt to kill Shevardnadze.[89] Clearly human rights in Georgia are not one of Shevardnadze's concerns.

The leadership of Azerbaidzhan is in a similar situation. In order to retain power and ward off threats from political enemies, President Aliev has dealt harshly with opponents. Not long after he gained power in 1993, human rights organizations were accusing Aliev of "reviving Stalin's repressions." According to a November 1993 report, Azerbaidzhan's Ministry of National Security was holding at least twenty political prisoners, some of whom had been denied lawyers.[90] Other reports claimed that security police were arresting journalists whose writings were critical of the government.[91]

Aliev had steadfastly maintained that he would not declare martial law in the country because "such steps would restrict democratic rights."[92] But, following an attempted coup in October 1994, led by the deputy minister of interior, he did just that. The result was further arrests and a crackdown on the press. Another coup attempt, again connected with Ministry of Interior police officers, occurred in March 1995, and yet another in August 1995. Both were followed, not surprisingly, by dozens of arrests by security police.[93] With the government run by Aliev, himself a former high-ranking KGB professional, and besieged by violent opposition, its observance of human rights, as in Georgia, was bound to be limited.

Armenia, which enjoys more political stability than its Transcaucasian neighbors and has a democratically elected president, had a relatively good record in the area of human rights until late 1994. At that time security police began cracking down on members of the opposition Dashnak Party and closed more than a dozen newspapers, wire services, and journals associated with Dashnak. Dashnak's operations were suspended, thus precluding its participation in the July 1995 parliamentary elections. On the grounds that they were hunting out terrorists, police burst into private premises without warrants and made widespread arrests.[94]

One of those arrested, Dashnak Party member Artavazd Manukyan, died in jail in May 1995, prompting a parliamentary inquiry and the resignation of Security Chief Davit Shakhnazaryan.[95] The former Armenian prime minister was pessimistic about these developments: "You can't say we are already a totalitarian state, but you can no longer say that this government is leading toward democracy."[96] Although this was probably an overstatement, it does seem clear that even reformist leaders are vulnerable to the temptation of using antidemocratic police methods.

HUMAN RIGHTS IN CENTRAL ASIA

With regard to the Central Asian States, most observers consider Kyrgyzstan to have made the most progress in the realm of political reform and human rights. Although Kyrgyzstan has a powerful State Committee for National Security, democracy there has developed to the point where this agency does not harass political opposition. Political parties are allowed to participate freely in politics and there are no political prisoners.[97]

A few developments have caused concern among those monitoring human rights, however. In May 1994, Kyrgyzstan enacted a sweeping law on state secrets, in which citizens are forbidden to discuss in public even such information as the condition of roads and certain aspects of public health.[98] Although the law appears to have had little practical impact thus far, its existence is nonetheless a potential threat to the freedom of expression. During the February 1995 parliamentary elections in Kyrgyzstan there were reports of pressure and intimidation against candidates and attempts by President Akaev to muzzle the press. Security authorities closed two papers that had been critical of the president. Since then there have been at least three prosecutions of members of the press for "insulting the honor and dignity of the president."[99] Although these developments do not signify a resurgence of the security police, they do point to clear limitations on freedom of the press in Kyrgyzstan.

Kazakhstan has made less progress in moving toward democracy. The 1992 Kazakh Law on the Organs of National Security gave its security committee a broad mandate to disallow constitutional rights in certain circumstances, and it stressed the obligation of citizens and government agencies to assist security bodies. The right of investigators to enter private premises without a warrant (with subsequent notification to the procurator) was enshrined in the new law, as was the authority to recruit informers.[100] A Law on Operational-Investigative Activity, published two years later, expanded considerably on these powers. A Kazakh police official defended the law in the same way that Russian security chief Stepashin sought to justify Russia's anticrime decree: "For the most part we violate housing laws (penetration of apartments) and we eavesdrop on telephone conversations. But all these measures do not affect the interests of law-abiding citizens."[101]

Several cases of police repression against writers and journalists have been reported in Kazakhstan since it became an independent state. In August 1992, Karishal Asanov, a writer and publisher, was arrested on charges of slandering President Nazarbaev after excerpts from his forthcoming book, which was highly critical of the president, appeared in a

Kazakh newspaper.[102] Asanov was not permitted to see a lawyer, even after the charges were filed, until human rights groups began protesting Asanov's detention and the authorities relented. When his case was tried in early November 1992, the judges declared that there was insufficient evidence against Asanov and threw the case out.[103]

In December 1992, a doctor named Ruslan Chukurov was tried on charges of "insulting the dignity" of a Supreme Soviet deputy, who happened to be a relative of Nazarbaev. He was eventually freed, but lost his job. In September 1994 Russian journalist Boris Supruniuk was found guilty of writing articles that "aroused ethnic discord" and given a suspended sentence of two years in prison. Supruniuk had described government policies that he considered discriminatory against Russians in Kazakhstan. He appealed to the Kazakh Supreme Court, which over-ruled the conviction in December 1994.[104] The arrest of Supruniuk and police actions against other prominent Russians in Kazakhstan prompted the Russian Duma in May 1995 to issue a protest to the Nazarbaev government against "persecutions and cruel repressions" of their countrymen.[105]

Kazakh security authorities continue to use Soviet-style legal statutes to suppress criticism of the government, although to a much lesser extent than in the past. That their attempts have in the end failed and the rights of their victims have prevailed in the cases described here is a positive sign. But individual rights are still fragile. As one source observed: "Kazakhstan is no democracy. Rather, to quote Nazarbaev, who apparently believes his country needs a period of at least five years of presidential rule, it is an 'authoritarian democracy.'"[106] This authoritarian democracy relies heavily on the services of the former KGB.

Still, Kazakhstan is further ahead in human rights than the three remaining Central Asian states. As noted earlier, Turkmenistan's security service, the Committee of National Security, is at the disposal of dictatorial President Niyazov, who imposes Soviet-style controls on the population. Political opposition is fiercely repressed. When Secretary of State James Baker visited the capital, Ashgabat, in February 1992, security police kept at least thirty oppositionists under house arrest. In KGB fashion, security police routinely harass and threaten oppositionists. They also reportedly arrange to have troublesome dissidents killed during staged provocations.[107]

Equally disturbing are the actions of Turkmen security officers abroad. In November 1994, they seized (with the help of their Uzbek colleagues) two Turkmen dissidents in Tashkent and took them to Ashgabat, where they were charged with a terrorist plot. In December 1994, Russian FSK officers arrested, on behalf of Turkmen authorities, another two Turkmen dissidents living in Moscow.[108] Although the latter case was dropped, it was nonetheless a disturbing development. According to a U.S. Helsinki Commission report: "The incident demonstrated the level of Ashgabat's unease about opposition activity, however distant and weak, as well as the willingness in some circles of Russia's government to cooperate with Turkmenistan's security services. Niyazov appears intent on continuing his campaign against the opposition and determined to prevent the open expression of dissent."[109]

The situation in Uzbekistan is even worse, because the political opposition to President Karimov's rule is more active, hence giving rise to extremely ruthless abuses on the part of the National Security Service. Karimov, in the words of an American journalist, "has stayed in power by locking up many of his opponents. Uzbeks and foreigners agree that his grip is absolute."[110] Security police operate the way they did in Soviet days because the laws have not been changed since independence, except in cases where they were made more severe. All public demonstrations are completely banned. In January 1992, when students demonstrated against price increases, security forces did not hesitate to crack down, killing two demonstrators.[111]

Uzbek law permits the detention of persons without charges for up to three days, during which time the detainee has no right to counsel. Authorities use this provision to harass and restrict the actions of political oppositionists, detaining them at will without a formal arrest. When U.S. Senator Arlen Specter visited Uzbekistan in June 1994, for example, four dissidents were detained to prevent them from meeting Specter. Police often beat prisoners and keep them in solitary confinement. Pulak Akhunov, leader of the opposition party Birlik, reported being severely beaten during an incarceration. Security police also detain political activists on trumped-up charges, accusing them falsely of drug possession or disorderly conduct. Although the law permits them to have a lawyer after being charged, in reality political defendants are often deprived of this right.[112]

In September 1994, the National Security Service completed an investigation of a criminal case against members of the opposition democratic party Erk. More than forty persons, including some who had fled the country, were charged with preparing a coup against the government. Several defendants had been arrested for possessing copies of the newspaper of the Erk Party, banned in early 1993, but with continued publication underground. Others were rounded up for alleged illegal possession of firearms. By April 1995, severe sentences had been meted out in the case. Uzbek writer and publicist Mamadan Makhmudov was given four years in prison, while the publisher of the paper Erk, Murad Dzhuraev (who was arrested by Uzbek security police in Kazakhstan), was sentenced to twelve years.[113]

Violent assaults on government critics, occurring in a pattern that suggests security police involvement, are common.[114] The security police also make life difficult for Westerners, tapping their telephones and putting them under surveillance. Things became so intolerable by early 1995 that several Western news agencies in Tashkent moved their bureaus to neighboring Kazakhstan.[115]

In Tadzhikistan, where a civil war was raging until late 1992 and Russian troops have a substantial presence, it is almost beside the point to discuss human rights. As in other CIS states, random violence against government oppositionists is common, although antigovernment groups also engage in violent acts. From spring 1992 to spring 1994, at least thirty-five journalists were killed in Tadzhikistan, along with other vocal oppositionists. The Tadzhik Ministry of Security has regularly persecuted critics by means of criminal sanctions. In early 1994, Mirbobo Mirrakhimov, a well-known leader of the Tadzhik opposition and a journalist, was arrested on spurious charges. Several months later security police took two other prominent journalists, Maksud Khuseynov and Mukhammadrakhim Saydar, into custody.[116] More recently, in October 1995, Tadzhik authorities arranged to have Russian security police in Moscow arrest Tadzhik journalist Abdukayum Kayumov and extradite him back to Tadzhikistan because of his criticisms of the Tadzhik leadership.[117]

Security police systematically beat and torture detainees in prison. They also rape female prisoners. The criminal laws, which have not been amended since independence, allow for lengthy pretrial detention (up to fifteen months), but there have been numerous reports of detentions over this time limit. Four journalists arrested in January 1993 were held for eighteen months before their trial. According to government opponents, security police routinely detain people without ever charging them.[118] Although the level of overt violence is slowly declining in Tadzhikistan, as the political situation stabilizes, the dictatorial policies of the current government, backed by a strong security police, have instilled fear in a large proportion of the population. This makes it unlikely that a strong human rights lobby, demanding an end to arbitrary police persecution, will develop in the near future.

Respect for the law and protection of individuals from police abuse remain largely elusive goals in many of the CIS states. The habits of the Soviet period die hard and, with ethnic conflict and economic crime on the rise, are not likely to disappear in the near future. As the dominant member of the CIS, Russia should, ideally, be taking the lead in establishing true democratic rights for its citizens. But Yeltsin's increasing propensity to deal with his critics by resorting to heavy-handed, undemocratic tactics and the assault on Chechnia have created serious doubts about the Russian model of political change.

The fact that Russia has not pressured CIS governments to stop their most egregious human rights abuses is an indication that this issue is not a high priority for the Yeltsin administration. On the contrary, Russian security authorities have abetted the repression of Central Asian political dissidents by arresting and extraditing them when they seek haven in Russia. And in the Transcaucasian states, Moscow has actively promoted the political instability that has motivated their governments to employ authoritarian methods. In light of these trends, it is difficult to view Russia's human rights record as separate from the record of the CIS states that Russia seeks to dominate.

Chapter Eight

GUARDIANS OF HISTORY

> The most important question at the moment is whether
> archival resources in the Russian Federation belong to society.
> *(Historian Iurii Afanas'ev, 1993)*

> The guardian of the materials on the [security police]
> repressions is the direct successor of the organization
> that inflicted the repressions, and, moreover, the files
> of the victims are examined in the very same buildings
> where they were tortured and executed.
> *(Arsenii Roginskii and Nikita Okhotin, "The KGB
> Archives: A Year after the Coup," 1992)*

ONE OF THE GREATEST obstacles to Russia's transforming it-self into a full-fledged democracy, and hence curtailing once and for all the powers of its security services, is the failure of Russian society to come to terms with its past. That past—the story of a totalitar-ian regime's subjugation of its people and its unrelenting efforts to under-mine democracy in the West—is still buried in the archives, which remain largely under the control of the security services. As Russian historian Iurii Afanas'ev observed: "The public consciousness has not yet reached the required level. That there existed a certain regime and that a return to it is out of the question is acknowledged only by individuals, not as yet by the society."[1]

No states, however democratic, have a perfect record in facing up to dark spots in their history. But Russia's record is particularly bad, and it is not difficult to understand why. First, an opening of the archives and a full societal recognition of what really happened might unleash broad demands for a complete change of guard—and a change of ways—at the top, particularly in the security and intelligence apparatus. This, in turn, could lead to trials of former officials, like those that were conducted in east Germany and Poland. Also, the profit motive is at play. Sometimes security authorities refuse to declassify historical documents because they want to use them for their own commercial purposes.

The archival issue, then, is not just about what is in the archives, but also about how the current gatekeepers of these archives—a coalition of former KGB officials and party apparatchiks—are perpetuating Russian society's "collective amnesia" about the past by controlling what documents are to be released and who has access to them. Whatever the motives, the end result is the same—a distortion of historical truth and of societal memory.

HISTORY AS POLITICS

The manipulation of history is hardly a new phenomenon in Russia. In the Soviet state, history, or rather historical interpretation, was fraught with political implications. This was because the regime lacked legitimacy. Having seized power by force and imposed their will on the people, the Bolsheviks had to come up with a justification for their rule. The ideology of Marxism-Leninism, persuasive though it might have been, was not enough, especially after Lenin died. History had to be reinterpreted to present party leaders as heroes of the radical movement that led to the fall of the monarchy.

Stalin was acutely aware of this, so aware that he presided over a complete revision of revolutionary history to glorify the role of the Bolsheviks, and himself in particular. In his famous letter, written in 1931, to the editor of the historical journal *Proletarskaia revoliutsiia*, Stalin demanded that historians evaluate the role of revolutionary figures, not on the basis of documents dredged up by "archive rats," but on what they knew a priori must be truth, that is, the "Bolshevik truth." From this time onward historical objectivity was no longer possible in the Soviet Union. Historians could use documents only to further the official version. While Stalin ruled, this meant furthering Stalin's personality cult. As Robert Tucker pointed out, idolatry of Stalin's historical role became one of "Russia's major growth industries," reaching ludicrous proportions.[2]

Stalin's successors were no less zealous in their use of history for propaganda and their consequent contempt for documented facts. After defeating Lavrentii Beria in a bitter Kremlin power struggle and overseeing his execution in 1953, Khrushchev declared him a traitor and had his name erased from the textbooks. Although he opened the door a crack on Stalin's crimes in his famous 1956 speech to the Communist Party's Central Committee, Khrushchev never came close to revealing the true extent of the purges of the thirties. Nor did Brezhnev, who presided over an ambitious effort by historians to make him into a daring World War II hero, when in fact, as a political commissar, he barely saw fighting. Until the advent of glasnost in the late 1980s, Soviet history remained a phantasmagoric effort to persuade readers of the infallibility of the Communist Party leadership. The archives were closed to all but the most carefully vetted researchers, who had been sanctioned by the party to document the official line.

Despite their predilection for hiding the facts, Soviet officials were meticulous record keepers and, to use Tucker's phrase, "arch archive rats." They knew the value of historical documents, which could always be pulled out selectively to suit some leader's political purpose, and thus kept their archives carefully preserved and well organized.[3] For researchers who have managed to gain access to these archives, this has proved to be a bonanza.

Like so many other reforms of the past few years, the opening of the archives has been a very uneven, arbitrary, and highly politicized process. As the official guardians of the state's secrets, the KGB and its successor agencies have been deeply involved. The 1992 Law on Federal Organs of State Security instructed these agencies "to participate in work and in the realization of measures to protect state secrets; to exercise control over their safekeeping in ministries, state committees and departments, and at enterprises, establishments, and organizations, regardless of ownership."[4] Not only do Russian security agencies protect their own archives; they also guard the archives belonging to other state bodies, including those from the party. Anyone entering a building that houses archival documents will run into representatives of the security services.

INSIDE THE ARCHIVES

Russian archives contain vast holdings, estimated at sixty-five million files, which are spread out among several agencies.[5] There is the extensive Central Party Archives, which hold Communist Party documents up to 1952; the Storage Center for Contemporary Documentation, holding Central Committee files from 1952 through August 1991; the Presidential Archives, which are closed but reportedly contain the most sensitive files of the party leadership, including the personal papers of Stalin; the State Archives; the Foreign Ministry Archives, the Defense Ministry Archives, and so on.[6] Because of their painstaking record keeping, the Soviets often made copies of important documents, so in all of these archives there are reports and memoranda from the KGB and its predecessors. But the full picture on many burning issues of the past is in the KGB Archives, which, aside from the Presidential Archives, represent the jewel in the crown for researchers on the Soviet period.

What is in the archives of the former KGB and why are they so important? These archives are not a single entity, but are divided among different repositories. In the Soviet period, not only the territorial branches of the KGB but also certain central directorates had their own archives. The foreign intelligence archives were separate from those of counterintelligence and domestic security (the KGB's Second Chief Directorate) and are housed out at Iasenevo, where FIS (Foreign Intelligence Service) headquarters are located. The Eighth Chief Directorate (now the Federal Agency for Government Communications) also had its own archives.[7]

Reportedly many files from the KGB archives in the republics were evacuated to Russia prior to August 1991. This was most certainly the case in Lithuania, for example, where there was free access to KGB archives after the coup attempt. An American scholar, Romuald Misiunas, who spent several weeks in these repositories, found evidence that large numbers of KGB files had been removed to the city of Omsk in Russia. Almost all of the files relating to KGB collaborators and secret agents were missing.[8] Misiunas also observed that large numbers of documents had been destroyed: "There is considerable evidence everywhere of the haste with which the final occupants departed in August 1991. The entire building [in Vilnius] was left strewn with debris, torn paper, burned and partially burned documents and abandoned intelligence operations equipment."[9]

In Moscow, the destruction of documents had begun much earlier and was more systematic. According to Memorial Society representatives, the security police routinely destroyed documents for housekeeping purposes from the 1920s onward. But there were certain periods where this process went beyond routine. Before and during the war, for example, many documents were burned in order to prevent them from falling into the hands of the Germans. During 1954–1955, in connection with post-Stalin amnesties, authorities burned thousands of case files.

Then in 1989, most of the 550-volume dossier on Andrei Sakharov, including his confiscated diaries, was destroyed, and at the end of that year KGB Chief Kriuchkov ordered the elimination of all files on those charged under Article 70 of the criminal code (anti-Soviet agitation and propaganda), which had recently been amended. As a result, thousands of dossiers on dissidents were burned or shredded. This was followed less than a year later by a purge of files on KGB agents, which continued until July 1991. Memorial Society researchers, noting that Kriuchkov was motivated by fear for the KGB's future, conclude: "The rumors circulating in Russian society that 'there was burning in the KGB' were to a great extent confirmed."[10]

Despite this destruction, however, there are still more than five million files in various KGB archives on Russian territory. At the Lubianka is all the documentation on police persecution of innocent victims throughout the Soviet period. The "operative collection" contains police dossiers on Soviet citizens, with records of secret surveillance and copies of denunciations, and agents' files, the working records of agents, and evaluations of their performance. It was this collection that suffered the most from the "purging" of documents carried out by the KGB. Another group of files, the criminal investigation collection, includes records of criminal cases investigated by the political police from the 1920s onward. This collection, which contains reports of arrests, interrogations, and trials, is massive, reportedly containing files on four million cases.[11]

A third collection at the Lubianka deals with business correspondence, including documents on the organization and administration of state security organs from 1917 onward. The files contain instructions and directives, statistics, plans and accounts of the various departments, and so on. There is also a personnel collection, which contains the personal files of security employees, and, finally, a "filtrations collection," which has materials that used to have operational significance but no longer do.[12]

The archives of the FIS, housed at Iasenevo, are not so controversial domestically as those relating to internal security because they cover the foreign operations of the KGB (carried out by its First Chief Directorate, or FCD, and its predecessors), and few Russians question the legitimacy of KGB activities in this sphere. Nonetheless, FIS archives could hardly be considered apolitical. They hold answers to questions that have preoccupied Western policymakers and historians for years. Because these archives remain closed, researchers can only guess at what they contain and how they are organized. But outside sources provide an idea. Former KGB officer Oleg Gordievsky copied several top secret First Chief Directorate documents before he defected to the West in 1985 and published them. These materials, which are in the FCD archives, include instructions from Moscow to KGB officers abroad on conducting disinformation campaigns and detailed methods for recruiting agents.[13]

In Lithuania, archives from the KGB's First Chief Directorate have been accessible, and some of these files emanated from Moscow. American scholar Misiunas found that, although many documents had been destroyed, the archives contain a mine of information on the KGB's foreign operations: "In addition to the insights on general facets of KGB activity such as disinformation, technology transfer, and the creation and maintenance of double identities for illegal agents abroad, which transcend Lithuania, the archive has so far also provided the only available primary source on the scope, purpose and success (or lack thereof) in Soviet relations with the emigrations of its national components."[14]

Misiunas found the Lithuanian FCD files organized into six main collections, presumably in a similar manner to the FCD files at Iasenevo. The first, called "files of preliminary study" (*dela predvaritelnogo izucheniia*), contains files on foreigners residing abroad who had attracted KGB attention and who had been under KGB surveillance. The second holds "agent-observation files," intelligence reports on Lithuanian or Baltic emigré groups and political organizations. In the third category there are instructions from Moscow and also files on the so-called Line S, the illegals department, which detail the establishment of double identities for undercover residents abroad. The fourth collection includes documents on persons targeted as objects of disinformation. The fifth collection contains "informational files" of a broad variety, most of which provided background information. The final collection covers "operative selection," files on foreigners who were under scrutiny as possible recruits by the KGB. In addition, Misiunas came across documents on technological espionage, including "shopping lists" for KGB officers and materials disclosing extensive disinformation efforts abroad.[15]

Judging from what is available in the Lithuanian archives, researchers would find documents of unprecedented historical value in the FIS files at Iasenevo, even if they were granted access to only a small portion of them. But this remains an elusive goal. Although FIS Chief Primakov promised that his agency would make files from his archives available to independent researchers, he has not done so. As is typically the case with foreign intelligence organizations, including those in the West, the FIS is reluctant to give up its secrets. In contrast with other state institutions like the Ministry of Foreign Affairs and Ministry of Defense, which have grudgingly granted limited access to files dating back several decades, the FIS has kept its history locked up, except in a few cases, which are discussed later in this chapter.

MOMENTS OF TRUTH

Most of the domestic pressure for opening up the archives has focused on those at the Lubianka rather than at Iasenevo. The pressure began under Gorbachev, when glasnost unleashed demands among democrats for historical truth and a reassessment of the Soviet past. As might have been expected, few of the entrenched *apparatchiks* favored the idea of making archival documents public, but it had become a central plank of the democrats' program. According to two members of the Memorial Society: "It is not an exaggeration to say that, in 1987–89, the main line of resistance in the struggle between those trying to preserve their positions through party ideology and the new social forces that appeared from nowhere, striving for change, was history."[16]

As usual, the KGB, feeling pressure from the reformers, was quick to jump on the bandwagon and take matters into its own hands. For many Soviet citizens the key historical issue was the purges of the thirties and subsequent Stalinist repressions. But the archives also held documentation on more recent police repressions, so the question of archival access had more current political implications. In an effort to contain the democrats' demand for potentially explosive information, the KGB encouraged the party's Politburo to form a Commission to Study Materials and Documents Related to the Repressions during the Stalin Era in the autumn of 1987. Although the commission included party luminaries, such as Aleksandr Iakovlev, one of the architects of perestroika, KGB officials predominated. Delving into their vast files, KGB officials began "rehabilitating" people who had been charged for various political crimes during the Stalin era—and in most cases had been executed or died in labor camps.

The KGB used the commission as a public relations gambit, portraying its organization as being in the forefront of efforts to come clean about past crimes and make amends with victims. In the words of a KGB deputy chairman, Vladimir Pirozhkov: "Work associated with restoring the honorable names of people and historic and social justice for the victims of repression is at present foremost in the operations of the state security organs. . . . For us Chekists of the new generation, the fate of every innocent victim is particularly painful . . . every falsified case goes through our hearts and our hands. Each contains a personal tragedy."[17] But the "personal tragedies" that occurred as a result of police repression in the early Soviet years, or after Stalin's death, were not mentioned. The process of rehabilitation was tightly controlled and highly selective.

The KGB went to great lengths to emphasize that Chekists who bore responsibility for the repressions were no longer part of their organization and that many had been punished for their illegalities. At a 1989 meeting with members of the Memorial Society, a KGB spokesperson stated emphatically: "There is not a single person in the USSR KGB at present who was in any way associated with implementing the repressions. . . . Since 1953 there have been 1,342 convictions (including death sentences) of NKVD–Ministry of State Security employees for breaching the socialist rule of law. . . . Some 2,370 have been dismissed, stripped of military ranks, and deprived of pensions and government awards. Each of the culprits was taken severely to task by the party."[18]

But there was the occasional embarrassment. Investigative journalist Yevgenia Albats discovered several former members of the Stalinist NKVD (People's Commissariat of Internal Affairs) who had "fallen through the cracks" and were enjoying prosperous post-NKVD careers. In 1988, she published a series of articles on Colonel Vladimir Boyarsky, a former NKVD investigator with an especially bloodthirsty past. He had tortured prisoners and was responsible for over a hundred deaths of innocent victims. As a state security officer in the reserves, Boyarsky was a respected professor of the history of technology at a prestigious academic institute when Albats exposed him. Why had he and others like him not been punished? According to Albats: "Because they were needed. They were needed as experts to work for the KGB under other 'covers'—in

Boyarksy's case, at the Academy of Sciences. They were needed as professional agents to keep people in their various institutes under surveillance (the amateur informers couldn't match them). They were needed to select and help promote people in all areas of science, culture, industry and government."[19]

Albats had obtained files on Boyarsky—through personal connections—in the archives of the Procuracy. Reading through the mounds of documents, she became convinced of the necessity to make all the files on the purges and their victims public: "I think that people should know what can be done—what has been done—to them in their own country, by their fellow citizens: *people like us*."[20] But KGB officials saw it differently. Although in 1990 they did begin providing victims of the NKVD and their relatives with certain documents relating to the criminal cases in question, they steadfastly refused to allow researchers access to archives on the purges. The reason, they said, was that information from the files could harm the reputations of victims because the latter were often forced to confess to crimes they did not commit. In Pirozhkov's words: "The main point is not to smear the honest name of a person who has sincerely devoted his life to the cause of the party, the people, and socialism by so-called 'confession testimony.'"[21] This rationale, although typical of any state bureaucracy that had something to hide, was obviously self-serving. Denying people access to files on the purges not only protected the victims, but also the executioners.

The KGB's line went unchallenged until August 1991, when the coup attempt tarnished its image so badly that angry crowds threatened to storm the Lubianka. Inside, nervous KGB staffers began shredding documents, especially those related to recent events. After a few days things calmed down and the threat abated. But the KGB would take no chances. Albats says that many important documents, in particular lists of KGB agents and their personal files, were transferred to military bases under KGB command in remote regions of Russia.[22] KGB officials worried about pressure to open their archives. And they were right. According to Vadim Bakatin, who took over as chairman of the KGB at this time, "There was probably no issue relating to the KGB that attracted such attention from journalists, scholars, and the public as the Committee's archives."[23]

ARCHIVAL ACCESS AFTER THE COUP ATTEMPT

One of the first aims of the democrats was to gain access to the KGB Archives by having them officially placed under the control of the new Russian government. In compliance with their demands, Yeltsin issued a decree on 24 August 1991 ordering the transfer of both KGB and Communist Party archives to the repositories of the Russian Republic. Significant portions of the party archives were placed under the jurisdiction of the newly formed Russian Committee on the Archives (Roskomarkhiv), which began to declassify documents for public availability. The KGB, however, was not prepared to comply with the decree, apparently because Yeltsin had no intention of forcing the issue. According to its new chief, Bakatin: "We have reached an agreement with Boris Nikolayevich, and he has agreed that we should not simply take everything and hand it over . . . this should most categorically not be done. Society should not be disrupted, nor should we yet again introduce into every family this sort of fear, this sort of settling of accounts. It is not to be tolerated."[24]

Democratic reformers nonetheless considered it essential to devise a set of rules and regulations governing access to KGB files, along with those of other Russian archives. With this goal in mind, several leading democrats, including historian Afanas'ev, became active members of the Commission on the Transfer of the CPSU and KGB Archives to State Use, which was set up by the Russian parliament in October 1991. The commission, headed by military historian and Yeltsin adviser Dmitrii Volkogonov, laid out procedures for transferring KGB documents to the public archives, but it did not deal with the sensitive question of access. The commission decided that the KGB should transfer all files dealing with "discontinued" criminal cases, those cases in which a decision had been made to rehabilitate the accused; active cases that dated back beyond fifteen years; the entire filtrations collection; "secret" business correspondence dating back fifteen years or more; and the personal files of KGB employees who had retired more than thirty years ago. This meant that almost 80 percent of the KGB archives would be handed over.[25]

The decision met with immediate resistance from the KGB, which proposed exceptions. For example, security officials claimed that, among the files dealing with active cases and secret business correspondence, there were documents that should not be transferred for reasons of security and because they were still being used for official purposes. They referred specifically to cases connected to espionage or organized crime. There were also problems with space, particularly in the regions away from Moscow, where people's deputies, workers' groups, archivists, and security officials were to carry out the transfer of local KGB files. In many regions the public archives were already full, and there was no space for KGB files. In these cases it was decided to allow the KGB to be the temporary custodian.[26]

Throughout 1992, while liberal members of the parliamentary commission were pressing to proceed with the transfer, security officials continued to prevaricate, using every possible excuse to obstruct the process. The Yeltsin government went right along with them, supporting their efforts to place brakes on the transfer. In early 1992 Roskomarkhiv (later named Rosarkhiv), headed by Yeltsin appointee Rudolf Pikhoia, issued a joint directive with the Ministry of Security, saying that the transfer of KGB files would take place in two stages. At first just the files on victims of police abuse who had been rehabilitated would take place. Only later would the Ministry of Security (MB) give up the other files. This decision was a blow to those who had hoped to expedite the transfer quickly.[27]

Having General Dmitrii Volkogonov at the head of the parliamentary archival commission hardly helped the democrats' cause. Although he had earned fame as a biographer of Stalin, Volkogonov's credentials as a scholar and a historian were of recent vintage. Most of his career had been spent in the military, where he specialized in ideological education and propaganda for soldiers. He wrote books like *The Psychological War*, a chilling diatribe against the West, in which he lambasted Americans for praising such "renegades" as Solzhenitsyn and Sakharov and called the courageous human rights activist Piotr Grigorenko (whose health was ruined during incarceration in KGB-run psychiatric hospitals) "a malicious anti-Soviet . . . who had completely gone out of his mind."[28]

Volkogonov was well connected in former KGB circles. Thus he had no trouble gaining personal access to top secret KGB files, which he used to write his highly profitable biographies of Stalin, Trotsky, and Lenin. Presumably he had little incentive to open up the KGB archives to other researchers, despite his leadership of the parliamentary commission on archives. Nor did Pikhoia, Yeltsin's chief archivist. Interviewed in *Literaturnaia gazeta* in the spring of 1993, he claimed disingenuously that the transfer of the KGB archives was "proceeding normally across Russia." When pressed, however, he admitted that nothing had been done with the central archives in Moscow. Pikhoia cited a number of vague technical reasons why these archives had not been moved and then volunteered feebly: "Incidentally, as compared with the massive bulk of party documents, the KGB archives are small in volume, trifling."[29]

Arsenii Roginskii, a member of the archival commission, complained at this time that the handover of the KGB archives was proceeding at a snail's pace and was hopelessly behind schedule. It was not just a matter of obstruction on the part of the Ministry of Security. Also, he said, Rosarkhiv was taking a "very passive stance." Russian authorities were not interested in the process because "it is a matter of indifference to them whether the documents from the Lubianka archives are stored in the left-hand 'pocket' or the right. In either case, the materials are fully at their disposal."[30]

The Ministry of Security's chief archivist, Anatolii Kraiushkin, put a different spin on the situation. Interviewed in April 1993, he boasted of the great progress that his agency had made in handing over KGB archives, although, like Pikhoia, he implied that the transfers were taking place in regional archives rather than in Moscow. Kraiushkin also claimed that declassification commissions had been set up in the Ministry of Security in Moscow and in its regional branches for the purpose of removing the secrecy restrictions on millions of documents. Researchers would be able to access these declassified materials at a public reading room in the Ministry of Security.[31]

The Legal Morass

Some researchers had pinned their hopes for access to KGB files on the long-promised Law on Archival Collections of the Russian Federation, which finally was passed by the parliament in July 1993.[32] But the law did not touch upon the issue of transferring KGB archives to the public domain. State security and foreign intelligence files continued to be subject to special procedures, which were set forth in the laws on the security services. Historian Mark Kramer has pointed out that, if anything, the archival law brought more restrictions on documents because it stated specifically that access to secret documents could not be granted until thirty years after they appeared. Before this law, there had been a thirty-year policy, but it was not always observed and archivists had some flexibility in declassifying documents.[33]

The law did stipulate that, by the decision of "appropriate departments" and the Russian state archive service, the thirty-year period could be shortened and documents could be declassified earlier. But this placed researchers at the mercy of bureaucrats who had little incentive to declassify documents in the first place. Moreover, the law also stated that the secrecy time limit could be extended. With regard to KGB archives, as Kramer concluded, "Most of the KGB's documents could end up being even less accessible than before, with files sealed off completely for 50 to 75 years or more."[34] Indeed, just days after the archive law was passed, the Russian parliament extended by another twenty years the limits on access to classified foreign intelligence documents. This meant that these documents would remain inaccessible for fifty years after their appearance.[35]

Countervailing forces were clearly at work when it came to archival access (a situation that researchers also encounter with documents from the security services of democratic countries). Things seemed to improve when, in September 1994, Yeltsin signed a directive (*razporiazhenie*) designed to speed up the procedure for declassifying Communist Party documents, in particular those more than thirty years old.[36] But in March 1995 the government issued a lengthy statute on "procedure for declassification of and extension of classification limits on USSR government archival documents." It established a laborious process for declassification of government archives (including those of the KGB), which would slow things down considerably.[37]

At the top of a large pyramid of officials to be involved in declassification (or reclassification) was the so-called Interagency Commission for the Protection of State Secrets. This commission, to have the ultimate say on removing secrecy restrictions, had under it an Interagency Group of Experts, including representatives from the counterintelligence service (successor to the Ministry of Security and soon to be renamed the Federal Security Service), the foreign intelligence service, and FAPSI (the communications and information agency), as well as officials from other ministries and archivists. These experts had to follow a complicated procedure for declassification, which involved a page-by-page review of all documents submitted for declassification and then approval by the state secrets commission. With this statute in effect, it hardly mattered whether KGB archives were still at the Lubianka or were transferred to Rosarkhiv. In either case, security officials could use the morass of bureaucratic regulations to prevent access.

How Much to Reveal

Despite these obstacles, the rehabilitation process has continued and some police investigative files (records of criminal cases and interrogations) from the Stalin period have been made available. The parliamentary archival commission, which is now defunct, had devoted a great deal of time to debating the issue of access to these files. The Law on Rehabilitation, passed by the Russian parliament in October 1991, stated that victims of police repression and relatives had the right to examine their investigation files. The law said nothing about access for others, which was to be covered in a more general law on archives. Not surprisingly, the security organs interpreted the rehabilitation law to mean that *only* relatives and victims could see these files. Thus, for example, historians could not look at the file on Nikolai Bukharin, the famous Bolshevik, or the file on Soviet poet Osip Mandelstam. [38]

Although the commission agreed that this interpretation by security officials was wrong, its members could not reach a consensus on the question of access to the investigative files. Some were in favor of unlimited access, but others were concerned that the files would contain information of a personal nature that could prove embarrassing to the victims and their families, or that false information in the files would damage reputations of innocent people. One example of this problem, cited by a Russian historian, was the publication of NKVD material on the interrogation in 1938 of the famous physicist and Nobel Prize winner Lev Landau; Landau had signed false accusations against himself and his colleagues during an NKVD interrogation.[39] Finally a compromise was reached, and in November 1992 the commission adopted a proposal whereby victims of repression and their relatives could not restrict access to investigative files, but could prevent publication of information of a personal nature that appeared in the file.[40]

What about the even more controversial operative files from the Lubianka archives (dossiers on citizens under secret surveillance, reports of agents, etc.)? Security officials were adamant that these would remain closed. They would not allow information on KGB agents, informers, and collaborators to be revealed. The Yeltsin administration agreed. In fact, some information from these files—that related to secret KGB collaborators in the Russian Orthodox Church—did find its way into the press. Parliamentary deputies Gleb Iakunin and Lev Ponomarev, who found copies of these documents in the CPSU Central Committee archives, leaked them to the media in early 1992. The security service responded by publishing a law on operative-investigative work, making it a crime to reveal the names of KGB agents, which were classified as state secrets.[41]

The controversy over the exposure of KGB agents and informers has sparked emotional debates in Russia. Although many people praised Iakunin and Ponomarev for publishing these incriminating documents, others expressed strong reservations. Former Gorbachev adviser Aleksandr Iakovlev, for one, feared that a campaign to expose former KGB agents would only serve to demoralize society. Others pointed out that KGB reports like the one that was published often were unreliable because KGB officers tended to exaggerate their achievements by listing even the most casual contacts as "agents." Often those named had no idea that the KGB regarded them as agents or as "trustworthy persons" who were put in the KGB card index. In the absence of any formalized agreement on cooperation, it was difficult to confirm that someone had indeed acted as a KGB agent or informer.[42]

Recognizing that they were dealing with a potentially explosive political issue, security officials did their best to defuse it by downplaying the importance of the operative files. Ministry of Security archivist Kraiushkin pointed out that the operative collection was actually quite small, because case files had been routinely destroyed over the years. There were, he said, only a few operational files left, primarily those that had been kept because they were of historical interest.[43] But this did not put an end to the debate. Many were convinced that information on KGB agents and informers had to be made public, mainly to prevent its being used to pressure politicians who had a KGB past. To quote journalist Albats: "If it is not done, these files will find their way onto the 'black market' and will be used by various forces to manipulate our politicians."[44]

THE LUSTRATION ISSUE

Some reformers pushed for a law on lustration (a term derived from the Latin *lustratio*, meaning purification by sacrifice), like the one passed in Czechoslovakia, where officials and politicians were screened for past association with the secret police—the Statni Bezpečnost, or StB. Such a law would regulate the release of KGB operational intelligence files and at the same time bar former KGB collaborators from certain government jobs. Members of the Democratic Russia movement proposed a law banning former KGB staffers and agents, as well as party officials, from serving in executive government posts and in teaching positions. However, those elected to the parliament or the presidency would not have to go through screening for KGB collaboration, since, in the words of parliamentary deputy Galina Starovoitova, "After all, we can leave the people a choice to vote for a totalitarian regime once again."[45]

But the Czechoslovak experience with lustration was far from positive. Indeed, the way the law was misused and the vengeance that it unleashed made many, including President Václav Havel, regret that it had been introduced in the first place.[46] There the files remained closed to the public, but special commissions were given access in order to screen candidates for public office. The biggest problem with lustration was that it relied on the registers and files of the secret police, which contained the names of some 140,000 secret police agents, collaborators, and contacts during the communist period. This meant putting faith in the very organization that had deceived the population for forty years. As it turned out, even some former dissidents who had spent their lives fighting for human rights found themselves listed as collaborators. The screening procedure became highly politicized and often was used as a means of attacking political figures.[47]

In Germany the files of the STASI (East German secret police) were opened up in late 1991. The German parliament adopted a law on the files, which stipulated the conditions of access and detailed the rights of both the victims of the STASI and those who were agents. It also set down regulations for the publication of STASI materials in the press. The opening of the STASI archives and the subsequent revelations of the names of thousands of police collaborators caused tremendous societal trauma and wrought havoc on the personal lives of many East German citizens. It raised complex legal, political, and ethical issues that politicians and government officials are still grappling with. But, as one expert pointed out, Germany had an advantage over other postcommunist states in that it had a well-developed judicial system.[48]

In Russia, with its weak tradition of legality, it would be even more difficult to deal with the complex issues arising from a lustration law, or even for that matter, a law that opened up KGB operative files containing the names of agents. More to the point, with the old *nomenklatura*—both party and KGB—still dominating politics, such laws were unlikely to be passed. Indeed, the communist-aligned paper *Pravda* and the weekly *Glasnost* both claimed that the drafters of the lustration law, which was presented at a conference on the KGB, were influenced by Western secret services. Ministry of Security public relations chief Aleksei Kondaurov, who appeared at the conference, objected that this law was discriminatory against KGB veterans because their official job descriptions, upon which the lustration would be based, did not necessarily mean that they had committed abuses.[49]

Even human rights activists like Sergei Kovalev were opposed to a lustration law. Kovalev worried that it would divide Russian society and deflect from the fact that the entire nation bore responsibility for what had occurred.[50] But the issue of past KGB collaboration would not go away. As the historian Iurii Afanas'ev expressed it:

> It has yet to be determined how many people collaborated with the KGB; but it is eminently clear that they number in the several millions. What shall we do about them? Should we reveal their names to society or, for various reasons, should we seal these documents, say for fifty or seventy years? . . . This is an enormous moral problem for all Russia and for the entire former Soviet Union; it reaches the level of nationwide repentance. How can we survive this disease, how can we overcome it, how do we get beyond totalitarianism, not chronologically but within ourselves?[51]

SPECIAL PRIVILEGES

As American historian Mark Kramer pointed out, the idea that archives and official documents are part of the public domain remains an alien one in Russia. According to Kramer, who spent several months doing research in the party and state archives there: "Archival policy in Russia is still determined by the prevailing political winds, and professional archivists find themselves obliged to respond to the demands and whims of high-level bureaucrats."[52]

There have been numerous reports of people being granted special access to documents that are unavailable to others. Representatives from the Memorial Society, for example, claimed that certain researchers and journalists with ties to the former KGB have been allowed to see files on victims of police repression, or at least obtain copies of documents.[53] Former KGB general Sergei Kondrashev sold secret police documents from the 1930s to the German newspaper *Die Zeit* for an undisclosed sum.[54] And Iurii Afanas'ev reported that Dmitrii Volkogonov "spends days and nights in the archives, working with documents labeled secret; other people come there as well—I don't know how many. So, while there is not universal access, a significant number of historians are granted access to documents still labeled secret. They photocopy them, collect data, prepare future publications."[55] These historians have a tremendous advantage over scholars who do not have special access and lack the money to buy it.[56]

The law on archives states rather ambiguously that "documents from the state section of the Archival Fund cannot be bought or sold or be the subject of other transactions, except by the decision of representative bodies of power or on the basis of a court verdict."[57] Yet if certain well-connected historians are able to cite these documents in their publications, it amounts to the same thing.

Another example of privileged access is that of Oleg Tsarev, a former KGB officer with the First Chief Directorate. Tsarev collaborated with British writer John Costello to write a book called *Deadly Illusions*, published in 1993, about the Soviet spy Alexander Orlov, who defected to the United States in 1953. While still working for the KGB (he eventually took early retirement and became a part-time KGB consultant), Tsarev got special permission from Chairman Kriuchkov to delve into the security archives for materials for his book. No holes were barred and he even got valuable assistance from KGB archivists. "The research for this book," Tsarev says in the preface, "had extended into scores of files, which under the strict new regulations could not be removed from the archive. This necessitated frequent trips to Yasenevo [FIS] headquarters to check and recheck documents."[58]

In an interview with *Pravda*, Tsarev refused to reveal how much money the American publisher, Crown Books, had agreed to pay him and Costello. But he made it clear that he was going to pocket his share of the profits: "The authors of the Orlov book, John Costello and yours truly, will receive royalties that are quite normal for this kind of work."[59] Why would the KGB—and its successor, the Foreign Intelligence Service—allow Tsarev to use the KGB archives for his book? One reason may have been that FIS officials got some of the profits. But they might have had another motive as well.

Deadly Illusions gave a new spin to the Orlov affair that the FIS probably liked. According to the book, which is based on the seventeen-volume Orlov dossier in the KGB files, Orlov was not the genuine defector the CIA and FBI thought he was, but instead remained a dedicated communist. He gave the Americans just enough information to convince them of his worth so that he could get asylum in the United States, but never told them anything of value:

> He succeeded in this challenging task by providing the CIA and FBI with a concoction of half truths, trivialities and disinformation which he skillfully passed off as a sincere confession. Just how cleverly he had deceived the FBI and CIA became evident to the KGB after a five-year search for Orlov, initiated in 1964, eventually resulted in two clandestine contacts with him in 1969 and 1971. The report of the KGB officer who conducted this operation proved beyond doubt Orlov's loyalty to the Soviet intelligence service, its agents and his mother country.[60]

If Tsarev and Costello are to be believed, the defection of Orlov, who the Americans had touted as a top prize for their intelligence services, was in fact a coup for the KGB. By not revealing the names of KGB agents in the United States, Orlov put the CIA and FBI off guard and enabled their agents to continue operating with impunity. *Deadly Illusions*, then, provided some favorable publicity for the former KGB and doubtless caused disquiet in American intelligence circles.

THE CROWN BOOK DEAL

Deadly Illusions was part of a close collaboration between the Foreign Intelligence Service and Crown Publishers. In the spring of 1992, a contract was signed whereby Crown agreed to publish at least five books compiled from documents in the foreign intelligence archives. Topics would cover the case of Leon Trotsky, the Berlin crisis, Soviet intelligence operations in the United States and in Great Britain, and the Cuban missile crisis. Apparently to avoid controversy, the FIS was not a direct party to the contract. Rather, it was the "Association of Intelligence Veterans," technically a private group, that represented the Russian side. But the person who conducted all the negotiations and signed the contract on behalf of the association was FIS public relations chief Iurii Kobaladze.[61]

According to the agreement, Crown Publishers paid an advance of over $1.8 million, thereby gaining exclusive rights to the KGB archival documents that would appear in these volumes. Public access to them would be closed for the next ten years. Naturally, scholars and historians saw this as a disturbing precedent. Not only would the documents be denied to all other scholars until publication, but the enormous sum of money paid by Crown would make it difficult for scholars to see other foreign intelligence files in the future unless they were able to pay a lot for them.[62]

Who would actually receive the money? The Association of Intelligence Veterans was to get a 10 percent cut and the authors of the books would receive large advances.[63] What about FIS officials like Kobaladze and his chief, Evgenii Primakov? In a June 1992 interview Kobaladze insisted: "We are not opening up the archives and we are not selling any documents. What we are doing and what we are guaranteeing to the authors of these books is that we shall supply them with materials which will allow them to write these books on the basis of documents."[64] Nonetheless, it is hard to imagine that Kobaladze and Primakov were not rewarded for their trouble.

Apparently because there was no law on archives at this time, those who maintained the archives were able to do what they wished with the files, acting as private entrepreneurs. According to parliamentary deputy Nikolai Arzhannikov, who voiced strong objections to the Crown deal: "Primakov thinks that he is the proprietor of the archives and that he has the right to dispose of them. I proceed on the basis that the archives are state property and national history. The FIS, however, has decided to engage in commerce with our national property."[65]

Aside from the issue of privileged access and money, another problem with the Crown deal was that, since FIS staffers would be selecting the documents, they would in effect be giving their version of history.[66] Clearly the Russian security and intelligence community had its own agenda as far as historical issues were concerned—to present itself, or its predecessors, in the best possible light. This involved dredging up documents showing that so-called intelligence failures or defections, like that of Orlov, were not as they seemed, that in fact the Soviet intelligence service knew what it was doing all along. It is no coincidence that, when the KGB started publishing materials from his files in the late 1980s, readers saw endless reports from the NKVD in 1940 and 1941 that warned about an imminent German attack on the Soviet Union, reports that Stalin chose to ignore.[67] Invariably, the documents published by the security services paint a romantic picture of episodes in the past, designed to glorify the operations of the security and intelligence apparatus. The exception is the documentation dealing with the Stalinist purges, which were carried out by the notorious internal security branch of the NKVD. Here the approach is simply to stress that after the death of Stalin and Beria in 1953, everything changed and the new police apparatus, the KGB, was reformed.[68]

Cold War Mysteries

The controversies that have arisen in the West over revelations from the KGB archives demonstrate the power that rests in the hands of those who have access to archival material. General Volkogonov's "revelations" about Alger Hiss in 1992 are a good example. Mr. Hiss, a former senior State Department official under Presidents Roosevelt and Truman, was accused in 1948 of having been a Soviet spy. After vehemently denying the charges, Hiss was eventually sentenced to four years in prison for perjury. The Hiss case generated a tremendous controversy that divided the American public between those who were convinced of his guilt and those who thought he had been framed by his accuser, Whittaker Chambers.

The dispute has never been resolved, but Mr. Hiss continued over the years to try to establish his innocence. In the summer of 1992 he decided to take advantage of glasnost and wrote to Volkogonov, asking him for materials on his case or on Whittaker Chambers that might be in the KGB archives and might clear his name. Hiss requested that the documents be handed over to an intermediary, a historian named John Lowenthal. In September 1992 the latter met with Volkogonov, who promised to search for the materials in the foreign intelligence archives and personally review them. When Lowenthal returned to Moscow in October, Volkogonov handed him a typewritten letter stating that a thorough archival search had yielded no documents to substantiate the claim that Hiss had been a Soviet spy: "On the basis of a very careful analysis of all the information available, I can inform you that Alger Hiss was never an agent of the intelligence services of the Soviet Union."[69]

Scholars of Soviet history were dubious about Volkogonov's claims, questioning how the alleged absence of documentation could be considered conclusive evidence, particularly since the general gave no specifics as to what archival files he had searched. How could he make a definitive statement about a case as complex as the Hiss one, which had generated such a vast amount of commentary and contradictory evidence over the years?[70] Moreover, as one Russian journalist pointed out, it was hard to believe that the intelligence archives did not contain a single report of the Hiss affair. Surely the Soviet foreign intelligence service had followed this sensational story closely at the time and its commentary would provide useful clues about the true status of Hiss.[71]

Apparently Volkogonov had not realized that he would open up a Pandora's box in addressing the Hiss case. Responding to the flurry of negative publicity, he decided upon a strategic retreat. In a 24 November letter to the Moscow daily *Independent Gazette*, he qualified his statements about Hiss considerably: "As to whether A. Hiss was or was not a 'spy,' I can render judgment only as a historian. The more so as, as far as I know, the agency in which those documents from the 1950s were reviewed was not the only one which was involved in intelligence. Furthermore, there are no guarantees that they all survived."[72]

The POW/MIA Story

Volkogonov was also involved with another issue—that of American POWs (prisoners of war) and MIAs (missing in action) from World War II, the Korean War, and the Vietnam War. He was co-chairman of the Russian-American Commission to investigate the fate of these POWs and MIAs, set up after Yeltsin's visit to Washington in June 1992. At that time Yeltsin had earned praise from the American public by promising that his government would provide conclusive information on POWs and MIAs who might have ended up in Russia. But, despite all the fanfare, the commission had produced few results by the autumn of 1992. American members of the commission complained of foot dragging on the part of those in charge of the archives, who had produced little data of any value.[73]

The information the Russians came up with was primarily from interviews rather than from archival documents. Nonetheless, Volkogonov maintained that the Americans were learning a great deal. In December 1993 he said: "We have managed to collect and communicate to the United States information on over 20,000 American citizens who were repatriated from German concentration camps. . . . Just a very small portion of them ended up on [Soviet] Union territory during the last war for various reasons."[74]

Whereas the Russian members of the commission preferred to focus on information about Americans lost during World War II, which was less politically sensitive, the concern on the American side was focused on those who disappeared in later years. Clearly important data were available in the files of the former KGB, both its domestic and foreign branches. More than fifty U.S. personnel remained unaccounted for after espionage flights were downed over or near Soviet airspace during the cold war period. The Soviet military intelligence agency, the GRU, may have initially been in charge of these cases and thus had information in its archives. (Former U.S. ambassador Malcolm Toon, the American co-chairman of the POW-MIA commission, alluded to this when he criticized the GRU for not providing information.) But the KGB would also have monitored the cases of these Americans closely because of their political significance, and the KGB was a meticulous record keeper. How then could Rudolf Pikhoia, Yeltsin's chief archivist, insist that it would take years to find information in the files about these missing men?[75]

Did Yeltsin and his subordinates Pikhoia and Volkogonov lack the authority to order those in charge of KGB archives—or the GRU archives for that matter—to produce the data, or did they not have a strong incentive to do so? At a news conference in September 1993, Volkogonov said that the United States had been supplied with all the information, including that from the intelligence services, about airplanes downed over Soviet territory during the cold war.[76] Yet the fate of those missing Americans, with a few exceptions, remained unknown.

Equally pressing from Washington's point of view was the problem of missing Americans from the Korean and Vietnam Wars. At this same news conference the commission chairmen stated that there was no evidence that American citizens taken prisoner in these wars were ever brought to the Soviet Union.[77] Nonetheless, given the close relationship that the Soviet Union had with North Korea and North Vietnam, it was not unreasonable to assume that the Russians had information on what had happened to these POWs and MIAs. In fact, this was the case, although it was merely by chance that a document on American POWs in Vietnam was discovered in Russia.

The document in question, unearthed in the party archives by a Harvard researcher named Stephen Morris, was a Russian translation of a report given by the deputy Vietnamese Army chief to the North Vietnamese Politburo in 1972. The report gave details on 1,205 American POWs who were in captivity, but the figure of POWs publicly cited by the North Vietnamese government at the time was 368 and the number released the next year was only 591. The report was accompanied by a cover memorandum from the head of the GRU, Piotr Ivashutin, who clearly accepted the larger figure as valid and said he was pleased with Vietnam's success at extracting valuable information on American military technology from the prisoners who were interrogated.[78]

Not surprisingly, the document, the first to shed significant light on POWs in Vietnam, created a stir in the United States. But, although most experts accepted it as a legitimate GRU report, they questioned the accuracy of the figures on POWs that were cited. Perhaps they had been exaggerated for some reason by the North Vietnamese. Some months later, rather curiously, the Russians took the initiative and produced another copy of a GRU archival document, again a translation of a Vietnamese Communist Party report and again discussing numbers of POWs. But the American commission members received only two pages of the report and, without the original from which it was translated, or any other documentation, it was impossible to verify the report's authenticity.[79]

THE WALLENBERG CASE

It seemed, then, that there was material in the archives that could shed valuable light on the POW-MIA issue. Even if the KGB and GRU refused to come up with relevant files, copies of many of their documents were in the archives of the Soviet Communist Party, under the direct control of Yeltsin's trusted subordinates Pikhoia and Volkogonov. These archives doubtless would clarify other cold war issues that have preoccupied historians and politicians for years, but members of the Yeltsin administration chose to be cautious.

Vladimir Abarimov, a Russian journalist who has researched a number of cold war mysteries, expressed his frustration in attempting to get facts from the Russian foreign intelligence archives:

> Anyone who has ever had to deal with archives in Russia knows that getting access to certain documents does not necessarily mean getting the documents themselves. At every step of the way, the researcher stumbles upon man-made obstacles. An examination of the most grisly chapters of our past is often blocked by the authorities, and even when we journalists already know all, or almost all of it, we are forced to wait for permission from the powers-that-be.[80]

A case in point is the story of Raoul Wallenberg, the Swedish diplomat who saved the lives of thousands of Hungarian Jews from the Nazis during World War II. After being arrested by the Soviets in Hungary in 1945, Wallenberg disappeared. The Soviets claimed to know nothing about his fate until 1957, when they acknowledged that they had taken him captive and said he had died of a heart attack in Lubianka Prison. Asked for archival information on Wallenberg after the breakup of the Soviet Union, the keepers of the KGB archives prevaricated. Wallenberg's personal file could not be found, they said. Then, inexplicibly, they produced several new documents connected with Wallenberg, including records of three interrogations of him. The pagination showed that the records were taken out of a larger file. Yet security officials continued to insist that they had no Wallenberg file.[81]

Later, in April 1993, some journalists from *Izvestiia* reported coming across a former NKVD officer who had direct knowledge of Wallenberg's execution in 1947. These journalists confronted General Anatolii Kraiushkin, chief of the Lubianka archives, with their story. All of the materials on Wallenberg had been dug up, Kraiushkin said, and it had been established that Wallenberg died suddenly in his cell. Nonetheless, he went on cryptically: "I certainly cannot discount another finale—execution without sentencing. Otherwise they would not have scratched his name out of the prison records, there would have been a medical certificate, an autopsy report, and a record of cremation."[82] Two months later, *Izvestiia* was able to confirm its hypothesis in another article, which cited a 1947 memorandum from Deputy Foreign Affairs Minister Andrei Vyshinskii to his boss, Viacheslav Molotov, on the proposed "liquidation" of Wallenberg.[83] Thus, it turned out that KGB archivists had been holding back after all. As British historian Christopher Andrew observed, the Russians' piecemeal release of information on the Wallenberg case was "a kind of obscene dance of the seven veils."[84]

THE SUDOPLATOV AFFAIR: MANIPULATING HISTORY

It goes without saying that serious historians cannot write objective history on the basis of documents that are spoon-fed to them from archives, or even worse, on the basis of typed excerpts of documents. The only way for scholars to be on solid ground in archives is to ferret out documents independently and to verify their authenticity. Otherwise they are vulnerable to forgeries or to misleading materials that distort the true picture. And, of course, the documents must be interpreted in context. A good example is the above-mentioned Vietnam document. It was indeed "authentic," but that does not mean that everything the report said represents the truth.

Unfortunately for historical scholarship on the Soviet period, however, writers do not always observe these precautions. And, judging from the reception that the book *Special Tasks: The Memoirs of an Unwanted Witness—A Soviet Spymaster* received in the West, the general public does not care whether they do, as long as they offer exciting revelations.[85] *Special Tasks*, which appeared in the spring of 1994, did just that. According to its title, the book represented the memoirs of Pavel Sudoplatov, formerly a senior official in the foreign intelligence branch of the Soviet security apparatus until his arrest as a protégé of the disgraced Lavrentii Beria in 1953. But in fact, *Special Tasks* was actually an "oral history," based on twenty hours of taped interviews of Pavel Sudoplatov, and co-written by his son Anatolii, together with two Americans, Jerrold and Leona Schecter. As historian Thomas Powers observed in a review of the book: "It is impossible to distinguish Sudoplatov's real memories, however confused by age and years, from the Schecters' own research and general editorial tidying up."[86]

The most shocking revelation in *Special Tasks*, for Western readers, was the claim that from 1942 onward Robert Oppenheimer and several other prominent nuclear scientists who were involved in the Manhattan Project were passing atomic secrets to the Soviets. As might have been expected, Sudoplatov's assertions created a furor. The book, which was excerpted in *Time* magazine, became an instant best seller. Many readers found it credible, especially the sections about Oppenheimer, who was stripped of his security clearance in 1954 and was known for his leftist views. But it was denounced by scholars and historians. They were able to point out myriad errors and inconsistencies in the account about Western atomic scientists that basically demolished Sudoplatov's charges.[87] When confronted with these mistakes, the American co-authors, the Schecters, said that they had documentation to back up Sudoplatov's assertions. In fact the book itself had appendices of documents from the Foreign Intelligence Archives that presumably were intended to add credence to the atomic spy story. But none of the documents were new—they had already been published—and none of them supported Sudoplatov's claims. The Schecters then insisted that other documents existed in the FIS archives that would confirm the allegations and promised that the FIS would release them soon. This never happened.

Sudoplatov, then, was the sole source of the allegations against Western scientists. This was a problem for two reasons. First, he had been one of the most bloodthirsty members of Stalin's secret police. His specialty was "wet affairs"—murder, terrorism, and sabotage directed against perceived opponents of the Soviet regime, especially the non-Russian nationalists who objected to Stalin's brutal policies of Sovietization. By his own account, he was a murderer and, like his NKVD colleagues, an expert at disinformation and lies. Yet readers were expected to take him at his word about Western atomic spies.

Second, most of his revelations about Western scientists, in particular those about Oppenheimer, concerned the period from 1941 to 1943. Contrary to what he said in his book, however, Sudoplatov had nothing to do with atomic espionage until late 1944 or 1945. The book mentions the creation of a Special Committee on the Atomic Bomb in 1942 and Sudoplatov's appointment as its "director of intelligence." But the committee was not even established until August 1945, when the Soviets began full-scale efforts to produce a bomb. Though Sudoplatov had indeed been a top official in the NKVD and thus knew a great deal about its operations, he (or perhaps the Schecters) grossly misrepresented his role in the gathering of intelligence on the bomb.[88]

Interestingly, this deception was confirmed by a statement from the Russian FIS shortly after the book came out: "Pavel Sudoplatov had access to atomic problems during a relatively brief period of time, a mere twelve months, from September 1945 to October 1946, when he was in charge of Special Department S. Department S had no direct contact with the agents' network."[89] Indeed, the FIS went even further: "Judging by the archival material which the FIS has, one can state that P. A. Sudoplatov's book 'Special Tasks' is a jumbled mosaic of authentic facts, half-truths, and obvious fabrications."[90]

Why would the FIS go out of its way to discredit the Sudoplatov book? After all, according to *Moscow News* journalist Nataliia Gevorkian, who spoke to FIS public relations chief Iurii Kobaladze about *Special Tasks*, the FIS does not disapprove, in principle, of memoirs or histories by its former officers. Indeed, as was the case with Sudoplatov, the FIS even allows them to use archival documents, as long as the FIS has a good idea of the book's contents and can see it before publication.[91] It is difficult to say what went wrong in the case of *Special Tasks*. Probably the FIS had not realized how blatantly inaccurate it was and had not expected the outcry that the allegations about atomic scientists would create in the West. Then it was time for damage control. FIS officials may have worried that the Western market for spy memoirs and espionage histories they sponsored could be hurt by having their agency associated with *Special Tasks*.

UNAUTHORIZED CONFESSIONS

As the Sudoplatov controversy illustrates, books about cold war espionage have the potential to attract a wide readership. Despite the fact that this war is over, its history is recent and there is still an immense interest in that era of spying and intrigue, described so well in fiction by John le Carré. Aware of the market for their trade secrets, numerous ex-KGB spies have embarked on literary careers without the sanction of their former employers. In these cases there are no documents from the archives, just their own recollections.[92]

There are several problems with this now-flourishing genre of spy memoirs. First, as with *Special Tasks*, there is the basic question of credibility. The reader is expected to believe an author who was trained in the KGB school of disinformation and who spent his entire career trying to undermine Western democracies with lies. What are the author's motives, aside from money, in telling his story? Ex-KGB spies are not usually very good writers (which is why their books are often co-authored), so in order to sell their books, they have to come up with sensational revelations. This can be a slippery slope. Even if they have left the intelligence service, they have to be careful not to arouse the ire of the service by telling too much, especially if they are still living in Russia.

This was General Oleg Kalugin's problem, when he wrote his memoirs, *The First Directorate: My 32 Years in Intelligence and Espionage against the West*, which appeared in 1994.[93] As noted earlier, Kalugin had been a top official in the KGB's foreign intelligence branch and was privy to some of the KGB's deepest secrets. But, anxious as he was to please Western audiences by sharing some of these secrets, he had to be careful. The result was a book that offered insights into KGB operations but, with its half-truths and things left unsaid, did not enlighten the reader on any key issues of East-West relations in the Soviet period. Indeed, in some respects the book confused these issues. Kalugin's book, for example, said repeatedly that Edward Lee Howard, a CIA spy who escaped to Moscow in 1985, was responsible for the subsequent exposures of several Russians working for the CIA. We know now, however, that it was not Howard but Aldrich Ames who betrayed these men. Kalugin also insisted that Vitalii Iurchenko, the KGB officer who defected to the United States in 1985 and then changed his mind, was a genuine defector and not a KGB plant. But, as noted earlier, the Ames affair has called this version into serious question.[94]

With KGB defector Iurii Shvets, author of *Washington Station: My Life as a KGB Spy in America*, the problem was different.[95] Shvets had not been high up in the KGB and thus did not know nearly as much as Kalugin did. But he had to come up with something to excite his readers. So he told them about his recruitment in 1985 of "Socrates," whom he billed as a top prize. According to Shvets, the KGB attached tremendous importance to this agent, a former Washington bureaucrat during the Carter administration. But when he was recruited Socrates had been out of the government for years and had no access to classified documents. What could he tell the KGB? All that he provided, it turns out, was information he had gleaned from talking with friends and neighbors who worked for the government. Yet Shvets claimed that the KGB valued this information so highly that the Politburo used it as the basis for decisions on U.S.-Soviet relations.

As these examples show, books by former KGB spies, either defectors or born-again dissidents living in Russia, cannot be taken as factual accounts. But even when archival documents are used, there is no guarantee of historical truth. The guardians of Soviet history are now retelling it, in some cases availing themselves of the KGB archives for their own publications, releasing selected documents to the press, and even selling documents to those willing to pay a high enough price. By law the FIS and its domestic counterpart are the ultimate arbiters in the declassification process and they can block access to archival documents on grounds of protecting secrecy whenever they see fit. This gives them considerable power.

Western scholars working in Russian archives, such as those housing Communist Party documents, have reported that, after the initial policy of openness that prevailed in 1991–93, access began to be curtailed. By early 1995 authorities had tightened restrictions considerably. And, even more ominously, the presence of security officers in archives and research institutes grew much more noticeable.[96]

These changes are in keeping with the general trends that have been discussed: the growing power of the security agencies; a willingness to use military force at home; a more aggressive foreign policy; increasing impatience with the independent media; and a distinct distrust of foreigners who come to Russia. All are trends that Yeltsin has endorsed. With regard to the archives specifically, he personally has issued the decrees and regulations that have conferred so much decision making on the KGB's successors. And he has, at the very least, turned a blind eye to what has become a system of special privileges when it comes to access. A Moscow journalist, bemoaning the fact that the presidential archives are closed to all except those with political connections, observed: "It's regrettable that this all is done in the president's name, in his domain, and with his help. One wants to believe that he's done it unintentionally and was ill-informed."[97] Unfortunately, this does not seem to be the case.

Chapter Nine

1995: THE KGB'S DOMAIN REVISITED

> Earlier the KGB was under the strict control of the party. . . .
> In the absence of the CPSU and in our state of undeveloped
> democracy, our security organs, left to their own devices
> in watching over the leadership of the country, are
> becoming especially dangerous.
> *(Journalist Rustam Sabirov in the*
> Independent Gazette, *March 1995)*

B Y THE SPRING OF 1995, shortly before President Clinton's trip to Moscow to commemorate VE-Day with President Yeltsin, Western experts had divided themselves into two distinct camps in their prognoses for democracy in Russia. The optimists saw considerable progress in Russia's political and economic transition since the Soviet Union had been dissolved three and a half years earlier, and they expected this progress to continue. To be sure, there had been a few setbacks, such as Yeltsin's bloody confrontation with the Russian parliament in October 1993 and the December 1994 invasion of Chechnia. Economic woes had taken their toll on the Russian people. And Russia's new assertiveness vis-à-vis the "near abroad" was disquieting. But the overall picture from the optimists' point of view was favorable. They cited the flourishing retail trade in Russia's cities, the shops filled with abundance, and the slowly decelerating inflation rate. The independent media were more vocal than ever; and political parties were already preparing for the parliamentary elections scheduled for December 1995.[1]

The pessimists saw things much differently; their prognosis for Russia's future was grim. The rising tide of street violence, ethnic disturbances, and organized crime, the growing impoverishment of what had become a large underclass in Russia, the decline in essential social services, and the steady environmental decay alarmed members of this camp. So too did Yeltsin's increasing authoritarianism, manifested by a flurry of presidential decrees strengthening the powers of the government to impose its will on the citizenry. For the pessimists, the invasion of Chechnia was part of an alarming and dangerous trend toward the use of force in dealing with domestic opposition. Worse still, it had ominous implications for Russia's policy toward the newly independent states that were once part of the Soviet Union.[2]

Of course, there were too many wild cards at play for anyone to make firm predictions. But developments involving the security services gave grist to the pessimists' mill, especially regarding authoritarian political trends and Russian aggressiveness abroad. The Chechnia war, which had been masterminded by the FSK (Federal Counterintelligence Service), was still raging, with Moscow giving no signs that it was prepared to make concessions beyond a cosmetic cease-fire during the Clinton visit. Security chief Stepashin, about to be promoted to an army general, continued to talk tough. Foreign intelligence director Primakov's line on such issues as NATO and the partnership for peace was holding firm. And, in early April 1995, a new law was passed that broadened the powers of the security organs significantly.

WHAT'S IN A NAME?

In the January 1995 interview mentioned earlier, FSK deputy public relations chief Tomarovskii spoke about the impending new law on his organization and lamented the inconvenience of the fact that, yet again, there would be a name change. The FSK was to be called the Federal Security Service (Federal'naia Sluzhba Bezopasnosti), or FSB. This meant, he pointed out with frustration, that all the stationery would have to be replaced with new letterheads. Once the law passed the state Duma and was enacted three months later, however, it became clear that the change in designation was not frivolous. It reflected a distinct expansion in the functions of the agency headquartered at the Lubianka. It was appropriate that this be a "security" agency, rather than simply a counterintelligence agency. As Tomarovskii's boss, public relations chief Mikhailov, put it: "Counterintelligence has a narrower definition and means just opposing foreign secret services. We have been gradually commissioned with other tasks."[3]

The new Law on Organs of the Federal Security Service was noticeably comprehensive in scope, even by Russian standards.[4] Why did the Russian government deem it necessary to enact and publish yet another detailed law on its security service? (There is no equivalent act in United States legislation, which instead has a series of different laws and executive orders dealing with national security, intelligence, and counterintelligence.)[5] Again, as with earlier such laws, the government wanted to demonstrate its adherence to legality, yet the regulations themselves actually enabled the new agency to exercise sweeping powers.

The FSB regained a number of the rights that had been lost during its various post-KGB reorganizations. Its investigative authority was now fully restored by the law—although, as mentioned, the FSK had already been conducting criminal investigations on the basis of a presidential edict issued months before—and investigative detention prisons (fourteen in all) were back under its rubric, along with several special troop detachments. As might have been expected, the liberal press reacted negatively. One Moscow paper reported that "a special service far more powerful than the now defunct KGB has been created under the law."[6]

Even more significant was that the law gave the FSB the right to conduct intelligence operations both within the country and abroad for the purpose of "enhancing the economic, scientific-technical, and defense potential" of Russia (Article 2). For some observers this was a disquieting development. As one journalist put it: "The FSB's powers within the country, even if impressive, cannot shock anybody; everybody has long been accustomed to a complete free-for-all with respect to the special services (regardless of various party resolutions or laws). But the expansion of the FSB's sphere of activity beyond Russian borders was without precedent."[7] Although FSB intelligence operations were to be carried out in collaboration with the Foreign Intelligence Service, the specifics of the collaboration were not provided. It is hard to imagine that the FIS reacted favorably to this infringement on its sphere.

The new service, according to this law, also encroached on the functions of the Federal Agency for Government Communications and Information (FAPSI). The law instructed the FSB to detect signals from radio-electronic transmitters, to carry out cipher work within its own agency, and to protect coded information in other state organizations and even in private enterprises. It was not clear how the lines would be drawn between the functions of the FSB and FAPSI in ciphering and communications, which may account for the speculation that the latter would be merged into the FSB.[8]

A presidential edict signed in early April 1995 shed some light on the new arrangements. Aimed at protecting telecommunications systems, the edict established a procedure whereby FAPSI was authorized to license all ciphering and information security devices, while the FSB and the GRU (military intelligence) were to ensure that the licensing regulations were observed.[9] Nonetheless, there would doubtless be some overlap—and competition—in an area that involved access to data of crucial economic and strategic significance. This was especially so, given that FAPSI Chief Starovoitov was pushing for a stronger role for FAPSI. He began issuing warnings, for example, about the intensified threat to secret economic data (including that of the Russian Central Bank) from Western special services, a threat which he said called for greater security measures.[10]

THE DUMA'S ROLE

The law did reflect some input from democratically minded delegates in the Duma, which passed it on the second reading with some changes. The law says, for example, that "the exercise of counterintelligence activity affecting the secrecy of correspondence, telephone conversations, postal, telegraphic, and other messages" is allowed only with permission from the courts (Article 9). But the law also authorizes security police to enter private residences without hindrance if "there is sufficient reason to suppose that a crime is being or has been perpetrated there . . . or if pursuing persons suspected of committing a crime." In these cases, in accordance with other laws, the officer need only inform the procurator within twenty-four hours (Article 13).

As was the case with the FSK statute, the new law states that the president "directs the activity" of the security service, which is a federal executive organ. Article 23 pays lip service to parliamentary oversight by noting that the president, the Federal Assembly, and the judicial organs "monitor" the security service. But the only right that Duma deputies have in this regard is vague: "to obtain information regarding the activity of FSB organs in accordance with procedure laid down by Russian Federation legislation." (By contrast, United States legislation is very specific on the system of congressional oversight.)[11] The impression of vagueness was compounded by the fact that, according to this law, unpublished "normative acts" govern much of the FSB's procedure.

Why did the Duma pass such a law, particularly when it gave the president direct control of the new Federal Security Service? The process was not entirely smooth. There had been disagreement between the president and the Duma on certain points. Indeed, both sides had produced different versions of the draft law. At Yeltsin's suggestion, a conciliation commission was set up, comprising representatives of the Duma, the Federation Council (the parliament's upper house), and the president's staff, to iron out these differences. The commission's head was Duma deputy Aleksei Aleksandrov, a former police investigator for the Ministry of Internal Affairs (MVD).[12] He was outspokenly in favor of a law strengthening the security organs, because, in his opinion, they were the last bastion in the struggle against crime. Corruption had not infiltrated their ranks, he said, so it was important to prevent this from happening by improving their morale and efficiency with this new law.[13]

Two other members of the commission were Viktor Iliukhin, chairman of the Duma Committee on Defense and Security, and Iurii Baturin, the president's national security adviser and a legal expert. The fact that

Iliukhin was a member of the communist faction of the Duma undoubtedly helped the passage of the law. Iliukhin is a strong law and order man, who worries about spies. In his words: "Many believe that Russia is so friendly with everyone today, and all states are also so friendly with Russia, that allegedly there is no need to have strong and efficient security bodies or special services. This is not so, however. I can cite a dozen examples of special services and intelligence services of foreign countries stepping up their activities nowadays all over the Russian border and inside Russia."[14]

Apparently many in the Duma agreed with him. This is not surprising, given the hard-line political bent of its deputies, and perhaps they had cause for concern.[15] Also, of course, the issue of crime and violence was paramount on the minds of Russian citizens, so a law giving the security police extra powers to combat the problem was popular both in the Duma and in the country as a whole. Concerns about police abuse of individual rights faded in the face of worries about public safety. According to one report, the sentiment in the Duma was as follows: "A car, even a state car, will go in the direction in which the wheel is turned. A well-oiled security system will not 'run over' a dawdling freethinker for no reason, but will be able to protect citizens from gangsters, society from upheavals, and the state from being undermined and destroyed by its open and covert enemies."[16]

YELTSIN'S EDICT AGAINST FASCISM

In addition to the specter of foreign subversion and criminalization of society, another threat to Russia was looming on the horizon—fascism. By the spring of 1995 the term "fascism" or "neo-fascism" had become a growing concern in Russian political circles, especially those close to the president. Fascism, according to the Yeltsinites, was spreading at an alarming rate and something had to be done about it. Authorities had tried unsuccessfully to prosecute Viktor Bezverkhi, a well-known St. Petersburg anti-Semite who wrote a book calling for the extermination of all Jews, and Aleksei Vedenkin, leader of the right-wing party, Russian National Unity, who threatened to kill two human rights activists in the Duma, Sergei Kovalev and Sergei Iushenkov. In the view of the Yeltsin administration, more effective measures were needed to combat the phenomenon of fascism.[17]

Was the government exaggerating the problem? To be sure, manifestations of fascism were becoming more and more noticeable. Jewelry and T-shirts emblazoned with swastikas were reportedly big sellers in Moscow shops. Journalist Yevgenia Albats claimed that, as of early May

1995, there were forty-three profascist organizations and 154 profascist newspapers operating in Russia.[18] Nonetheless, as Valerii Solovei observed in *Nezavisimaia gazeta*, fascist groups exist in almost every state, and their mere existence does not mean they represent a danger to society. The groups that were considered fascist in Russia lacked the necessary strategies, organization, and political objectives to achieve real influence. In Solovei's view, the Yeltsin administration was using the antifascist campaign to "demonize political opponents" and also to repair the damage in relations between Yeltsin and the democrats, who had lost faith in Yeltsin because of the Chechnia invasion. Fighting fascism was a cause that appealed to democrats and, in drawing attention to Russian fascists, Yeltsin made his own authoritarianism and nationalism seem moderate by comparison.[19]

However serious the disease of fascism was in Russia, Yeltsin's proposed cure offered little solace to democratic reformers. His sweeping Edict on Combatting Fascism and Other Forms of Political Extremism, issued at the end of March 1995, was a glaring example of the arbitrary approach to lawmaking that had characterized his administration since its inception.[20] The edict began with a broad indictment of those who "fuel social, racial, ethnic, and religious hatred" and political extremists who carry out other "anticonstitutional activities." Among other things, the edict ordered the security police to arrest and prosecute people "disseminating printed matter, film, photographic, audio and video material designed to propagate fascism, and incite social, racial, ethnic, or religious hatred." It also instructed security authorities to prohibit public meetings and demonstrations organized by groups that arouse such hatred.

Using these broad categories, security police could round up not just people like Bezverkhi and Vedenkin, but anyone who voiced opposition to the Yeltsin regime. They could, in theory, prevent any political group from publicly demonstrating. Apparently anticipating criticism of the edict on these grounds, the authors included a clause stating that the Russian Academy of Sciences should within two weeks submit to the president's State-Law Administration a "scientific explanation of the concept of 'fascism' and other concepts and terms" so that the required amendments to criminal legislation could be made. This would be a challenging task. How would they give a precise legal definition to such terms as "fascism" and "political extremism"? What does it mean "to arouse social hatred"?

Meanwhile, because the edict went into effect the day that it was signed, it was up to the security police to define these terms. Stepashin showed no hesitation in implementing Yeltsin's edict immediately. Just a few days after it appeared, he chaired a conference at the Lubianka on fighting fascism and political extremism. Even before the Duma acted upon the legislation, he said, manifestations of fascism had to be quelled. His agency would begin right away by tracking down the financial sources of fascist periodicals and seizing extremist printed matter.[21] With the new law changing the FSK into the Federal Security Service about to be enacted, Stepashin and his men would be equipped with unprecedented legal powers to pursue Yeltsin's agenda.

STEPASHIN'S NEW TITLE

The directorship of the new Federal Security Service carried with it the title of army general, the highest military rank. No security chief had achieved this rank since the last KGB leader, Kriuchkov, so this was a major achievement for Stepashin, who only a few years earlier had been a minor official in the MVD. Stepashin's promotion came as a surprise to those who had been predicting his dismissal because of the botched Chechnia invasion. A Moscow journalist had reported in early January: "A frantic search has begun for scapegoats to blame for the bungling of the operation. . . . Although the chiefs of the internal affairs and defense ministries have at least one card to play—their soldiers are dying—the FSK has nothing to hide behind. Even the CIA did a better job of handling the Contras."[22]

In February 1995, a Russian general, Evgenii Podkolzin, had stated publicly that the heavy losses among military troops in Chechnia and their failures in battle were largely attributable to faulty intelligence information provided by the FSK. The timing was bad, he said. Public opinion had not been adequately prepared for the invasion, and it was pointless to start hostilities at a time of year when conscripts who had served their time were discharged. This meant that trained servicemen were replaced by inexperienced ones. Also, the severe winter months in the Caucasus were the worst time to wage a campaign. As for reports on the fighting capability and armaments of the enemy, they were misleading. This too was the fault of the FSK, the general said, because the GRU (the military intelligence agency) had not become involved with intelligence gathering in Chechnia until after the invasion began.[23]

FSK public relations chief Mikhailov had been quick to respond to the charges, pointing out that General Podkolzin did not take part in the operation and therefore did not know the facts. The generals directly in charge, he claimed, had praised the FSK for its intelligence.[24] Indeed, it did seem far-fetched to blame the FSK for failing to draw the above-mentioned considerations about timing to the attention of military generals. These were facts about which the latter should have been aware. And it is hard to imagine that the GRU was not gathering military intelligence before the invasion. Military intelligence was, after all, the job of the GRU, not the FSK. (In fact, another source made the equally unlikely claim that presidential bodyguard Korzhakov had prevented GRU intelligence reports from reaching the president, because the GRU was recommending against the invasion.)[25] But the failure to anticipate the fierce Chechen resistance to the invasion could be blamed, in part at least, on Stepashin and his agency. Even a fleeting knowledge of the Chechen people and the impact that past Russian repressions had on the Chechen attitude toward Russia would have been enough to predict that they would fight to the death.[26]

Nonetheless, if Yeltsin had lost faith in Stepashin because of Chechnia, he was not showing it. Stepashin's high public visibility in the months after the invasion and his authoritative statements on Chechnia defied speculation that he was about to lose his job. And he exhibited no signs that he regretted the decision for an all-out assault. In January, at the very time Russian Prime Minister Viktor Chernomyrdin of Russia was meeting with a delegation of Chechen officials in Moscow to discuss terms of a possible cease-fire, Stepashin, from his outpost in Mozdok, dismissed the possibility of any negotiations: "I'm categorically against carrying on political talks with people representing Dudaev's regime," he told reporters.[27] In May 1995 he discounted the possibility of a quick resolution to the Chechen war: "I would like to note that we do not hope for an easy settlement of the conflict. That is why the FSB [successor to the FSK] has created a department for the Chechen republic, one of the biggest territorial divisions, to include a task force to fight banditisim."[28] That Stepashin's uncompromising line on Chechnia held sway over the more dovish views of others in the Yeltsin administration gave the impression that his status in the government had not declined. But, as events would show, he was actually on shaky ground, and the predictions of his demise eventually proved true.

KORZHAKOV'S BYZANTINE COURT

Adding to the speculation about Stepashin were rumors of his intense competition with Korzhakov, the éminence grise of the Kremlin, whose influence over Yeltsin—often compared by Russians with that of Rasputin over Tsar Nicholas II—had become the talk of Moscow by this time. The Russian media's obsession with Korzhakov had begun with the raid on the Most Bank in early December 1994, which was carried out by his security forces. As Korzhakov himself noted in a January interview with the paper *Argumenty i fakty*, "I can name the date when this 'tidal wave' [of negative publicity] began—2 December of last year, when our personnel neutralized the Most Group security personnel."[29]

The Most affair continued to have repercussions, with the liberal press decrying Korzhakov's attempts to intimidate Yeltsin's critics. The media also reacted strongly to a publication in *Izvestiia* of a memorandum from Korzhakov to Chernomyrdin, outlining the reasons why the Russian government should not allow free access to Russian oil pipelines by abolishing state licensing and quotas on protection and export of oil.[30] What business, it was asked, did Korzhakov, the president's bodyguard, have with oil? Korzhakov again tried to defend himself, in a letter to *Izvestiia*, saying that everyone, including the chief of the president's security service, had the right to express his opinion freely.[31] But his explanations did not persuade the independent media. As *Izvestiia* put it: "When it is a question of oil—a commodity that brings in billions of dollars every year—the preservation of a system of privileges in this field, instead of equal rights for all, makes it possible for a bureaucrat 'to make a millionaire' of a businessman, at his own discretion. It also gives the bureaucrat himself such opportunities for selling his favors that all talk of a struggle against corruption becomes simply laughable."[32]

The hue and cry over Korzhakov's involvement in the government's economic affairs continued. In early February *Izvestiia* published an article on the creation of a special joint stock company for oil exports that was to fund the presidential staff's Administration of Affairs.[33] It was quite a coincidence, the author observed, that this new stock company was included on the list of oil traders just a month after Korzhakov's memorandum to Chernomyrdin. The author also claimed that Korzhakov was overseeing the state company, Rosvooruzhenie, set up in late 1993 for selling government arms abroad. These reports prompted the following commentary on Korzhakov from *Nezavisimaia gazeta*:

> Authoritative political observers continue to state that the effect of this government official on Russian policy is growing. The country's chief bodyguard is determining the strategy of oil industry development; is dealing with arms trade issues; is an expert in the banking business, nuclear power engineering, nonferrous metallurgy; has his own opinion on privatization and so forth. . . . Aleksandr Korzhakov is no longer satisfied with his task of only providing physical security for the head of state.[34]

Next came a claim that Korzhakov had created an election "slush fund" for Yeltsin out of his alleged illegal earnings. According to the journalist Sergei Parkhomenko, the upcoming parliamentary and presidential elections would require large sums of money for the Yeltsin camp, money that was to come from "rake-offs" from the arms, oil, and precious-metals trade. Parkhomenko offered further evidence that Korzhakov was deeply involved in controlling arms sales abroad, citing the creation in late December 1995 of a State Committee for Military Technology Policy which was directly under the president and run by Korzhakov and his protégés.[35] Moreover, all key jobs in Rosvooruzhenie, according to Parkhomenko and other sources, were in the hands of former Chekists who were Korzhakov men. By this time Rosvooruzhenie was being investigated by the procurator-general in connection with the unexplained disappearance of large sums of money, but few expected the investigation to result in charges, because the acting procurator-general, Iliushenko, was a Yeltsin loyalist.[36]

Although Korzhakov was the ultimate sponsor of these operations on behalf of Yeltsin, the man actually running things, according to Parkhomenko, was another "Rasputin," General Georgii Rogozin, who was "feared and hated by hundreds of people."[37] Rogozin, dubbed the "Black Magician" in Yeltsin's circles, was a longtime veteran of the KGB. He had earned his stripes in military counterintelligence and then worked in the late 1980s in the KGB Institute for the Study of Security Problems. Having survived the upheaval of the August 1991 coup attempt, Rogozin moved into the presidential apparatus, becoming a deputy to Korzhakov in the Presidential Security Service (SBP) and heading the team of experts that provide advice to Yeltsin. Described by Yeltsin insiders as a devotee of the occult, Rogozin reportedly studied the stars in producing policy analyses and recommending appointments. More ominous, however, was his habit of spying on other members of the administration, creating an atmosphere of paranoia among Yeltsin's advisers.

Parkhomenko, a proreform journalist with a solid reputation, based his story on interviews with numerous officials close to the Yeltsin administration, so it cannot be dismissed as a fantasy. Even allowing for exaggerations, we can conclude that Korzhakov and his men were doing a great deal more than just guarding the president. If the reports of financial illegalities had any credence, Yeltsin was surrounded with corrupt power seekers whose main concern was keeping him in office so they could reap financial rewards. Yeltsin's health problems—which led to a lengthy hospital stay in July 1995 because of a heart ailment—offered the Korzhakov group even more latitude in pursuing its aims.

DEVELOPMENTS WITHIN THE GUARD DIRECTORATE

What role were Barsukov and the GUO (Main Guard Directorate) playing in these Byzantine intrigues? As noted earlier, Korzhakov's Presidential Security Service was now independent from Barsukov's guard directorate, and Korzhakov was no longer Barsukov's deputy. From the operational point of view, however, this change was not all that significant. The two officials had worked together for a long time—Barsukov had been Korzhakov's boss in the "ninth"—and still cooperated closely. They shared the analytical department that had begun monitoring the political and economic situation in the country. As one observer wrote: "It is difficult to understand where the GUO ends and the Presidential Security Service begins; the two conduct joint measures and have a common press service and certain other subdivisions."[38]

As the successor to the KGB's Ninth Directorate, the GUO, together with Korzhakov's service, had continued to grow. Its staff reportedly had increased from 8,000 to more than 20,000 by late 1994 in order to guard Russia's highest leadership, its offices, cars, apartments, dachas, and a variety of secret "objects of state importance." As mentioned earlier, the GUO was authorized by law to engage in investigative operations. GUO officers thus could shadow people, tap telephones, and so on. According to press reports, Barsukov's GUO had an unlimited budget and was even buying sophisticated Western technology in order to bug offices within the Kremlin.[39] Whose offices were these? Asked in an interview whether he was one of the targets, Yeltsin's national security adviser Iurii Baturin responded discreetly: "Because of my position, I know the technical possibilities of different special services. For this reason, I follow this rule: neither in my office, nor on the telephone, nor anywhere else do I say anything that I could not say publicly."[40]

The GUO, then, was yet another agency with functions overlapping those of Stepashin's service. With the powerful FAPSI (communications and information), which reportedly had unlimited technical capabilities for monitoring communications and gathering intelligence, the security and intelligence bureaucracy of the Russian Federation was more bloated than ever.[41] Indeed, yet another department for "information gathering" by technical means had cropped up at around this time: the so-called Administration of Informational and Documentational Security for the President's Administration. This department, under the authority of Chief of Staff Sergei Filatov, reportedly was asserting itself over FAPSI.[42]

The proliferation of agencies that guarded, carried out surveillance and wiretapping, or conducted other "operational-investigative measures" was confusing, to say the least. As one Russian commentator observed wryly, "it used to be simpler and easier to understand: you were being bugged either by the KGB or the MVD. But currently one cannot be sure."[43]

Why had the Yeltsin administration created such a large and seemingly unwieldy security structure? To be sure, there was also overemployment in the KGB during the Soviet period, thanks to spy-mania and the intolerance for political dissent. But the KGB was a hierarchical organization where responsibilities were at least clearly delineated. And there was so much fear of the KGB in society that a little went a long way when it came to internal political controls. The Yeltsin administration, by contrast, felt itself besieged by political opposition and threatened by the growing violence in the country. Hence, the more security, the better. According to one source:

> The "niners" [staff of the KGB's Ninth Directorate] sufficed to guard persons and facilities across the entire territory of the Soviet Union. Since that time, the country has diminished perceptibly, but the guard has spread out. Previously, for example, ten or twenty guards were sufficient for the entire *nomenklatura* dacha settlement, whereas today, every individual dacha is guarded by up to 20 GUO officers. . . . In addition, the number of specialists engaged in electronic surveillance and wiretapping has recently risen sharply.[44]

This is not to mention the heightened security presence required in certain "hotspots" on Russian territory, particularly in the North Caucasus and of course in Chechnia, where Stepashin's service had opened a large office.

FURTHER STEPS TOWARD REINTEGRATION

In addition to expanding its domestic security agenda, the Russian government was becoming more ambitious in the "near abroad." This may explain why the April 1995 law authorized the FSB to engage in intelligence gathering along with the FIS and to establish formal relationships with the special services of foreign states, concluding treaties with them in accordance with FSB "normative acts" (Article 13). Here "foreign states" refers primarily to the former republics of the Soviet Union that are part of the CIS.

In fact, the CIS security services had already decided "to pool their efforts" before the law was enacted. In mid-March 1995, a two-day conference of the heads of the twelve CIS services was held in Moscow. Before the conference, a KGB official, Iurii Demin, had said that there would be no organized structure, just loose cooperation, among the different services.[45] But things turned out differently. The participants voted unanimously to set up a permanent secretariat, headquartered in Moscow and chaired by Stepashin, to coordinate their operations. Sharing a common data bank (also based in Moscow), they agreed to cooperate in fighting organized crime, drug smuggling, terrorism, and espionage on the part of "nearby foreign countries." A final accord, dealing with such issues as extradition of criminals and other legal problems, was signed at a meeting of CIS security chiefs in Georgia at the end of May.[46]

These agreements hardly came as a surprise, since the Russians had been cooperating bilaterally with their fellow CIS services all along. Nonetheless, the signing of formal accords was significant because it meant that Moscow has abandoned all pretense of noninterference in the domestic security affairs of other CIS states. How, it might be asked, could a state maintain its independence if it shared with other states its information on suspected criminals, spies, and other security threats, even allowing these states to have legal jurisdiction on its territory? Would not the exchange of security personnel among the CIS states create opportunities for them to gather intelligence on each other? Given that the Russians would be directing this common security effort and coordinating its operations, they of course had the most to gain. Indeed, this is doubtless why Stepashin had been promoting cooperation so vigorously. But his CIS counterparts probably needed little persuading, since they were used to cooperating with the Russians from KGB days and may have welcomed Moscow's support. In Stepashin's words: "It is no chance occurrence that the special services of republics of the former USSR got together recently and reached agreement on a whole range of issues . . . that will coordinate the efforts of our special services. No one came out a winner as a result of the collapse of the service's former system—everyone lost."[47] Now things were returning to normal. The KGB was gone in name, but it was returning in spirit.

A similar process was continuing with the border services, although there were sticking points that prevented a CIS border treaty from being adopted by all states. At the end of May 1995 in Minsk, representatives from seven CIS states initialed cooperative agreements on guarding external CIS borders.[48] Turkmenistan, Uzbekistan, Azerbaidzhan, Moldova, and Ukraine did not sign the draft. Turkmenistan already had a bilateral agreement with Russia, so its failure to sign meant little in practice. Ukrainian officials adhered to their stance that, as an independent state, Ukraine found the idea of a formal CIS external border unacceptable.[49] But Chief Nikolaev of the Russian border troops was optimistic that the remaining states would join the treaty in the near future. As he expressed the situation earlier: "Unlike a united Europe, for example, we do not need to unite: we used to be one state and many ties have not yet been disrupted, inter alia, a single border has been preserved to a large decree."[50]

The conflict along the Tadzhik-Afghan border intensified during the first months of 1995. Despite efforts at maintaining a cease-fire, armed clashes between Russian border guards and Afghan-supported Tadzhik rebels were occurring with increasing frequency.[51] Moscow continued to declare its unswerving support for the communist Tadzhik government of President Rakhmanov by means of economic aid, military backing for the Tadzhik Army, and a CIS "peacekeeping" force of over 1,500 men. For his part, Nikolaev made it clear that his 18,000 troops had no intention of withdrawing from the Tadzhik border.

His views were supported by members of different Duma factions who visited the Tadzhik border in April 1995. The group, which included the right-wing political leader Zhirinovskii, favored strengthening the border force there. Russia had a tremendous stake in preserving its dominance in this area by preventing a possible political takeover by the anticommunist, Islamic oppositionists, especially since there are close to twenty million Muslims within Russia who deeply resent Russian policies after the war in Afghanistan, the Tadzhik conflict, and the Chechnia invasion. "If we abandon Tadzhikistan today," Nikolaev stressed, "new sponsors will immediately come on the scene."[52]

The belief that Russia's strategic interests extended to the CIS states and the consequent "urge to reintegrate" was not confined to Russia's security and intelligence apparatus. This was a sentiment that was widely shared in the Yeltsin administration, although it was not always expressed so explicitly. Even Foreign Minister Andrei Kozyrev, who had a reputation for being moderate and democratically minded, had begun talking about Russia's interests in the "near abroad" with a new assertiveness. He surprised many in the West, for example, by stating in April 1995 that Russia would not hestitate to send its troops into any CIS country where the rights of Russian minorities were being violated.[53] This was unusually tough talk for Kozyrev, but it was in keeping with a general trend in the government that could be called "neo-imperialist," a trend that had become especially noticeable since the invasion of Chechnia. Although Chechnia is part of the Russian Federation and so technically cannot be termed a victim of Russian imperialism, Russia's war against Chechnia has illustrated that it would not hestitate to use military force to defend its interests against recalcitrant non-Russian national groups.

THE FOREIGN INTELLIGENCE SERVICE ON THE OFFENSIVE

Judging from their statements, FIS Chief Primakov and his colleagues at Iasenevo have been strong supporters of this neo-imperialist trend. Although Primakov has not said much about Chechnia, he made a point of warning about Muslim extremism in his above-mentioned public report of September 1994. In fact, this report, an unprecedentedly forceful assertion of Russian prerogatives toward other nationalities, presaged the Chechnia invasion and the subsequent hawkish stand on the CIS taken by officials like Kozyrev.[54] Once the Chechnia war began, the FIS turned to the problem of repairing Russia's damaged image abroad. In the words of one official: "We see our task as making sure that public figures abroad understand correctly the events in Chechnia. We are trying to somehow keep them away from incorrect appraisals, unreasoned responses, hasty political decisions." Another important task, this official added, was "to facilitate the integration process in the near abroad."[55]

When Primakov first took his job as head of the FIS, political observers viewed him as a transitional figure, a holdover from the Gorbachev era who would soon disappear from the scene. By early 1995, however, he had been in his post for over three years, had given three major foreign policy statements, and, as a full member of the Security Council, was a key player on Yeltsin's national security team, meeting with Yeltsin every Monday morning to brief him on developments abroad. How to explain Primakov's staying power and his obvious success at maintaining the influence of the FIS on policymaking? According to one source: "An experienced analyst at the head of the secret service, ready to work for the new power, he was of obvious use. Furthermore, it is risky to pester intelligence services too much—the authorities realize well to what international and domestic scandals the secret service is susceptible."[56] As a longtime member of the foreign policy establishment who was used to working with the KGB, Primakov had brought continuity to the FIS during the difficult transitional period. While taking into account the dramatic changes in the international environment, he gave the foreign intelligence service a mission that carried on many of the KGB's traditional functions.

Economic intelligence gathering is a good example of this continuity of mission. Toward the end of the Soviet period, as the Kremlin leadership became aware that the country was falling behind the West in many key technological areas, the KGB's First Chief Directorate (FCD), together with the GRU (military intelligence agency), developed an ambitious program of acquiring Western technological secrets, for both military and nonmilitary use.[57] According to Primakov's first deputy, Trubnikov, by 1995 the FIS had broadened this type of intelligence gathering to include the entire range of economic relations between Russian enterprises and Western economic firms. FIS officers were busy studying markets, brokering deals, especially in the area of arms and strategic raw materials, and keeping track of Russian capital going abroad.[58] In principle, the FIS performs these services only for enterprises belonging to the Russian state. Its spokespersons have denied reports, for example, that the FIS supplies intelligence to private firms like the Most group or Menatop Bank.[59] Nonetheless, former foreign intelligence officers who are now working for these firms at the very least use their contacts with the FIS to gain inside information.

This new economic mission may explain why the FIS took an active role in the controversial deal Russia made to sell nuclear reactors to Iran.

Despite strong objections from the United States, which has continuously expressed concern about Iran developing a nuclear military potential, Russia decided to proceed with the sale in the spring of 1995. (The Russian government did, however, concede to American requests for certain restrictions that would make it more difficult for Iran to use the reactors for military purposes.) The FIS had actively promoted the deal, launching a strong propaganda campaign in its defense. In late March, when the FIS issued a report on the proposed extension of the Nuclear Non-Proliferation Treaty (which was about to expire), FIS leaders took the opportunity to speak out strongly in favor of the Iran deal.

General Gennadii Evstaf'ev, head of the FIS directorate dealing with arms and nuclear proliferation, claimed that the proposed nuclear reactors did not contain weapons-grade plutonium and therefore could not be used for developing a bomb. Furthermore, he said, Iran was a signatory to the nonproliferation treaty and consequently its nuclear activity could be supervised by the International Atomic Energy Agency. And finally, according to data collected by his agency, the Iranian nuclear weapons program was in an embryonic state and would not produce results for years.[60] Taking a more forceful stance, Primakov stated unequivocally: "The FIS has clearly defined its position on this delicate problem, which is now a bone of contention in Russian-U.S. relations. If the Americans again manage to impose their will on us and to thwart the deal . . . no one will be able to accuse the FIS of disregarding national interests."[61] Here again Primakov was issuing a strong statement of opposition to American attempts to influence Russian policy shortly before a planned meeting between Yeltsin and Clinton.

Primakov also protested again against American plans to expand NATO. These plans, he said, "sprang from the desire of certain forces to deprive Russia of great-power status." In order to create favorable conditions for reform, he explained, Russia had to retain this status.[62] Primakov's views on NATO were hardly unique; most of Yeltsin's advisers and members of his administration voiced similar objections to NATO expansion.[63] But the implication of his comments was clear: the FIS was not going to be silent when it came to key foreign policy decisions.

It was remarkable that the Foreign Intelligence Service was exerting such influence on Russian policy when, in comparison with its manpower and resources in the Soviet period, it was operating on a significantly lesser scale, without a vast agent network in eastern Europe at its disposal and cooperation from the security services of Soviet satellite states. In this respect the FIS was worse off than its domestic counterpart. Although, in aftermath of the dissolution of the Soviet Union, Russia's internal security services lost the territorial branches that belonged to the Soviet republics, by 1995 they had accomplished a great deal toward reconstituting their former organization. The only clear losses were the services of the former KGB in the Baltic states. By contrast, the adjunct organizations of the KGB in eastern Europe were now under the control of truly independent states. Nonetheless, the FIS had not been subjected to the continual reorganizations and changes at the top that the internal security services had endured. And Primakov was seemingly able to insulate his organization from the intense political struggles that were going on in government circles. From this standpoint, his main domestic counterpart, Stepashin, was much more vulnerable.

THE BUDENNOVSK CRISIS AND THE FALL OF STEPASHIN

Counterterrorism was a key function of Stepashin's service, and he and his colleagues frequently boasted of how well trained and well equipped their men were for counterterrorist missions. In the autumn of 1994 Stepashin personally presided over special exercises to prepare antiterrorist units for operational combat, and his agency (both the FSK and its successor, the FSB) even had a special directorate for combatting terrorism. Its activities were coordinated with the special units of the MVD and with the Alpha group, which was still under the formal command of Barsukov's GUO, but apparently was at the disposal of the other security agencies for special missions.[64]

Stepashin thus had considerable responsibility on his shoulders when faced with the terrorist crisis that erupted on 14 June 1995—the seizing of several hundred hostages by Chechen rebels in the North Caucasus city of Budennovsk. The crisis was eventually resolved by Prime Minister Chernomyrdin, who talked the rebels, led by Shamil Basaev, into releasing their captives in exchange for being allowed to escape back into Chechnia. But resolution came only after an unsuccessful storming of the hospital where the hostages were held, a storming which resulted in several deaths and injuries. (Altogether, 120 people were killed during the hostage crisis.) The episode caused a storm of protest within the general population, which saw it as further proof that the war in Chechnia was a mistake, and led the Duma to declare a vote of no-confidence in the Chernomyrdin government on 21 June.

Clearly Yeltsin had to do something to appease the parliament and avert a deeper crisis. Following a session of his Security Council on 29 June, Yeltsin announced the resignation of three federal officials—MVD Chief Erin, Deputy Prime Minister for Nationalities Nikolai Egorov, and Stepashin, along with the governor of the Stavropol region (where Budennovsk is located). The gambit worked and the Duma subsequently backed down on its no-confidence measure.[65]

Interestingly, the Duma had demanded the resignation of Erin, Egorov, and Defense Minister Grachev, but not that of Stepashin. Why was he sacrificed? Stepashin clearly bore some blame for the Budennovsk crisis. He had flown there along with Egorov and Erin, who directed the operation, to help with the hostage situation, so it might have been difficult for Yeltsin to keep him on while firing the other two. According to experts on terrorism, it was a serious mistake to have the Alpha troops storm the hospital. First, conditions did not call for it: hostages were not being murdered and negotiations on their release had not yet reached a deadlock. Furthermore, the situation was unfavorable for the troops, since the hospital complex could not be taken in one quick strike. The Alpha unit was also ill-equipped, with only rifles and no other armor, and did not have sufficient time to prepare for the attack on the hospital.[66]

Stepashin could also be blamed for his agency's failure to detect plans for the attack on Budennovsk beforehand. Men from the FSB were everywhere in Chechnia. Why had they not managed to infiltrate this group of rebels or at least gather some intelligence on them? As a critic from the government-controlled paper *Rossiiskaia gazeta* put it:

> How did the bandits manage to travel hundreds of kilometers unhampered? Representatives of the MVD and FSB kept emphasizing to journalists at press conferences: the bandits had prepared carefully for their operation. It is strange to hear that. Dudaev and his crew had declared many times that they would take the hostilities from Chechnia to Russia and had publicly threated terrorism. So they were prepared, but not, it appears, the MVD and the FSB?[67]

Although Stepashin's culpability in the Budennovsk affair was undeniable, this was probably not the only reason for his dismissal, especially since the Duma was not demanding his resignation, so it could not be used by Yeltsin as a "bargaining chip." Stepashin had, after all, committed an even greater blunder in late 1994 when his officers had failed abysmally in their covert attempts to topple the Dudaev regime, and Yeltsin had not fired him. Neither had Yeltsin fired Erin, whose troops, responsible for policing captured areas of Chechnia, have been accused of looting and committing atrocities against the civilian population. Yeltsin had overlooked their mistakes until the Budennovsk debacle, which may have been the last straw.

Nonetheless, he saved Pavel Grachev (at least for the time being), whose public credibility was much lower than that of Stepashin. Grachev's alleged involvement in corruption and the failure of the Russian Army to subdue the Chechens successfully and quickly had aroused universal scorn. And, as he admitted in a subsequent interview, Grachev too bore responsibility for the Budennovsk tragedy. His reconnaissance troops had let Basaev's men pass freely across Chechen territory, and the local army garrison in Budennovsk was unable to give sufficient support to the militia in the initial attack. Grachev claimed that he had in fact offered to resign at the fateful Security Council meeting. Yeltsin, he said, had accepted his proposal, along with Border Guards Chief Nikolaev, Prime Minister Chernomyrdin, and Federation Council Speaker Shumeiko, only to be outvoted by the others.[68] But if Yeltsin had really wanted to fire Grachev he could of course have done so; the Constitution gives him the right to appoint and remove the high command of the Russian armed forces. Yeltsin might also have dismissed Korzhakov and Barsukov, to whom the Alpha group was subordinated, but they escaped completely unscathed.[69]

Although Stepashin and Erin had served Yeltsin well, they were, in the end, dispensable. This was particularly true of Stepashin, who, unlike Korzhakov, Barsukov, and Grachev, had never been been close to Yeltsin personally. (There were no reports of his accompanying Yeltsin to the sauna, for example, as his predecessor Barannikov had done.) Grachev, moreover, for all his prevaricating during the October 1993 crisis, had in the end come through for Yeltsin. With the military playing an increasing role in suppressing internal disorder within the Russian Federation—there were 30,000 army troops guarding Moscow's streets and government installations at this time—Yeltsin had to have a minister of defense whom he could count on.[70]

As for Erin, Yeltsin did not toss him out into the cold. Much to everyone's surprise, he was appointed deputy chief of the Foreign Intelligence Service, supervising the struggle against organized crime internationally. According to one source:

> Yeltsin could not just say "no" to a Hero of Russia. [the title awarded to Erin after October 1993.] The last wish of a dismissed minister (just like somebody sentenced to execution) is a command. Soon afterward he had a conversation with FIS director Evgenii Primakov. Being well aware of the fact that there is no use being too uncompromising in such cases, Primakov decided to meet Yeltsin halfway by finding a special sinecure for his former colleague.[71]

For Stephasin there was no such redemption. As the fourth security chief to be fired in less than four years, he was out of a job. His dismissal, so soon after he had been made an army general and seemed to be riding high, revealed once again the vulnerability of this post. The chief of security and counterintelligence (MB, FSK, and FSB) was always on the "hot seat," particularly under a president like Yeltsin, who drew this agency into unsavory battles with his opponents and gave it carte blanche in risky domestic military operations. Given that he was not a veteran Chekist and brought little experience to the job, it is hardly surprising that Stepashin ran into problems. Although he vigorously and successfully fought to increase the powers of his agency, he did not have a group of loyal supporters within the FSB to support him. Below him were seasoned Chekist professionals, many of whom had resented the imposition of a young outsider as their chief.[72] Most important, however, was the increasing power and influence of the "Niners," led by Korzhakov and Barsukov, who, as events would show, had strong reasons for wanting Stepashin out of the picture.

MIKHAIL BARSUKOV'S NEW JOB

In keeping with its intense preoccupation with police and security matters, the Russian press was filled with speculation about who would replace the two fallen power ministers. The news about Erin's successor was not long in coming and not particularly surprising: he was Anatolii Kulikov, commander of the Russian forces in Chechnia and a deputy minister of internal affairs since 1992. Kulikov, widely perceived as a hawk, had been the MVD's commander in the North Caucasus before the collapse of the Soviet Union. As the man-on-the-spot in Chechnia, Kulikov seemingly bore direct responsibility for the behavior of MVD troops there. But the Yeltsin administration apparently did not see it that way.

The decision on Stepashin's successor was not announced officially until 24 July, when members of the FSB Collegium were invited to the sanatorium where Yeltsin was recuperating from his heart problem, so that the president personally could present the new director to them. This was none other than forty-seven-year-old Colonel General Mikhail Barsukov, erstwhile chief of the GUO. Barsukov's nomination was somewhat unusual. Barsukov had worked for years in the security services, but he had always served in the guards directorate, whose personnel were more like soldiers than policemen or spies. Indeed, by training Barsukov, who attended the Supreme Soviet Combined Arms Command School (Kremlin Cadets) and the Frunze Military Academy, before serving in the Kremlin Regiment, was a military man. Although crucial to the physical and political security of the leadership, the guards were traditionally on the periphery of the security services in the sense that they were not part of the investigative, counterintelligence, or intelligence apparatus. Under Yeltsin, however, the role of the guards had evolved from physical protection into broader security and intelligence functions. And, if Barsukov found himself lacking in experience, his new first deputy, Viktor Zorin, who would simultaneously be in charge of the FSB's Antiterrorist Directorate, would be a valuable asset. Zorin had headed the KGB's Seventh Directorate (surveillance) in the 1980s.[73]

Barsukov, by all accounts, was not in Yeltsin's confidence to the extent that Korzhakov was. Indeed, at first his only *entré* to Yeltsin was through Korzhakov. But, after the stormy period in the autumn of 1993, when Barsukov's troops had shown reluctance to support Yeltsin, Barsukov reportedly had gained Yeltsin's ear and began to accompany him on trips—both business and personal. In a portrait of Barsukov in *Komsomol'skaia pravda*, he was described as a lover of vodka who enjoyed presiding over receptions with foreign guests, during which he would get them drunk.[74] This brought to mind the infamous dinners at Stalin's dacha, when Beria, who oversaw the political police, would be the official toastmaster and force guests to imbibe more than they could handle. Indeed, the machinations of Korzhakov, Barsukov, Rogozin, et al. and their alleged attempts to influence decision making and appointments by underhanded means resembled the politics of the late Stalin period, when, with Stalin's mental and physical health declining, intrigue and infighting among Stalin's subordinates became especially intense.

The Barsukov appointment, which was accompanied by the transfer of the elite Alpha troop unit to the FSB, suggested that the men from the "Ninth" enjoyed unprecedented influence in the Yeltsin administration. For Korzhakov personally this was an especially important victory; he now had a trusted ally at the helm of the FSB. Stepashin may not have been an enemy, but he was his own person with his own agenda, which doubtless interfered with Korzhakov's plans at times. The new arrangement brought Yeltsin's guards and the FSB under a united leadership.

The real fruits of Korzhakov's victory came a week later, when a major reorganization within the president's administration was announced. According to a presidential edict, the "Russian Federation Presidential Security Service [SBP] is to be considered a state organ within the Russian Federation Presidential staff and an organ of day-to-day management in the system of federal organs of state protection." Unlike other bodies within the president's administration, however, the SBP would not be supervised by the chief of staff (Sergei Filatov), but would answer directly to the president. Furthermore, a simultaneous edict placed the management of the GUO, now headed by Barsukov's former deputy, Iurii Krapivin, under the control of the SBP, thus greatly enhancing Korzhakov's authority.[75]

Korzhakov, who had been promoted to the rank of Lieutenant General just three days earlier, was now the head of a significantly more powerful security service, and, with his friend Barsukov running the Lubianka, he had a direct line of influence over the FSB. In fact, some analysts interpreted the edict on the SBP, which conferred on it the management of "the system of federal organs of state protection," to mean that Korzhakov had gained control of all the security agencies. In the words of one journalist: "Is it possible that this colossal structure has been transferred to the jurisdiction of Mr. Korzhakov? This is not just a strengthening; it is nearly unlimited power on the verge of usurpation."[76]

What did all this mean for Yeltsin? In retrospect, it appears that his concession to the Duma was a convenient means of removing officials who might oppose the consolidation of the security apparatus under his administration. The SBP, which had no legal foundation in the Russian state—its statute was secret—and was totally removed from government controls, was now at the helm of the security services. Neither Filatov (who reportedly was close to Stepashin) nor Chernomyrdin, let alone the parliament had the authority to influence its operations.

In just a short time the balance of power among the security agencies had changed dramatically. The much-vaunted separation of functions and paring down of operations had become a fiction. With the elections looming just a few months away, Yeltsin's "security monster" would doubtless do all in its power to influence events in its favor. As *Segodnia* journalist Vera Selivanova observed not long after the law on the FSB was passed:

> In the context of the approaching election campaign, under cover of much-publicized political and economic events, absolutely uncontrolled by democratic mechanisms of any kind, and behind the backs of the population, a question is being decided that is, in fact, very important to that population—whether the state security system will become a system of state protection of citizens' security or whether it will gain strength and remain a system for the protection of the state against all citizens together and each of them individually.[77]

PARLIAMENT VERSUS THE YELTSINITES

However ominous these developments appeared, they must be viewed in the broader political context, which by the summer of 1995 featured the parliament in an increasingly activist role, particularly regarding Chechnia. Budennovsk was a catalyst for strengthening the opposition to Yeltsin's Chechnia policy from all sides of the political spectrum. Among the 241 deputies who voted in favor of dismissing the Chernomyrdin government in late June were not only those from the ultra-right parties, but also those from liberal groups like "Yabloko" and even some from Yeltsin's own party, Russia's Choice.[78]

It was at the Duma's insistence that the Russian Constitutional Court, led by Chairman Vladimir Tumanov, agreed to conduct hearings on the legality of two secret decrees issued by Yeltsin in December 1994 to authorize the assault on Chechnia. The hearings, which began on 10 July, amounted to a showdown between parliamentarians and representatives of the executive branch who defended Yeltsin's edicts before the court. One of those called by Duma deputies to testify against the president was his erstwhile human rights commissioner, Sergei Kovalev, who, rather ironically, had been dismissed from his human rights post as a result of a Duma vote against him in March 1995. Now the Duma was on his side. In retaliation for Kovalev's scathing criticism before the court, the Yeltsin administration announced in early August that the Human Rights Commission was dissolved, to be replaced by a "Division on Letters and Complaints Connected with Violations of Citizens' Rights" within the president's staff. Thus there would no longer be an independent watchdog agency to monitor abuses by the security police.[79]

Although the Constitutional Court ruled in favor of Yeltsin, the fact that the parliament was able to initiate a hearing at all was in itself encouraging. And clearly, the mounting parliamentary opposition to the war in Chechnia was what prompted the Yeltsin administration to set about brokering a peace agreement with Chechen leaders in late July 1995. The Duma, furthermore, had made some progress in the area of legislation, passing, on 20 July, the long-awaited new criminal code. The code, although criticized for its ambiguity in several areas, would theoretically enable law enforcement officers to prosecute those guilty of economic illegalities more effectively because it introduced a wide range of crimes previously unknown in Soviet jurisprudence.[80]

The urgency of the crime and corruption problem was an issue that most Russian politicians, in the parliament and in the Yeltsin administration, agreed on publicly. In early August 1995, the deputy director of the MVD's Department for Combatting Organized Crime reported that there were more than 8,000 gangs with 35,000 members in Russia. But would the new law actually improve things? This was not the view of a group of leading business people who attended the funeral of a prominent banker named Ivan Kivelidi, murdered on 4 August 1995 by an unknown assailant. They angrily criticized the government's failure to combat contract killings, suggesting that, since there had been virtually no convictions for these murders, the police might often be in league with the criminals.[81] The sentiment in the Duma was similar, but members had been able to do little about the problem, beyond calling for the resignation of police officials like Erin and creating a special commission on corruption, which seemed to have little effect. They had also refused to confirm Yeltsin's appointee Iliushenko as procurator-general, on the grounds that he was corrupt and ineffective. When the corruption reports about Iliushenko began to mount, Yeltsin was finally forced to let him go from his post as acting procurator in October 1995. But there was little reason to assume that his successor, Oleg Gaidanov, would do any better in the job.[82]

The Invisible Hand of the KGB?

In the view of many observers, corruption went well beyond the police; it was so widespread among the political leadership that it was motivating much of the Kremlin's domestic and foreign policy. Writing in *Moskovskii komsomolets*, Aleksandr Budberg discussed the tremendous profits that were made by arms trading to those involved in civil conflicts in places like Chechnia, Georgia, and Nagornyi-Karabakh. Drug smuggling, too, flourished during violent conflicts, because of more transparent borders and weaker controls. Thus, Budberg said, certain influential military and civilian officials had a strong incentive to keep conflicts smoldering and to suppress investigations of corruption and organized crime.[83]

Whoever the members of this "war lobby" were, beyond the obvious officials like Grachev and his cronies, the security services would be valuable and essential allies in such ventures.[84] Indeed, Korzhakov's involvement with arms and oil exports and the covert operations of Stepashin's service in the various conflicts within the CIS, as well as in Chechnia, lend credence to the theory that illegal profits were motivating many of the operations carried out by the security services.

But this was a murky picture, made all the more murky by the obsession of the Russian media with stories of conspiracy and villainy on the part of the former KGB. A group called "Feliks" (after the first chief of the political police), for example, was allegedly created in late 1991 by former KGB and GRU officers for the purpose of turning the course of Russian politics away from reform. Their plans were said to include the assassination of "insufficiently patriotic" and corrupt government officials, including Prime Minister Chernomyrdin.[85]

The "Feliks" group may well have been a phantom, conjured up for purposes of disinformation—indeed, some claimed that Korzhakov was behind the story. But the numerous unsolved killings of prominent public figures continued to suggest that the security services, like their KGB predecessors, were still in the business of political murder. This was the view of human rights activist Sergei Grigoriants, who announced at a press conference in mid-July that he saw the hand of the FSK/FSB in several recent suspicious deaths.[86] Public relations officials in the FSB of course vehemently denied Grigoriants's allegations. As FSB spokesman Sergei Vasilev put it: "The defenders of legality don't like us. We don't want them to like us, but we do ask for their respect. To go into detail with such gibberish as Grigoriants puts forth, we consider unwarranted. We have declared many times and we declare now: the FSB does not engage in political murders. Don't confuse us with the KGB."[87]

Among the more disturbing unsolved murders was that of American disaster relief expert Frederick Cuny, who was killed in April 1995 while on a mission to assess the needs of Chechen refugees. According to members of Cuny's family, who spent considerable time in Chechnia trying to ascertain what had happened to Cuny, the FSK/FSB deliberately spread disinformation to Chechen rebels that Cuny was a spy, so that they would kill him. What were the motivations? Cuny had written an article that was highly critical of the Russian military operation in Chechnia and he was working on behalf of the Soros Foundation, which Stepashin's service had on more than one occasion accused of being a cover for the CIA. Again the charges against the FSB met with a firm and indignant denial, this time by the chief of FSB public relations, Aleksandr Mikhailov. He dismissed the allegations as "nonsense" and even made the highly unlikely claim that Mr. Cuny was still alive, hinting that he worked for the CIA.[88]

If the security services were in fact behind any of these murders—and this probably will never be known for certain—their involvement had ominous implications for Russian politics, particularly with the elections looming. The rampant crime and violence were destabilizing enough in itself, but the possibility that some of it was generated from those in power was even more disturbing. Regardless of who was responsible, the authorities, in particular the FSB and MVD, seemed determined to prevent the crimes from being investigated effectively. Speaking of what of he called a "system of unsolved murders," the chairman of the Duma Subcommittee on Legislation in the Sphere of National Security, Aleksei Aleksandrov, said that he was convinced that these crimes could easily have been investigated successfully if the authorities had wanted to do so: "This situation makes me leery. It is generally not the growth of crime in the country that is frightening—this is ultimately objective—but the growth of unsolved crimes in respect to well-known persons. . . . I have the impression that someone is already prepared to say to the people: 'Well, now, have you had enough of democracy? It has brought you nothing but blood and screwups.'"[89]

Doing little to dispel the growing fears of police-inspired violence, the FSB began to show its mettle by openly employing some old, KGB-style tactics. In early August, for example, FSB authorities detained a Russian journalist at Groznyi Airport when she refused to hand over the film from her camera.[90] Then came the disturbing news that Viktor Orekhov, a hero to former dissidents, had been sentenced to three years in a strict-regime labor camp for illegal possession of firearms. (A gun had been found by the FSB in his home during an illegal search.) As a KGB officer in the 1970s, Orekhov had warned dissidents of imminent searches and arrests by the KGB, thereby saving many from prison. After being discovered by his employers, he was tried and sentenced to eight years in the camps, completing his term under Gorbachev. The investigator in his case, ironically, had been the current FSB deputy director and chief of the Moscow FSB, Anatolii Trofimov.[91] The KGB was getting its revenge for a second time.

There was a difference now, however. Whereas the story of Orekhov's initial arrest and sentence was circulated secretly in *samizdat* publications for the consumption of a small group of human rights activists, news of his second conviction appeared prominently on the pages of several popular and respected Russian newspapers—for the entire Russian public to read about. The message was clear: if the security services were going to resort to KGB methods, they would not enjoy the KGB's immunity from publicity. The press would call them to account for their actions.

If the forthcoming elections result in a parliament—and a president—with greater resolve to curb police powers and protect individual rights, such publicity may give rise to concrete and long-lasting measures to reform the Russian security apparatus. The security services, however, cannot be expected to stand by complacently and allow this to happen without a fight. They may conclude that Yeltsin's chances to remain Russian president are slim. But they can be counted on to do their utmost to preserve the political influence of other officials and politicians who want the KGB's successors to be just as powerful as the KGB.

Chapter Ten

CONCLUSION

> Sometimes one gets the impression that all of Russian life
> has been contaminated by these human by-products of
> the decomposition of communism.
> *(Vassily Aksyonov, 1994)*

FOUR YEARS after a euphoric Russian crowd, on 27 August 1991, desecrated the statue of Feliks Dzerzhinskii in front of KGB headquarters, the Lubianka, their action seemed more like an empty gesture than the symbol of the KGB's demise that it was meant to be. Lubianka still stood and, although there had been changes at the helm inside, the long-awaited reform of the security services had yet to happen. Indeed, by August 1995, the security services had recaptured much of the ground lost in the first days after the August 1991 coup.

This book, in tracing the evolution of the post-KGB security apparatus in Russia since 1991, has described the numerous reorganizations of the security services and the many and varied laws that have been passed to govern their activities. As the book demonstrates, instead of curbing the powers of the security services and narrowing their functions, these measures have only served to broaden their role.

Democratization has proceeded in Russia nonetheless. And, with parliamentary elections to take place in December 1995 and presidential elections coming in June 1996, there is reason to hope that Russia's political transition will continue in that direction. But, whatever democratic institutions are developed, they will remain fragile until the security services are reformed. Real, lasting democracy is incompatible with a security apparatus wielding the power and influence that it still holds in Russia.

As was pointed out at the beginning of this book, it is no simple matter to reform a security and intelligence apparatus that for decades had such a commanding role in politics and society. If we consider the countries that have made successful transitions to democracy in the late twentieth century, it becomes clear that it is much easier for a democratizing regime to come to terms with a powerful military than with a powerful security police. Samuel Huntington, in his book *The Third Wave*, describes how in Latin America the key force that reforming political leaders had to reckon with was the military. Reducing military involvement in politics was what Huntington calls the "praetorian problem" faced by these leaders. In order to depoliticize the military, the new governments—in countries like Brazil, Peru, and Uruguay—allowed the military to retain its autonomy and professionalism, while gearing it toward purely military missions. They removed internal security functions from the armed forces, but at the same time remained sensitive to concerns about the material status and resources of the military.[1]

It is much more difficult for democratic leaders to make such bargains with a repressive security police because, unlike the military, it has no legitimate role to play in a stable, democratic society beyond counterintelligence and fighting organized crime (ordinary law and order being a task of the regular police). Security police have a vested interest in preserving the old, totalitarian, or authoritarian system.[2]

Russia, then, cannot easily be compared with countries in Latin America that made transitions from authoritarianism to democracy because one of the main obstacles to democracy has been its security services. But what about the East European states, whose political structures were modeled after that of the Soviet Union? They too have had to deal with powerful secret police in overcoming the praetorian problem. How successful have the governments of eastern Europe been in reforming their security and intelligence services? Did four decades of police control permanently corrupt their societies? A brief look at the experiences of the these states may shed light on the problems Russia faces in making the transition to democracy and the possible course of its future political development.

THE EAST EUROPEAN EXPERIENCE

The new, postcommunist states in eastern Europe wanted to start with a clean slate and demonstrate their sincere efforts to create security agencies that conformed to democracy, but they also, like Russia, needed effective forces against terrorism, drug trafficking, and crime. And they relied on the security services for a host of other practical tasks. As one Czech official expressed it: "People are asking that we immediately dismantle the secret police, and they are right from a moral and legal point of view. But it would mean that there would be no passports or visas issued since they control those services, and so much more."[3] Clearly the new governments could not spend years creating new services from scratch, but neither could they allow their secret police to thwart the process of political reform.

The degree of success in meeting this challenge has varied considerably from country to country, depending of course on the extent to which democracy has been established.[4] All of the former Soviet satellite states have eliminated their old bureaucracies and abandoned communism as the official ideology. In the process of building new, democratic institutions, they have sought to redefine their security interests and establish legal structures that support real reforms in the security services. This has been a formidable task, given their past histories of secret-police repression. As one expert observed: "No other aspect of dismantling the communist structure has caused as much irritation and polarization of public opinion as deciding the fate of the secret services."[5]

Romania and Bulgaria, which had particularly ruthless and omnipotent security police in the communist period, have been the least successful in facing up to and overcoming the legacy of police repression. Only with regard to these two states do specialists consider it possible that the security police could recover its former power. Romania's Securitate was a machine of political terror that successfully subdued the population by instilling widespread fear.[6] As with the Soviet KGB, the main elements of Romania's Securitate were transformed after the collapse of the communist regime into separate agencies, but continued to function with the same personnel. They retained control of the secret-police archives and thus were able to keep a lid on public demands for retribution.[7]

Romania now has a relatively independent press, opposition parties, and a parliament, which has a special body for overseeing the revamped security services. But the proliferation of security and intelligence agencies operating under various government institutions—at least nine—has made parliamentary control difficult. Moreover, the ruling National Salvation Front is led by former communists who have been unwilling to rein in the security police. Gone are the days when innocent civilians were arrested in the night to disappear in Securitate prisons. But Romania still has a long way to go before its citizens can stop being concerned about the possibility of police repression.

Bulgaria's situation is similar. Efforts by its postcommunist government to reform the secret services have yielded mixed results. Because Bulgarian communism had a long, indigenous history and Bulgaria traditionally had friendly relations with Russia, postwar Soviet domination was not universally resented as it was in other satellite states.[8] Bulgaria was the Soviet Union's most obedient client state, and its secret police, whose organization and structure mirrored that of the KGB, never hesitated to carry out the KGB's orders. The majority of secret police officers were educated and trained in the Soviet Union, where they established personal contacts with their Soviet counterparts. The fact that there have been practically no dismissals means that many security personnel today have ties with their old colleagues in Russia. This may be one reason why police files remain inaccessible.

The restructured security services are now nominally controlled by the National Assembly, which is dominated by former communists who continue to resist full-scale reforms. Given that many Bulgarian government officials today worked closely with the secret police in the past, they have good reason to keep the archives closed and to avoid offending the security services by attempts to restrict their powers.[9]

However divisive the issue of confronting their history has been, the countries that have faced their pasts head on and rid themselves of the legacy of communism have been the most successful in achieving lasting reforms. The legacy of totalitarianism has been most decisively routed in Poland, Hungary, and the former Czechoslovakia, all of which had experience with democracy and Western-style legal systems before the Soviets imposed communism on them. Of the three countries, Poland has come the farthest in making the transition from communism. This is a reflection of the fact that communism was never as brutal in Poland as it was elsewhere and that throughout the 1980s Poland had a highly developed dissident movement. Even before the transfer of power from the communists to the dissidents in 1989, the Polish government had taken steps to undo the legacy of a Soviet-inspired totalitarian regime by introducing democratic freedoms and releasing political prisoners.[10]

Once the Solidarity-led government took charge, reform of the Polish Security Service began in earnest. In 1990 the Polish parliament disbanded the service, divided its functions among four new agencies, and introduced effective legal constraints on the activities of these agencies. Poland has not passed a lustration law, but it is grappling openly with the issue of what to do with its former secret police and collaborators. In the view of many Poles, if the government attempts to expose them all, it will unleash endless recriminations, but if it closes the door on the past completely it creates a hunting ground for blackmailers.[11]

The surprising victory of the communists in the September 1993 elections led to concerns that the process of democratic reform in Poland was reversing itself. But Poland is unlikely to witness a resurgence of old-style communists who would allow the police to regain their former powers and commit human rights abuses. Poland's dissident activity was so widespread that it resembled a genuinely grass-roots movement, striking a deep chord throughout the country. This experience made people conscious of the need to defend human rights and should have a lasting effect on the Polish people.

Czechoslovakia, which had experienced extreme political repression during the postwar years, was equally determined to destroy the legacy of its security services after the collapse of communism. During the first months after the "Velvet Revolution," the new government under President Václav Havel took significant steps to ensure human rights. Czechoslovakia's secret police, the StB, was officially disbanded in February 1990. The government then began the more fundamental task of establishing some of the basic pillars of a state based on the rule of law, such as an independent judiciary and a court system that would protect individual rights.[12]

The one dark spot in this otherwise bright picture of a successful transition to democracy was the lustration law, passed in October 1991 with the aim of preventing former communists, secret police, and collaborators from entering government service. As discussed earlier, the law was heavily criticized because it opened the way for human rights abuses. It introduced the idea of collective guilt and punishment for prior status rather than actions. And it relied on the files of the police which often were purposefully misleading. Within less than two years, over 200,000 people had been subjected to lustration.[13]

How is it that, in a country where democratic legal principles had been declared a top priority, a witch hunt of this nature could ensue? As the American writer Laurence Wechsler pointed out, the legacy of the StB was very much alive in Czechoslovakia and there was a general feeling that its former employees were still manipulating things behind the scenes.[14] When this collective paranoia wears off, the new Czech Republic, now separate from Slovakia, will doubtless tire of its anticommunist crusade. The fact that its new security services have been completely revamped and are under the firm control of a special council under the prime minister should help this process.

Hungary began reforming its security services in 1990, by dismantling its political police and purging those security officers who had abused human rights. A former Hungarian dissident observed: "The dissidents are now in the government; our enemies are now our friends. A big security force will be hard to justify."[15] Hungary introduced a tight system of controls on the former secret police. In the words of a Hungarian parliamentarian: "We need a system far stricter than those in well-established democracies. We have to watch our step."[16]

Although many secret police files in Hungary were destroyed, the issue of past collaboration with the communist regime and the police became the focus of intense debate. In the spring of 1993 the Hungarian National Assembly adopted a law on screening certain categories of former police and collaborators and banning them from key government positions.[17] Fortunately, however, Hungary has been able to avoid a "witch hunt" of the type experienced in the former Czechoslovakia.

Lithuania, Estonia, and Latvia have also had to grapple with their heritage of police repression. In their cases, however, the secret police had not even nominally been their own, but were adjuncts of the Moscow-based KGB. Although the KGB chief was, as a rule, a member of the indigenous nationality, the rest of the organization was staffed heavily with

Russians or other Slavs. As for the native KGB staffers, they were screened carefully to make sure that their loyalties were with Moscow. The KGB in these republics was the main instrument through which the Soviet government ensured its domination. To be sure, the party apparatus and the military troops stationed in the Baltics also served to keep these republics in line. But the KGB represented the eyes and ears of the Kremlin, monitoring society for any signs of political disloyalty and suppressing all forms of independent expression. This is not to mention the extreme brutality of the KGB's predecessor, the NKVD, which was responsible for the arrest and execution of thousands of Baltic peoples in 1941 and again after the war.

It is no wonder, then, that the people of the newly independent Baltic states vented so much of their anti-Russian sentiments upon the KGB. When new security services were set up in the Baltic states after they achieved independence, KGB officers were fired and new people were brought in. The new governments passed laws restricting the employment and activities of former KGB personnel, and in Latvia they even initiated prosecutions.[18]

Former KGB officials, either Russian or native, are treated as outcasts in the Baltic states. It is more than a matter of resentment over the past. The substantial Russian population living in the Baltics and the presence of Russian troops in Latvia and Estonia until 1994 created a sense of insecurity vis-à-vis Russia that was not unjustified. Although few expected the Russians to reclaim the Baltics or to be overtly aggressive, they realized that Moscow had plenty of opportunity for covert operations against these states, especially if they drew upon the services of former KGB employees there.

These same concerns motivated the hunts for former KGB collaborators in all three states, which resembled the anticommunist campaigns in eastern Europe. The collaboration issue strikes a deep chord in the Baltics because of the large numbers of people under suspicion.[19] Although this has cast a shadow over the process of political reform, all three Baltic states, driven by their urge to rid themselves of a past dominated by Russians, have made substantial progress in dismantling the old Soviet governmental structures and establishing democratic institutions.

RUSSIA'S ANTIREVOLUTION

What does the varied postcommunist experience in eastern Europe and the Baltic states tell us about the possible future course of democracy in Russia? In the Baltics and eastern Europe the legacy of police repression and citizen collaboration has been the greatest obstacle to democratization. This is not to diminish the significance of their tremendous economic problems, environmental devastation, ethnic discontent and rising crime. But the problem of the past—the vicious circle of police surveillance, repression, and collaboration that permeated these societies—is what has caused the deepest dissension within these countries and conflicted most directly with the establishment of a rule of law. As a report on the Czech Republic from the U.S. Helsinki Commission expressed the problem: "If new governments are overzealous in their efforts to expose collaborators and agents of the former secret police and exclude them from government, they open themselves up to the criticism that they are engaging in a witch hunt, fomenting reactionary backlash and using the same tactics their predecessors used to execute political purges."[20]

Yet at least some attempt to address the problem of past injustices may be an unavoidable process, without which lasting democracy cannot be built. As the writer Tina Rosenberg said of Germany today, which is struggling with the double historical burden of fascism and communism: "A successful *Geschichtsaufarbeitung* [working through of history] is crucial to democracy's long-term health."[21] If a new regime simply glosses over the past abuses because of vested interests within the government or the continued influence exerted by the old leaders, then it takes on the moral corruption of the old regime.[22]

This is what has happened in Russia. Indeed, it is ironic that, while states in eastern Europe and the Baltics are grappling openly with the legacy of police repression, Russia, which had the largest and most powerful secret police organization of all, has barely confronted this issue. It is much more than a question of the terror under Stalin, the perpetrators of which are largely dead. Equally important is the post-Stalin era, when KGB officials deprived citizens of basic freedoms, murdered and incarcerated innocent people, and created a society of spies and informers. Who bears responsibility? Why is no one asking, "How could they have done that?"

The Russian émigré writer Vassily Aksyonov pondered this question when he visited Russia in the summer of 1994 and ran into a former KGB officer who had supervised the expulsion of dissident writers (including Aksyonov) from the Soviet Writers' Union. Now this same officer was organizing a literary event in honor of Andrei Sakharov and inviting Aksyonov. He had metamorphosed overnight into a democrat and no one was questioning his credentials. He was not the only one; Aksyonov found that many of those who held powerful posts in the KGB and the party were at the top of society again. His observations are revealing:

> Without denazification, Germany would not have reached its glamorous democracy and prosperity so quickly. But debolshevization is inconceivable in Russia. The Soviet Union was not defeated on the battlefield, it was not occupied by the forces of democracy. Nor was it ruined as a result of popular up-

rising. Even the expected storming of the KGB headquarters in August 1991 did not take place; the crowd was talked out of it. . . . Somehow or other this strange version of a mass upheaval, with its inspirational as well as farcical elements, has helped Russia avoid another horrid Stalinist bloodletting. But it has created extreme ambiguity. The breakup of one leviathan of a totalitarian mafia has given birth to numerous smaller gangs running the gamut of politics.[23]

In contrast to the efforts at political justice that have occurred in eastern Europe, all the postcommunist regime did in Russia was to stage a show trial of those accused of attempting a coup in August 1991. Call it what you will, the defeat of the coup attempt was no revolution, and the subsequent demise of the party and the union did not result in a renewal of the ruling elite. The fact that the old *apparatchiks*, including Yeltsin, are still at the helm is one of the main reasons why Russia has not reformed its security services. The party leadership and the KGB were closely allied, running the country together. One could hardly expect former party bureaucrats to turn against their loyal supporters. In these turbulent times men like Yeltsin need men like Korzhakov more than ever. Yeltsin has avoided real reform of the security services by instigating one reorganization and name change after another, leaving it up to security officials themselves to work out the details and write their own charters. In these circumstances it is hardly surprising that they would cling to their powers and prerogatives. As one observer put it: "Much in the same way that nobody seriously considered in 1945 assigning the Gestapo to the task of denazification, likewise one cannot reasonably expect the present-day KGB to carry out desovietification."[24]

Even if Russian leaders make sincere efforts to reform the security services, they face a daunting task. It is not enough merely to make changes in the way these bodies operate and to bring in new personnel. What is required is the legal infrastructure—criminal codes, procedural laws, judicial system, lawyers—to support restraints on the security police, as well as an effective system of parliamentary oversight. Although the government and parliament have made progress in reforming the laws, this has been a painfully slow process, and Russia still lacks many of the fundamentals necessary for an effective and democratic system of justice.

Russia does not have a tradition of legality to build upon. Unlike the Baltics and east European states, Russia never experienced a period of democratic rule. Throughout the nineteenth and early twentieth centuries, as the tsarist government struggled to modernize and bring order to its society, it never was able to go beyond authoritarianism and establish a rule of law. Once the Bolsheviks gained power in 1917, all hopes of this happening disappeared. Socialist legality, upheld by a ruthless and arbitrary political police, took over and imposed itself on the society. Russians now have to create a rule of law from scratch.

But this also requires a society that is prepared for democratic changes. Seventy years of a communist dictatorship has not only created severe economic, political, and ecological problems in Russia, it has also done considerable moral and psychological harm. Accustomed to having many of their decisions made for them, people will need to develop the sense of public responsibility, the inclination to political activism, and, most importantly, the necessary faith in the new system that they are establishing.

It is difficult for people to trust a government filled with corrupt officials who are holdovers from the past communist regime. Bribery and stealing state property are not a new phenomenon. In the Soviet period they served as the modus operandi for party and state officials. It could not have been otherwise, given that the economic system was too inflexible and unresponsive to demand to function without these back channels and an underground economy. What were accepted practices in the Soviet period are now crimes, and those who engage in these practices are criminals. The result, compounded by the absence of regulations governing the process of privatization, is a society where a large proportion of officials are engaged in illegal business deals. This has generated an upsurge in ordinary crime and a real breakdown in law and order, creating a widespread feeling of what Huntington has termed "authoritarian nostalgia." The need to fight crime and corruption is used to justify a strengthening of police powers and the consequent curtailment of individual rights. This is what Yeltsin has done with his anticrime campaign and the harsh new laws he has introduced in the name of law and order.

There is also the problem of loss of empire and the consequent resurgence of unhealthy Russian nationalist tendencies, which have an adverse effect on the development of democracy. As it turns out, the collapse of the Soviet Union was not welcomed universally, either by Russians or non-Russians. A great many people, including those in the Yeltsin administration, had a stake in the Soviet Union and were not happy to see it disbanded. Even ordinary Russians did not like to see Russia lose its vast empire and have its great power status threatened. They are receptive when they hear FIS chief Primakov say that Russia has every right to defend Russian interests in the near abroad and when they hear domestic security officials assert that reintegration is inevitable. For many Russians, democracy and self-determination do not necessarily have to extend to the other CIS states.

As Huntington points out, the development of a democratic political culture depends largely on the extent to which people believe in democratic values. Judging from their apparent willingness to succumb to authoritarian laws and to allow the security services to play larger-than-life roles in society, the Russian people may say that they want democracy, but they do not necessarily believe in it. And democratic institutions such as elections and a parliament do not automatically result in a society based on the rule of law. In the words of one Russian observer: "Democracy is only an outward form, which can be used for good or evil. Hitler came to power democratically, and so could Zhirinovsky. . . . If we don't have the moral tradition, we have no future."[25]

Perhaps, as in eastern Europe, this moral tradition can be developed, enabling people in Russia to move along the path of other states that have democratized successfully. This may take time, but the exposure to a free press and the experiences of popular elections could eventually create a populace that understands more than the outer forms of democracy. As a result, Russia will have a new generation of leaders who are untainted by past histories of collaboration with the KGB and can finally achieve a break with the old regime. If and when this happens, there will still be a Russian security and intelligence apparatus, but it will no longer be a successor to the KGB.

NOTES

INTRODUCTION

1. Iurii Arakcheev in *Nezavisimaia gazeta*, 18 March 1993, p. 1.

2. The figure of 420,000 is given in a book, recently published by a group of former and current security officials: *Belaia Kniga Rossiiskikh Spetssluzhb* (Moscow: Obozrevatel', 1995), p. 38. This book provides an extensive account of the post-1991 history of the security services from an insider's point of view.

3. Valentin Korolev, "'Sekrety' Sekretnykh Sluzhb," *Ogonek*, no. 43, October 1990, p. 30.

CHAPTER ONE
THE KGB AND THE MYTH OF THE AUGUST COUP

1. Other members of the SCSE were Prime Minister Valentin Pavlov; Vice-Chairman of the Defense Council Oleg Baklanov; and two lesser officials, V. Starodubtsev and A. Tiziakov.

2. For a Western account, see Stuart Loory and Ann Imse, *Seven Days That Shook the World* (Atlanta: Turner Publishing, 1991).

3. For a good example of the glorification of the August coup in Western literature, see James H. Billington, *Russia Transformed—Breakthrough to Hope: Moscow, August 1991* (New York: The Free Press, 1991).

4. The poll results appeared in *Moskovskaia pravda*, 3 August 1994, p. 3.

5. In fact, skepticism about the coup had developed earlier. In early March 1993, the Moscow paper *Independent Gazette* observed: "Over time public opinion has changed sharply regarding the players, the extras, and the scenery of this already distant drama. The initial scenario, which featured the evil secret police, the victim Gorbachev, the hero on top of the tanks Yeltsin, and the courageous defenders of the White House, has collapsed. Now a completely opposite picture prevails." *Nezavisimaia gazeta* 4, March 1993, p. 5.

6. I have analyzed Gorbachev's policy toward the KGB in earlier writings. See Amy Knight, *The KGB: Police and Politics in the Soviet Union* (Boston: Unwin-Hyman, 1990); idem, "The KGB and Soviet Reform," *Problems of Communism* 35, no. 5 (September–October 1988): 61–70; idem, "The Future of the KGB," *Problems of Communism* 39, no. 6 (November–December 1990): 20–33; and idem, "The Coup That Never Was: Gorbachev and the Forces of Reaction," *Problems of Communism*, 40, no. 6 (November–December 1991): 36–43.

7. See, for example, Alexander Rahr, "'New Thinking' Takes Hold in Foreign-Policy Establishment," *Radio Liberty Report on the USSR* 1, no. 1, 6 January 1989, pp. 3–5; and "Gorbachev and the Post-Chebrikov KGB," *Report on the USSR* 1, no. 51, 22 December 1989, pp. 16–20.

8. Major General Oleg Kalugin, a former high-ranking KGB official who denounced his former organization in a dramatic public appearance in June 1990,

was the most illustrious KGB renegade. But there were several others. See Knight, "The Future of the KGB."

9. See *Komsomol'skaia pravda*, 7 March 1990, p. 1, for the staffers' appeal, and *Pravda*, 5 July 1990, p. 1, for Kriuchkov's speech. Among those who expressed alarm about reform was Nikolai Golushko, at the time chief of the Ukrainian KGB and later, in 1993, chief of the Russian Ministry of Security.

10. The law, which was published in *Izvestiia*, 25 May 1991, aroused concern among Russian democrats.

11. Unpublished stenographic report of the session of the parliamentary commission investigating the role of the KGB in the coup, chaired by L. A. Ponomarev, Moscow, 4 February 1992 (in Russian), pp. 35–40.

12. Colonel General Evgennii Podkolzin interviewed in *Argumenty i Fakty*, no. 12, 1993, p. 7.

13. Yevgenia Albats, *The State within a State: The KGB and Its Hold on Russia—Past, Present, and Future*, trans. Catherine A. Fitzpatrick (New York: Farrar, Straus, Giroux, 1994), pp. 276–278.

14. Ponomarev Commission report, pp. 105–107; John B. Dunlop, *The Rise of Russia and the Fall of the Soviet Empire* (Princeton: Princeton University Press, 1993), p. 193. Also see N. Belan in *Sovetskaia Rossiia*, 17 January 1992, p. 2.

15. Report of Ponomarev Commission, pp. 7–8. Western analysts also accepted this argument. See, for example, David Remnick, *Lenin's Tomb: The Last Days of the Soviet Empire* (New York: Random House, 1993), p. 426, where he mentions the bad information that Gorbachev was getting and the "betrayals all around him."

16. Gorbachev admitted at Varennikov's trial that he was not enthusiastic about the Union Treaty. See *Nezavisimaia gazeta*, 1 September 1994, p. 2. Yeltsin describes the Novo-Ogarevo meetings in his memoirs, *Struggle for Russia*, trans. Catherine A. Fitzpatrick (New York: Random House, 1994), pp. 36–39. He does not explain why other republican leaders were excluded from the secret talks. He also gives the impression that Gorbachev was in favor of the treaty.

17. Valery Boldin, *Ten Years That Shook the World: The Gorbachev Era as Witnessed by His Chief of Staff*, trans. Evelyn Rossite (New York: Basic Books, 1994), p. 278. Boldin was one of those arrested for plotting the coup. Transcripts of tapes of the secret Novo-Ogarevo meetings were subsequently found in Boldin's safe. See note 56 below. Also, in a highly charged memorandum to Gorbachev written shortly before 19 August, presidential aide Georgii Shakhnazarov urged restraint on the matter of sovereignty for the republics: "Of course its easier and more pleasant to give everyone what he wants. But what will be the result? After all, right after the Tatars, who want full control over their oil, after the Iakuts, who are claiming ownership of diamonds and gold, things will reach the point where one of the Moscow regions will claim ownership to a portion of the sky over Moscow. This is the road to chaos, collapse, civil war." See Shakhnazarov's memoirs, *Tsena svobody: Reformatsiia Gorbacheva glazami ego pomoshchnika* (Moscow: Rossika Zevs, 1993), p. 553.

18. For the official Russian story, see the book by the prosecutors in the case against the plotters, purportedly based on the evidence they gathered, including

interrogations of the accused: V. Stepankov and E. Lisov, *Kremlevskii zagovor* (Moscow: Ogonek, 1992).

19. Moscow Radio, 26 December 1990, in *Foreign Broadcast Information Service Daily Report, Soviet Union* (hereafter *FBIS-SOV*), 27 December 1990, pp. 12–13.

20. Loory and Imse, *Seven Days That Shook the World*, p. 52; *Times* (London), 22 January 1992. The substance of these telephone calls has never been revealed.

21. Michael Dobbs, "Moscow Mayor Sought U.S. Help to Head Off Suspected Coup," *Washington Post*, 17 February 1993, p. A21.

22. Interview with Lukianov in *Pravda*, 21 July 1992, p. 1.

23. Aleksei Adzhubei in *Izvestiia*, 3 September 1991, p. 1.

24. Interview with Pavlov, Moscow Television, 24 August 1991, in *FBIS-SOV*, 26 August 1991, p. 31.

25. "Avgustovskii prolog," *Nezavisimaia gazeta*, 19 August 1994, p. 5. Interview with Senior Russian Procurator Arkadii Danilov, based on Varennikov's testimony. Boldin, in his memoirs, gives a slightly different account, saying that in the end the president outlined a more democratic approach for them to follow. See *Ten Years That Shook the World*, pp. 27–28. Oleg Shenin, on the other hand, testified that Gorbachev gave them the go-ahead to declare a state of emergency.

26. *Avgust-91* (Moscow: Politizdat, 1991), pp. 116–117.

27. See a report on a news conference with Shakhnazarov and others, in *Rossiiskaia gazeta*, 23 August 1991, p. 2.

28. Stepankov and Lisov, *Kremlevskii zagovor*, p. 17.

29. Mikhail Gorbachev, *The August Coup: The Truth and the Lessons* (New York: HarperCollins, 1991), pp. 17–18.

30. See an interview with a senior KGB communications officer in *Pravda*, 6 November 1991, p. 1.

31. Interview with Klimov, *Literaturnaia gazeta*, no. 8, 24 February 1993, p. 12.

32. See Dunlop, *The Rise of Russia*, pp. 202–206. Dunlop leaves open, pending further evidence, the question of whether or not Gorbachev was telling the truth. Interestingly, although Vol'skii said initially that he called Gorbachev at 6 P.M. on 18 August (thus after the telephones were allegedly closed), he later changed his story and said the call was around 4 P.M. See *Nezavisimaia gazeta*, 19 August 1994, p. 5.

33. See *Nezavisimaia gazeta*, 13 July 1994, p. 3, and 19 August 1994, p. 5. Kriuchkov's lawyer, Iurii Ivanov, also asked why Gorbachev did not use the telephone in his car. See Dunlop, *The Rise of Russia*, p. 203.

34. "Avgustovskii prolog." Also see *Pravda*, 6 November 1991, pp. 1–2.

35. Two separate Russian papers mentioned a 20 August report that Shakhnazarov and his family were with Gorbachev at Foros. See *The Coup: Underground Moscow Newspapers* (Minneapolis: Eastview Press, 1991), p. 46. Shakhnazarov himself, who never mentioned the visit to Gorbachev's dacha, claimed in one statement that he returned to Moscow with Gorbachev adviser Evgenii Primakov on the 19th (interview in *Rossiiskaia gazeta*, 23 August 1991,

p. 2), and in another that he returned on the 20th (*Yomiuri Shimbun*, Tokyo, 22 August 1991, p. 3, in *FBIS-SOV*, 23 August 1991, p. 3). In his memoirs, Shakhnazarov is vague about when he returned, but he makes it clear that he did not fly back with Primakov. See Shakhnazarov, *Tsena svobody*, pp. 263–265. Shakhnazarov goes out of his way to dispute the theory that Gorbachev was feigning his captivity.

36. *Avgust-91*, p. 80.

37. Loory and Imse, *Seven Days That Shook the World*, pp. 62–68. According to this account, "The two groups avoided trouble even though both were armed. Gorbachev's bodyguards kept their weapons in the guesthouse near the dacha, and the security troops never did anything to disarm them. All of the workers on the compound, loyal to Gorbachev or not, ate in the same dining room" (p. 68).

38. Ibid.

39. See Dunlop, *The Rise of Russia*, p. 205. If, as Gorbachev indicates, the border guards did turn against him, then why was their chief not punished?

40. Yeltsin, *Struggle for Russia*, p. 53.

41. London *Daily Telegraph*, 28 January 1993, in *FBIS-SOV*, 12 February 1993, p. 13.

42. *Pravda*, 11 July 1992, pp. 1–2.

43. Yeltsin, *Struggle for Russia*, pp. 72–73, 88.

44. *Komsomol'skaia pravda*, 24 August 1991. Karpukhin subsequently retracted his statement and said that he had refused orders to attack the White House, but this smacked of improvisation. See an interview with him by *Asahi Evening News* (Tokyo), 13 September 1991, in *FBIS-SOV*, 16 September 1991, p. 2.

45. Ponomarev Commission hearings, p. 10.

46. Russian historian Roy Medvedev suggested that, already at the time of their news conference on 19 August, the emergency committee members were trying to extricate themselves from the trap they had fallen into. See an interview with Medvedev in *La Stampa*, 27 August 1991, p. 4, in *FBIS-SOV*, 3 September 1991, p. 13.

47. Yeltsin, *Struggle for Russia*, pp. 76, 101. Yeltsin's entire depiction of the coup episode in his memoirs is fraught with ambiguity. At one point he even says that he considered the possibility that Gorbachev was implicated in the plot: "Gorbachev knew about the whole situation, and the coup was being executed according to a scenario he had prepared. The idea was to have other people do the dirty work to clear Gorbachev's path, then he could return from vacation to a new country under a state of emergency" (p. 65).

48. Loory and Imse, *Seven Days That Shook the World*, pp. 148–149; "GKPCh: Armiia privlekalas' no ne uchastvovala," *Armiia*, nos. 7–8 (April 1992): 27.

49. *Avgust-91*, pp. 175–177.

50. *Putch: Khronika trevozhnykh dnei* (Moscow: Progress, 1991), p. 155, cited in Dunlop, *The Rise of Russia*, p. 203. It may have been even earlier. Dunlop cites a report of a conversation between Gorbachev and Arkadii Vol'kskii that took place at 3:12 P.M.!

51. Michael R. Beschloss and Strobe Talbott, *At the Highest Levels: The In-*

side Story of the End of the Cold War (Boston: Little, Brown, 1993), pp. 436–437. Beschloss and Talbott claim that it was Bush who put through a call to Gorbachev, and not vice versa.

52. *Avgust-91*, pp. 170–175. Interestingly, Leonid Shebarshin, named acting KGB chairman by Gorbachev on the latter's return from Foros, observed after meeting with Gorbachev on 22 August: "Mikhail Sergeevich looked terrific. He was full of energy, speaking concisely and clearly. His eyes shone. He looked just like someone who had had a restful vacation on the shore of a soft, warm sea, not at all like a person who had just been freed from captivity." See Shebarshin's memoirs, *Sekretnye missii: Iz zhizni nachal'nika razvedki* (Moscow: "Mezhdunarodnye otnosheniia," 1994), p. 106.

53. See a report on the verdict in *Pravda*, 13 August 1994, p. 1.

54. These men were Kriuchkov, Iazov, Baklanov, Boldin, Pavlov, Lukianov, Tiziakov, Ianaev, Starodubtsev, Shenin, Varennikov, and four other KGB officials: Iurii Plekhanov, Viktor Grushko, Viacheslav Generalov, and Genii Ageev. (Ageev, a deputy chairman of the KGB, was for some reason not arrested until late September 1991.) Boldin, Grushko, and Shenin were subsequently released from custody and their cases halted temporarily because of ill health. Later, cases against Tiziakov, Baklanov, and Ianaev were also postponed. This left nine defendants facing trial in November 1993.

55. An analogous case in Poland was that of General Wojciech Jaruzelsi, who was charged in 1992 with treason for declaring martial law in Poland in 1981. The legal grounds were feeble, since Jaruzelski in fact had not disobeyed any laws existing at the time. See Tina Rosenberg, *The Haunted Land: Facing Europe's Ghosts after Communism* (New York: Random House, 1995), pp. 125–129, 250–258.

56. *Times* (London), 13 November 1991, as cited in Dunlop, *The Rise of Russia*, p. 195. One such conversation occurred on 29 July 1994 among Gorbachev, Yeltsin, and Nazarbaev. Gorbachev agreed to Yeltsin's demands that he remove Kriuchkov and other hard-liners from the leadership. According to Yeltsin, the tapes found their way into Boldin's safe. He does not say how they got there, but it is entirely possible that Gorbachev himself gave them to Boldin. See Yeltsin, *The Struggle for Russia*, p. 39.

57. Moscow Radio in Russian, 23 August 1991, in *FBIS-SOV*, 26 August 1991, p. 32.

58. *Armiia*, nos. 7–8, April 1992, pp. 22–38; *Komsomol'skaia pravda*, 2 December 1991, p. 3. Also see the printed version of Grachev's testimony to investigators in the coup case, on 25 October 1992, reprinted in *Moskovskii novosti*, no. 19, 17–24 July 1994, p. 8.

59. For an official account of the Pugo death, see Stepankov and Lisov, *Kremlevskii zagovor*, pp. 245–254. Pugo's deputy, Viktor Erin, was the first to arrive on the scene after Pugo and his wife were shot. Erin later became minister of internal affairs for the Russian Federation.

60. *Sekretnye missii*, p. 106.

61. *Sovetskaia Rossiia*, 18 July 1992, p. 1.

62. See ibid. and an interview with former Soviet prosecutor Telman Gdlian, *Argumenty i fakty*, no. 39 (October 1991): 2.

63. Stepankov and Lisov, *Kremlevskii zagovor*.

64. On this last point see, Peter Reddaway, "On the Eve," *The New York Review of Books*, 2 December 1993, p. 20.

65. Albats, *State within a State*, p. 295.

66. Shebarshin says in his memoirs that he was greatly relieved to learn that he would not retain his acting appointment. This was not an easy time for anyone to take on such a job. Upon hearing the news that Bakatin would take over, Shebarshin responded to Gorbachev: "Thank you very much. Tonight I will sleep soundly." *Sekretnye missii*, p. 117.

67. Judging from what Bakatin says in his memoirs, he was chosen because he was the one candidate that both Gorbachev and Yeltsin could agree on. Bakatin says that he was not appointed by Gorbachev alone, but by the State Council, which included presidents of the all the republics. See Vadim Bakatin, *Izbavlenie ot KGB* (Moscow: Novosti, 1992), p. 22; and an interview with Bakatin in *Izvestiia*, 2 January 1992, p. 6.

68. Moscow Radio, 30 August 1991, in *FBIS-SOV*, 3 September 1991, pp. 34–44.

69. As quoted in David Wise, "Closing Down the KGB," *The New York Times Magazine* 47, November 24, 1991, p. 71.

70. Ibid., p. 66.

71. *Literaturnaia gazeta*, no. 14 (April 1994): 11.

72. Bakatin, *Izbavlenie*, pp. 66–68.

73. Ibid., pp. 77–78.

74. Ia. V. Karpovich in *Nevskoe vremia*, 31 July 1992, p. 3.

75. William Saffire in *The New York Times*, 11 November 1991, p. A15.

76. Bakatin, *Izbavlenie*, pp. 77–78.

77. *Izvestiia*, 26 October 1991; INTERFAX, 24 October 1991, in *FBIS-SOV*, 25 October 1991, p. 13.

78. Bakatin, *Izbavlenie*, pp. 90–91.

79. Yevgenia Albats, "KGB-MSB-MBVD: Substantive Changes?" *Moscow News*, no. 2, 1992, p. 5.

80. Ibid.

81. Bakatin, *Izbavlenie*, p. 88.

82. Ibid., p. 177.

83. See Knight, "The Coup That Never Was," p. 41. Also see an interview with former KGB first deputy chief (and accused coup plotter) Viktor Grushko in *Nezavisimaia gazeta*, 14 April 1994, p. 6. Grushko negotiated with Skokov on Kriuchkov's behalf for several months in 1991.

84. Bakatin, *Izbavlenie*, p. 92. Bakatin is careful in his book not to blame Yeltsin, but the parliamentary commission was clearly acting on Yeltsin's behalf.

85. Moscow Radio Rossii, 5 October 1991, in *FBIS-SOV*, 7 October 1991, p. 54.

86. *Rossiiskaia gazeta*, 4 December 1991 (interview with Ivanenko). Albats, *State within a State*, p. 305. Albats observed that in the autumn of 1991 "already, the tastier morsels of the Soviet Union's state security had been swallowed up by Russian state security. Yeltsin was stealing from Gorbachev's plate" (p. 302).

87. Bakatin, *Izbavlenie*, pp. 234–238.

88. For a detailed account of the last months of the Soviet Union and Gorbachev's struggle to keep it together, see Dunlop, *The Rise of Russia*, pp. 255–284.

89. Some say that Bakatin was retired because he handed over to U.S. Ambassador to Russia, Robert Strauss, technical documentation on equipment used earlier for bugging the U.S. Embassy in Moscow. But, although he aroused the displeasure of Russian security officials, Bakatin had the approval of both Yeltsin and Gorbachev in making this gesture of "openness" to the Americans. See an interview with Bakatin in *Izvestiia*, 2 January 1992, p. 6.

90. According to one source, Barannikov had become a sort of "aide-de-camp" to Yeltsin in 1990, "washing Yeltsin's back in the bathtub." Leonid Radzikhovskii, "Deviatnadtsatyi? Dvadtsatyi? Dvadtsat' pervyi? (Bslety i padeniia khoziaev Lubianki)," *Stolitsa*, no. 35 (1993): 16.

91. See *Rossiiskaia gazeta*, 28 December 1991, p. 2. According to a former employee of FAPSI, it incorporated two additional KGB technical directorates, along with the Eighth CD. See I. Baryshnikov, "Sekrety?" *Segodnia*, no. 43, 17 August 1993, p. 7. During the period between August and December 1991, this agency was known as the Government Communications Directorate. See Bakatin, *Izbavlenie*, p. 83.

92. In his memoirs Yeltsin made it clear how much he trusted Korzhakov, observing that "his job forces him to be near me twenty-four hours a day." Yeltsin, *Struggle for Russia*, p. xix.

93. See *Komsomol'skaia pravda*, 20 October 1992; an interview with Deputy Minister of Security Andrei Bykov in *Trud*, 22 May 1993; *Rossiiskaia gazeta*, 10 July 1992, p. 5, and 18 September 1993, p. 2 (article by Viktor Suslov); and an interview with Baruskov in *Izvestiia*, 8 October 1993, p. 2.

94. The decree placing the border guards under the MB was signed by Yeltsin on 12 June 1992. See *Rossiiskaia gazeta*, 16 June 1992, p. 5.

95. See, for example, Korolev in *Ogonek*, no. 43 (October 1990): 28–31.

96. Yeltsin news conference, as reported on Moscow Russian Television, 7 September 1991, *FBIS-SOV*, 9 September 1991, p. 71.

CHAPTER TWO
BUILDING RUSSIA'S SECURITY APPARATUS

1. "Krakh agenturnoi razvedki" [author anonymous], *Den'*, no. 30, 26 July–1 August, 1992, p. 3.

2. Michael Voslensky made this point in his seminal book on the Soviet ruling class: "In their accounts of the crimes of the Cheka-GPU-NKVD-MGB-KGB, these authors [of books on the political police] create the impression, whether deliberately or not, that the 'organs' consist of fiends possessing almost supernatural powers. That is wrong, and it was wrong even in Stalin's time, when there was more reason to believe it. . . . The KGB is a Soviet government department, and so its work is subject to planning and it must render an account of how the plan has been carried out." Michael Voslensky, *Nomenklatura: Anatomy of the Soviet Ruling Class*, trans. Eric Mosbacher (London: The Bodley Head, 1984), pp. 281–283.

3. See Igor Amvrosov, "Who Will Control the KGB Successor Organization?" *Moscow News*, no. 11, 15 March 1992, p. 8. For a good general picture of the different political groupings in the Russian parliament at this time, see John Dunlop, *The Rise of Russia and the Fall of the Soviet Union* (Princeton: Princeton University Press, 1993), pp. 288–300.

4. *Vedomosti S'ezda Narodnykh Deputatov Rossiiskoi Federatsii i Verhovnogo Soveta Rossiiskoi Federatsii*, no. 10 (March 1992): 642.

5. Ibid., p. 664.

6. A copy of the draft, dated December 1992, was given to this author.

7. See a report in *Izvestiia*, 30 July 1993, p. 1.

8. The other three security officials on the committee were Nikolai Kuznetsov, Igor Nikulin, and Georgii Kuts.

9. From an interview with Yakunin, published in *Perspective* 3, no. 2 (November 1992): 1.

10. As quoted in *Rabochaia tribuna*, 17 April 1992, p. 4.

11. Interview with Stepashin in *Segodnia*, 18 May 1993, p. 11.

12. *Vedomosti S'ezda Narodnykh Deputatov i Verkhovnogo Soveta Rossiiskoi Federatsii*, no. 4 (January 1992): 219–220. Also see Iu. Sorokin in *Komsomol'skaia pravda*, 5 February 1992, p. 1, in *FBIS-SOV*, 10 February 1992, p. 53; and an interview with Vladimir Rubanov in *Novaia ezhednevnaia gazeta*, no. 7, 21–27 May 1993, p. 2.

13. Published in *Rossiiskaia gazeta*, 29 April 1992, p. 3.

14. *KGB: Vchera, segodnia, zavtra. Plenarnoe zasedanie. Doklady i diskusii*, Moscow, 19–21 February 1993, p. 7.

15. Published in *Rossiiskaia gazeta*, 6 May 1992, p. 5.

16. See Article 10 of the Russian Federation Law on Security, ibid.

17. See *Rossiiskaia gazeta*, 12 August 1992, for the text of the law.

18. Thus, for example, the May 1991 law (*Izvestiia*, 25 May 1991) ordered the KGB "to combat the intelligence-gathering and subversive activity of the special services of foreign states and foreign organizations, directed against the USSR and the republics, to protect the constitutional structure of the USSR and the republics against illegal infringements, and protect the sovereignty and territorial integrity of the state and its economic, scientific-technical and defense potential." The 1992 law directed the MB "to detect, prevent, and cut short the intelligence and subversive activity of foreign intelligence services and organizations against the Russian Federation, and also unlawful encroachment on the constitutional order, sovereignty, territorial integrity, and defense capability of the Russian Federation."

19. See *Rossiiskaia gazeta*, 29 September 1992, p. 1, for the presidential decree on such secondment. Also see a later interview with Nikolai Golushko, who mentions the "operational reserve officers," in *Izvestiia*, 3 February 1994, p. 1.

20. Yevgenia Albats, talk at Johns Hopkins University, SAIS, Washington, D.C., 20 November 1992. An MB official, General Andrei Chernenko, denied that his ministry sent staff to work under cover as journalists: "Such a practice of implantation is simply meaningless today. This made sense only at the time when there was a monopoly on thought and all newspapers were the same." Interview with Chernenko in *Literaturnaia gazeta*, no. 51 (December 1992): 10.

21. See, for example, *Nezavisimaia gazeta*, 25 February 1992, p. 6 (on the law on operational-investigative procedures).

22. See *Izvestiia*, 1 October 1992, where an appeal from the newly founded front was published.

23. These amendments were introduced by Yeltsin on 9 October 1992 and published in *Rossiiskaia gazeta*, 27 October 1992. For further details, see p. 168.

24. *Rossiiskaia gazeta*, 30 October 1992, p. 1.

25. *Kommersant-Daily*, 29 October 1992, p. 8.

26. Unattributed report in *Krasnaia zvezda*, 28 October 1992. When it came to challenges from democrats and human rights advocates—traditional enemies of the KGB—the MB was more inclined to show its mettle. The case of Vil Mirzaianov, a scientist arrested in 1992 on charges of revealing state secrets, is a good example. For a discussion of the Mirzaianov case, see chapter 7.

27. *Krasnaia zvezda*, 14 May 1992, p. 2. These complaints were reiterated by security professionals in the book *Belaia Kniga Rossiiskikh Spetssluzhb* (Moscow: Obozrevatel', 1995). According to this book (p. 40), 20,000 KGB staffers resigned between August 1991 and June 1992.

28. Ibid.

29. "Krakh agenturnoi razvedki," *Den'*, 28 July 1992, p. 3.

30. Ibid.

31. See, for example, Valentin Korolev, "'Sekrety' Sekretnykh Sluzhb," *Ogonek*, no. 43, October 1990, pp. 28–31.

32. M. Deytch, "Lubianka: Vse v prodazhe?" *Literaturnaia gazeta*, no. 26, 24 June 1992, p. 13.

33. See *Rossiiskaia gazeta*, 5 June 1992, p. 2; *Izvestiia*, 10 June 1992, p. 2.

34. *Rossiiskaia gazeta*, 10 June 1992, p. 2; Moscow, INTERFAX, 11 June 1992, in *FBIS-SOV*, 12 June 1992, p. 49.

35. Viktor Yasmann, "Corruption in Russia: A Threat to Democracy?" *RFE/RL Research Report* 2, no. 10, 5 March 1993, p. 17.

36. See *Kuranty*, 19 June 1993, p. 1.

37. *Argumenty i fakty*, no. 26 (June 1993): 2, and no. 27 (July 1993): 3.

38. On Golushko's career, see *Argumenty i fakty*, no. 39 (September 1993): 2.

39. For details on the Fifth Directorate, see "The Anatomy of the Fifth Directorate," *New Times*, no. 11 (1992): 12–13.

40. See Amy Knight, "Russian Security Services under Yeltsin," *Post-Soviet Affairs* 9, no. 1 (January–March 1993): 40–65 (esp. p. 60).

41. Author's interview with Golushko, Moscow, 12 January 1995.

42. The interview was broadcast on Moscow Russian Television, 27 April 1992, in *FBIS-SOV*, 28 April 1992, pp. 34–36.

43. *Nezavismaia gazeta*, 17 February 1993, p. 6.

44. See an interview with Chernenko in *Nezavisimaia gazeta*, 26 August 1992, p. 6.

45. Moscow Central Television, 15 October 1992, in *FBIS-SOV*, 22 October 1992, pp. 23–24. It may be that this colonel was a victim of the collaboration between CIA officer Aldrich Ames and the Russian security services. See chapter 5.

46. Moscow Radio, 10 December 1992, in *FBIS-SOV*, 10 December 1992.

47. S. Turchenko, "Chuzhim spetssluzham vol'gotno v Rossii," *Sovetskaia Rossiia*, 30 January 1993.

48. For a discussion of Kozyrev's views at this time, see Dunlop, *The Rise of Russia*, pp. 287–288.

49. Stephen White and Ol'ga Kryshtanovskaia, "Public Attitudes to the KGB: A Research Note," *Europe-Asia Studies* 45, no. 1 (1993): 169–175.

50. Jim Leitzel, Clifford Gaddy, and Michael Alexeev, "Mafiosi and Matrioshki: Organized Crime and Russian Reform," *The Brookings Review* 13 (Winter 1995): 26–29 (on p. 27).

51. As cited in Claire Sterling, *Thieves' World: The Threat of the New Global Network of Organized Crime* (New York: Simon and Schuster, 1994), p. 93. Also see Arkady Vaksberg, *The Soviet Mafia* (New York: St. Martin's Press, 1992).

52. For recent studies of the connection between government and organized crime, see Christopher J. Ulrich, "The Price of Freedom: The Criminal Threat in Russia, Eastern Europe and the Baltic Region," *Conflict Studies*, no. 275 (October 1994); and Stephen Handelman, *Comrade Criminal: Russia's New Mafia* (New Haven and London: Yale University Press, 1995).

53. Gaddy, Leitzel, and Alexeev contend that, in fact, the mafias provide a much-needed service to businessmen in the chaotic Russian environment.

54. See an interview with Gaidar's assistant, Mikhail Gurtovoi, in *Nezavisimaia gazeta*, 8 October 1992, p. 2.

55. See a report by Andrei Shilov in *Kommersant-Daily*, 23 October 1992, p. 9.

56. S. Sergeev, "Skol'ko shchupalets u spruta?" *Sovetskaia Rossiia*, 17 November 1992, p. 4.

57. Moscow Radio, 10 December 1992, in *FBIS-SOV*, 10 December 1992.

58. *Vechernii Rostov*, 17 May 1993, in *FBIS-SOV*, 1 July 1993, pp. 37–38.

59. See reports in *Nezavisimaia gazeta*, 28 April 1993, p. 6; 25 May 1993, p. 6.

60. Yasmann, "Corruption in Russia," p. 17.

61. See an interview with Gurov and MB Deputy Chief Chernenko in *Vek*, no. 15, 27 November–4 December 1992, p. 10.

62. *Krasnaia zvezda*, 10 January 1993, p. 1.

63. His report was reprinted in *Nezavisimaia gazeta*, 16 February 1993, pp. 1–2.

64. ITAR-TASS World Service in Russian, 12 February 1993, in *FBIS-SOV*, 12 February 1993, pp. 24–25.

65. *Izvestiia*, 11 February 1993, p. 1.

66. Interview with Rubanov in *Novaia ezhednevnaia gazeta*, no. 7, 21–27 May 1993, p. 2.

67. See Yasmann, "Corruption in Russia"; and Julia Wishnevsky, "Corruption Allegations Undermine Russia's Leaders," *RFE-RL Research Report* 2, no. 37, 17 September 1993, pp. 16–18. The issue of corruption in the Western Group of Forces was to create a scandal touching Minister of Defense Pavel Grachev in 1994. See chapter 4.

68. *Pravda*, 17 April 1993, pp. 1, 3.

69. Georgii Portnov and Stanislav Shumilov, "El'tsingate," *Pravda*, 17 April 1993, pp. 1, 3.

70. *Nezavisimaia gazeta*, 21 April 1993, p. 2.

71. Interview with O. Sadykov, Moscow Russian Television, 22 April 1993, in *Foreign Broadcast Information Service Report: Central Eurasia* (hereafter *FBIS-USR*), 12 May 1993, pp. 6–7.

72. Yevgenia Albats, "Lubianka: Budet li etomu konets?" *Izvestiia*, 3 December 1993, p. 2.

73. Olga Kryshtanovskaia, "Nadoelo zanimat'sia politikoi—nado delo delat'," *Nezavisimaia gazeta*, 16 June 1993, p. 6; E. Vladimirova, "KGB: Vchera, segodnia . . . Zavtra?" *Znanie-sila*, no. 8, 1994, p. 34.

74. See Deytch, "Lubianka."

75. As cited by TASS, 14 November 1991, in *FBIS-SOV*, 15 November 1991, p. 66.

76. The Law on Federal Organs of Government Communications and Information was published in *Rossiiskaia gazeta*, 7 April 1993, p. 4.

77. Baryshnikov, "Sekretnaia kommertsiia."

78. *Pravda*, 2 March 1993, p. 1.

79. Kryshtanovskaia, "Nadoelo zanimat'sia politikoi."

80. See the Law on Private Detective and Security Activities, *Rossiiskaia gazeta*, 30 April 1992, p. 3.

81. Handelman, *Comrade Criminal*, p. 140.

82. See Viktor Yasmann, "The Role of the Security Agencies in the October Uprising," *RFE/RL Research Report* 2, no. 44, 5 November 1993, p. 15.

83. *Novosti razvedki i kontrrazvedki*, nos. 3–4 (1995): 2.

84. Interview in *Nezavisimaia gazeta*, 26 May 1994, p. 1.

85. *Izvestiia*, 26 January 1995, p. 5.

86. See an interview with Viacheslav Trubnikov in *Nezavisimaia gazeta*, 23 December 1993, p. 1.

87. See an interview with Shebarshin in *Komsomol'skaia pravda*, 9 September 1993, p. 2; and an interview with Leonov in *Moskovskaia pravda*, 30 December 1993, p. 2. Leonov also gave a personal interview in Moscow, 11 January 1995.

88. Yegor Alexyev, "Ex-KGB People Work with Businessmen," *New Times International*, no. 18 (May 1992): 30.

89. Interview with Drozhdov in *Nezavisimaia gazeta*, 24 May 1995, p. 4. Author's interview with Vasilii Gatov, independent consultant for Western media in Russia and an expert on the former KGB, Moscow, May 1994. Another member of this firm is Gleb Nechiporenko, brother of Oleg. Both were top spies for Soviet foreign intelligence.

90. Author's interview with Leonov, 11 January 1995, Moscow; Leonid Shebarshin, *Ryka moskvy: Zapiski nachal'nika sovetskoi razvedki* (Kiev: Stodola, 1993), pp. 39–40. Like Shebarshin, Leonov has written memoirs about his intelligence work abroad: *Likholet'e* (Moscow: "Mezhdunarodnoe otnosheniia," 1994).

91. Evgenii Tarasov, Aleksandr Usanov, and Boris Neskorodov, "Zagnanye v ugol," *Nezavisimaia gazeta*, 27 July 1994, p. 6.

92. See, for example, Handelman, *Comrade Criminal*, pp. 296–316.

93. *Novosti razvedki i kontrrazvedki,* nos. 5–6 (1995): 8.

94. Aleksandr Chistov, "FAPSI: Zakon bol'shogo brata," *Nezavisimaia gazeta,* 21 April 1993, p. 1.

95. *Rossiiskaia gazeta,* 18 September 1993, p. 2.

96. Ibid.

97. They included "predicting and exposing threats to the interests of the objects of protection and measures for their prevention and neutralization." Thus, GUO officers could independently pursue investigative operations. The law was published in *Rossiiskaia gazeta,* 22 May 1993, p. 5.

98. Interview with Bykov in *Trud,* 22 May 1993, pp. 1, 5.

99. According to Aleksandr Zhilin, deputy chief of the MB's operational and technical directorate, five agencies had the right to tap telephones: the MVD, the MB, the FIS, subunits of the Main Guard Directorate, and the tax service. See *Nezavisimaia gazeta,* 9 April 1993, p. 2.

100. CHASPIK in Russian, 14 April 1993, p. 10, in *FBIS-USR,* 31 May 1993, p. 23

CHAPTER THREE
SECURITY SERVICES PUT TO THE TEST

1. "Yeltsin and Russia: Two Views," *The New York Review of Books,* 22 April 1993, p. 17.

2. Dialogue between Igor Kliamkin and Iurii Shchekochikhin in *Literaturnaia gazeta,* no. 21, 26 May 1993, p. 11.

3. Moscow Ostankino Television, 20 March 1993, in *FBIS-SOV,* 22 March 1993, pp. 13–15.

4. Moscow Russian Television, 21 March 1993, in *FBIS-SOV,* 22 March 1993, p. 39.

5. Ibid.

6. INTERFAX, 22 March 1993, in *FBIS-SOV,* 23 March 1993, p. 20. MOD spokespeople were reported as making similar disclaimers about Grachev.

7. *Krasnaia zvezda,* 24 March 1993, p. 1.

8. Boris Yeltsin, *Struggle for Russia,* trans. Catherine A. Fitzpatrick (New York: Random House, 1994), p. 212.

9. *Komsomol'skaia pravda,* 30 March 1993, p. 1.

10. Ibid.

11. Ibid.

12. *Rossiiskaia gazeta,* 2 April 1993, p. 1.

13. Interview in *Nezavisimaia gazeta,* 10 April 1993, p. 1.

14. See *Izvestiia,* 8 May 1993, p. 2; and *Izvestiia,* 15 May 1993, p. 8 (report by MB public relations chief Aleksei Kondaurov). Also see an interview with Lieutenant Colonel A. Mikhailov in *Argumenty i fakty,* no. 18 (May 1993): p. 2.

15. *Nezavisimaia gazeta,* 10 April 1993, p. 1.

16. *Komsomol'skaia pravda,* 30 March 1993, p. 1.

17. Russian Procurator-General Valentin Stepankov mentioned this in March 1993, complaining that nothing had been done to prosecute these cases. See

Nezavisimaia gazeta, 16 March 1993, p. 6. Was he putting pressure on Barannikov and the MB to do something?

18. ITAR-TASS, 22 April 1993, in *FBIS-USR*, 12 May 1993, p. 6.

19. *Sovetskaia Rossiia*, 26 June 1993, p. 3. Also see Wishnevsky, "Corruption Allegations." Grachev later admitted that he had in fact obtained the two Mercedes. See p. 101 below.

20. *Sovetskaia Rossiia*, 26 June 1993, p. 3.

21. "Chistka neugodnykh?" *Literaturnaia Rossiia*, nos. 26–27, 9 July 1993, p. 1.

22. Ibid.

23. Ibid.

24. See an interview with parliament deputy Evgenii Kozhokin, head of the subcommittee for international security and intelligence, in *Novaia ezhednevnaia gazeta*, 23 July 1993, p. 1.

25. *Argumenty i fakty*, no. 29, July 1993, p. 2.

26. ITAR-TASS in English, 24 September 1993, in *FBIS-SOV*, 28 September 1993, p. 27.

27. *Pravda*, 31 July 1993, pp. 1–2.

28. The two were lawyer Andrei Makarov and Aleksei Iliushenko, who would later be appointed acting procurator-general of the Russian Federation by Yeltsin.

29. See *Izvestiia*, 29 July 1993, pp. 1–2; and *Komsomol'skaia pravda*, 31 July 1993, p. 1.

30. For a detailed account of Iakubovskii's secret visit and dramatic escape, see excerpts from a book by Eduard Topol and Aleksandr Grant, reprinted in *Izvestiia*, 3 November 1993, p. 5; and 4 November 1993, p. 5. Iakubovskii apparently knew too much for the comfort of the Yeltsin administration, however. In early 1995 he was arrested in Moscow on charges of stealing ancient manuscripts. In late September 1995 his defense lawyer was murdered. See *Moskovskie novosti*, no. 67, 1–8 October 1995, p. 2.

31. Interview with former People's Deputy and member of the presidential administration, Galina Starovoitova, Washington, D.C., 15 March 1994. According to journalist Yevgenia Albats, "It was known even before Barannikov was appointed as the Chekists' head that he had sticky fingers." *Izvestiia*, 3 December 1993, p. 7.

32. Although Yeltsin did dismiss Shumeiko, along with Rutskoi, in early September 1993 (see later this chapter), he eventually brought Shumeiko back into his administration. See *Rossiiskie vesti*, 3 September 1993, p. 1.

33. Yeltsin, *Struggle for Russia*, p. 226. His account of the appointment of Iakubovskii to oversee the security services also seems disingenuous. He claims to have discovered the appointment at the last minute and then quashed it, but he never explains why; see pp. 228–229 of his book.

34. *Novaia ezhednevnaia gazeta*, no. 21, 30 July 1993, p. 2.

35. See, for example, a commentary by Aleksandr Mozgovoi in *Rossiiskaia gazeta*, 29 July 1993, p. 1; and *Pravda*, 29 July 1993, p. 1, and 30 July 1993, p. 1. This is also the view expressed by security professionals in the book *Belaia Kniga Rossiiskikh Spetssluzhb* (Moscow: Obozrevatel', 1995), p. 41.

36. Aleksei Fedorov, "V Kremle nespokoino," *Pravda*, 4 August 1993, p. 1.

37. Sergei Iushenkov, "Why Was Minister Barannikov Sacked?" *New Times International*, no. 32, August 1993, p. 8.

38. *Nezavisimaia gazeta*, 1 September 1993, p. 1.

39. Ibid.

40. *Rossiiskaia gazeta*, 31 July 1993, p. 2.

41. *Nezavisimaia gazeta*, 11 August 1993, p. 1.

42. Moscow Maiak Radio, 12 August 1993, in *FBIS-SOV*, 12 August 1993, p. 13.

43. See Wishnevsky, "Corruption Allegations," pp. 20–21.

44. *Izvestiia*, 27 August, 1993, p. 1; Moscow Radio Rossii, 4 September 1993, in *FBIS-SOV*, 7 September 1993, p. 32.

45. *Moskovskii komsomolets*, 2 September 1993, p. 1.

46. *RFE/RL Daily Report*, no. 111, 15 June 1993, p. 1.

47. For a good discussion of the army's political role in 1993, see Stephen Foye, "Russia's Fragmented Army Drawn into the Political Fray," *RFE/RL Research Report* 2, no. 15, 9 April 1993, pp. 1–7.

48. *Rossiiskaia gazeta*, 31 July 1993, p. 2.

49. *Pravda*, 29 July 1993, p. 1.

50. *Pravda*, 13 August 1993, p. 2.

51. As reported in *Rossiiskaia gazeta*, 17 September 1993, p. 2.

52. *Moskovskie novosti*, no. 42, 17 October 1993, pp. A4–A5.

53. *Moskovskii komsomolets*, 12 August 1993, p. 1.

54. For an analysis of the Golushko appointment, see *Nezavisimaia gazeta*, 21 September 1993, pp. 1–2.

55. Yeltsin, *Struggle for Russia*, p. 245.

56. Moscow Ostankino Television, 22 September 1993, in *FBIS-SOV*, 23 September 1993, p. 19.

57. Author's interview with Golushko, Moscow, 12 January 1995.

58. *Moskovskii komsomolets*, 23 September 1993, p. 3.

59. As reported in *Nezavisimaia gazeta*, 30 September 1993, p. 1.

60. See an interview with Savostianov in *Kuranty*, 22 October 1992, p. 10.

61. *Nezavisimaia gazeta*, 11 October 1993, p. 2.

62. Interview with Erin, Moscow Ostankino Television, 23 September 1993, in *FBIS-SOV*, 24 September 1993, pp. 21–22; *Kommersant-Daily*, 24 September 1993, p. 2.

63. INTERFAX, 4 October 1993, in *FBIS-SOV*, 5 October 1993, p. 9; *Moskovskie novosti*, no. 42, 17 October 1993, pp. A4–A5. *New York Times*, 11 October 1993, p. 1.

64. *Izvestiia*, 2 November 1993, p. 5.

65. Interview with German television, 12 November 1993, in *FBIS-SOV*, 15 November 1993, p. 12.

66. *Komsomol'skaia pravda*, 8 October 1993, p. 2.

67. See Vladimir Lopatin, "O roli sily v ispolnenii zakona," *Nezavisimaia gazeta*, 19 October 1993, pp. 1–2.

68. Interview with Savostianov in *Izvestiia*, 2 November 1993, p. 5.

69. Interview in *La Repubblica*, 8 October 1993, p. 13, in *FBIS-SOV*, 13 October 1993, p. 46.

70. See an interview with Grachev in *Moskovskii komsomolets*, 8 October 1993, p. 1; *Trud*, 9 October 1993, p. 3. On Yeltsin's problems with Vympel and Alpha, see *Struggle for Russia*, pp. 11–14.

71. INTERFAX, 19 October 1993, in *FBIS-SOV*, 20 October 1993, p. 31.

72. Moscow Maiak Radio, 6 October 1993, in *FBIS-SOV*, 6 October 1993, p. 7. Gaidar had been made first deputy prime minister in September 1993.

73. *Izvestiia*, 12 October 1993, p. 3. Also see Georgii Rozhov, "Za obnovlenie. Gde ono?" *Ogonek*, nos. 42–43, October 1993, p. 3.

74. INTERFAX, 2 November 1993, in *FBIS-SOV*, 3 November 1993.

75. *Rossiiskaia gazeta*, 15 October 1993, p. 2.

76. *Nezavisimaia gazeta*, 9 October 1993, p. 1; *Argumenty i fakty*, no. 41 (October 1993): 3.

77. Interview with Poltoranin, Moscow Russian Television, 16 October 1993, in *FBIS-SOV*, 18 October 1993, p. 21.

78. *Argumenty i fakty*, no. 47 (November 1993): 6.

79. *Novaia ezhednevaia gazeta*, 20 October 1993, p. 1.

80. Interview with Stepashin, *Rossiiskaia gazeta*, 13 November 1993, pp. 1–2.

81. The draft constitution, approved by voters on 12 December, was published in *Rossiiskie vesti*, 10 November 1993.

82. The decree was published in *Krasnaia zvezda*, 25 December 1993, p. 1.

83. Moscow Ostankino Television, 22 December 1993, in *FBIS-SOV*, 23 December 1993.

84. See, for example, Sergei Grigoriants, "Kuda idet KGB?" *Izvestiia*, 12 January 1993, p. 5; and Yevgenia Albats, "Lubianka: Budet li etomu konets?" *Izvestiia*, 3, 4, 7 December 1993.

85. *Krasnaia zvezda*, 11 January 1994, p. 1.

86. *Izvestiia*, 29 December 1993, p. 2.

87. See a report by Aleksandr Kudakaev in *Segodnia*, 23 December 1993, p. 1.

88. St. Petersburg Television, 30 January 1994, in *FBIS-SOV*, 7 February 1994, p. 21.

89. *Izvestiia*, 29 December 1993, p. 1. Golushko confirmed in a personal interview that he was unhappy about the changes.

90. Moscow Radio Rossii, 5 January 1994, in *FBIS-SOV*, 6 January 1994, p. 19; interview with Stepashin in *Rossiiskaia gazeta*, 12 January 1994, p. 2.

91. ITAR-TASS, 6 January 1994, in *FBIS-SOV*, 6 January 1994, p. 19. The irony that the MB was handing over its responsibilities for fighting corruption to the Procuracy, an agency that reputedly collaborated with the local mafia, was not lost on the media: "We can congratulate the mafiosi on its unexpected New Year's present," noted *Komsomol'skaia pravda*. "For its interrogators are employees of an organization that, in legal terms, no longer exists." *Komsomol'skaia pravda*, 29 December 1993, p. 3.

92. Interview with Viktor Zorin, head of the Counterintelligence Operations Directorate, *Moskovskii komsomolets*, 2 March 1994, p. 2.

93. *Rossiiskaia gazeta*, 12 January 1994, p. 2.

94. *Izvestiia*, 11 January 1994, p. 1.

95. *Izvestiia*, 29 December 1993, p. 1.

96. *Krasnaia zvezda*, 11 January 1994, p. 1.

97. ITAR-TASS, 10 January 1994, p. 26, in *FBIS-SOV*, 11 January 1994, p. 26.

98. *Rossiiskaia gazeta*, 11 January 1994, as cited in Viktor Yasmann, "Security Services Reorganized: All Power to the Russian President," *RFE/RL Research Report* 3, no. 6 (February 1994): 12. In February 1994, Yeltsin signed an edict abolishing the Administration for Information Resources, under the president's staff, and handing over its functions to FAPSI. See *Kommersant-Daily*, 23 February 1994, p. 2.

99. See two articles by Vera Selivanova in *Segodnia*, 30 July 1993, p. 2; and 19 February 1994, p. 2.

100. See Radio Rossii, 17 December 1993, in *FBIS-SOV*, 20 December 1993, p. 64; and Sergei Parkomenko, "Bashnia Merlina," *Moskovskie novosti*, no. 31, 30 April-7 May 1995, pp. 1, 8–9.

101. *Izvestiia*, 11 January 1994, p. 3.

102. Nonetheless, both Korzhakov and Guard Directorate chief Barsukov had difficulty persuading their elite Alpha and Vympel units to back up Yeltsin during the October crisis. Yeltsin retaliated against Vympel, which had been subordinated to the Guard Directorate in the summer of 1993, by transferring it to the MVD. This led to the resignation of 110 out of 180 officers. The remaining Vympel employees were reorganized to form a special force for combatting nuclear terrorism, under the direct control of the Minister of Internal Affairs. INTERFAX, 19 April 1994, in *FBIS-SOV*, 20 April 1994, p. 41. As for Alpha, it remained under Barsukov's service. See *Obshchaia gazeta*, 12 January 1995, p. 8.

103. *Komsomol'skaia pravda*, 23 December 1993, p. 1.

104. Iurii Buida, "Russkii dekabr: Nichego neozhidannogo," *Nezavisimaia gazeta*, 4 January 1991, p. 1.

105. For background on Baturin, see a profile of him by Nataliia Gevorkian in *Moskovskie novosti*, no. 32, 8 August 1993, pp. 8–9, and *Novoe vremia*, no. 3 (January 1994): 10–11.

106. Ibid.

107. INTERFAX, 7 January 1994, in *FBIS-SOV*, 7 January 1994, p. 16.

108. *Izvestiia*, 11 January 1994, p. 3.

109. *Nezavisimaia gazeta*, 2 February 1994, p. 4; Albats, *State within a State*, p. 350.

110. Moscow Russian Television, 8 November 1993, in *FBIS-SOV*, 10 November 1993, p. 39.

111. See *Kuranty*, 6 April 1994, pp. 4, 5; and Susan Cavan, "Presidential Apparatus: Constant Change," *Perspective* 5, no. 1 (September–October 1994): 5–8.

112. The statute, which was approved by Yeltsin in early January, was published for the first time in *Rossiiskaia gazeta*, 30 March 1994, p. 4.

CHAPTER FOUR
1994: AN EXPANDING ROLE FOR DOMESTIC SECURITY

1. Michael McFaul, "Eurasia Letter: Russian Politics after Chechnya," *Foreign Policy*, no. 99 (Summer 1995): 149–165 (on p. 151).

2. As McFaul observes: "By the end of November, the 'party of war,' as it was dubbed by the liberal Russian press, was in control of the Kremlin and was determined to resolve the Chechen crisis by force." Ibid., p. 153.

3. See *Rossiiskaia gazeta*, 30 March 1994, p. 4.

4. Iurii Baturin, "The Special Service That Came in from the Cold," *Kuranty*, 6 April 1994, pp. 4–5, in *FBIS-SOV*, 28 April 1994, pp. 29–35.

5. *Rossiiskie vesti*, 6 July 1994, p. 2.

6. Moscow, INTERFAX, 8 October 1994, p. 1, in *FBIS-SOV*, 19 September 1994, p. 33.

7. See *Segodnia*, 24 November 1994, p. 1.

8. Interview with Stepashin, *Komsomol'skaia pravda*, 29 November 1994, p. 10.

9. Author's interview with Golushko, Moscow, 12 January 1995. Moscow Radio, 1 March 1994; INTERFAX, 28 February 1994, in *FBIS-SOV*, 1 March 1994, p. 17. Also see *Segodnia*, 1 March 1994, p. 1.

10. Yevgenia Albats, *The State within a State: The KGB and Its Hold on Russia—Past, Present and Future*, trans. Catherine A. Fitzpatrick (New York: Farrar, Straus, Giroux, 1994), p. 357.

11. Author's interview with Albats, Moscow, May 23, 1994.

12. On Stepashin's background, see *Segodnia*, 18 May 1993, p. 1, and 4 March 1994, p. 1. Also see author's interview with Golushko.

13. *Zavtra*, no. 11, March 1994, p. 1.

14. Baturin in *Kuranty*, 6 April 1994, pp. 4–5.

15. Ibid.

16. Ibid.

17. ITAR-TASS, 5 April 1994, in *FBIS-SOV*, 5 April 1994, p. 8.

18. *Komsomol'skaia pravda*, 5 April 1994, p. 3.

19. *Nezavisimaia gazeta*, 26 May 1994, pp. 1, 5.

20. Ibid., p. 5.

21. His speech was reprinted in *Rossiiskaia gazeta*, 28 May 1994, pp. 1, 4.

22. *Kommersant-Daily*, 1 June 1994, p. 14, in *FBIS-SOV*, 2 June 1994, p. 18.

23. *Rossiiskaia gazeta*, 1 June 1994, p. 4.

24. The majority of the new recruits would come from the regular armed forces. According to one recent estimate, the MVD's internal troops numbered 70,000 at the time the additional 52,000 were to be added. See Mark Galeotti, "Russia's Internal Security Forces—Does More Mean Better?" *Jane's Intelligence Review*, no. 6 (June 1994): 271–272.

25. *Izvestiia*, 26 January 1994, p. 1.

26. The crime problem in the former Soviet Union has not been limited to Russia. Mafia activities have spread to other CIS countries and to the Baltic and east European states. Porous borders and other problems relating to the transition

to democracy and free-market economies have caused organized crime to become endemic throughout the former Soviet empire. See Christopher J. Ulrich, "The Price of Freedom: The Criminal Threat in Russia, Eastern Europe and the Baltic Region," *Conflict Studies*, no. 275 (October 1994).

27. Moscow Ostankino Television, 11 June 1994, in *FBIS-SOV*, 13 June 1994, p. 34.

28. Yevgenia Albats, "Ne poletiat li tol'ko shchepli?" *Izvestiia*, 17 June 1994, p. 3.

29. Ibid.

30. *Izvestiia*, 15 June 1994, p. 1.

31. *Izvestiia*, 16 June 1994, pp. 1–2.

32. *Nezavisimaia gazeta*, 18 June 1994, p. 2.

33. *Moskovskie novosti*, no. 25, 19–26 June 1994, p. A5.

34. *Nezavisimaia gazeta*, 16 June 1994, p. 1.

35. *Sovetskaia Rossiia*, 21 June 1994, pp. 1–2.

36. Ibid.

37. *Pravda*, 16 June 1994, p. 1; *Nezavisimaia gazeta*, 18 June 1994, p. 1.

38. Published in *Rossiiskaia gazeta*, 7 July 1994, p. 1.

39. *Izvestiia*, 24 June 1994, p. 2.

40. ITAR-TASS, 22 June 1994, in *FBIS-SOV*, 23 June 1994, p. 15.

41. Moscow Russian Television, 23 June 1994, in *FBIS-SOV*, 24 June 1994, pp. 21–22.

42. INTERFAX, 28 June 1994, in *FBIS-SOV*, 29 June 1994, p. 21; *Rossiiskie vesti*, 6 July 1994, p. 2.

43. *Rossiiskaia gazeta*, 30 June 1994, p. 3.

44. INTERFAX, 7 July 1994, in *FBIS-SOV*, 8 July 1994, p. 14.

45. *Rossiiskaia gazeta*, 21 July 1994, pp. 1, 2.

46. As cited in *Newsweek*, 25 July 1994, p. 28.

47. *Kommersant-Daily*, 21 June 1994, p. 14.

48. Ivan Putilin, "FBR sozdaet zashchitnyi poias ot russkoi mafii," *Nezavisimaia gazeta*, 1 July 1994, pp. 1, 3.

49. *Nezavisimaia gazeta*, 5 July 1994, p. 1.

50. Moscow Ostankino Television, 22 June 1994, in *FBIS-SOV*, 23 June 1994, p. 18.

51. *Segodnia*, 6 July 1994, p. 7.

52. Igor Baranovskii, "Terror kak fakt rossiiskoi konkurentsii," *Moskovskie novosti*, no. 29, 17–24 July 1994, p. 4.

53. *Segodnia*, 23 July 1994, p. 7.

54. INTERFAX in English, 2 April 1994, in *FBIS-SOV*, 4 April 1994, p. 28.

55. *Pravda*, 25 March 1994, p. 1.

56. Barannikov died of a heart attack, at age fifty-four, in July 1995. It was rumored that Barannikov had compiled a list of over two thousand public figures who had served secretly as agents for the KGB. See an article by Nataliia Gevorkian in *Moskovskie novosti*, no. 59, 3–10 September 1995, p. 21.

57. *RFE/RL Daily Report*, no. 198, 18 October 1994, p. 1.

58. Ibid., no. 199, 19 October 1994, p. 1.

59. Moscow, Maiak Radio in Russian, 18 November 1994, in *FBIS-SOV*, 18 November 1994, p. 35.

60. *Izvestiia*, 4 November 1994, p. 5; Moscow Television, 17 November 1994, in *FBIS-SOV*, 17 November 1994, p. 17; ITAR-TASS, 2 December 1994, in *FBIS-SOV*, 2 December 1994, p. 21.

61. *Rossiia*, no. 43, 9 November 1994, p. 1, in *FBIS-SOV*, 6 December 1994, p. 3.

62. *Izvestiia*, 16 November 1994, p. 1.

63. Interview with Stepashin in *Komsomol'skaia pravda*, 29 November 1994, p. 10.

64. See, for example, an article by J. Michael Waller, "Russia's Biggest 'Mafia' Is the KGB," in *Wall Street Journal, Europe*, 22 June 1994. Waller paints a picture of a vast KGB criminal conspiracy to control commercial and trade ventures.

65. *Moskovskie novosti*, no. 24, 12–19 June 1994, p. 2; *New York Times*, 12 August 1994, p. 1. Later, the German weekly *Der Spiegel* claimed that the plutonium seized by German agents was not from Russia after all and was part of a "setup" by the German secret services. As reported in *Krasnaia zvezda*, 29 April 1995, p. 2. Also see a chronology (1994–1995) of reported thefts and illicit exports of nuclear materials in *Nuclear Successor States of the Soviet Union: Nuclear Weapon and Sensitive Export Status Report*, published by the Carnegie Endowment for International Peace and the Monterey Institute of International Studies, Washington, D.C., no. 3 (July 1995): 58–79.

66. See the Statute on the FSK, *Rossiiskaia gazeta*, 30 March 1994, p. 4. The MB and its predecessor, the KGB, had similar responsibilities. The MVD's Eighth Chief Directorate supported the FSK in guarding nuclear facilities.

67. INTERFAX, 28 January 1993, in *FBIS-SOV*, 29 January 1993, p. 23.

68. ITAR-TASS, 28 January 1993, in *FBIS-SOV*, 28 January 1993, p. 21.

69. INTERFAX, 19 April 1994, in *FBIS-SOV*, 20 April 1994, pp. 41–42.

70. ITAR-TASS, 4 July 1994, in *FBIS-SOV*, 5 July 1994, p. 6; INTERFAX, 5 July 1994, in *FBIS-SOV*, 6 July 1994, p. 27. It is interesting that just a few weeks earlier Stepashin said in an interview that "the problem of holes in the borders is directly tied to the plundering of the national wealth of Russia. It is common knowledge on what an immense scale raw materials, components, and products are illegally exported abroad . . . the 'transparency' of the borders makes it impossible to fight contraband effectively" (*Nezavisimaia gazeta*, 26 May 1994, p. 1).

71. Interview with FSK official Vladimir Tomarovskii in *Le Point*, 20 August 1994, p. 11, in *FBIS-SOV*, 22 August 1994, p. 6. Also see *Krasnaia zvezda*, 20 August 1994, p. 2, and an interview with FSK spokesman Aleksandr Mikhailov, Moscow Russian Television, 29 August 1994, in *FBIS-SOV*, 30 August 1994, pp. 22–23.

72. ITAR-TASS, 22 August 1994, in *FBIS-SOV*, 23 August 1994, p. 2. *RFE/RL Daily Report*, no. 179, 20 September 1994, p. 1.

73. Moscow Ostankino Television, 23 August 1994, in *FBIS-SOV*, 25 August 1994, p. 9.

74. *Nezavisimaia gazeta*, 25 August 1994, p. 1; and Paris AFP, 30 August 1994, in *FBIS-SOV*, 31 August 1994, p. 35.

75. *Izvestiia*, 31 August 1994, p. 1.

76. Berlin RRP/ADN Radio in German, in *FBIS-SOV*, 23 September 1994, p. 15.

77. *Kommersant-Daily*, 9 September 1994, p. 3; and ITAR-TASS in English, 2 November 1994, in *FBIS-SOV*, 3 November 1994, p. 42.

78. *Moskovskie novosti*, no. 61, 4–11 December 1994, p. 14.

79. ITAR-TASS, 24 May 1995, in *FBIS-SOV*, 24 May 1995, p. 17.

80. See an interview with Dudaev in *Moskovskie novosti*, no. 31, 31 July–7 August 1994, p. 10.

81. *Kommersant-Daily*, 5 July 1994, p. 3, in *FBIS-SOV*, 6 July 1994, p. 31; *Nezavisimaia gazeta*, 30 July 1994, p. 3.

82. *Kommersant-Daily*, 4 May 1994, p. 14, in *FBIS-SOV*, 4 May 1994, p. 21; *Nezavisimaia gazeta*, 10 August 1994, p. 1.

83. *Izvestiia*, 7 September 1994, p. 2.

84. See, for example, ITAR-TASS, 4 August 1994, in *FBIS-SOV*, 5 August 1994, p. 22.

85. Moscow, Ostankino Television, 17 September 1994, in *FBIS-SOV*, 19 September 1994, p. 18.

86. *Kommersant-Daily*, 3 December 1994, p. 3.

87. ITAR-TASS, 8 December 1994, in *FBIS-SOV*, 8 December 1994, p. 38.

88. Moscow Radio, 10 December 1994, in *FBIS-SOV*, 12 December 1994, p. 45.

89. *Nezavisimaia gazeta*, 14 December 1994, p. 2.

90. Interview with Stepashin, Moscow Radio, 10 December 1994, in *FBIS-SOV*, 12 December 1994, p. 45.

91. Author's interview with Vladimir Tomarovskii, deputy chief of FSK public relations, 10 January 1995. Also see Amy Knight, "The Real Winner in Chechnya: The KGB," *New York Times Op-Ed*, 3 February 1995.

92. David Remnick, "Letter from Chechnia," *The New Yorker*, 24 July 1995, p. 55. Also see McFaul, "Eurasia Letter."

93. Interview in *Obshchaia gazeta*, no. 19, 11–17 May 1995, p. 8.

94. Interview in *Komsomol'skaia pravda*, 29 November 1994, p. 10.

95. *New York Times*, 12 December 1994, p. A8.

96. Andrei Zhdankinin in *Komsomol'skaia pravda*, 10 February 1995, p. 7, in *FBIS-SOV*, 15 February 1995, pp. 14–16.

97. Ibid., p. 16.

98. As quoted in the *New York Times*, 5 January 1995, p. A8.

99. *Belaia Kniga Rossiiskikh Spetssluzhb* (Moscow: Obozrevatel,' 1995), pp. 45–48.

100. *Nezavisimaia gazeta*, 6 December 1994, p. 3; *Segodnia*, 8 December 1994, p. 1.

101. Journalist Nataliia Gevorkian says that he was dismissed because he was the scapegoat for the botched Chechnia operation. See *Moskovskie novosti*, no. 61, 4–11 December 1994, p. 2.

102. See *Ekspress khronika*, 16–23 March 1995, no. 9, p. 8.

103. See, for example, *Izvestiia*, 7 December 1994, pp. 1, 4.

104. Korzhakov interview in *Argumenty i fakty*, no. 3 (January 1995): 3.

105. *Obshchaia gazeta*, no. 4, 26 January 1995, p. 8; *Moscow News*, no. 4, 27 January–2 February 1995, pp. 1,4. Also see *Segodnia*, 19 January 1995, p. 2.

CHAPTER FIVE
FOREIGN INTELLIGENCE

1. Actually, this is not entirely accurate. In 1979 Kalugin had a falling out with Vladimir Kriuchkov, chief of foreign intelligence at the time, and was transferred to the Second Chief Directorate (internal counterintelligence). He served in the Leningrad KGB administration from 1980 through 1987. See a brief biography of him in *Argumenty i fakty*, no. 26, 30 June–6 July 1990, p. 6.

2. To Bonner's comment Kalugin responded: "What is so strange? Her husband [Andrei Sakharov] is the father of the Soviet hydrogen bomb. He was a total Stalinist in his time. . . . Am I not allowed to change? Is this the right of Sakharov only?" See Kalugin's book, *The First Directorate: My 32 Years in Intelligence and Espionage against the West*. With Fen Montaigne (New York: St. Martin's Press, 1994), pp. 335–336.

3. See Kalugin, *The First Directorate*, pp. 178–183. Also see an interview with Kalugin in *Demokraticheskaia Rossiia*, no. 5, 19 April 1991, pp. 6–7, in which he reveals that the Bulgarians gave him a Browning pistol for his role in the murder.

4. John le Carré, "My New Friends in the New Russia: In Search of a Few Good Crooks, Cops and Former Agents," *New York Times Book Review*, 19 February 1995, p. 33.

5. One of the first times Kobaladze cited these figures was in a talk at the Kennan Institute, Washington, D.C., 12 January 1993.

6. Kobaladze said this when he appeared at a conference on "The KGB: Yesterday, Today and Tomorrow," Central House of Writers, Moscow, 28 May 1994.

7. She claims to have had no connection with the KGB: "I was totally removed from that organization. I never had an intelligence or counterintelligence officer among my acquaintances." See *Novosti razvedki i kontrrazvedki*, no. 1 (February 1993): 7.

8. Interview in *Segodnia*, 24 December 1993, p. 3.

9. See *Patriot*, no. 33, August 1992, p. 4.

10. *Krasnaia zvezda*, 24 July 1992, p. 2.

11. Interview in *Krasnaia zvezda*, 30 October 1993, p. 6.

12. Moscow Radio, 26 April 1992, in *FBIS-SOV*, 28 April 1992, p. 23.

13. "Pochemu nam nuzhna razvedka?" *Krasnaia zvezda*, 21 December 1993, p. 3.

14. Ibid.

15. Radio Rossii, Moscow, 24 January 1993, in *FBIS-SOV*, 26 January 1993, p. 19.

16. *Izvestiia*, 14 January 1993, p. 3.

17. Interview with Kobaladze, Moscow Central Television, First Program, 10 August 1992, in *FBIS-SOV*, 13 August 1992, pp. 24–27.

18. Moscow, Russian Television, 28 February, 9 March and 11 March 1994, in *FBIS-SOV*, 16 March 1994, pp. 13–14.

19. See Nataliia Gevorkian and Azer Mursaliev, "The Four Lives of Yevgeniy Primakov," *Moscow News*, no. 23, 16–22 June 1995, p. 7.

20. Yevgenia Albats, *The State within a State*, Trans. Catherine A. Fitzpatrick

(New York: Farrar, Straus, Giroux, 1994), p. 462. According to *Moscow News*: "The rumors that Primakov was involved with the intelligence service since that time are not groundless. The retired KGB general Oleg Kalugin maintains that about two thirds of Soviet correspondents abroad were linked to the KGB." See "The Four Lives of Yevgeniy Primakov."

21. Primakov's boss at the Peace Committee was Gennadii Borovik, a former *Novosti* journalist and a recognized official of the KGB. Borovik's brother-in-law was erstwhile KGB chief, Vladimir Kriuchkov. On the activities of the Peace Committee, see secret CPSU documents published in *Izvestiia*, 29 July 1992, p. 7.

22. According to some reports, Primakov had earlier, when he served as correspondent in the Middle East, coordinated KGB contacts with Palestinian terrorist organizations. See *World Press Review*, March 1992, p. 7.

23. *Rossiiskaia gazeta*, 3 October 1991, p. 1.

24. Gevorkian and Mursaliev, "The Four Lives of Yevgeniy Primakov."

25. Interview with Primakov in *Nezavisimaia gazeta*, 21 December 1991, pp. 1, 5; Moscow Radio, 26 February 1992, in *FBIS-SOV*, 27 February 1992, p. 34.

26. *Nezavisimaia gazeta*, 21 December 1991, p. 5.

27. Leonid Mlechlin, "Into the Forest and out of the Forest: Russian Intelligence Service in Search of Its Lost Identity," *New Times*, no. 22 (June 1992): 34–38 (on p. 35).

28. *Rossiiskaia gazeta*, 17 June 1993, p. 7.

29. The visit was disrupted by the murder in Georgia of CIA employee Fred Woodruff, which led to speculation in Moscow that the CIA was lending support to the government of Eduard Shevardnadze. See *Krasnaia zvezda*, 12 August 1993, p. 3, and pp. 126–127 below.

30. *Rossiiskie vesti*, 4 August 1993, in *FBIS-SOV*, 4 August 1993, p. 24.

31. This figure was cited in ibid.

32. In November 1992, for example, both the Ministry of Security and the FIS requested increases in their budgetary allocations, but President Yeltsin reportedly refused. Moscow, Ostankino Television, 16 November 1992, in *FBIS-SOV*, 17 November 1992, p. 12.

33. Albats, *State within a State*, p. 37.

34. He first said this at a press conference he gave after being appointed head of the KGB's Foreign Intelligence Directorate in the autumn of 1991. TASS, international service, 2 October 1991, in *FBIS-SOV*, 3 October 1991, pp. 17–18.

35. Albats, *State within a State*, p. 462.

36. *Nezavisimia gazeta*, 26 February 1994, p. 2.

37. Interview with Deputy FIS Director Grigorii Rapota, *Nezavisimaia gazeta*, 28 January 1995, p. 2.

38. For a discussion of this practice, see Mlechin, "Into the Forest," p. 35; and an article by Arkadii Voropaev in *Sovetskaia Rossiia*, 4 February 1993, p. 6, which argues that the whole idea of curtailing foreign intelligence operations under diplomatic cover is absurd.

39. Stanislav Levchenko, "Is the KGB Dead?" *The World and I* (August 1992): 44.

40. See Adam Zagorin, "Still Spying after All These Years," *Time*, 29 June 1992, p. 58, citing a statement by FBI counterintelligence chief Wayne Gilbert.

41. Moscow, INTERFAX, 5 January 1993, in *FBIS-SOV*, 6 January 1993, p. 7.

42. The law was published in *Rossiiskaia gazeta*, 11 August 1992, p. 4.

43. Larisa Petukhova, "Shtirlits udivilsia by . . .," *Chelovek i zakon*, nos. 11–12 (1992): 21.

44. *Novaia ezhednevnaia gazeta*, 16 July 1993, p. 3.

45. Petukhova, "Shtirlits udivilsia by."

46. Interview in *Komsomol'skaia pravda*, 22 December 1994, p. 6.

47. *Kuranty*, 27 October 1992, p. 4.

48. *Izvestiia*, 15 April 1992, p. 5.

49. Aleksandr Vasil'ev, "Pochemu 'ushel' polkovnik KGB," *Komsomol'skaia pravda*, 9 May 1992, p. 4.

50. Ibid.

51. *Izvestiia*, 14 August 1992, p. 4; and 20 October 1992, p. 4.

52. See *Rabochaia tribuna*, 4 December 1993, p. 1.

53. Moscow, TASS, 26 October 1990, in *FBIS-SOV*, 29 October 1990, p. 64.

54. Moscow, Ostankino Television, 9 September 1992, in *FBIS-SOV*, 10 September 1992, p. 21.

55. ITAR-TASS, 10 January 1994, in *FBIS-SOV*, 10 January 1994, p. 38.

56. *Kommersant-Daily*, 24 February 1994, p. 14.

57. Interview in *Nezavisimaia gazeta*, 23 December 1993, pp. 1, 6.

58. Interview in *Sobesednik*, no. 36, September 1990, pp. 6–7.

59. For an informative Western story of the Ames affair, see David Wise, *Nightmover: How Aldrich Ames Sold the CIA for $4.6 Million* (New York: HarperCollins, 1995).

60. Ibid. and interview with a KGB colonel, Boris Nikodimovich, whose last name was not revealed, *Kommunist vooruzhennykh sil*, no. 13 (July 1990): 67–71.

61. *New York Times*, 2 March 1994, pp. A1, B7.

62. *Izvestiia*, 25 February 1994, p. 6.

63. *Kommersant-Daily*, 24 February 1994, p. 14.

64. "Skandal v Amerike: Dve tochki zreniia na prichiny i sledstviia," *Literaturnaia gazeta*, 3 March 1994, p. 14.

65. See an interview with him in *La Repubblica*, 26 February 1994, p. 17, in *FBIS-SOV*, 1 March 1994, p. 5.

66. In an interview with this author on 24 November 1993, Washington, D.C., Kalugin said that no moles had been recruited in the CIA. "in his time in the KGB." According to Edward Jay Epstein, Kalugin stated categorically in 1992 that "no responsible politician or government employee was ever recruited by the Soviets in Europe or America in the last twenty years." See *The New Republic*, 28 March 1994, p. 14.

67. See Kalugin, *The First Directorate*, pp. 202–206; and an interview with Iurchenko in *Moskovskaia pravda*, 9 August 1986, p. 4.

68. In fact, this idea had been raised earlier in a lengthy series of articles by a Russian journalist. See Vladimir Snigirev, "The KGB Colonel's Version," *Trud*, 13, 15, 18 August 1992, in *FBIS-USR*, 18 September 1992, pp. 1–9.

69. For a discussion of Ames's ties with Iurchenko, see Walter Pincus, "Ames's Role with Soviet Defector under Review," *Washington Post*, 4 April 1994, p. A6. Also see Wise, *Nightmover*, pp. 133–140. Kalugin, in his recent book, goes out of his way to stress that it was Howard's information that led to the arrest and exposure of several KGB officers who had been spying for the United States. Kalugin finished his book just at the time that Ames was arrested, so, not surprisingly, he makes no mention of Ames, but this does not mean that he did not know about him. See a review of his book by this author in the *Washington Post*, 13 October 1994, p. D3; and an exchange of letters with Kalugin in *Washington Post Book World*, 18 December 1994, p. 14.

70. Mikhail Liubimov, "Dlia TsRU 'krasnaia seledka,'" *Sovershenno sekretno*, no. 3 (1994): 3. Gordievsky now says that he is sure that he was exposed by Ames. Ames received his first payment from the KGB on 18 May 1985, the day after Gordievsky was recalled to Moscow because he had fallen under suspicion of being a traitor. See a report in *Izvestiia*, 1 April 1994, p. 3.

71. See *New York Times*, 20 March 1994, p. 12; Dmitrii Radyshevskii, "Eims, Iurchenko i smert' agenta TsRU v Gruzii," *Moskovskie novosti*, no. 12, 20–27 March 1994, p. 13.

72. Interview with Kobaladze, Moscow Radio, 23 February 1994, in *FBIS-SOV*, 24 February 1994, p. 2.

73. As reported in the *Washington Post*, 27 February 1994, p. A21.

74. Vladimir Abarinov, "Skandal s Eimsami kak 'aktivnoe meropriatie' TsRU i FBR," *Segodnia*, 18 March 1994, p. 3.

75. Moscow Radio, 23 February 1994, in *FBIS-SOV*, 24 February 1994.

76. *Segodnia*, 2 March 1994, p. 1.

77. Later, in June 1995, a former Russian counterintelligence officer claimed that Ames's contribution to the success of Russian counterintelligence had been exaggerated. Ames, for example, had nothing to do with the exposure of GRU general Poliakov. ITAR-TASS, 13 June 1995, in *FBIS-SOV*, 14 June 1995, pp. 10–11. Was this "sour grapes," since Ames was a prize of the foreign intelligence service?

78. *Izvestiia*, 25 February 1994, p. 6.

79. Interview with Solomatin in *Trud*, 26 February 1994, p. 6.

80. *Kuranty*, 18 December 1993, p. 3.

81. *Moskovskii komsomolets*, 28 December 1993, p. 1.

82. ITAR-TASS, 14 June 1994, in *FBIS-SOV*, 15 June 1994, pp. 18–19.

83. His speech was reprinted in *Rossiiskaia gazeta*, 29 April 1994, p. 3. On the reaction at Iasenevo, see *Kuranty*, 13 May 1994, p. 4.

84. *Rossiiskaia gazeta*, 29 April 1994, p. 3.

85. *Izvestiia*, 3 August 1993, p. 1.

86. *Nezavisimaia gazeta*, 18 February 1993, p. 1.

87. ITAR-TASS, 23 June 1994, in *FBIS-SOV*, 24 June 1994, p. 15.

88. As reported in *Defense News*, 8–14 March 1993, p. 1.

89. *Perspektivy rashireniia NATO i interesy Rossii*, Moscow, 1993, in *FBIS-SOV*, 8 December 1993, pp. 61–71.

90. Interview with Trubnikov in *Nezavisimaia gazeta*, 23 December 1993, p. 1.

91. The main portions of the report were reproduced in *Nezavisimaia gazeta*, 22 September 1994, p. 1.

92. Interview with Evstaf'ev, *Moskovskie novosti*, no. 2, 9–16 January 1994, p. 14.

93. *Izvestiia*, 24 June 1994, p. 1.

94. ITAR-TASS, 4 June 1994, in *FBIS-SOV*, 7 June 1994, p. 5; and ITAR-TASS, 29 June 1994, in *FBIS-SOV*, 1 July 1994, p. 7.

95. See, for example, the new military doctrine of the Russian Federation, *Osnovnyye polozheniia voennoi doktriny rossiiskoi federatsii (izlozhenie)*, Moscow, 1993.

96. For analysis of the shift in Russian foreign policy, see Suzanne Crow, "Why Has Russian Foreign Policy Changed?" *RFE/RL Research Report* 3, no. 18, 6 May 1994, pp. 1–6.

97. Fiona Hill and Pamela Jewett, "Back in the USSR: Russian Intervention in the Internal Affairs of the Former Soviet Republics and the Implications for United States Policy toward Russia," Ethnic Conflict Project, Harvard University, Cambridge, Mass., January 1994, p. 86. Also see ibid.; Stuart D. Goldman, "Russia's Emerging Foreign and Defense Policy," Congressional Research Report for Congress, Washington, D.C., June 8, 1994; and William Odom and Robert Dujarric, *Commonwealth or Empire? Russia, Central Asia and the Transcaucasus* (Indianapolis: The Hudson Institute, 1995).

98. *Krasnaia zvezda*, 8 April 1992, p. 1.

99. *Komsomol'skaia pravda*, 14 September 1993, p. 7; INTERFAX, 6 April 1994, in *FBIS-SOV*, 8 April 1994, p. 4. Belorussia and Uzbekistan signed further agreements with the FIS in September 1992 and July 1993, respectively. See INTERFAX, 3 September 1992, in *FBIS-SOV*, 4 September 1992, p. 38; and ITAR-TASS, 23 July 1993, in *FBIS-SOV*, 23 July 1993, p. 12.

100. INTERFAX, 18 April 1994, in *FBIS-SOV*, 19 April 1994, p. 58.

101. For a discussion of the security services in the states of the former Soviet Union, see chapter 6.

102. See Oleg Stekal, "Ukraine: The New Secret Service," *Transition* 1, no. 10 (June 1995): 1–4.

103. See *Ukraina moloda*, 19 May 1992, pp. 4–5, in *FBIS-SOV*, 19 June 1992, p. 59; and *Molod Ukrainy*, 18 August 1992, in *FBIS-SOV*, 2 October 1992. Also see chapter 6.

104. The border troops, which were under the authority of the Ministry of Security until late 1993, are a semi-independent agency. See chapter 6.

105. See Odom and Dujarric, *Commonwealth or Empire*, pp. 84–86; and Gevorkian and Mursaliev, "The Four Lives of Yevgeniy Primakov." For more on Giorgadze, see pp. 157–158.

106. Erevan, SNARK radio, in *FBIS-SOV*, 21 March 1994, pp. 60–61.

107. Armen Khanbabian, "Kto ubil byvshego predsedatelia KGB respubliki?" *Nezavisimaia gazeta*, 26 January 1994, p. 3. In July 1992, Iuzbashian had publicly declared that the leader of the political opposition to President Ter-Petrossian, Grayr Marukhian, had been an agent for the KGB. See *Rossiiskaia gazeta*, 28 July 1992, p. 7.

108. *Argumenty i fakty*, no. 15 (May 1993).

109. INTERFAX, 6 April 1994, in *FBIS-SOV*, 8 April 1994, p. 3.

110. *Paevaleht*, 2 March 1993, pp. 6–7, in *FBIS-SOV*, 22 May 1993, pp. 86–89; *Krasnaia zvezda*, 16 June 1992, p. 2.

111. *Diyena*, 20 January 1993, p. 1, in *FBIS-SOV*, 24 February 1993, pp. 146–147; and Tallin BNS (radio), 26 February 1993, in *FBIS-SOV*, 2 March 1993, p. 72.

112. Kalugin in *Demokraticheskaia rossiia*, 19 April 1991.

113. Wolfe was sentenced in December 1993 to six years in prison, but in June 1995 the German high court overturned the sentence. See *New York Times*, 6 June 1995, p. A11.

114. *New York Times*, 12 September 1993, p. 1.

115. *Nezavisimaia gazeta*, 18 February 1993, p. 1

116. Anna Sabbat-Swidlicka, "Problems of Poland's State Security Office," *RFE/RL Research Report*, 28 February 1992, pp. 15–20.

117. *RFE/RL Daily Report*, no. 93, 17 May 1993; *Nezavisimaia gazeta*, 18 May 1993, p. 1.

118. *Izvestiia*, 7 December 1993, p. 3.

119. See an unpublished monograph by Victor Yasmann, "Restructuring the Secret Services in Eastern Europe," Munich, 1995.

CHAPTER SIX
RUSSIA'S BORDERS AND BEYOND

1. In addition to Russia, the CIS includes Azerbaidzhan, Armenia, Belarus, Georgia, Kazakhstan, Kyrgyzstan, Moldova, Tadzhikistan, Turkmenistan, Ukraine, and Uzbekistan. The three other former Soviet republics, Latvia, Lithuania, and Estonia, which did not join, are discussed briefly in the concluding chapter.

2. For a discussion of border administration in the Soviet period, see Amy Knight, *The KGB* (Boston: Unwin-Hyman, 1990), pp. 221–247.

3. See Richard Woff, "The Border Troops of the Russian Federation," *Jane's Intelligence Review* 7, no. 2, February 1995, pp. 70–73.

4. See an interview with border troops commander Andrei Nikolaev in *Komsomol'skaia pravda*, 28 May 1994, p. 2.

5. The law was reproduced in *Federatsiia*, no. 47, 27 April 1993, pp. 4–5.

6. Moscow, INTERFAX, 26 January 1995, in *FBIS-SOV*, 27 January 1995, p. 9.

7. *Golos Ukrainy*, 18 December 1991, p. 13, in *FBIS-USR*, 28 April 1992, pp. 74–77.

8. ITAR-TASS, 4 August 1994, in *FBIS-SOV*, 5 August 1994, p. 9. *Demokratychna ukrayna*, 10 November 1994, p. 3, in *FBIS-SOV*, 21 November 1994, p. 50, and INTERFAX, 30 January 1995, in *FBIS-SOV*, 31 January 1995, p. 26.

9. Woff, "The Border Troops," pp. 71–72.

10. *Moskovskie novosti*, no. 3, 15–22 January 1995, p. 10; *Segodnia*, 4 February 1995, p. 3.

11. Moscow, RIA in English, 22 December 1994, in *FBIS-SOV*, 28 December 1994, p. 13.

12. ITAR-TASS, 27 December 1994, in *FBIS-SOV*, 28 December 1994, p. 7; *Rossiiskaia gazeta*, 29 December 1994, p. 2.

13. Tadzhikistan announced in early June 1994 that it was creating its own border guards. See ITAR-TASS, 7 June 1994, in *FBIS-SOV*, 7 June 1994, p. 60.

14. ITAR-TASS, Moscow, 4 March 1993, in *FBIS-SOV*, 5 March 1993, p. 23.

15. The agreement was published in *Turkmenskaia iskra*, 28 August 1992, pp. 1–2. Also see *Rossiiskaia gazeta*, 25 January 1994, p. 6.

16. INTERFAX, 29 July 1994, in *FBIS-SOV*, 2 August 1994, p. 1. Also see *Krasnaia zvezda*, 19 July 1994, p. 3.

17. The Kyrgyz government reaffirmed in late 1994 that Russian border troops would continue exercising this function. *Vecherniy Bishkek*, 17 November 1994, p. 2, in *FBIS-SOV*, 21 November 1994, p. 62.

18. Moscow Maiak Radio, 17 January 1994, in *FBIS-SOV*, 18 January 1994, p. 1. In July 1994 Russia signed agreements with Uzbekistan, Tadzhikistan, and Turkmenistan on joint control of the CIS outer border. Moscow Radio, 16 July, 1994, in *FBIS-SOV*, 18 July 1994, p. 59.

19. INTERFAX, 8 June 1995, in *FBIS-SOV*, 9 June 1995, pp. 96–97.

20. See Yeltsin's speech to the border guards, reproduced in *Rossiiskaia gazeta*, 31 May 1994, p. 1; and *RFE/RL Daily Report*, no. 173, 12 September 1994, p. 6.

21. Interview with Nikolaev in *Moskovskii komsomolets*, 12 May 1994, p. 1. On the pull-out of Russian border troops from the Azerbaidzhan-Iran border, see *Rossiiskaia gazeta*, 18 November 1992, p. 7.

22. INTERFAX, 30 January 1995, in *FBIS-SOV*, 31 January 1995, p. 26.

23. The statute on the Federal Border Service was not actually signed by Yeltsin until early March 1995. See an article by border chief Nikolaev in *Rossiiskie vesti*, 11 May 1995, p. 2, in *FBIS-SOV*, 11 May 1995, p. 2.

24. Interview with Nikolaev in *Komsomol'skaia pravda*, 28 May 1994, p. 2. The Soviet border troops were estimated to number about 230,000 in the late 1980s. See Knight, *The KGB*, p. 232.

25. *Moskovskii komsomolets*, 15 June 1994, p. 1, in *FBIS-SOV*, 15 June 1994, p. 24. By late 1994, the Border Service had seven border districts and three groups of border troops, as well as an independent border control detachment that operates at the major airports. Woff, "The Border Troops," p. 72.

26. *Rossiiskie vesti*, 11 May 1995, p. 2.

27. *Nezavisimaia gazeta*, 9 February 1995, p. 2.

28. *Krasnaia zvezda*, 21 July 1994, p. 3; *Nezavisimaia gazeta*, February 1995, p. 2.

29. *Selskaia zhizn*, 4 February 1993, p. 3.

30. See *Rossiiskaia gazeta*, 19 January 1995, p. 2; and *Nezavisimaia gazeta*, 1 February 1995, p. 2.

31. Interview with deputy chief of the Federal Border Service Nikolai Bordiuzha, RIA Radio, 24 December 1994, in *FBIS-SOV*, 29 December 1994, pp. 3–4; Woff, "The Border Troops," p. 72.

32. See his biography in *Krasnaia zvezda*, 16 September 1993, p. 1; and *Jane's Intelligence Review*, November 1993, p. 7.

33. *Izvestiia*, 14 July 1994, p. 1. After the Security Council meeting, Nikolaev announced that the new policy would increase the number of border troops over

the next few years, as opposed to a continued cut in the number of military troops. See *Segodnia*, 20 July 1994, p. 2.

34. RFE/RL Daily report, no. 132, 14 July 1994, p. 1. Grachev was also angered by the fact that Nikolaev had decided to stage a "strategic command exercise," involving both border and regular military officers, without consulting Grachev. See Woff, "The Border Troops," p. 73.

35. *Nezavisimaia gazeta*, 5 October 1994, p. 1.

36. Interview in *Rossiiskie vesti*, 30 December 1994, p. 1.

37. Ibid.

38. See *Segodnia*, 4 February 1995, p. 3.

39. INTERFAX, 10 February 1995, in *FBIS-SOV*, 13 February 1995, pp. 3–4. For further developments, see chapter 9.

40. *Samostiyna ukrayina*, no. 14, October 1991, p. 6, in *FBIS-SOV*, 15 November 1991, pp. 13–14.

41. Ibid.

42. The figure of 18,000 was given to this author by Nikolai Golushko, former Ukrainian security chief, in an interview in Moscow, January 10, 1995.

43. See an interview with SBU chief Evhen Marchuk, *Vecherniy Kiyev*, 17 March 1992, p. 1, in *FBIS-SOV*, 15 April 1992, p. 65.

44. *Molod ukrayiny*, 7 May 1992, p. 2, in *FBIS-SOV*, 5 June 1992, pp. 71–72.

45. Oleg Strekal, "The New Secret Services," *Transition* 1, no. 10 (June 1995), p. 1. Also see *BBC Summary of World Broadcasts*, SU/1363, 24 April 1992, p. B7, which cited Marchuk as saying that two-thirds of the department heads in the service had been replaced.

46. Interview with first deputy chief of the SBU, Major General Vasily Gorbatyuk, *Narodnaia armiia*, 17 July 1992, pp. 1, 3.

47. *Narodnaia armiia*, 22 April 1992, p. 1.

48. Interview in *Vecherniy Kiyev*, 17 March 1992, pp. 1–2, in *FBIS-USR*, 15 April 1992, pp. 65–70.

49. As told to this author by Western observers living in Ukraine.

50. The law was published in *Golos Ukrainy*, 13 May 1992, pp. 6–8, in *FBIS-USR*, 30 June 1992, pp. 33–40.

51. *Nezavisimost*, 16 June 1995, pp. 1, 6, in *FBIS-SOV*, 10 July 1995, p. 60.

52. *Rossiiskaia gazeta*, 12 August 1992, pp. 1, 4.

53. Interview with Marchuk, Kiev Radio, 16 March 1994, in *FBIS-SOV*, 17 March 1994, pp. 29–30.

54. INTERFAX, 23 July 1992, in *FBIS-SOV*, 23 July 1992, p. 54.

55. Interview with Marchuk, *Uryadovyy Kuryer*, 25 March 1993, p. 5, in *FBIS-USR*, 10 May 1993, pp. 50–51; INTERFAX, 12 April 1993, in *FBIS-SOV*, 13 April 1993, pp. 59–60.

56. See, for example, an interview with Donetsk SBU Chief Anatolii Chumak, *Aksent*, 17 January 1995, pp. 1–2, in *FBIS-SOV*, 20 January 1995, pp. 39–40.

57. *Uryadovyy kuryer*, 21 August 1993, p. 11, in *FBIS-SOV*, 4 October 1993, p. 17.

58. *Ukrayinska hazeta*, 7–20 July 1994, p. 8, in *FBIS-SOV*, 13 July 1994, pp. 32–35.

59. Strekal, "The New Secret Service," p. 3.

60. Ibid.

61. See *Moskovskie novosti*, no. 11, 13–20 March 1994, p. 10.

62. *Demokratychna ukrayina*, 16 June 1993, p. 3, in *FBIS-SOV*, 21 June 1993, pp. 63–65.

63. See Karen Dawisha and Bruce Parrott, *Russia and the New States of Eurasia: The Politics of Upheaval* (Cambridge, U.K.: Cambridge University Press, 1994), pp. 247–250.

64. On the Union of Ukrainian Officers and the SBU, see ibid., pp. 137–138.

65. Moscow Radio, 27 November 1993, in *FBIS-SOV*, 29 November 1993, p. 62.

66. *Uryadovyy kuryer*, 30 July 1994, pp. 1, 3, cited in *FBIS-SOV*, 4 August 1994, p. 34.

67. INTELNEWS, Kiev, 21 February 1995, in *FBIS-SOV*, 23 February 1995, pp. 57–58.

68. In one of his first public pronouncements, Malikov claimed that the interests of foreign special services in Ukraine had become stronger and that his service had to counteract aggressively their efforts at spying and subversion. See *Rabochaia tribuna*, 26 March 1993, p. 3, in *FBIS-USR*, 23 April 1993, pp. 72–73.

69. *Molod ukrayiny*, 29 July 1994, p. 1, in *FBIS-SOV*, 2 August 1994, p. 33.

70. See *Krasnaia zvezda*, 21 July 1992, p. 1; *Komsomol'skaia pravda*, 4 October 1993, p. 7.

71. *Molod Ukrayiny*, 4 March 1994, pp. 1, 3.

72. See, for example, an article in *Demokratychna Ukrayina*, 10 June 1995, p. 1, in *FBIS-SOV*, 15 June 1995, pp. 40–41.

73. See Alexander Lukashuk, "Belarus's KGB: In Search of an Identity," *RFE/RL Research Report* 1, no. 47, 27 November 1992, pp. 17–21.

74. For a good survey of politics in Belarus, see Ustina Markus, "Belarus: You Can't Go Home Again?" *Current History* (October 1994): 337–341.

75. Ibid. and INTERFAX, 13 November 1992, in *FBIS-SOV*, 16 November 1992, p. 72; *Narodnaia gazeta*, 11 November 1993, p. 2.

76. *Nezavisimaia gazeta*, 17 November 1992, p. 3.

77. *Zvyazda*, 20 November 1992, in *FBIS-SOV*, 8 January 1993, pp. 26–28.

78. Radio Minsk, 16 December 1993, in *FBIS-SOV*, 16 December 1993, p. 73; Minsk, Belepan News, 29 March 1994, in *FBIS-SOV*, 30 March 1994, p. 51.

79. *Komsomol'skaia pravda*, 25 April 1995, p. 2, in *FBIS-SOV*, 5 May 1995, p. 38.

80. *Svaboda*, 23–29 August 1994, p. 1, in *FBIS-SOV*, 30 August 1994, p. 41.

81. *Zvyazda*, 28 January 1995, pp. 1, 3, in *FBIS-SOV*, 23 February 1995, pp. 68–70.

82. Lukashuk, "Belarus's KGB," p. 20.

83. INTERFAX, 29 August 1994, in *FBIS-SOV*, 30 August 1994, p. 41; Minsk, Belapan News, 24 May 1995, in *FBIS-SOV*, 25 May 1995, p. 60.

84. See Fiona Hill and Pamela Jewett, "Back in the USSR: Russian Intervention in the Internal Affairs of the Former Soviet Republics and the Implications for United States Policy toward Russia" (Ethnic Conflict Project, Harvard University, Cambridge, Mass., 1994), pp. 59–65.

85. Willian Crowther, "Moldova after Independence," *Current History* (October 1994): 342–347 (pp. 346–347).

86. ITAR-TASS, 24 June 1994, in *FBIS-SOV*, 27 June 1994, p. 58; *Moskovskie novosti*, no. 27, 3–10 July 1994, p. 1.

87. On general developments regarding these republics and their relationship with Moscow, see William E. Odom and Robert Dujarric, *Commonwealth or Empire? Russia, Central Asia and the Transcaucasus* (Indianapolis: The Hudson Institute, 1995).

88. See Azer Mursaliev, "Narkoperevorot," *Moskovskie novosti*, no. 61, 4–11 December 1994, p. 11; *Moskovskii komsomolets*, 14 June 1995, p. 4, and 11 August 1995, p. 2; *Izvestiia*, 4 October 1995, p. 2.

89. Elizabeth Fuller, "Security as Achilles' Heel in Georgia and Armenia," *RFE/RL Research Report* 3, no. 30, 29 July 1994, pp. 23–26.

90. Ibid.; *Izvestiia*, 4 October 1995, p. 2.

91. Interview with Giorgadze in *Sakartvelos respublika*, 24 March 1994, pp. 1, 2, in *FBIS-SOV*, 11 April 1994, pp. 61–63.

92. See *New York Times*, 30 August 1995, p. A7.

93. Tbilisi Radio, 13 October 1993; INTERFAX, 13 October 1993, in *FBIS-SOV*, 14 October 1993, p. 100.

94. *Obshchaia gazeta*, no. 16, 22–28 April 1994, p. 8.

95. *Izvestiia*, 4 October 1995, p. 2; *Moskovskii komsomolets*, 26 September 1995, pp. 1, 7.

96. *Rabochaia tribuna*, 11 November 1992, p. 2.

97. Baku, TURAN, 2 June 1995, in *FBIS-SOV*, 5 June 1995, p. 84.

98. ITAR-TASS, 2 June 1995, in *FBIS-SOV*, 5 June 1995, p. 84.

99. *Moskovskii komsomolets*, 14 June 1995, p. 4.

100. *Izvestiia*, 4 August 1993, p. 5. Aliev has reiterated his commitment to close relations with Russia on numerous occasions since then. See, for example, an interview with Aliev in *Rossiiskaia gazeta*, 15 June 1994, pp. 1–2.

101. See *Izvestiia*, 10 October 1995, p. 2.

102. *Izvestiia*, 7 July 1992, p. 3; *Nezavisimaia gazeta*, 26 January 1994, p. 3; INTERFAX, 18 January 1994, in *FBIS-SOV*, 19 January 1994, p. 61.

103. Fuller, "Security as Achilles' Heel"; ITAR-TASS, 7 August 1994, in *FBIS-SOV*, 10 August 1994, p. 50.

104. ITAR-TASS, 6 January 1995, in *FBIS-SOV*, 9 January 1995, p. 63.

105. For background on these states, see Odom and Dujarric, *Commonwealth or Empire?*, and Jim Nichol, "Central Asia's New States: Political Developments and Implications for U.S. Interests," CRS Issue Brief, Congressional Research Service, 13 May 1994.

106. For background on Akaev and his handling of political opposition, see *Literaturnaia gazeta*, no. 8, 22 February 1995, p. 11.

107. For a general analysis of recent Kyrgyz politics, see *Report on the Parliamentary Election in Kyrgyzstan*, prepared by the staff of the Commission on Security and Cooperation in Europe, Washington, D.C., April 1995.

108. INTERFAX, 1 February 1995, in *FBIS-SOV*, 2 February 1995, p. 45.

109. *Kazakhstanskaia pravda*, 7 July 1992, pp. 1,3; Moscow, Radio Rossii, 14 July 1992, in *FBIS-SOV*, 16 July 1992, p. 66.

110. ITAR-TASS, 16 June 1993, in *FBIS-SOV*, 17 June 1993, p. 63. Also see an earlier interview with Baekenov in *Kazakhstanskaia pravda*, 7 May 1992, p. 3.

111. *Kommersant-Daily*, 27 February 1993, p. 20, in *FBIS-SOV*, 2 March 1993, p. 56.

112. ITAR-TASS, 17 May 1994, in *FBIS-SOV*, 18 May 1994, p. 56.

113. *Segodnia*, 4 August 1994, p. 4.

114. See, for example, *Nezavisimaia gazeta*, 27 May 1994, p. 3, on the persecution of Turkmen dissident Murad Essenov.

115. *New York Times*, 16 April 1995, p. 6.

116. *Narodnoe slovo*, 24 September 1994, p. 1, in *FBIS-SOV*, 27 September 1994, p. 71.

117. Ibid.

118. See Nichol, "Central Asia's New States."

119. Dushanbe Radio, 1 November 1994, in *FBIS-SOV*, 2 November 1994, p. 45.

120. For a discussion of Moscow's changing CIS policy, see *Nezavisimaia gazeta*, 9 February 1995, pp. 1-2.

CHAPTER SEVEN
THE SECURITY SERVICES AND HUMAN RIGHTS

1. *Delovoi mir*, 13 May 1995, p. 12, in *FBIS-SOV*, 8 June 1995, pp. 20-21.

2. See Valery Chalidze, *The Soviet Human Rights Movement: A Memoir* (New York: The American Jewish Committee, 1984), for a concise overview of the movement in its early stages.

3. See *Reform and Human Rights: The Gorbachev Record*, report by the Commission on Security and Cooperation in Europe (Washington, D.C.: Government Printing Office, 1988), p. 31. Also see Robert B. Cullen, "Human Rights: A Millennial Year," *The Harriman Institute Forum* 1, no. 12 (1988): 1-8.

4. See Amy Knight, "The KGB and Democratization: A New Legal Order?" in Uri Ra'anan, *The Soviet Empire: The Challenge of National and Democratic Movements* (Lexington, Mass.: Lexington Books, 1990), pp. 41-62; and Amy Knight, "The Future of the KGB," *Problems of Communism* 39, no. 6 (November-December 1990): 20-33.

5. Ibid.

6. Robert Sharlet, "Soviet Legal Reform in Historical Context," *Columbia Journal of Transnational Law* 28, no. 1 (1990): 5-18 (p. 7).

7. See *Rossiiskaia gazeta*, 17 June 1992, p. 5.

8. The Law on the Status of Judges was published in *Rossiiskaia gazeta*, 29 July 1992, p. 5, and the draft Constitution first appeared in *Rossiiskaia gazeta*, 10 November 1993, pp. 3-6. For an analysis of the Constitution's effects, see Robert Sharlet, "Reinventing the Russian State: Problems of Constitutional Implementation," *The John Marshall Law Review* 28, no. 4 (Summer 1995): 775-786.

9. On the debate over this law in the Duma, see *Segodnia*, 8 June 1995, p. 2. The current law on the procuracy was enacted in January 1992.

10. For details on this edict, see chapter 9.

11. See *Nezavisimaia gazeta*, 15 October 1994, pp. 1, 3, for an analysis of the draft code.

12. Article 70 was revised to prohibit "public calls for the forcible change of the constitutional system or for the seizure of power, and likewise the mass dissemination of materials containing such calls." *Rossiiskaia gazeta*, 27 October 1992, p. 5.

13. See *Rossiiskaia gazeta*, 18 August 1995, p. 1. In the words of *Moskovskii komsomolets*: "Now the list of permitted operational investigative measures includes virtually all possible methods of operational activity against citizens." *Moskovskii komsomolets*, 15 August 1995, p. 1.

14. See *Pravda*, 7 March 1995, p. 2. As of September 1995, the draft was still awaiting final approval by Yeltsin.

15. Article 277 prohibited "acts directed at the incitement of social, national, racial, or religious hostility or discord; the abasement of national dignity and likewise, the promotion of propaganda furthering the discrimination or inferiority of citizens on the basis of their religious, national, or racial affiliation if said acts are committed publicly or using the mass media."

16. See an analysis of the law: Iurii Feofanov, "Prestupleniia i nakazaniia v svete rynochnykh otnoshenii," *Izvestiia*, 25 July 1995, pp. 1, 2; and *Kommersant-Daily*, 21 July 1995, p. 14.

17. George Ginsburgs and Armins Rusis, "Soviet Criminal Law and the Protection of State Secrets," in *Law in Eastern Europe*, vol. 7 (Leyden: A. W. Sythoff, 1963), pp. 3–48.

18. For the Law on State Secrets, see *Rossiiskaia gazeta*, 21 September 1993, pp. 5–6.

19. See *Segodnia*, 18 May 1993, p. 2; and *Rossiiskie vesti*, 3 March 1994, p. 4, for a critical response to the law.

20. "Otravlennaia politika," *Moskovskie novosti*, no. 38, 20–27 September 1992, p. 16.

21. *Izvestiia*, 3 November 1992, pp. 1–2; *Kuranty*, 23 January 1993, p. 5, in *FBIS-SOV*, 26 January 1993, pp. 2–4.

22. Ibid., and *Nezavisimaia gazeta*, 23 October 1992, p. 1.

23. Moscow, Central Television, 5 November 1992, in *FBIS-SOV*, 12 November 1991, p. 52.

24. *New York Times*, 8 April 1993, p. A8.

25. *Moskovskie novosti*, no. 5, 30 January–6 February 1994, p. A6.

26. Ibid.; *Nezavisimaia gazeta*, 5 February 1994, p. 1; *Moskovskie novosti*, no. 11, 13–20 March 1994, p. 1.

27. Vil S. Mirzaianov, "Chemical Weapons: An Exposé," *Perspective* 4, no. 4 (April-May 1994): 1–4.

28. MB investigator Shkarin clearly understood the broader implications of the case. He even explained to Mirzaianov that, since the Chemical Weapons Convention did not go into effect until 1995, Russia should develop and produce as many chemical weapons as possible. See *Izvestiia*, 22 January 1994, p. 1.

29. The state has, however, used courts to suppress freedom of the press. In August 1992, before the initial arrest of Mirzaianov, authorities had arrested Gennadii Maiorov for alleged libel. Maiorov had written a newspaper article

exposing abuses at the notorious Special Psychiatric Hospital in Orel and was found guilty of slander. *Human Rights and Democratization in the Newly Independent States of the Former Soviet Union*, Commission on Security and Cooperation in Europe, Washington, D.C., January 1993, p. 30.

30. See one of the reports on persecution of journalists in the former Soviet Union, published monthly in the *Independent Gazette: Nezavisimaia gazeta*, 14 April 1995, p. 2.

31. ITAR-TASS, 28 and 29 December 1994, in *FBIS-SOV*, 29 December 1994, p. 25.

32. *Izvestiia*, 30 December 1994, p. 2.

33. ITAR-TASS, 29 December 1994, in *FBIS-SOV*, 30 December 1994, pp. 10–11.

34. *Nezavisimaia gazeta*, 10 January 1995, p. 3. Also see Amy Knight, "The Real Winner in Chechnya: The KGB," *New York Times*, Op-Ed, 3 February 1995.

35. *Moskovskii komsomolets*, 20 January 1995, p. 1.

36. ITAR-TASS, 23 January 1995, in *FBIS-SOV*, 23 January 1995, pp. 12–13.

37. *Rossiiskaia gazeta*, 28 May 1994, p. 1.

38. *Rossiiskaia gazeta*, 4 January 1993, p. 6, and 1 September 1993, pp. 1–2; *Country Reports on Human Rights Practices, 1993*, U.S. Department of State (Washington, D.C.: Government Printing Office, 1994), pp. 1029–1030.

39. *Human Rights and Democratization*, p. 27.

40. On the *propiska* system and its history, see Kronid Liubarskii, "Pasportnaia systema i sistema propiski v Rossii," *Rossiiskii biulleten' po pravam cheloveka*, vol. 2 (Moscow: Project Group on Human Rights, 1994), pp. 14–24.

41. *The Situation in Russia*, briefing of the Commission on Security and Cooperation in Europe, Washington, D.C., October 1993, p. 5 (testimony by Paul Goble).

42. *Komsomol'skaia pravda*, 25 January 1995, p. 1.

43. See *Country Reports on Human Rights Practices*, 1993, p. 1027.

44. See Vera Tolz, "The Moscow Crisis and the Future of Democracy in Russia, *RFE/RL Research Report* 2, no. 42, 22 October 1993, pp. 1–2.

45. See *Country Reports on Human Rights Practices*, 1994, U.S. Department of State, February 1995 (Washington, D.C.: Goverment Printing Office, 1995, p. 936.

46. See a segment of the *Independent Gazette's* regular reports on the persecution of journalists: *Nezavisimaia gazeta*, 21 April 1995, p. 2.

47. *Human Rights and Democratization*, p. 31.

48. See *Kommersant-Daily*, 24 January 1995, p. 14.

49. *Nezavisimaia gazeta*, 8 October 1994, p. 3.

50. *Zavtra*, no. 41, October 1994, p. 1; INTERFAX, 11 January 1995, in *FBIS-SOV*, 12 January 1995, p. 20. The U.S. State Department's Human Rights Report for 1994 states with regard to the Kholodov murder that "the line between politically motivated killings and criminal activities has become difficult to distinguish" (p. 930).

51. *Segodnia*, 14 March 1995, p. 1.

52. See *Izvestiia*, 4 March 1995, pp. 1–2, for a discussion of the role of the FSK in the murder. It is worth noting that, following the Listev murder, several television figures connected to him received death threats. INTERFAX, 21 March 1995, in *FBIS-SOV*, 22 March 1995, p. 22.

53. *Izvestiia*, 3 December 1993, p. 7.

54. *Rossiiskaia gazeta*, 28 May 1994, p. 1.

55. As *Moscow News* pointed out, Yeltsin's Security Council voted unanimously for the presidential decree that authorized the invasion and "the Security Council does not carry responsibility independently from the president." See *Moskovskie novosti*, no. 63, 11–18 December 1994, p. 4.

56. See Knight, "The Real Winner in Chechnya."

57. *Rossiiskaia gazeta*, 25 January 1995, p. 1.

58. Testimony of Professor Mohammad Shashani before the U.S. Commission on Security and Cooperation in Europe, Washington, D.C., 19 January 1995.

59. Testimony of Paul A. Goble before the CSCE Commission, Washington, D.C., 19 January 1995.

60. Sharlet, "Reinventing the Russian State," p. 782.

61. Author's interview with Tomarovskii, Lubianka, Moscow, 10 January 1995. Stepashin expressed similar views. See, for example, an interview in *Delovoi mir*, 25 February 1995, p. 2. According to Stepashin, 90 percent of counterfeit Russian bank notes discovered in recent years was connected with Chechen criminal groups.

62. *Rossiiskaia gazeta*, 23 February 1995, p. 2.

63. The Russian Duma issued a decree granting amnesty to those who took part in armed resistance to the invasion up until 18 December 1994, but who then laid down their arms. Clearly, this amnesty would cover only a small portion of the adult population. See *Rossiiskaia gazeta*, 1 March 1995, p. 15.

64. *Rossiiskaia gazeta*, 28 January 1995, p. 1; INTERFAX, 31 January 1995, in *FBIS-SOV*, 1 February 1995, p. 19.

65. Testimony of Mohammad Shashani; ITAR-TASS, 22 March 1995, in *FBIS-SOV*, 23 March 1995, p. 37.

66. Amnesty International, "Human Rights Concerns in Chechnia," testimony before the Organization on Security and Cooperation in Europe, Washington, D.C., 19 January 1995, pp. 7–8.

67. *Moskovskie novosti*, no. 26, 16–23 April 1995, p. 1; David Remnick, "Letter from Chechnya: In Stalin's Wake," *The New Yorker*, 24 July 1995, p. 62.

68. Remnick, "Letter from Chechnya," p. 48.

69. Moscow, Russian Television, 24 February 1995, in *FBIS-SOV*, 24 February 1995, p. 28; Remnick, "Letter from Chechnya."

70. *Human Rights and Democratization*, p. 50.

71. The law, dated December 1993, was published in *Holos Ukrayiny*, 21 January 1994, p. 3, in *FBIS-SOV*, 25 January 1994, pp. 44–45.

72. The Ukrainian law was published in *Holos Ukrayiny*, 10 March 1994, pp. 6–8, in *FBIS-USR*, 28 April 1994, pp. 39–46. The Russian law appeared in *Rossiiskaia gazeta*, 21 September 1993, pp. 5–6.

73. *Country Reports on Human Rights Practices for 1994*, p. 1019; Kiev Radio, 8 July 1993, in *FBIS-SOV*, 12 July 1993, p. 43.

74. *Country Reports on Human Rights Practices*, 1994, p. 1017; *Golos Ukrainy*, 13 May 1992, pp. 6–8, in *FBIS-SOV*, 30 June 1992, p. 37 (Law on the Security Service). *Uryadovyy kuryer*, 6 October 1994, in *FBIS-SOV*, 14 October 1994, p. 40.

75. *Human Rights and Democratization*, p. 55; *Nezavisimost*, 18 November 1992, p. 1, in *FBIS-SOV*, 9 December 1992, p. 60.

76. *Nezavisimaia gazeta*, 13 March 1995, p. 2. His case had not come up for trial by the end of the summer of 1995.

77. *Narodna hazeta*, no. 21 (152), May 1994, p. 5, in *FBIS-SOV*, 23 May 1994, p. 70.

78. *Komsomol'skaia pravda*, 27 October 1993, p. 2.

79. *Country Reports on Human Rights Practices*, 1994, p. 1017.

80. *Nezavisimaia gazeta*, 14 April 1995, p. 2.

81. Minsk, Belarus Radio, 28 December 1994, in *FBIS-SOV*, 29 December 1994, pp. 37–38.

82. See Minsk, Belapan News, 27 April 1995, in *FBIS-SOV*, 27 April 1995, p. 62; *Nezavisimaia gazeta*, 13 April 1995, p. 2.

83. *Human Rights and Democratization*, pp. 85–95.

84. William Crowther, "Moldova after Independence," *Current History* (October 1994): 342–347 (on p. 347).

85. See Jim Nichol, "Georgia in Transition: Situation Update," CRS Report for Congress, 10 December 1993.

86. Tbilisi Radio, 14 March 1994, in *FBIS-SOV*, 15 March 1994, p. 51.

87. Tbilisi, *Akhali Taoba*, 26 August 1994, p. 3, in *FBIS-SOV*, 2 September 1994, p. 56.

88. *Rezonansi*, 9–10 February 1995, p. 1, in *FBIS-SOV*, 15 February 1995, p. 82.

89. At a June 1995 meeting of Georgian parliamentary deputies, Shevardnadze remarked that "no state needs an inactive security service." Tbilisi, SAKINFORM, 23 June 1995, in *FBIS-SOV*, 26 June 1995, p. 96.

90. *Segodnia*, 30 November 1993, p. 4.

91. *Nezavisimaia gazeta*, 7 May 1994, p. 3; and 8 October 1994, p. 1.

92. Interview with Aliev, INTERFAX, 16 June 1994, in *FBIS-SOV*, 17 June 1994, p. 53.

93. Aliev alluded to the involvement of the Russian security services in the latest plot to unseat him. See *Segodnia*, 18 August 1995, p. 7.

94. See an article by Fred Hiatt in *Washington Post*, 8 June 1995, p. 1.

95. Erevan, SNARK, 18 May 1995; Aragil Electronic News Bulletin, 18 May 1995, in *FBIS-SOV*, 19 May 1995, pp. 83–84.

96. Hiatt in *Washington Post*.

97. *Report on the Parliamentary Election in Kyrgyzstan*, prepared by the staff of the Commission on Security and Cooperation in Europe, April 1995.

98. ITAR-TASS, 17 May 1994, in *FBIS-SOV*, 17 May 1994, p. 50.

99. *Nezavisimaia gazeta*, 13 April 1995, p. 2; *Omri Daily Digest*, 1, no. 134, 12 July 1995, p. 6.

100. For further discussion of this law, see *Human Rights and Democratization*, p. 198.

101. *Sovet Kazakhstana*, 18 October 1994, p. 2, in *FBIS-SOV*, 10 November 1994, pp. 79–87. This law, again, was very similar to the 1992 Russian law on operational investigation.

102. Karishal Asanov, "Ne ver' ulybke presidenta," *Khak*, no. 3, 1992, pp. 1–2.

103. *Human Rights and Democratization*, pp. 201–202.

104. Ibid., p. 202; *Nezavisimaia gazeta*, 8 November 1994, p. 3; *Kazakhstanskaia pravda*, 19 November 1994, p. 3, in *FBIS-SOV*, 25 November 1994, pp. 56–57.

105. ITAR-TASS, 26 May 1995, in *FBIS-SOV*, 30 May 1995, p. 43.

106. *Report on the March 7, 1994, Parliamentary Elections in Kazakhstan*, Commission on Security and Cooperation in Europe, March 1994, p. 14.

107. *Human Rights and Democratization*, pp. 184–185; *Segodnia*, 4 August 1994, p. 4.

108. *Report on Parliamentary Elections in Turkmenistan*, Commission on Security and Cooperation iin Europe, February 1995, p. 5; *RFE/RL Daily Report*, no. 196, 14 October 1994, p. 2.

109. *Report on Parliamentary Elections in Turkmenistan*, p. 1.

110. *New York Times*, 16 April 1995, p. 6.

111. *Human Rights and Democratization*, p. 210.

112. *Country Reports on Human Rights for 1994*, pp. 1039–1040. Abdumannov Pulatov, a prominent human rights campaigner, was tried in January 1993 on charges of "insulting the honor" of President Karimov. His lawyer was not allowed to see materials on the case until shortly before the trial. See *Izvestiia*, 23 January 1993, pp. 1–2.

113. *Country Reports on Human Rights*, 1994, pp. 1039–1040; *Nezavisimaia gazeta*, 23 September 1994, p. 3; 16 March 1995, p. 2; 5 April 1995, p. 2.

114. See *Human Rights and Democratization*, pp. 211–212; *Country Reports on Human Rights*, 1993, p. 1140; *Izvestiia*, 17 May 1994, p. 2; *Nezavisimaia gazeta*, 16 March 1995, p. 2.

115. *Nezavisimaia gazeta*, 16 February 1995, p. 2.

116. *Rossiiskii biulleten' po pravam cheloveka*, no. 2, Working Group on Human Rights, Moscow 1994, pp. 105–130; *RFE/RL Daily Report*, no. 99, 26 May 1994, p. 3; *Nezavisimaia gazeta*, 16 August 1994, p. 3.

117. *Omri Daily Digest*, part 1, no. 197, 10 October 1995.

118. *Rossiiskii biulleten'*, no. 2; *Country Reports on Human Rights*, 1994, pp. 983–987.

CHAPTER EIGHT
GUARDIANS OF HISTORY

1. "The Case of the Russian Archives: An Interview with Iurii N. Afanas'ev," *Slavic Review* 52, no. 2 (Summer 1993): 338–352 (on p. 351).

2. See Robert C. Tucker, "The Rise of Stalin's Personality Cult," *The American Historical Review* 84 (April 1979): 347–366.

3. This observation is based on the personnel experience of doing research in the party archives in the summer of 1992. It has been confirmed by other Western scholars.

4. *Rossiiskaia gazeta*, 12 August 1992, p. 1.

5. This figure comes from Serge Schmemann, "Soviet Archives: Half-Open, Dirty Windows on Past," *New York Times*, 26 April 1995, p. A10. It does not include files in the regional archives.

6. Western scholars have described Russian archival holdings in detail. See, for example, Patricia Kennedy Grimstead, "Russian Archives in Transition: Caught between Political Crossfire and Economic Crisis," *The American Archivist* 56, no. 4 (Fall 1993): 614–663; and Mark Kramer, "Archival Research in Moscow: Progress and Pitfalls," *Cold War International History Project Bulletin*, Fall 1993.

7. Arsenii Roginskii and Nikita Okhotin, "Arkhivy KGB: God posle putcha," unpublished manuscript, Moscow, 1992, p. 7. Also see Amy Knight, "The Fate of the KGB Archives," *The Slavic Review* 52, no. 3 (Fall 1993): 582–586, which draws on this manuscript.

8. Romuald J. Misiunas, "The Archives of the Lithuanian KGB," *Report of the Bundesinstitut für Ostwissenschaftliche und Internationale Studien*, no. 3, 1994, p. 8.

9. Ibid.

10. Roginskii and Okhotin, "Arkhivy KGB," p. 11. Also see an interview with former KGB chief Vadim Bakatin in *Literaturnaia gazeta*, 18 December 1991; and Vadim Bakatin, *Izbavlenie ot KGB* (Moscow: Novosti, 1992), pp. 158–160.

11. Roginskii and Okhotin, "Arkhivy KGB," pp. 8–9.

12. Ibid.

13. Christopher Andrew and Oleg Gordievsky, eds., *Comrade Kryuchkov's Instructions: Top Secret Files on KGB Foreign Operations, 1975–1985* (Stanford, Calif.: Stanford University Press, 1993).

14. Misiunas, "Archives of the Lithuanian KGB," p. 42.

15. Ibid., pp. 15–42.

16. Roginskii and Okhotin, "Arkhivy KGB," p. 1.

17. *Nedelia*, no. 26, 26 June–2 July 1989, p. 1. This was not the first time that the KGB and the party rehabilitated victims of Stalin's purges. In the mid-1950s, shortly after Stalin died, the Khrushchev leadership initiated rehabilitations.

18. *Moskovskaia pravda*, 26 August 1989, p. 2.

19. Yevgenia Albats, *The State within a State* (New York: Farrar, Straus, Giroux, 1994) pp. 112–167 (quotation on p. 131). Also an interview with an official of the Procuracy, V. G. Provotorov, who helped to reveal some of the facts about Boyarsky's past, in *Sovetskaia kultura*, 25 February 1989, p. 8.

20. Albats, *State within a State*, p. 150.

21. *Nedelia*, no. 26, 1989, p. 1.

22. Albats, *State within a State*, p. 295. Similarly, the Czech secret police, the StB, destroyed large numbers of its files in 1989. See Tina Rosenberg, *The Haunted Land: Facing Europe's Ghosts after Communism* (New York: Random House, 1995), pp. 85–86.

23. Bakatin, *Izbavlenie ot KGB*, p. 149.

24. Moscow Russian Television, 28 August 1991, in *FBIS-SOV*, 29 August 1991, p. 43.

25. Roginskii and Okhotin, "Arkhivy KGB," pp. 14–15. Also see Ella Maksi-

mova, "Poka arkhivy KGB bez khoziaina, sekrety uplyvaiut na zapad," *Izvestiia*, 24 January 1992, pp. 1, 7.

26. Rosinskii and Okhotin, "Arkhivy KGB," pp. 14–15.

27. Ibid., pp. 16–17.

28. D. Volkogonov, *The Psychological War* (Moscow: Progress Publishers, 1986), p. 105.

29. *Literaturnaia gazeta*, no. 17, 28 April 1993, p. 10.

30. ITAR-TASS, 29 May 1993, in *FBIS-SOV*, 2 June 1993, p. 39.

31. *Rossiiskaia gazeta*, 17 April 1993, p. 13.

32. See *Rossiiskaia gazeta*, 14 August 1993, p. 5. For an analysis of the law, see *Izvestiia*, 14 July 1993, p. 5.

33. Kramer, "Archival Research," p. 19.

34. Ibid., p. 12.

35. ITAR-TASS, 23 July 1993, in *FBIS-SOV*, 23 July 1993, p. 36.

36. Published in *Rossiiskaia gazeta*, 27 September 1994, p. 4. For details on the directive, see *Moskovskie novosti*, no. 44, 2–9 October 1994, p. 4; and see a translation and analysis by Mark Kramer in *Cold War International History Project Bulletin*, Fall 1994, pp. 89, 100. Kramer interprets the directive to include nonparty documents. But in light of a subsequent statute (see below) of March 1995, it seems that the directive was only referring to party documents housed both in party and government archives. It created a commission to declassify party documents, which included the chief archivists of the FIS and the counterintelligence service, thus giving the security services a say in what party documents could be declassified.

37. *Rossiiskaia gazeta*, 1 March 1995, p. 16. A Federal Law on Information Systems and the Protection of Information, signed by Yeltsin in February 1995, strengthened the impression that archives were becoming more restrictive. It gave government agencies broader say in setting policies for access to documents under their control. See the *Cold War International History Bulletin*, no. 5, Spring 1995, p. 77.

38. Roginskii and Okhotin, "Arkhivy KGB," pp. 16–17.

39. Vera Tolz, "Access to KGB and CPSU Archives in Russia," *RFE/RL Research Report* 1, no. 16, 17 April 1992, p. 4, citing *Izvestiia TsK KPSS*, no. 3, 1991.

40. Ibid., pp. 17–22.

41. According to the law: "Information about people who are cooperating or who have cooperated with organs conducting operational investigation activity [i.e., the security police] on a confidential basis is a state secret and can be publicized only with those persons' written consent or in other cases directly envisaged by the law."

42. Tolz, "Access to KGB and CPSU Archives," pp. 4–5. This was a major problem with opening the police archives in eastern Europe. See Rosenberg, *The Haunted Land*.

43. *Rossiiskaia gazeta*, 17 April 1993, p. 13.

44. Quoted in Tolz, "Access to KGB and CPSU Archives," p. 6.

45. Transcript of conference, "KGB: Yesterday, Today, Tomorrow," Moscow, February 1992, p. 24.

46. "We have not yet found a dignified and civilized way to reckon with our past," Havel observed in 1992. "The lustration act affects the small fish. The big ones are laughing at us." See Jeri Laber, "Witch Hunt in Prague," *The New York Review of Books* 39, no. 8, 23 April 1992, p. 8. Also see Rosenberg, *The Haunted Land*, pp. 3–121.

47. Laber, "Witch Hunt," pp. 5–8.

48. See Kjell Engelbrekt, "The Stasi Revisited," *RFE/RL Research Report* 2, no. 46, 19 November 1993, pp. 19–24; and idem, "Germany's Experience with the Stasi Archives," *RFE/RL Research Report* 3, no. 18, 6 May 1994, pp. 11–13.

49. See Viktor Yasmann, "Legislation on Screening and State Security in Russia," *RFE/RL Research Report* 2, no. 32, 13 August 1993, pp. 11–16.

50. Ibid., 13–14.

51. "The Case of the Russian Archives," p. 340.

52. Kramer, "Archival Research," p. 19.

53. Roginskii and Okhotin, "Arkhivy KGB," p. 16.

54. See Maksimova, "Poka Arkhivy KGB," and Kondrashev's subsequent defense of himself in *Izvestiia*, 4 February 1992, p. 8.

55. "The Case of the Russian Archives," p. 341.

56. This was pointed out by journalist Ella Maksimova, "Prodavtsy sensatsii." For Volkogonov's response, see *Izvestiia*, 19 July 1994, p. 5.

57. *Izvestiia*, 14 July 1993, p. 5.

58. John Costello and Oleg Tsarev, *Deadly Illusions* (New York: Crown Publishers, 1993), p. xx.

59. *Pravda*, 16 October 1992, p. 6.

60. Costello and Tsarev, *Deadly Illusions*, p. xii.

61. See *Komsomol'skaia pravda*, 3 November 1992, p. 4.

62. See, for example, Kramer, "Archival Research," pp. 12–13; and Grimstead, "Russian Archives in Transition," p. 629.

63. *Komsomol'skaia pravda*, 3 November 1992, p. 4.

64. Moscow, Ostankino Television, 26 June 1992, in *FBIS-SOV*, 30 June 1992, pp. 16–17.

65. *Komsomol'skaia pravda*, 3 November 1992, p. 4.

66. This point was made by Mark Kramer in "Archival Research," p. 12.

67. Among the periodicals that publish KGB archival material are *Sovershenno sekretno* and *Novosti razvedki i kontrrazvedki*.

68. See, for example, an article by Aleksandr Bitkovskii, "Legendy i byl'," *Sluzhba bezopasnosti*, no. 1 (August 1992): 77–80, which describes conditions for those incarcerated in the Lubianka during the Stalin era and reproduces secret NKVD orders.

69. Both Hiss's letter and Volkogonov's letter are reproduced in *The Cold War International History Project Bulletin*, no. 2, Fall 1992, p. 33.

70. See, for example, an article by Allen Weinstein, author of a book on the Hiss-Chambers case, in *Washington Post*, 4 November 1992, p. A19.

71. Vladmir Abarinov in *Nezavisimaia gazeta*, 20 November 1992, p. 4.

72. *Nezavisimaia gazeta*, 24 November 1994, p. 4.

73. See Grimstead, "Russian Archives," pp. 629–630.

74. *Komsomol'skaia pravda*, 6 December 1993, p. 7, in *FBIS-SOV*, 13 December 1992, p. 73.

75. See the *Bulletin* of the Cold War International History Project, Fall 1992, p. 37, for reports on the POW-MIA issue. Also see Grimstead, "Russian Archives," p. 630, for the Toon comment.

76. ITAR-TASS, 2 September 1993, in *FBIS-SOV*, 3 September 1993, p. 7.

77. Ibid.

78. On the Morris affair, see Kramer, "Archival Research"; and Stephen Morris, "Ghosts in the Archives," *Washington Post*, 12 September 1993, p. C3.

79. Ibid.

80. Vladimir Abarinov, "More Troubled Waters in the KGB Archives," *Demokratizatsiia* 11, no. 2 (1992): 41.

81. Ibid., pp. 43-44.

82. Ella Maksimova and Valeriy Reshetnikov, "Prava k versiiu," *Izvestiia*, 6 April 1993, p. 7.

83. Ella Maksimova, "Vallenberg mertv," *Izvestiia*, 3 June 1993, p. 5. Former KGB chief Bakatin referred to the existence of a memorandum to Molotov, but said that the document in question could not be located. See Bakatin, *Izbavlenie ot KGB*, p. 169.

84. "Glasnost with a Vengeance," *Insight* 7, no. 44, November 3, 1991, p. 29.

85. Pavel Sudoplatov and Anatoli Sudoplatov, with Jerrold and Leona Schecter, *Special Tasks: The Memoirs of an Unwanted Witness—A Soviet Spymaster* (New York: Little, Brown, 1994).

86. Thomas Powers, "Were the Atomic Scientists Spies?" *The New York Review of Books*, 9 June 1994, p. 14.

87. See, for example, ibid.; Priscilla McMillan, "They Weren't Spies," *Washington Post*, 26 April 1994, p. A15; Richard Rhodes, "Atomic Spies or Atomic Lies?" *New York Times*, OP-ED, 3 May 1994; a review of the book by Roald Sagdeev in *Washington Post Book World*, 1 May 1994, p. 8; and the *F.A.S. Public Interest Report*, journal of the American Federation of Scientists, vol. 47, no. 3 (May/June 1994). The book generated an unprecedented amount of commentary in the press.

88. See Amy Knight, "The Man Who Wasn't There," *New York Times*, OP-ED, 3 May 1994. Sudoplatov actually recanted much of what he said about the atomic scientists in a 1995 interview in Russia, shortly before his book was to appear there: "The great scientists of that period were never our agents and never cooperated with our people." See *Novosti razvedki i kontrrazvedki*, no. 11–12 (44–45) (1995): 6.

89. As cited in Walter Schneir, "Sudo-History," *The Nation*, 6 June 1994, p. 805.

90. *Nezavisimaia gazeta*, 6 May 1994, p. 1.

91. Personal interview with Nataliia Gevorkian, Moscow, May 1994.

92. KGB defector Oleg Gordievsky's book, *KGB: The Inside Story of Its Foreign Operations from Lenin to Gorbachev* (London: Hodder and Stoughton, 1990), written with Christopher Andrew, is not really in this genre. Although he talks about his own personal experience, he uses KGB documents that he secretly copied and many secondary sources to produce a history rather than memoirs.

93. Oleg Kalugin with Fen Montaigne, *The First Directorate: My 32 Years in Intelligence and Espionage against the West* (New York: St. Martin's Press, 1994).

94. See my review of the Kalugin book in *Washington Post*, 14 October 1994, and an exchange of letters between Kalugin and me in *Washington Post Book World*, 18 December 1994, p. 14.

95. Yuri B. Shvets, *Washington Station: My Life as a KGB Spy in America*, trans. from the Russian by Eugene Ostrovsky (New York: Simon and Schuster, 1994). Also see my review in *Washington Post Book World*, 29 January 1995, p. 6.

96. See Schmemann in *New York Times*, 26 April 1995, p. A10.

97. Maksimova, "Prodavtsy sensatsii."

CHAPTER NINE
1995: THE KGB'S DOMAIN REVISITED

1. See, for example, Anders Aslund, "Ruble Awakening: Why the Economic News from Russia Is—Suprise!—Good," *Washington Post*, 23 April 1995, p. C4; *U.S. Assistance and Related Programs for the Newly Independent States of the Former Soviet Union*, 1994 Annual Report, Washington, D.C., January 1995. Also see Anders Aslund, *How Russia Became a Market Economy* (Washington, D.C.: The Brookings Institution, 1995). Although Aslund acknowledges that Russia lacks an effective rule of law and that the state has too much power, he nonetheless thinks that "Russia has become a democratic society."

2. See, for example, Peter Reddaway, "Cancel the IMF Loan to Russia," *Asian Wall Street Journal*, 10 March 1995.

3. ITAR-TASS, 6 April 1995, p. 16 in *FBIS-SOV*, 7 April 1995, p. 16.

4. Published in *Rossiiskaia gazeta*, 12 April 1995, pp. 9–10.

5. See *A Compilation of Intelligence Laws and Related Laws and Executive Orders of Interest to the National Intelligence Community, Prepared for the Use of the House Permanent Select Committee on Intelligence* (Washington, D.C.: Government Printing Office, 1987). This compilation includes the National Security Act of 1947 and the Central Intelligence Agency Act of 1949.

6. *Moskovskii komsomolets*, 7 April 1995, p. 1, in *FBIS-SOV*, 12 April 1995.

7. *Kommersant-Daily*, 23 February 1995, p. 1, in *FBIS-SOV*, 23 February 1995, p. 24.

8. *Izvestiia*, 18 March 1995, pp. 1, 2.

9. INTERFAX, 3 April 1995, in *FBIS-SOV*, 11 April 1995, p. 20; *Moskovskii komsomolets*, 8 July 1995, p. 1, in *FBIS-SOV*, 10 July 1995, p. 24.

10. See, for example, a report on statements by Starovoitov made at a cabinet meeting, *Kommersant-Daily*, 28 July 1995, p. 3, in *Eastview Press Digest*, part 1, 28 July 1995.

11. See *Compilation of Intelligence Laws*, pp. 14–17, 257–261.

12. For a brief biography of Aleksandrov and an interview with him on the question of law and order, see *Nezavisimaia gazeta*, 15 March 1995, p. 4.

13. *Izvestiia*, 18 March 1995, p. 1.

14. Moscow, NTV, 7 April 1995, in *FBIS-SOV*, 12 April 1995, p. 18.

15. For an analysis of the political composition of the Duma following the December 1993 elections, see *Russia's Parliamentary Election and Constitutional Referendum*, 12 December 1993, prepared by the staff of the CSCE, Washington, D.C., January 1994.

16. *Rossiiskaia gazeta*, 12 April 1995, p. 1.

17. On the growth of fascism, see, for example, Aleksei Chelnokov, "Fashisty ne skryvaiut svoego litsa," *Izvestiia*, 23 February 1995, pp. 1–2.

18. Yevgenia Albats, talk delivered at the Hudson Institute, Washington, D.C., 1 May 1995.

19. See Valerii Solovei, "Rossiia ne obrechena na fashizm," *Nezavisimaia gazeta*, 29 March 1995, pp. 1–2.

20. Published in *Rossiiskie vesti*, 28 March 1995, p. 1.

21. INTERFAX, 27 March 1995, in *FBIS-SOV*, 31 March 1995, p. 18.

22. *Moskovskii komsomolets*, 31 December 1994, p. 1.

23. Moscow Radio, 20 February 1995; INTERFAX, 20 February 1995, in *FBIS-SOV*, 21 February 1995, pp. 19–20.

24. Moscow, Ostankino Television, 20 February 1995, in *FBIS-SOV*, 21 February 1995, p. 20.

25. Rustam Sabirov, "Reanimatsiia KGB vpolne real'na," *Nezavisimaia gazeta*, 30 March 1995, p. 1.

26. For a good Western analysis of the initial stages of the Chechen war, see Mark Galeotti, "Decline and Fall—Moscow's Chechen War," *Jane's Intelligence Review* 7, no. 2 (February 1995): 50–56.

27. *Washington Post*, 18 January 1995, p. A11.

28. INTERFAX, 10 May 1995, in *FBIS-SOV*, 11 May 1995, p. 35.

29. Interview with Korzhakov in *Argumenty i fakty*, no. 3, January 1995, p. 3.

30. *Izvestiia*, 22 December 1994, p. 1.

31. *Izvestiia*, 28 December 1994, p. 2.

32. Ibid.

33. *Izvestiia*, 1 February 1995, pp. 1–2.

34. Sabirov, "Reanimatsiia KGB."

35. See a two-part article by Parkhomenko, "Bashnia Merlina," *Moskovskie novosti*, no. 29, 23–30 April 1995, pp. 1, 8–9; and no. 31, 30 April 1995, pp. 18–19.

36. Moscow NTV, 23 April 1995, in *FBIS-SOV*, 11 May 1993, pp. 28–30; and *Segodnia*, 18 May 1995, p. 2. The publicity about Rosvooruzhenie had already led the Yeltsin administration, probably Korzhakov in particular, to try to muzzle the press by claiming that arms exports were a state secret. See chapter 7, p. 172

37. Parkhomenko, "Bashnia Merlina," p. 8.

38. *Obshchaia gazeta*, no. 2, 12 January 1995, p. 8.

39. Ibid.; *Komsomol'skaia pravda*, 9–16 June 1995, p. 5. A former KGB officer, who was the head of a commercial firm that sold Western-made monitoring devices, told *Moscow News* that Barsukov had bought millions of dollars worth of cameras and bugging equipment from his firm during 1992–1993, after which Barsukov then purchased equipment from an American firm with

connections to the CIA. See *Moskovskie novosti*, no. 50, 23–30 July 1995, p. 7.

40. *Obshchaia gazeta*, no. 19, 11–17 May 1995, p. 8.

41. There have been complaints about lack of funds for salaries and equipment, especially since the Yeltsin administration may have curtailed FAPSI's commercial activities. One anonymous FAPSI colonel expressed his resentment about this in an April 1994 interview: "I recall how we rejoiced at first when we were removed from the Committee of State Security to be a separate structure. . . . Now we have a feeling that we have been left high and dry. There is neither the money nor the prestige." *Obshchaia gazeta*, no. 14, 8–14 April 1994, p. 8.

42. See an article by Vera Selivanova, "I na FAPSI est' UIDO," *Segodnia*, 5 May 1995, p. 2.

43. Vladimir Murashkin, "The Electronic Ear Is Sometimes Sensitive and Sometimes Deaf," *Rossiia*, no. 39, 12–18 October 1994, p. 8, in *FBIS-SOV*, 8 November 1994, p. 30.

44. *Obshchaia gazeta*, no. 2, 12 January 1995, p. 8.

45. *Nezavisimaia gazeta*, 15 March 1995, p. 2.

46. ITAR-TASS, 15 March 1995, in *FBIS-SOV*, 17 March 1995, pp. 1–2. *Izvestiia*, 17 March 1995, p. 2; Tbilisi, *Iprinda*, 1 June 1995, in *FBIS-SOV*, 1 June 1995, p. 1.

47. Kazan, *Respublika Tatarstan*, 4 April 1995, in *FBIS-SOV*, 10 April 1995, p. 27.

48. ITAR-TASS, 26 May 1995, in *FBIS-SOV*, 30 May 1995, p. 7.

49. Kiev, UNIAN, 21 April 1995, in *FBIS-SOV*, 24 April 1995, p. 56.

50. Moscow Radio, 31 March 1995, in *FBIS-SOV*, 7 April 1995, p. 17. Also see ITAR-TASS, 30 March 1995, in *FBIS-SOV*, 31 March 1995, p. 2, and ITAR-TASS, 25 May 1995, in *FBIS-SOV*, 26 May 1995, pp. 2–3.

51. See a report in *Krasnaia zvezda*, 14 April 1995, p. 3.

52. *Moskovskie novosti*, no. 31, 30 April–7 May 1995, p. 4. Moscow Television first channel (interview with Nikolaev), 17 April 1995, in *FBIS-SOV*, 18 April 1995, pp. 17–18.

53. *Washington Post*, 19 April 1995, p. A28.

54. See chapter 5, p. 131.

55. Interview with FIS Deputy Director Grigorii Rapota, *Nezavisimaia gazeta*, 28 January 1995, p. 2.

56. Nataliia Gevorkian and Azer Mursaliev, "The Four Lives of Yevgeniy Primakov," *Moscow News*, no. 23, 16–22 June 1995, p. 7.

57. See Amy Knight, *The KGB: Police and Politics in the Soviet Union* (Boston: Unwin-Hyman, 1990), pp. 282–283.

58. Interview with Trubnikov in *Trud*, 11 January 1995, p. 6.

59. Rapota interview, *Nezavisimaia gazeta*.

60. Moscow, Voice of Russia World Service, 25 March 1995, in *FBIS-SOV*, 30 March 1995, p. 13.

61. *Rossiiskaia gazeta*, 25 March 1995, p. 6.

62. *Segodnia*, 21 April 1995, p. 3.

63. See *Moskovskie novosti*, no. 22, 2–9 April 1995, p. 13; *Izvestiia*, 28 April 1995, p. 3.

64. See *Rossiia*, Moscow, no. 39, 12–18 October 1994, p. 8, in *FBIS-SOV*, 8 November 1994, pp. 31–32. For a reference to the Alpha group's subordination to the GUO, see *Obshchaia gazeta*, no. 2, 12 January 1995, p. 8.

65. *Kommersant-Daily*, 4 July 1995, p. 3, in *Eastview Press Digest*, part 2, 4 July 1995.

66. *Segodnia*, 30 June 1995, p. 3; and *Moskovskie novosti*, no. 44, 25 June–2 July 1995, p. 9 (interview with the head of Alpha, Aleksandr Gusev).

67. Vladimir Klimov in *Rossiiskaia gazeta*, 23 June 1995, p. 2, in *FBIS-SOV*, 23 June 1995, p. 33.

68. Interview in *Moskovskaia pravda*, 2 August 1995, p. 16, in *Eastview Press Digest*, part 2, 2 August 1995.

69. Both Barsukov and Korzhakov attended the funeral, along with Stepashin and Erin, of the three Alpha members who were killed in the attempt to free the hostages at Budennovsk—an indication that Alpha was still under their subordination. See the report on the funeral in *Moskovskie novosti*, no. 44, p. 9. Grachev was reported here as saying that he could have carried out the operation better had he been in charge.

70. For a report on the military presence in Moscow, see INTERFAX, 6 July 1995, in *FBIS-SOV*, 7 July 1995, p. 20.

71. *Moskovskii komsomolets*, 7 July 1995, p. 1, in *Eastview Press Digest*, part 1, 7 July 1995.

72. This was the impression conveyed to this author in interviews with former KGB officials in Moscow. Also see an interview with FIS Deputy Director Trubnikov, who alludes to Stepashin's lack of experience, in *Argumenty i fakty*, no. 23, June 1995, p. 3.

73. On Barsukov's background, see *Komsomol'skaia pravda*, 9–16 June 1995, p. 5. On Zorin, see *Izvestiia*, 16 September 1995, p. 1.

74. *Komsomol'skaia pravda*, 9–16 June 1995, p. 5.

75. See *Rossiiskaia gazeta*, 1 August 1995, p. 4.

76. Nikolai Troitskii in *Obshschaia gazeta*, no. 31, 3–9 August 1995, p. 8, in *Eastview Press Digest*, part 1, 2 August 1995. Also see a report by Vladimir Kartashkov in *Moskovskii komsomolets*, 1 August 1995, pp. 1, 2, in *Eastview Press Digest*, part 1, 1 August 1995.

77. *Segodnia*, 29 April 1995, p. 2.

78. See *Sovetskaia Rossiia*, 22 June 1995, p. 1, for a record of the voting.

79. See *Omri Daily Digest*, no. 136, part 1, 14 July 1995; and *Segodnia*, 1 August 1995, p. 2.

80. See an analysis of the law, which was awaiting Yeltsin's signature and thus had yet to be published: Iurii Feofanov, "Prestupleniia i nakazaniia v svete rynochnykh otnoshenii," *Izvestiia*, 25 July 1995, pp. 1, 2.

81. *OMRI Daily Digest* 1, no. 154, 9 August 1995.

82. See *New York Times*, 9 October 1995, p. A7. On the Duma's anticorruption commission, see *Moskovskie novosti*, no. 24, 9–16 April 1995, p. 6.

83. *Moskovskii komsomolets*, 11 August 1995, p. 2.

84. One of those mentioned by the author of the *Moskovskii komsomolets* article as a leading member of the corrupt "war lobby" was Fedor Ladygin, chief of the GRU, the military intelligence agency of the army's General Staff. The au-

thor linked Ladygin to the killing of journalist Dmitrii Kholodov, who, he said, had been investigating illegal arms trading and was killed by explosives belonging to the special troops of the GRU. But there has been no confirmation of these allegations.

85. See the interview with an anonymous retired KGB officer who claimed to be a member of "Feliks," in *Komsomol'skaia pravda*, 7-14 July 1995, p. 3; and Aleksandr Minkin, "Vyshel Feliks iz tumana, bynul pravdy iz karmana," *Moskovskii komsomolets*, 22 July 1995, pp. 1, 3.

86. Grigoriants cited the probable murders of Andrei Tamburi, an Italian who was connected with the Helsinki group monitoring the situation in Moldova and that of the editor and owner of the paper "Literary News," Edmund Iodkovskii. See "Sueta vokrug Lubianki," *Obshchaia gazeta*, no. 29, 20-26 July 1995, p. 7. Also see *Segodnia*, 13 July 1995, p. 6.

87. "Sueta vokrug Lubianki."

88. See *New York Times*, 18 August 1995, p. A3.

89. Interview with Aleksandrov in *Nezavisimaia gazeta*, 15 March 1995, p. 4.

90. *Segodnia*, 3 August 1995, p. 3.

91. *Izvestiia*, 3 August 1995, p. 1.

CHAPTER TEN
CONCLUSION

1. Samuel Huntington, *The Third Wave: Democratization in the Late Twentieth Century* (Norman and London: University of Oklahoma Press, 1991), pp. 209-250.

2. It should be noted, however, that Yeltsin's tendency to use the military to suppress internal disorder, as in October 1993 and in Chechnia, as well as the deployment of army troops to preserve order in cities like Moscow has drawn the military into a greater political role.

3. *Washington Post*, 25 January 1990, p. 19.

4. For general surveys of political change in eastern Europe, see Vladimir Tismaneanu, *Reinventing Politics: Eastern Europe from Stalin to Havel* (New York: Free Press, 1992); and Gail Stokes, *The Walls Came Tumbling Down: The Collapse of Communism in Eastern Europe* (New York: Oxford University Press, 1993).

5. Victor Yasmann, "Restructuring the Secret Services in Eastern Europe," unpublished manuscript, Munich 1995, pp. 2-3.

6. *Los Angeles Times*, 22 March 1990, p. 1; Dennis Deletant, "The Securitate and the Police State in Romania: 1948-64," *Intelligence and National Security* 8, no. 4 (October 1993): 1-25; and "The Securitate and the Police State in Romania, 1964-89," *Intelligence and National Security* 9, no. 1 (January 1994): 22-49.

7. Dan Ionescu, "Romania's Public War over Secret Police Files," *RFE/RL Research Report* 1, no. 29, 17 July 1992, pp. 9-15.

8. On postwar Bulgaria, see Stokes, *The Walls Came Tumbling Down*, pp. 46-50.

9. See Kjell Engelbrekt, "Reinventing the Bulgarian Secret Services," *RFE/RL Report* 2, no. 47, 26 November 1993, pp. 41–49.

10. See *Human Rights and Democratization in Poland*, Commission on Security and Cooperation in Europe, Washington, D.C., January 1994.

11. Yasmann, "Restructuring the Secret Services"; Anna Sabbat-Swidlicka, "Problems of Poland's State Security Office," *RFE/RL Research Report*, 28 February 1992, pp. 15–18.

12. *Human Rights and Democratization in the Czech Republic*, prepared by the Staff of the Commission on Security and Cooperation in Europe, Washington, D.C., September 1994, pp. 6–10; Jiri Pehe, "Czechoslovakia: Building a State Based on the Rule of Law," *Report on Eastern Europe*, 1 March 1991, pp. 7–12.

13. *Human Rights in the Czech Republic*, pp. 12–15.

14. Laurence Wechsler, "The Velvet Purge: The Trials of Jan Kavan," *The New Yorker*, 19 October 1992, p. 68.

15. *Los Angeles Times*, 22 March 1990, p. 1.

16. Ibid.

17. Yasmann, "Restructuring the Secret Services," pp. 13–15.

18. Tallin BNS, 17 March 1994, in *FBIS-SOV*, 18 March 1994, p. 57.

19. In Estonia alone 16,000 persons were estimated to have cooperated secretly with the KGB during the years from 1980 to 1988. Report from Conference of Memento and Estonian Heritage Society, Tallinn, 25–26 March 1994, p. 3.

20. *Human Rights and Democratization in the Czech Republic*, p. 13.

21. Tina Rosenberg, *The Haunted Land* (New York: Random House, 1995), p. 306.

22. For an excellent analysis of the debate over decommunizing in eastern Europe and whether or not to punish officials from the old regimes, see Christopher H. Rhoads, "The German Democratic Republic on Trial: The Cases of Erich Honecker, Erich Mielke and Marcus Wolfe, and the Pursuit of Political Justice," The Johns Hopkins School of Advanced International Studies, Occasional Papers in Russian Area and East European Studies, 1995.

23. Vassily Aksyonov, "My Search for Russia's Revolution," *New York Times*, OP-ED, 22 November 1994.

24. Joel-François Dumont in *Intelligence and the New World Order: Former Cold War Adversaries Look Towards the 21st Century*, ed. Carl Runde and G. Voss (Washington, D.C.: International Freedom Foundation, 1992), p. 80.

25. As cited in Barbara von der Heydt, "Corruption in Russia: No Democracy without Morality," a special report to the Senate Foreign Relations Committee, 21 June 1995, p. 3.

INDEX

Government agencies are entered under the appropriate jurisdiction, e.g., Russian Ministry of Defense; Ukrainian Security Service; United States Central Intelligence Agency, etc. Legislation is entered directly under title, e.g., Law on Foreign Intelligence (Russia: 1992). Headings beginning "Russian" signify the Russian Federation unless they are qualified by the abbreviation for the former Russian republic: RSFSR.

Amy Knight is Senior Research Analyst at the Library of Congress and Professorial Lecturer in Russian History and Politics at the Johns Hopkins School of Advanced International Studies, Washington, D.C. She is the author of *The KGB: Police and Politics in the Soviet Union* and *Beria: Stalin's First Lieutenant* (Princeton).